D0821135

SEX, DRUGS, AND ROCK 'N' ROLL

SEX, DRUGS, AND ROCK 'N' ROLL

The Rise of America's 1960s Counterculture

Robert C. Cottrell

ROWMAN & LITTLEFIELD
Lanham • Boulder • New York • London

Published by Rowman & Littlefield
A wholly owned subsidary of The Rowman & Littlefield Publishing Group, Inc.
4501 Forbes Boulevard, Suite 200, Lanham, Maryland 20706
www.rowman.com

Unit A, Whitacre Mews, 26-34 Stannary Street, London SE11 4AB

British Library Cataloguing in Publication Information Available

Library of Congress Cataloging-in-Publication Data Available

Cottrell, Robert C.
Sex, drugs, and rock 'n' roll: The rise of America's 1960s counterculture / by Robert C. Cottrell.
p. cm.
Includes bibliographical references and index.
ISBN 978-1-4422-4606-5 (cloth : alk. paper) -- ISBN 978-1-4422-4607-2 (electronic)

∞ ™ The paper used in this publication meets the minimum requirements of
American National Standard for Information Sciences Permanence of Paper for
Printed Library Materials, ANSI/NISO Z39.48-1992.

Printed in the United States of America

To Harry, Edie, Ruthie, Steve, Sharon, Bill, and Sue,
children of the 1960s
and to Jordan, a child of children of the 1960s

CONTENTS

PREFACE

They believed, like good sons and daughters of a new American frontier, in the possibility of rebirth, of renewal, of regeneration. They saw themselves as born anew, ironically, in the manner of religious fundamentalists, as spirits whose souls had been cleansed once more. Some considered their quest to be very much in the American vein; others likened it to a sacred journey to the East. Many sought to rekindle a democratic and communitarian tradition that had apparently long since dissipated. Their example, they keenly reasoned, would help to revitalize not only their fellow citizens but humankind in general.

There was certain innocence in their quest, and yes, a very real naiveté and arrogance as well. They presumed that they could transform society and achieve spiritual bliss in a manner only the sanctified few had ever accomplished. They deemed their way as wholly righteous, drawing as it did on religious preachments of both the occidental and oriental variety. They were sure that their path toward illumination was eased or ensured altogether by lifestyle changes they effected, by their discarding of the competitive and rational ways that had brought so much misery to so many, and by the ingesting of pharmacological substances that seemingly promised instant enlightenment.

They were the hippies of the 1960s, the proponents of a counterculture, which stood in opposition to established ways, values, and verities, and to the so-called Establishment itself. Indeed, they saw themselves and were viewed by others as a group apart, as either the progenitors of a new and better means of making one's way in the world or a faddish, ungrateful, and aberrational force in the midst of American plenty. Again, each side had it right, at least from the perspective of its celebrants. For the hippies proved to be a short-lived phenomenon, perhaps because they were considered ingrates and freaks in the eyes of others, with their rejection of the American way. Yet for a time, the best, the most idealistic of them strove to attain something both more elemental and purer, no matter how frivolous and lighthearted they appeared to others.

Perhaps the intensity of the reaction to the hippies, both laudatory and accusatory, indicates as much. They were likened by some to a band of new Christs and Madonnas, and by others as the latest brand of American Adams and Eves, out to chart a new course in the wilderness of human existence. They were viewed as such by millions of the young in age and in spirit, who desperately sought new answers or a guiding light as an apparent age of darkness threatened to apocalyptically envelope the national landscape. They were damned by others as diabolical creatures, more Satanic than God-like, or at the very least as wholly irresponsible sorts, who were determined to waste their own lives, while leading youthful cohorts astray and perverting America. They were seen as little likely to usher in a new millennium, but rather as bound to bring about the collapse of the social order, which was already more tenuous than it had been for decades or longer, and hardly required anything akin to a misguided children's crusade.

The hippies, like the antebellum communitarians, Greenwich Village bohemians of the pre–World War I period, and the beats who haunted Eisenhower's America, were an integral part of their age. The utopians were part of the spate of reform movements that flourished in the United States before the Civil War. The bohemians characteristically exuded the innocence and exuberance of the Lyrical Left of John Reed, Mabel Dodge, Floyd Dell, and Bill Haywood, which developed during the progressive era. The beats stood in stark contrast to the complacency, conservatism, and conformity of the 1950s, a security-riddled period seemingly haunted by ever-present communists, both authentic and phantasmagoric. The hippies appeared during the same period that the New Left supposedly threatened the ideological hegemony of the liberal center, which shone briefly thanks to the appeal of the New Frontier and the Great Society.

Thus, all but one of the countercultures of the nineteenth and twentieth centuries, including that of the 1960s, evolved when the reform spirit was ascendant and an American left present. Indeed, the hopefulness and expectations raised by presidents John Fitzgerald Kennedy and Lyndon Baines Johnson, as much as disillusionment spawned by fading dreams and visions of the early part of the decade, set the stage for the arrival of the cultural rebels of the mid- and late sixties. Still, those rebels were undoubtedly influenced by images from Birmingham and Dallas, Watts and Saigon, Memphis and Los Angeles, which filled the pages of local newspapers and the small screens of television sets. Likewise, they took to heart tales of the new Greenwich and Liverpool, Golden Gate Park and Monterey, Paris and Chicago. The hippies truly were children of a media-driven age, with its panoply of adrenalin-like fixes and its haunting images from the McLuhanesque global village.

Their icons were multifold, and, notwithstanding suggestions to the contrary, not all were of the simplistic or nonliterate variety. Some, at least, read widely, including Buddhist masters, European Nobel laureates, Middle Eastern poets, British folklorists, American science-fiction writers, popular novelists, beats, and sexologists, in addition to Timothy Leary's instructional manual *The Psychedelic Experience* or Ken Kesey's *One Flew over the Cuckoo's Nest*. Many idealized rock musicians, with none more revered than four young Englishmen and a tousle-haired former folk musician from America's heartland. A good number venerated the ways, the style, the social patterns, and the grace of those often depicted as outsiders, particularly Native Americans and outlaws of one kind or another. Indeed, many of their heroes boasted antiheroic stripes.

The hippies attempted to shape an idealized existence, through their own music and poetry, their communes and collectives, their underground press and other alternative institutions, their clothing and dietary habits, their drug and sexual experimentation, and their religiosity and spirituality. Some of their endeavors were more successful than others, and some longer-lived. All, for better or worse, influenced how Americans came to interact with one another in their most intimate relationships, in educational and recreational spheres, and even in the corporate world. Similarly, hippie modes and manners affected apparel and hair styles, foods consumed or refused, as well as language and general patterns of thought.

Ultimately, the grand expectations and equally large fears that the hippies engendered bespoke the revolutionary possibilities that swirled about them. The hippies themselves and those who championed them hoped that utopian, even millennial results could emanate from their lifestyle experiments and transformations. Their foes worried that the hippies' rejection of the American way could imperil the nation itself, thus seeing in the long-haired, colorful denizens of a new frontier seeds of an apocalypse in which Hell, not Heaven, would result. What follows is something of this cultural clash, but more the story, albeit abbreviated, of the new American missionaries of the 1960s.

ACKNOWLEDGMENTS

Decades of reading about, reflecting on, and analyzing the events that took place have informed *Sex, Drugs, and Rock 'n Roll*. The bibliography admittedly only lightly covers the books, articles, and discography that have helped to shape this manuscript.

I do want to express my unbounded appreciation to five individuals in particular. My sister Sharon Gerson read through the entirety of *Sex, Drugs, and Rock 'n Roll*, and spent considerable time conversing with me about it. My daughter Jordan, notwithstanding her critical illness, served as a sounding board and read through some of the early offerings. My sister Edie Kreisler delivered emotional support, and my brother-in-law Steve Gerson provided his usual good cheer and sound advice. And my wife Sue was there, as always, fully supportive of this endeavor.

I am also grateful to the production team at Rowman & Littlefield, particularly Elaine McGarraugh and Jon Sisk.

I

THE PRECURSORS: FROM UTOPIA TO HUXLEY

The hippies of the 1960s, of course, were hardly the first countercultural figures to appear in the United States. A wave of utopian experiments cropped up during the antebellum period, amid an abundance of reform movements. Similar to the hippies, the utopians sought to regenerate their society, often by withdrawing to perfect particular communities of like-minded individuals. Again, in the manner of the hippies, many utopians stood in opposition to the capitalist economic order, engaged in sexual practices outside the mainstream, and hoped to bring about heaven on earth.

Among the most intriguing of the early communitarian endeavors in-volved the Shakers, New Harmony, Oneida, Brook Farm, the Icarians, and the Mormons. The Shakers, an offshoot of the Quakers, were headed by Ann Lee, and emerged during the American Revolution. Economic conservatives, they engaged in handicrafts; social radicals, they afforded women equal opportunities to head their operations. Believing that sin entered the world through sexual intercourse, they adopted the practice of celibacy, a distinctly self-defeating proposition. Robert Owen, a Scottish philanthropist, sought to carve out a socialist paradise in the American Midwest. The colony of New Harmony he founded at first thrived, but when its founder transferred control to its inhabitants, squabbling ensued along with economic ruin.

Oneida proved among the most controversial of the antebellum com-munitarian experiences, thanks to its leader, John Humphrey Noyes, who determined to adopt communal ways involving the sharing of private property and "communism of love." Noyes's decision to personally initiate young women into the rites of sexuality and his disdainful attitude toward monogamous relationships made Oneida notorious in the eyes of many. Brook Farm welcomed some of America's greatest intellectuals, including Ralph Waldo Emerson, Henry David Thoreau, Nathaniel Hawthorne, and Margaret Fuller, during its brief existence. The presence of so many strong-willed individuals, plus a crippling fire, brought that experiment in communalism to a close. Led by Etienne Cabet, European utopians—many of them French—established their first permanent Icarian colony in Nauvoo, Illinois, envisioning egalitarianism. A schism soon occurred and financial problems resulted in the disbanding of the Nauvoo colony.

Guided first by Joseph Smith, then by Brigham Young, the Mormons crafted the most enduring of the pre–Civil War communitarian efforts. Ostracized and vilified because of their practice of polygamy, the Mormons undertook a westward trek, eventually settling in the Great Salt Lake region where they proved enormously influential. They soon discarded both their early communitarian orientation and polygamy, for a seemingly benevolent, corporate thrust, which nevertheless retained something of the Mormon founders' messianic bent.

Along with the remaining communitarian enterprises and new ones that emerged, bohemians were sprinkled across the American landscape from the early nineteenth century onward. The literary and artistic worlds boasted such rebellious sorts, including Thomas Paine, Edgar Allan Poe, Walt Whitman, Mark Twain, Stephen Crane, Ambrose Bierce, O. Henry, Isadora Duncan, Ben Hecht, and Jack London. The firebrand British radical Paine, both reviled and lauded by the likes of William Blake, lived in Greenwich Village when it was still largely pastoral at the beginning of the nineteenth century. The tormented genius Poe, following a departure from the U.S. Military Academy at West Point, delivered short stories and poems riddled with mysteries, tales of the macabre, and personal anguish, such as "The Pit and the Pendulum," "The Tell-Tale Heart," and "The Raven." He dwelled for several years in Greenwich Village, before his untimely death in 1849, a fate perhaps induced by his affinity for alcohol and drugs. Poe had frequented literary salons in the Village, including the one hosted by Anne Charlotte Lynch, which also welcomed Herman Melville, Margaret Fuller, and William Cullen Bryant. The

French writer Charles Baudelaire helped to ensure Poe's fame, translating his work and asserting that "every lyric poet by virtue of his nature inevitably effects a return to the lost Eden."[1]

"The capital of Bohemia," Pfaff's Saloon in Greenwich Village proved welcoming to curious artists, with Henry Clapp Jr., the so-called King of the Bohemians, and the actress-writer Ada Clare frequently holding court there. Figures like William Dean Howells and Walt Whitman were sometimes in attendance, although Howells purportedly considered the salon "a sham Bohemia." Whitman had already garnered certain notoriety with the 1855 publication of the first edition of *Leaves of Grass*, which opened with the declaration, "I celebrate myself, / And what I assume you shall assume, / For every atom belonging to me as good belongs to you." Lionizing the American spirit, Whitman wrote, "And I know the spirit of God is the eldest brother of my own / And that all the men ever born are also my brothers . . . and the women my sisters and lovers." In the fashion of Poe and Baudelaire, Whitman reported, "The opium eater reclines with rigid head and just-opened lips, / The prostitute draggles her shawl, / her bonnet bobs on her tipsy and pimpled neck."[2]

The young Bret Harte, a New Yorker transplanted to San Francisco, produced a series of essays, referring to himself as "The Bohemian"; many of his writings appeared in the San Francisco newspaper, *Golden Era*. There, on November 11, 1860, Harte heralded Bohemia: "a fairy land, full of flowers, with a clear, unclouded sky. All day long the people go up and down the walks and pick boquests [sic]. . . . Then they travel away from Bohemia, and rove about trying to sell their flowers. Sometimes people don't like flowers, and then the poor Bohemians are in a bad way. Then again, perhaps, there's a taste for roses, and the poor Bohemian only has a few violets. Or people want Leaves of Grass, dirt and all."[3]

The Irishman John Boyle O'Reilly helped to usher bohemia into Boston, delivering an open proclamation in 1885, "In Bohemia."

> I'd rather live in Bohemia than in any other land,
> For only there are the values true,
> And the laurels gathered in all men's view. . . .
> Here, pilgrims stream with a faith sublime
> From every class and clime and time,
> Aspiring only to be enrolled

With the names that are writ in the book of gold;
And each one bears in mind or hand
A palm of the dear Bohemian land. [4]

In 1893, the realist novelist William Dean Howells, best known for *The Rise of Silas Lapham*, produced *The Coast of Bohemia*. As Stephen Crane would in *The Third Violet*, Howells, through one of his leading figures, Charmain Maybough, acknowledged the difficulty of explaining what Bohemia amounted to, and questioned its very existence. "Charmain herself, who aimed to be a perfect Bohemian, was uncertain of the ways and means of operating the Bohemian life, when she had apparently thrown off all the restrictions."[5] Ironically, in that very decade, bohemianism proved increasingly popular in certain circles in the United States.

Right before the advent of World War I, Greenwich Village became the center of American bohemianism, the site where poets and political agitators comingled in sometimes uneasy alliances. There, the *Masses*, the radical magazine, became a literary touchstone, and there could be found John Reed, Max Eastman, Floyd Dell, Randolph Bourne, and Mabel Dodge. Spirited conversation abounded regarding socialism, anarchism, syndicalism, antimilitarism, free love, and women's rights. Participants belonged, however informally, to the Lyrical Left of the early twentieth century, with its political, labor, and cultural layers.

The Socialist Party of America and the saintly Eugene V. Debs, a former state legislator from Terre Haute, Indiana, propounded the gospel of democratic socialism. The American socialists, under Debs's guidance, contended that political democracy in the United States had to be extended, particularly apart from corporate encroachments, and a measure of economic democracy offered, to prevent massive exploitation and help usher in the good society. Most lyrical leftists considered themselves socialists of one variety or another, condemning both laissez-faire economics and mild reform palliatives, although they seldom were organization men or women.

For a time, they identified—even more than they did with the Socialist Party—with the Industrial Workers of the World (IWW), whose Wobblies were spearheaded by the hulking, one-eyed Big Bill Haywood, a former leader of the American Federation of Miners, which necessarily waged a form of class warfare along the West Coast. Haywood showed up at Mabel Dodge's immaculately drawn salon at 23 Fifth Avenue in

Greenwich Village, along with writers, artists, and others involved in an early version of Radical Chic. Some supposedly identified with the IWW, which sought to represent the group Karl Marx and Frederich Engels had referred to as the lumpenproletariat: miners, lumberjacks, tenant farmers, and the like. Or they thrilled to Haywood's discussion of the Wobbly vision of anarcho-syndicalism and One Big Union's orchestrating a general strike to overturn the capitalist system.

Lyrical Leftists were best known for their vision of cultural emancipation and personal liberation, which might entail support for women's empowerment, sexual experimentation, and open marriage. Relationships were initiated and sometimes too easily broken, often leaving behind bruised egos and shattered psyches, notwithstanding supposed efforts to overcome bourgeois sensibilities. Yes, Lyrical Leftists quoted from Freud as from Marx and Engels, but often men more lightly carried out affairs, to the dismay of their female partners, who were encouraged to experiment in their own fashion. Old-fashioned jealousies and hurt feelings frequently resulted, affecting couples, their friends, even whole neighborhoods. At the same time, the belief in emancipatory possibilities ensured that Lyrical Leftists did not easily subscribe to doctrines or dogma, even if delivered by Marx, Engels, or Freud. Reed, Bourne, Dell, Max Eastman, Crystal Eastman, and other contributors to such publications as *The Masses*, *The Seven Arts*, and *The Liberator* expressed support for socialism, anarchism, sexual liberation, and peace. They continued to do so even as European socialist parliamentarians supported military budgets and party members marched off to war, while mounting discontent fostered talk of mutiny and revolution that filtered through army regiments and into cities from St. Petersburg to Paris.

U.S. intervention in World War I proved shattering on the home front, destroying the relatively nurturing environment that progressive era America had afforded some of its sharpest critics. Moreover, the United States failed to produce anything akin to the Dada cultural movement that emerged in Switzerland during the war, which drew from antiwar and anarchistic sensibilities. The administration of Woodrow Wilson, earlier considered even by many Lyrical Leftists as a genuine reformer, harshly dealt with its critics, at least those emanating from the left side of the ideological spectrum. Prosecutions of leading radicals, including Debs, Haywood, Reed, Max Eastman, Dell, and the anarchists Emma Goldman and Alexander Berkman, soon followed. The deaths of Bourne and Reed, both at the age of thirty-two, in 1918 and 1920, respectively, and the torturous connection to the new communist state in Russia, where Goldman, Berkman, and Haywood headed into forced exile, cemented the demise of the Lyrical Left. So too did Eastman's decision to reside for a handful of years in Russia, and the physical ailments that weakened and eventually took the life of his gifted sister Crystal, who had coedited *The Liberator* with him. Robert Minor's immersion in the communist movement transformed the career of another noted artist who had sparked the early enthusiasm for *The Masses*. As Reed had warned, "This class struggle plays hell with your poetry."[6] Other bohemian-tinged writers, like Joseph Freeman and Mike Gold, also joined the Communist Party, which insisted, in the fashion of the Soviet Union under Joseph Stalin, that socialist realism dominate artistic works.

A type of black bohemia had also surfaced during the 1910s and proved somewhat more enduring, as exemplified by the Harlem Renaissance of the 1920s. Talk of both a New Negro and a New Woman abounded throughout that later decade, and an underground culture flourished in speakeasies, gin joints, and literary salons. Musicians such as Bessie Smith and Louis "Satchmo" Armstrong, and poets on the order of Langston Hughes and Claude McKay, contested racial barriers, or sexual ones as well. Hughes's 1923 poem, "The Weary Blues," referred to a black musician's "drowsy syncopated tune," wafting through "a lazy sway. . . . To the tune o' those Weary Blues."[7] The phenomenon of the New Woman, exemplified in very different fashions by both Bessie Smith and the actress Clara Bow, the It Girl, suggested a greater acceptance of sensuousness and even sexuality somewhat in keeping with the emancipatory possibilities associated with the Lyrical Left. However, the continued hold of Victorian sensibilities during the early twentieth century ensured that the very idea of a New Woman, more spirited, assertive, and, yes, sexually engaged, remained enormously controversial.

A small number of utopian communities appeared during the Great Depression, including some established by the Resettlement Administration, headed by Rexford Tugwell, designed to assist small farmers and shape suburban greenbelt towns. Those again resulted in large-scale opposition, with accusations that the New Deal administration of Franklin Delano Roosevelt was trying to foster socialism or communism. Consequently, the Resettlement Administration assisted only a few thousand families, not the half-million originally envisaged. Rather than a counterculture, critics of the existing social order gravitated to political organizations like the Communist Party of the United States, with its utopian ideology, no matter how genuinely marred by its inextricable connection to the Soviet-directed Comintern and Joseph Stalin.

The hipster, as *New York Times* columnist Anatole Broyard referred to him in a *Partisan Review* essay, emerged at some point during the interwar period. As Broyard saw it, because the hipster "was the illegitimate son of the Lost Generation," he "was really *nowhere*" but wanted "to be *somewhere*." Something of an outsider by "race or feeling," he unhappily adopted a type of unrooted delinquency. This simply led to problems involving ever present legal forces, ultimately requiring him to convey his resentment "*symbolically*." A philosophy emerged, one "of *somewhereness* called *jive*," and the adoption of a minimalist but expressive language on the order of "*solid, gone, out of this world, or nowhere, sad, beat, a drag*." Jive language was inherently aggressive, even sexual. Boasting his coined verbiage and philosophy, the hipster attempted "to conquer the world," while holding himself apart from others. The hipster's look was distinctive too, including padded shoulders, a high collar, white-streaked hair, and sunglasses. He appeared as "an underground man," a seeming "creature of the darkness," who was familiar with the world of "sex, gambling, crime." Important to the hipster were both jive music, ranging from the blues to jazz and bebop, and "tea" or marijuana. Drugs afforded "an indispensable outlet . . . a free world to expatiate in." When the life of the hipster proved troubling, he could "dreamily" float "into the richer world of tea." Moreover, getting high "became a *raison d'etre*, a calling, an experience shared with fellow believers, a respite, a heaven or haven." Residents of Greenwich Village treated him "as an oracle," as "the great instinctual man, an ambassador from the Id." He viewed himself as "a poet, a seer, a hero." However, at some point, the hipster "stopped protesting, reacting," became "pretentious," lost his subversive quality, and reentered "the American womb."[8]

During and immediately following World War II, a small circle of hipster-like friends, many attending or graduates of Ivy League institutions, contested numerous cultural norms in the United States, while setting the stage for the counterculture that emerged in the 1960s. Allen Ginsberg, Jack Kerouac, William Burroughs, and Lucien Carr linked up with the Denver native, high school dropout Neal Cassady, and later, San Francisco–based Gary Snyder, Michael McClure, and Lawrence Ferlin-

ghetti, to articulate what Carr referred to as the New Vision and to experience what Ginsberg called the Libertine Circle. Proclaimed members of a
"beat generation" by Kerouac around 1950, these writers and their associates challenged standard mores, along with prevailing literary styles and
themes. Little appeared sacrosanct, including religion, politics, the work
ethic, the nuclear family, marriage, monogamy, education, and, at times,
Western thought altogether.

Before the beats made much of a mark, a pair of European intellectuals, along with American intelligence operatives, provided additional
seeds for an American counterculture. On November 16, 1938, the Swiss
research chemist Albert Hoffman initially synthesized lysergic acid die-
thylamide, LSD-25, a much more potent drug than mescaline, in a laboratory operated in Basel, Switzerland, by the Sandoz Company. Nearly five
years passed before Dr. Hoffman resynthesized LSD on Friday, April 16,
1943, then inadvertently ingested it. He later recalled "a remarkable rest-
lessness, combined with a slight dizziness. At home I lay down and sank
into a not unpleasant intoxicated-like condition, characterized by an extremely stimulated imagination." Then, "in a dreamlike state, with eyes
closed (I found the daylight to be unpleasantly glaring), I perceived an
uninterrupted stream of fantastic pictures, extraordinary shapes with intense, kaleidoscopic play of colours. After some two hours this condition
faded away." The next workday, Hoffman deliberately took a quarter of a
milligram of LSD, soon experiencing, as he recorded, "dizziness, feeling
of anxiety, visual distortions, symptoms of paralysis, desire to laugh."
Encountering difficulty in continuing to write, he requested that his assistant accompany him home on a bicycle. More remarkable sensations
ensued during the period subsequently referred to as "Bicycle Day." "On
the way home, my condition began to assume threatening forms. Everything in my field of vision wavered and was distorted as if seen in a
curved mirror. I also had the sensation of being unable to move from the
spot. Nevertheless, my assistant later told me that we had travelled very
rapidly." Feeling paranoid and witnessing "demonic transformations" on
arriving home, Hoffman also underwent "the dissolution of my ego. A
demon had invaded me, had taken possession of my body, mind, and
soul." He was overwhelmed "by the dreadful fear of going insane. I was
taken to another world, another place, another time." Eventually those
worries and sensations subsided, replaced by "a feeling of good fortune
and gratitude." The effects wore off after a half-dozen hours in which

Hoffman underwent tremendous mood swings. During the final hour, Hoffman partook of images "opening and then closing themselves in circles and spirals, exploding in coloured foundations," with sounds producing colors. He awakened refreshed the following morning, as his "senses vibrated in a condition of heightened sensitivity."[9]

The previous spring, General William Donovan, who headed the Office of Strategic Services, the precursor to the Central Intelligence Agency, had urged a group of leading American scientists to carry out a covert research program. The purpose was to devise a drug that would induce foreign spies and prisoners of war to relinquish information. A research committee was formed, which tested a variety of substances, including barbiturates and peyote, before a potent marijuana extract was deemed the most effective agent. Following World War II, the U.S. military and the CIA launched their own quests to discover what Martin A. Lee and Bruce Shlain refer to as "a truth serum." In 1947, the Navy Project undertook Project CHATTER, which resulted in experiments involving mescaline. Two years later, Sandoz Laboratories introduced LSD to the United States through the research psychiatrist Max Rinkel, hoping that clinical applications might be available. Rinkel soon reported that the ingesting of LSD resulted in "a transitory psychotic disturbance." Another psychiatrist, Dr. Paul Hoch of the Psychiatric Institute of New York, revealed that "LSD and Mescaline disorganize the psychic integration of the individual"; it was Hoch who contended "that LSD was a 'psychotomimetic' or 'madness-mimicking' agent," Lee and Shlain note. In 1951, the CIA, interested in mind-altering drugs, began experimenting with LSD. Two years later, the CIA, with Director Allen Dulles and Richard Helms of Clandestine Services taking the lead, initiated Project MKULTRA, involving the administering of LSD, often to unknowing subjects, including the U.S. Army biochemist Frank Olson, who died under mysterious circumstances in November 1953. Sessions with Olson had convinced a top agency LSD researcher, Dr. Harold Abramson, that the scientist suffered from "a psychotic state" exemplifying "delusions of grandeur . . . crystallized by the LSD experience."[10] The CIA soon began conducting additional experiments involving unsuspecting participants.

As early as the latter stages of the 1940s, popular publications in the United States presented articles on peyote, mescaline, and LSD. On May 25, 1947, the *New York Times* reported the use of mescaline to help better understand mental illness, especially hallucinations associated with schizophrenia. *New York Times* reporter Lucy Freeman, on May 11, 1951, discussed "2 Drugs Expected to Aid Mind Study": mescaline and LSD. She wrote about a presentation by Dr. Hoch before the American Psychiatric Association. He and fellow researchers at the Psychiatric Institute of New York had employed the drugs on volunteers to conduct "diagnostic, prognostic and therapeutic" studies, but considered their work to be at the "experimental" stage. They were seeking to discover if "normal and abnormal" individuals reacted similarly to drugs, and if "apparent psychoses" induced in "normal people" replicated those experienced "spontaneously" by others.[11] A June 18, 1951, article in *Time* referred to the use of peyote buttons by Navajo Indians. Derived from the mescal cactus, found throughout Mexico and various sections of Texas, peyote had proven popular for a decade-and-a-half. Peyote temporarily emancipated the impoverished Navajos, affording "visions and hallucinations" with "dreams in Technicolor." Peyote purportedly induced sexual frenzies, *Time* indicated, as well as possible damage to the heart and kidneys. Nevertheless, it remained outside federal jurisdiction.[12]

Appearing in the February 23, 1953, issue of *Newsweek*, "Mescal Madness" discussed mescaline's efficacy in exploring schizophrenia. Mescaline, the essay indicated, could induce "hallucinations of sight and sound . . . at will," but without the addictive qualities that characterized drugs such as morphine and cocaine. Additionally, the patient on mescaline could explain "his bizarre experiences with unblurred consciousness." The *Newsweek* article examined the impact of mescaline, including "a constant stream of scenes of incredible beautiful colors, grandeur, and variety," but also "grotesque shapes." One psychiatrist indicated that mescaline affected "the celebration circulation," thereby approximating "the dream state." The article concluded with the suggestion that mescaline might prove even more useful in the field of experimental psychology, particularly in detecting schizophrenia. Accompanying the article were several intriguing images, including one with a woman witnessing demonic hallucinations, another encountering large cobwebs that transmuted into song, and yet another experiencing "dazzling crystals." Consequently, the English psychiatrist G. Taylor Stockings, writing in the *Journal of Mental Science*, affirmed that mescaline was vitally important in helping to comprehend "the nature of mental disorder." "Mescal Madness" explored the history of the drug, at least over the previous five centuries, hearkening back to the Spanish explorer Hernando Cortez's discovery of Indians using mescal cactus to induce intoxication during religious rites. A Spanish priest referred to the plant as "an evil mushroom which intoxicates like wine." Native Americans in Texas and New Mexico also later partook of peyote during ceremonial explorations. In the mid-1890s, the English physician and psychologist Henry Havelock Ellis became one of the first Westerners to undergo a peyote trip. [13]

The July 13, 1953, issue of *Time* offered an essay titled "Medicine: Mescaline and the Mad Hatter." It referred to the British psychiatrist John Smythies, who, on taking the drug, experienced "visions of 'the utmost poetical integrity.'" Maintaining one's eyes shut, the article reported, enabled the mescaline user to witness color-laden "mosaics, networks, flowing arabesques, interlaced spirals, wonderful tapestries . . . great butterflies gently moving their wings, fields of glittering jewels . . . soaring architecture . . . and finally human figures and fully formed scenes where coherent histories are enacted." Distorted sensibilities occurred too, as the "teatime goes on forever," and the mescaline user "will feel quite literally that he is at the Mad Hatter's tea party," Smythies reported. But now working at the Saskatchewan Hospital in Weyburn, Canada, alongside Dr. Humphry Osmond, Smythies was most interested in examining the roots causes of schizophrenia. [14]

Ironically, the world famous English writer Aldous Huxley, to Albert Hoffman's delight, became another early proselytizer regarding psychedelics. On October 10, 1931, Huxley's essay, "A Treatise on Drugs," had appeared in the *Chicago Herald and Examiner*, warning, "All existing drugs are treacherous and harmful. The heaven into which they usher their victims soon turns into a hell of sickness and moral degradation." Prohibition proved ineffective, necessitating another solution. To prevent individuals from becoming addicted to alcohol, morphine, or cocaine required providing a substitute, Huxley wrote. "The man who invents such a substance will be counted among the greatest benefactors of suffering humanity." [15] Huxley's most acclaimed work, *Brave New World*, published in 1932, offered a dystopian vision of a future world in which the psychedelic drug soma was used by government to narcotize the general populace. Soma possessed "all the advantages of Christianity and alcohol; none of their defects," Huxley wrote. [16]

Huxley later became aware of studies into hallucinogenic drugs undertaken by Humphry Osmond and John Smythies. The brilliant author, having probably already experienced cocaine or hashish as early as the

1920s, contacted Osmond, who "did not relish the possibility, however remote, of being the man who drove Aldous Huxley mad." Nevertheless, in May 1953, only weeks after the CIA began MKULTRA, Osmond supervised Huxley's first mescaline experience. Huxley knew that the British physician and sexologist Havelock Ellis, the French poet Henri Michaux, and the Anglo-Irish poet William Butler Yeats had taken mescaline or peyote, apparently without deleterious results. Yeats recalled seeing "the most delightful dragons, puffing out their breath straight in front of them, like rigid lines of steam."[17] On the other hand, Huxley had recently published *The Devils of Loudun*, a novel in which he warned, "There are probably moments in the course of intoxication by almost any drug, when awareness of a non-self superior to the disintegrating ego becomes briefly possible. But these occasional flashes of revelation are bought at an enormous price. For the drugtaker, the moment of spiritual awareness (if it comes at all!) gives place very soon to a subhuman stupor, frenzy or hallucination, followed by dismal hangover."[18] Nevertheless, Huxley willingly ingested the mescaline Osmond handed him.

In 1954 and 1956, respectively, Huxley published *The Doors of Perception* and *Heaven and Hell*, extolling such psychoactive drugs as mescaline and LSD. In the first volume, Huxley discussed his own experiences with mescaline, which, he offered, proved enlightening in the manner that the great English poet William Blake had written: "If the doors of perception were cleansed every thing would appear to man as it is, infinite."[19] Blake is also said to have declared, "In the universe, there are things known and there are things unknown, and in between, there are doors." Drawing on theological, artistic, literary, and philosophical tenets, the Oxford-educated Huxley underwent a "trip" undoubtedly different than those later experienced by less brilliantly educated psychedelic users. Discussing the need to surmount the social dysfunctionality associated with alcohol and tobacco, Huxley insisted on "the universal and ever-present urge to self-transcendence" and the need of "other, better doors" to help usher in such transformation, which he called "a principal appetite of the soul." At the same time, Huxley acknowledged he was "not so foolish as to equate what happens under the influence of mescaline or of any other drug . . . with the realization of the end and ultimate purpose of human life: Enlightenment, the Beatific Vision." And yet he believed that a mescaline experience could be likened to "a gratuitous grace," helping to demonstrate greater possibilities "as they are apprehended, directly and unconditionally, by Mind at Large." This, he considered "an experience of inestimable value to everyone and especially to the intellectual." The individual who went "through the Door in the Wall," Huxley suggested, "will be wiser but less cocksure, happier but less self-satisfied, humbler . . . yet better equipped to understand the relationship of words to things, of systematic reasoning to the unfathomable Mystery which it tries, forever vainly, to comprehend."[20]

The response to Huxley's proselytizing about psychedelic drugs proved mixed, at best. Alistair Sutherland dismissively indicated, "The Witch Doctor of California produces another prescription for his suffering tribe."[21] *Time* magazine stated that no psychiatrist would replicate Huxley's supposed prescription of "mescaline for all mankind as a specific against unhappiness," but again offered that it could prove greatly beneficial for mental patients. In reviewing *The Doors of Perception* in the *British Medical Journal*, the British psychiatrist William Sargant referred to its author's "brilliant mind and pen." At a minimum, Sargant believed, the book should induce his fellow doctors to examine more closely "the physiological aspects of psychiatry."[22] Berton Roueche, the originator of "The Annals of Medicine," which appeared regularly in *The New Yorker*, referred to Huxley as a member of a "small, introspective company" that had partaken of mescaline. In a review of *The Doors of Perception* that appeared in the *New York Times*, Roueche praised "this small, introspective book," while wishing Huxley had presented "a somewhat fuller account of what exactly happened, objectively and mechanistically," when he took mescaline.[23] By contrast, the great German writer Thomas Mann, on receiving a copy of *The Doors of Perception*, deemed Huxley's latest brand of "escapism . . . rather scandalous," which would only convince "many young Englishmen and especially Americans [to] try the experiment." All of this amounted to "unscrupulous aesthetic self-indulgence." Dismissing him as "a dilettante," Mann tagged the book as "irresponsible" and leading "to the stupefaction of the world."[24] Such criticisms foreshadowed many later to be visited on progenitors of psychedelia.

In 1955, Huxley took mescaline for the second time, in the presence of his good friend Gerald Heard, and Captain Alfred M. Hubbard, a top OSS operative who underwent his own original LSD experience four years earlier. As Hubbard recalled, "It was the deepest mystical thing I've ever seen." Like Huxley, Hubbard was also in touch with Humphry Osmond.

Also in 1955, Huxley, again with Hubbard present, took LSD for the initial time. He discovered "love as the primary and fundamental cosmic fact."[25] In *Heaven and Hell*, Huxley, who had now "taken psychedelics nearly a dozen times," acknowledged, as Hoffman had, that the taking of mescaline or LSD could result in either a "blissful" or an "appalling" visionary experience.[26] As for Osmond and Hubbard, they envisioned LSD being employed to change the thinking of leaders around the globe. Huxley continued to reflect on the full merits of psychedelics, indicating to Osmond, "My own view is that it would be important to break off experimentation from time to time and permit the participants to go on, on their own, towards the Clear Light." He declared, "The opening of the door by mescaline or LSD is too precious an opportunity, too high a privilege to be neglected for the sake of experimentation" alone.[27]

In its December 19, 1955, issue, *Time* magazine included an article on Albert Hoffman and LSD research experiments. It referred to Hoffman's "Bicycle Day," and to a series of medical teams employing LSD in their psychiatric research. One twenty-three-year-old college student, who participated in a pair of LSD experiments, reported that he awakened "to a new world—my life, my mental state had been altered. I was a stranger in this world." Dr. Harold A. Abramson, a psychiatrist at the Cold Springs Harbor Biological Laboratory in New York City, warned that LSD should only be employed "under strictest medical supervision."[28] On April 8, 1956, John Dollard, a psychology professor at Yale, reviewing *Heaven and Hell* for the *New York Times*, referred to it as a "lovely fairy tale" regarding "beauty, ineffable and transporting beauty." Dollard spoke of Huxley's colorful "Eden of the mind," and the quest for a "supernal inner world" that could be attained only through "ascetic practices, meditation, drugs like peyote, the hypnotic trance, glittering objects and mundane works of art." For his part, Dollard denied that man required "otherworldly help" to comprehend mystery and uncertainty. After all, young children experienced "pure vision . . . uncontaminated by the rubrics of language."[29] Writing in the *British Medical Journal*, D. V. Hubble praised "Huxley's erudition . . . his ingenious hypotheses, and . . . the fine clarity of his writing."[30] The architect and art historian Paul Zucker deemed Huxley's approach in *Heaven and Hell* "tremendously exciting," combining as it did an examination of physiological, psychological, chemistry, and pharmacological research.[31] In mid-1958, *Time* discussed "Mushroom Madness," with a more extensive discussion of Albert Hoffman, the research director of the Swiss company, Sandoz, who was producing synthetic psilocybin pills. That corporation, *Time* offered, would "release psilocybin only to highly reputable medical investigators." Thus three psychedelics—LSD, mescaline, and psilocybin—might help "to induce controllable symptoms like those of uncontrolled mental illness."[32]

Meanwhile, government operatives continued to conduct their own research into the efficacy of hallucinogenics. CIA officials worried that foreign adversaries might use LSD "to produce anxiety or terror in medically unsophisticated subjects unable to distinguish drug-induced psychosis from actual insanity." To avoid such a scenario, several agents tried LSD, some numerous times. Top figures in the U.S. Army, such as Major General William Creasy, also believed in psychochemical warfare. Creasy considered the possibility of spiking water supplies with hallucinogenics. Justifying that very idea, Creasy asked, "Would you rather be temporarily deranged, blinded, or paralyzed by a chemical agent, or burned alive by a conventional fire bomb?" Soldiers in the U.S. Armed Forces were given doses of LSD, then compelled to undergo a battery of questions from intelligence officers. Members of Congress were sometimes apprised of such examinations, resulting in generous funds for the Chemical Corps.[33]

By the latter stages of the 1950s, LSD proved popular in the Los Angeles area, with the psychiatrists Oscar Janiger and Sidney Cohen helping to turn on Hollywood actors and other luminaries. Over the span of eight years, beginning in 1954, Janiger issued approximately three thousand doses of LSD to about one thousand volunteers. Those introduced to the drug included the French-born writer Anais Nin, who now felt she could comprehend "the infinite"; the Rand Corporation's Herman Kahn, the futurist and proponent of the hydrogen bomb; and British actor Cary Grant, who informed reporters, "I have been born again. . . . I found I was hiding behind all kinds of defenses, hypocrisies and vanities. I had to get rid of them layer by layer. The moment when your conscious meets your subconscious is a hell of a wrench. With me there came a day when I saw the light."[34] Among others turning on by the end of the decade were the highly conservative publisher and president of *Time* and *Life* magazines, Henry Luce, and his wife, Clare Boothe Luce, doing so under the tutelage of Sidney Cohen. Once more, *Time* magazine delivered a report on LSD, this time in its March 28, 1960, issue, which referred to its use by "such glossy public personalities as Cary Grant." *Time* indicated that the taking of LSD could produce "fantasies of seeing God and the Devil 'locked in mortal cosmic conflict.'" LSD enabled the user to "report vividly observed conflicts, dredged out from his deepest unconscious and acted out before him." The article suggested that two groups, long resistant to treatment, appeared to benefit from LSD use: "addicts and obsessive-compulsives." The drug continued to be closely monitored by its manufacturer, Sandoz, but more than twenty physicians were conducting research employing the drug. Experiments ranged from group encounters spearheaded by Dr. Harlad A. Abramson in Manhattan, to Dr. Abram Hoffer's attempt to treat alcoholics in British Columbia. Meanwhile, in Hollywood, *Time* noted, "word of LSD's power . . . led to a fad to try it." The magazine pointed to both Huxley and Grant, with the latter indicating he had finally discovered "a tough inner core of strength."[35]

2

TROUBADOURS FOR A NEW AMERICAN BOHEMIA: ALLEN GINSBERG, JACK KEROUAC, AND THE BEATS

While individuals from Edgar Allan Poe and John Reed to Albert Hoffman and Aldous Huxley provided models for a counterculture in the United States, Allen Ginsberg, Jack Kerouac, Timothy Leary, and Ken Kesey served as troubadours for a new American bohemia. Like key participants in the Lyrical Left, all four were products of elite schooling, then ascended to the top rungs of their chosen fields of endeavor but proved determined to challenge prevailing norms and sensibilities. That resulted in ostracism and even incarceration, however temporarily, as well as the cultivating of an outlaw image in keeping with denizens of bohemia, both within and beyond the United States.

No one moved more seamlessly among both the beats of the early postwar era and the hippies who flourished during the 1960s and early 1970s than Allen Ginsberg. Born on June 3, 1926, in Newark, New Jersey, he was the child of second generation Russian-Jewish immigrants, the poet Louis Ginsburg, who taught high school English and believed in socialism, and Naomi Ginsberg, a Communist Party member afflicted with severe paranoia. Acutely sensitive, Allen early experienced sexual feelings for other boys, during a period when homosexuality was considered a cardinal sin. He was also politically aware, considering himself shortly before he turned fifteen "an atheist and a combination of Jeffersonian Democrat-Socialist Communist." He idealized the martyred anarchists Nicola Sacco and Bartolomeo Vanzetti, Italian immigrant laborers who may have been victims of the post–World War I red scare or might have been involved in the felony murder for which they were prosecuted during a famous trial in the 1920s. Ginsberg also revered the longtime American Socialist Party presidential candidate, Eugene V. Debs, and thus not surprisingly was both disdainful of Stalinism and fearful of fascism during the 1930s. He was drawn to Walt Whitman's "Song of Myself," William Butler Yeats, and Carl Sandburg, but adhering to his father's wishes, planned to become a labor lawyer. However, Ginsberg switched to English at Columbia University, studying under Lionel Trilling, a former Trotskyist and the first Jew to be named a full professor in Columbia's Department of English, and he gravitated to a small, intimate circle of friends, whom he considered "the wild young barbarians and the savages," Jack Kerouac and Lucien Carr, among them.[1] It later broadened to include Harvard graduate William Burroughs, Neal Cassady, who had frequently been in trouble with the law in his hometown of Denver, and Gregory Corso, fresh out of jail following a robbery conviction. All, as Andrew Jamison and Ron Eyerman note in *Seeds of the Sixties*, "were sitting out a popular war while their fellows rushed to participate."[2]

Kerouac was born on March 12, 1922, in a working-class district of Lowell, Massachusetts, to Leo-Alcide Kerouac, a printer and businessman, and the fervently Catholic Gabrielle-Ange Levesque, both natives of Quebec, Canada. Raised speaking a French dialect, the intense child—known as Ti Jean—aspired to write stories, influenced by the radio program, *The Shadow*, and the novels of Herman Melville, Thomas Wolfe, Honore de Balzac, James Joyce, Fyodor Dostoyevsky, and Marcel Proust. He became enamored with jazz, producing his first article about Count Basie's Band. A high school football star, Kerouac attended Horace Mann Preparatory School, which he declared was "96 percent Jewish," before entering Columbia University on an athletic scholarship. A lengthy touchdown scamper merited a write-up in the *New York Times*, with Kerouac referred to as "a shifty, flat-footed back."[3] During his first two games, Kerouac starred, running back one kickoff ninety yards, but he ended up on crutches after cracking his right tibia. Popular because of his athleticism and smoldering good looks, Kerouac became class vice president and a member of the status-laden Phi Gamma Delta fraternity. Beset by mixed grades in the classroom and unable to get along with the football coach, Kerouac left Columbia. In a letter to a close high school friend, written in March 1943, Kerouac called for heading to France after the war to support the revolution, blasted the bourgeoisie, and referred to capitalist pigs in French. He entered the U.S. Navy that same month, but proved unable and unwilling to abide by the discipline required, and received an honorable discharge from military service only months later, having been diagnosed as possessing "indifferent character" and as "psychoneurotic."[4] He subsequently returned to the Upper West Side, hanging out near Columbia University, soon encountering Ginsberg.

By Christmas of 1943, a group of friends had begun to congregate in the city, including Ginsberg, Kerouac, Carr, Burroughs, Joan Vollmer Burroughs, Edie Parker, Herbert Huncke, Ed White, Hal Chase, Clellon Holmes, Ed Stringham, and Alan Harrington. Within a short time, Ginsberg, Kerouac, and Carr were conversing about "the New Vision" or "the New Consciousness," each of which heralded, to some degree, both youth and the avant-garde. The French Romantic poets Charles Baudelaire and Arthur Rimbaud particularly influenced Ginsberg and Kerouac, but so did William Blake, Jean Cocteau, Hart Crane, W. B. Yeats, W. H. Auden, Franz Kafka, Ándre Gide, and Albert Camus, all of whom Burroughs recommended. Ginsberg also delved into the writings of T. S. Eliot, Thomas Mann, Fyodor Dostoyevsky, and Leo Tolstoy, while Kerouac, Carr, and Ginsberg examined the works of Giovanni Vico, Vilfredo Prado, James Joyce, and Oswald Spengler. In his journal, Ginsberg attempted to define the New Vision: "Since Art is merely and ultimately self-expressive, we conclude that the fullest art, the most individual, uninfluenced, unrepressed, uninhibited expression of art is true expression and the true art."[5] The New Vision, Ginsberg later recalled, sought to quash standard morality altogether and cultivate, instead, creativity. Nevertheless, as Ginsberg informed the writer Martin Torgoff, "from the beginning, it wasn't a party drug scene. It was aesthetic, more of a curiosity as to the nature, the texture, of consciousness itself."[6] At the same time, they began to appreciate their "perceptions . . . were separate from the official vision of history and reality." The New Vision lost momentum when Lucien Carr pled guilty to a charge of first-degree manslaughter, after killing an older man, David Kammerer, who had long made sexual passes at him. Kerouac was briefly detained as a material witness, then bailed out by Edie Parker, whom he soon married. That marriage, like two subsequent ones, proved troubled and short-lived.

Drugs, including marijuana and amphetamines, were indeed part of the scene from the beginning. Ginsberg recalled an early pot experience during which he went to the Metropolitan Museum of Art to visit an exhibition by the postimpressionist painter Paul Cezanne.

> I was studying art at the time, and made sure to take along a couple of sticks of grass and smoked some before going in, and there they were, the Cezannes. I kept staring at them, and somehow, just looking at them in that state of consciousness I was able to discern his use of space. . . . For me it was only the beginning of the exploration of the senses, the first scratchings of the Buddhist meditation exercises I would learn—the actual observation of how the senses operate, and the exploration of the wall of the senses of sight, smell, sound, taste, touch and mind.

At the same time, Ginsberg was cognizant of "the association of what society was laying on you, the notion of the 'dope fiend.' If you altered consciousness, there was something wrong with you."[7] For his part, Kerouac was drawn to Benzedrine, which recast his cinematic-like appearance, as he sought an ideal writing "method," while frequently pounding on his typewriter in seemingly spontaneous fashion. Kerouac, aspiring to a novel "artistic morality," informed Ginsberg, "Out of the humankind materials of art, I tell myself, the new vision springs."[8] Suffering from a blood clot, Kerouac ended up in Queens VA Hospital, before moving to Ozone Park, Queens, where he resided with his parents. His father had terminal stomach cancer, and Kerouac helped to support his family, taking a job at a shoe factory, while writing at nighttime, loaded up on speed.

While at Columbia, Ginsberg undertook his first homosexual affairs, some furtive encounters. The nineteen-year-old Ginsberg, a self-professed Jewish atheist, was suspended for posting nasty notes about President Nicholas Murray Butler, "Butler has no balls," and "FUCK THE JEWS," on his dormitory window, and for being discovered in bed one morning with Kerouac.[9] Temporarily expelled from Columbia, Ginsberg resided in "a communal apartment" at East 115th Street with Kerouac and Burroughs for a time, and followed Burroughs's lead and that of Herbert Huncke in exploring the seamy underside of Manhattan around Times Square. It was Huncke, an inveterate street hustler, small-time thief, and drug addict, complete with "radiant," but "despairing eyes," who said to Kerouac at one point, "I'm beat."[10] Other hipsters in the Times Square area were spouting "a new language," adapted from black jargon, which involved a continuous "jazzy" delivery. Ginsberg joined the U.S. Maritime Service, hanging out at Brooklyn's Sheepshead Bay. Readmitted to Columbia, he passionately crafted poems, became assistant editor of the *Columbia Review*, and captured a pair of prestigious poetry awards at the university. He also met Neal Cassady in 1946, falling in love with him as he had Kerouac. Suffering from a breakup with Cassady, with whom he had a sadomasochistic relationship, Ginsberg took a steamer to West Africa, but soon returned to resume his undergraduate studies at Columbia.

He smoked dope with Kerouac and Cassady in early January 1947, an encounter that led Kerouac to write in *On the Road*, "Two piercing eyes glancing into two piercing eyes—the holy con-man with the shining mind, and the sorrowful poetic con-man with the dark mind."[11] The three spent time in Denver, along with Neal's new bride, Carolyn Robinson Cassady. Ginsberg and Cassady eventually headed for New Waverly, Texas, visiting William and Joan Burroughs, as more of the events that Kerouac subsequently recorded took place. During the summer of 1948, before his final year at Columbia, Ginsberg purportedly had a religious experience as he masturbated, in which he heard William Blake deliver his poem, "Ah, Sunflower," among other works, whereupon Ginsberg determined to become a poet himself. His experience appeared similar to the ones Albert Hoffman had and like those Aldous Huxley later underwent.

> I began noticing in every corner where I looked evidence of a living hand, even in the bricks, in the arrangement of each brick, some hand placed them there—that some hand had placed the whole universe in front of me. . . . Or that God was in front of my eyes-existence itself was God . . . what I was seeing was a visionary thing, it was a lightness in my body . . . my body suddenly felt light, and a sense of cosmic consciousness, vibrations, understanding, awe, and wonder and surprise. And it was a sudden awakening into a totally deeper real universe that I'd been existing in.[12]

For the next decade-and-a-half, Ginsberg attempted to replicate that experience, employing all sorts of drugs in the process. Various critics, including both Paul Berman and Jonah Raskin, have called into question, at least to a certain extent, whether Ginsberg actually underwent the transformative experience he later spoke freely about, but curiously, failed to chronicle in his journals. Ginsberg would acknowledge, "I cooked it up, somehow." No matter, Ginsberg would tag 1948 as "the turning point," when "the psychological fallout from the bomb—the consciousness . . . hit." In addition to "the splitting of the bomb," there was "the splitting of the old structure in society and also a sense of the inner world splitting up and coming apart." Subsequently, Ginsberg attempted to duplicate the Blake-induced hallucination, which did or did not occur, to bring about "an exalted state of mind," through the use of marijuana or nitrous oxide.[13]

By late 1948, Kerouac and Ginsberg, with more nominal input from another writer, John Clellon Holmes, had devised their own vision of what came to be known as the beat generation. The two spoke of a "Found" generation, an "Angelic" generation, or the "generation of furtives," but Kerouac finally said it was a "beat generation" while hoping it remained unnamed.[14] As Kerouac later recalled, that involved "a generation of crazy, illuminated hipsters suddenly rising and roaming America, serious, curious, bumming and hitchhiking everywhere, ragged, beatific, beautiful in an ugly graceful new way—a vision gleaned from the way we had heard the way the word 'beat' spoken on streetcorners in Times Square and in the Village, in other cities in the downtown city night of post America—beat, meaning down and out but full of intense conviction." Kerouac felt compelled to point out this "never meant juvenile delinquents, it meant characters of a special spirituality who didn't gang up but were solitary Bartlebies staring out the dead wall window of our civilization."[15] And yet, as Holmes documented by early 1949, he and Kerouac recognized that "the beat generation" included drug addicts, drug peddlers, thieves, even murderers. Huncke and Ginsberg identified with "Dostoyevskian" sensibilities because they were "underground."[16]

Ginsberg was arrested when stolen goods, stored by petty criminals like Herbert Huncke, were discovered at his apartment, resulting in his placement at the Columbia Presbyterian Psychiatric Institute in mid-1949, which enabled Allen to avoid a jail sentence. A horrified Lionel Trilling had urged Ginsberg to speak with Herbert Wechsler, who taught in the law school and advised Allen to plead insanity. While at Columbia Presbyterian, he met the hipster intellectual Carl Solomon, who had resided in Paris for an extended period, and like Jean-Paul Sartre, contended, "There is no room for an honest man on either side of the Iron

Curtain."[17] A female friend, Joan Vollmer Burroughs, indicated she was hardly surprised about Ginsberg's hospitalization, then stated, "I've been claiming for years that anyone who doesn't blow his top once is no damn good."[18] Released in early 1950, Ginsberg, after attending a poetry session of William Carlos Williams in New York City, attempted to ingratiate himself with the aging poet, who had recently asserted that "absolute freedom is the artist's birthright."[19] Ginsberg also told Kerouac he was "no longer going to have homosexual affairs," and that homosexuality was "camp, unnecessary, morbid." It was "so lacking in completion and sharing of love as to be almost as bad as impotence and celibacy, which it almost was anyway."[20] He sought fulfillment in heterosexual relationships, and spent considerable time in Greenwich Village. He and Kerouac hung out at the San Remo Bar, located at 189 Bleecker Street, encountering the Welsh poet Dylan Thomas there. Ginsberg and Kerouac referred to the people at the San Remo Bar as the "subterraneans."[21] Through book editor Robert Giroux, of Harcourt, Brace & Co., Kerouac met Pulitzer Prize–winning author Carl Sandburg.

Kerouac completed his first novel, *The Town and the City*, based on his family saga and the beat circle, and published in 1950 by Harcourt. *New York Times* reviewer Charles Poore, who had delivered a rave review of Albert Camus's *The Stranger*, referred to Kerouac as "a brilliantly promising young novelist" in his account of Jack's book. Poore acknowledged Kerouac's affinity for Thomas Wolfe, but deemed him an original with his own "expansive spirit and a sharp eye," who possessed "a magnificent grasp of the disorderly splendor and squalor of existence."[22] The novelist John Brooks, who also worked for *The New Yorker*, reviewed *The Town and the City* for the *Times* too, calling it "a rough diamond of a book." Kerouac's novel, Brooks wrote, presented a "somewhat Dostoevskian view of New York City life," which, though "exaggerated . . . is powerful and disturbing."[23] In his mid-year examination of books, Poore included *The Town and the City* as one of the first novels that he recommended, along with, among others, three previously published books by George Orwell.[24]

Having moved to 454 West 20th Street in Manhattan, Kerouac, employing "bop prosody," finished his next novel, *On the Road*, in April 1951, with the assistance of his second wife, Joan Haverty, who would divorce him in a matter of months; a myth, which Kerouac played into, had it written in twenty or so days, but historian Douglas Brinkley has given lie to that notion.[25] As Kerouac later explained, that book "was really a story about two Catholic buddies roaming the country in search of God. And we found him. I found him in the sky, in Market Street San Francisco (those two visions), and Dean (Neal) had God sweating on his forehead all the way." Kerouac proved unable to attain a publisher for *On the Road* for half a dozen years.[26]

Ginsberg struggled to find his own voice, expressing his frustration in correspondence with William Carlos Williams, the acclaimed modernist poet who befriended him. Ginsberg had sent Williams a batch of poems, along with a song that was "to be sung by Groucho Marx to a Bop background." Ginsberg explained, "I envision for myself some kind of new speech."[27] In early January 1952, Ginsberg mailed journal entries to Williams, who responded gushingly, "You *must* have a book, I shall see that you get it. Don't throw anything away. These are *it*."[28] He also continued to read widely, devouring Joseph Conrad's *Heart of Darkness*, Hermann Hesse's *Steppenwolf*, Jean Genet's *The Miracle of the Rose*, Paul Bowles's *The Sheltering Sky*, and other works. In an entry in his journal dated April 17, 1952, Ginsberg mentioned carrying "the god (small peyote god)" in a briefcase. In another entry, he declared that peyote was "not God—but is a powerful force" that could enable individuals to reveal family secrets to one another.[29]

In the fall of 1952, a series of reviews appeared, examining John Clellon Holmes's novel, *Go*, an early, full-length treatment of the beats, with characters based on Kerouac, Ginsberg, Neal Cassady, William S. Burroughs, Herbert Huncke, and Holmes himself. Gilbert Millstein of the *New York Times* called up Holmes to ask about the meaning of "the beat generation": "What the hell is this?" Holmes had hardly reflected about that, simply recalling that was what Kerouac once stated. Millstein subsequently noted that Holmes wrote about marijuana smokers or heroin addicts, with several figures quoting from "Blake, Dostoevsky and the Bible," and continually on the go from Greenwich Village to the West Side, the East Side, and Harlem.[30]

In an article appearing in the *New York Times Magazine* on November 16, 1952, titled "This Is the Beat Generation," Holmes called attention to the budding counterculture associated with Ginsberg, Kerouac, and their small circle of friends. Holmes related stories about young people smoking marijuana, belonging to a "non-virgin club," and exuding "an instinctive individuality." Holmes credited Kerouac with having exclaimed, several years earlier, "You know, *this is* really a *beat* generation." Holmes defined the idea of "beat" as involving a sense "of having been used, of being raw," and pertaining to "a sort of nakedness of mind, and, ultimately, of soul; a feeling of being reduced to the bedrock of consciousness." He continued, "A man is beat whenever he goes for broke and wagers the sum of his resources on a single number, and the young generation has done that continually from early youth." Possessing "instinctive individuality," members of that generation required no bohemian or eccentric behavior, Holmes offered. They had endured the Great Depression and a world war, thus intimately encountering emotional highs and lows. The insecure peace that followed helped spur their "lust for freedom, and the ability to live at a pace that kills," resulting in a fondness for jazz, drugs, sex, and existentialism. But Holmes denied that today's "wild boys" were "lost," lacking an eloquent sense of loss and the "shattered ideals" characteristic of the Lost Generation of the 1920s. Instead, they took such "things frighteningly for granted," and delved into drugs or sex for curiosity's sake.[31]

"Only the most bitter" of the beats, Holmes indicated, would consider their existence nightmarish and bemoan a dearth of future possibilities. They appeared more concerned about "how to live," rather "than why," while displaying "a perfect craving to believe." At the same time, its members possessed no desire to transform "'square' society" but rather to evade it. They adhered to no particular philosophy, political party, or attitude, recognizing that the inability of standard moral and social ideals to encapsulate one's own experiences required each individual "to meet the problem of being young in a seemingly helpless world in his own way, or at least to endure." Holmes likened the Beat Generation to the "Young Russia" movement of the 1880s, which, thirty years later, turned to bombs, but he predicted that was not likely to occur in America. And yet he considered hopeful the recognition that modern life was beset by spiritual ailments, and the fact that there existed among the young, "clear, challenging faces."[32]

The early beats, moving beyond the quest for self-liberation desired by the Lyrical Left two generations earlier, explored sex of a seemingly unrestrained sort, alcoholic consumption, and drugs, including pot, hashish, heroin, and psychedelics. Ginsberg himself took peyote in early 1952, producing this entry in his notebook: "Heavens the universe is in order." He wrote, "I have been going around grinning idiotically at people, almost afraid they'll ask, 'What's the matter with you this minute?' But they seem to me also—so strange in their momentary consciousness." Like many of the beats, Ginsberg became attracted to Eastern religions, including Zen Buddhism; he urged Kerouac to read Japanese professor D. T. Suzuki's offerings on Zen.[33]

Burroughs became the next writer close to the New Vision crowd to see his book manuscript in print, but before that occurred his publisher, Ace Books, desired biographical information. He found this impossible to deliver, as he informed Ginsberg, who was acting as his literary agent and had sold *Junkie: Confessions of an Unredeemed Drug Addict* to Carl Solomon, working at Ace Books, in a letter dated April 22, 1952. It was difficult to believe, Burroughs suggested, that the publisher wanted truthful information such as "I have worked . . . as towel boy in a Kalamazoo whore house, lavatory attendant, male whore and part-time stool pigeon." Tell Solomon, Burroughs wrote, "I don't mind being called queer." After all, T. E. Lawrence and so many well-regarded sorts were "queer." However, he would castrate Solomon before accepting the characterization of being "a Fag." Burroughs drew "a distinction between us strong, manly, noble types and the leaping, jumping, window dressing cocksucker."[34]

The semi-autobiographical *Junkie* appeared in 1953, and despite non-existent reviews, sold more than one hundred thousand copies during its first year in print. In an unpublished examination of *Junkie*, Ginsberg lauded it as "an important document; an archive of the underground; a true history of the true horrors of a vice."[35] Later that year, Burroughs moved to Tangiers to initiate a four-year stay, while Ginsberg traveled to Mexico for five months, a glimmer of the peripatetic quality that characterized beat writers. There, Ginsberg engaged in the same quest for yage that Burroughs was undertaking, coming back to New York in the late summer, with "a gallon bottle of liquid infusion of the hallucinogenic vine ayahuasaca." Ginsberg was also reading *The Tibetan Book of the Dead*.[36]

In a harbinger of what lay ahead, the San Francisco poet Kenneth Rexroth, a veteran of the Old Left political battles of the 1930s and a conscientious objector during World War II, produced a poem, "Thou Shalt Not Kill," in tribute following the death of Dylan Thomas in November 1953. Rexroth bemoaned the murder of "all the young men," who had been hunted down on a daily basis for half-a-century. "They are killing the young men," having devised ten thousand means to do so,

Rexroth wailed. This was happening across Asia, in Siberian "slave pens," in European slums, and in American nightclubs. Those who bore witness, favored the poor, remained steadfast notwithstanding persecution, and bohemian spirits suffered vilification and worse at the hands of smooth individuals appearing like "the hyena" doing the bidding of big business or "the jackal" operating through the United Nations. There were the embittered red baiters and the countless numbers who suffered "prefontal Lobotomies in the Communist Party." The result: "Three generations of infants / Stuff down the maw of Moloch." Angrily, Rexroth wrapped up his magnum opus. "You killed him. / In your God damned Brooks Brother suit, / You son of a bitch."[37]

Viking Press, encouraged by Malcolm Cowley, who had earlier brilliantly chronicled the Lost Generation and helped to refurbish the literary reputations of both William Faulkner and F. Scott Fitzgerald, seriously considered the possibility of publishing Kerouac's *On the Road* manuscript. Editor Helen K. Taylor wrote to Cowley in late 1953, conveying her full agreement with his assessment that Kerouac's work was "a 'classic of our times.'" She lauded Kerouac's "bold writing talent," terming it "lavish, reckless," seemingly careless but "almost always effective." Taylor also considered the book "a piece of raw sociology" regarding the hipster generation, proclaiming it "a life slice so raw and bleeding that it makes me terribly sad." *On the Road* explored present-day "trickles of evil," exhibited by several young people who were, literally, "irretrievably gone." Indeed, "there is no redemption for these psychopaths and hopeless neurotics, for they don't want any," aspiring as they were wont to "the violences of sensation." Another editor at Viking, Evelyn Levine, believed *On the Road* "must be and will be eventually published." In an in-house memo, she declared, "I loved Kerouac's prose style, and the sense of poetic rhythm in the prose . . . throughout there is a Whitmanesque style for the US."[38]

In the August 21, 1954, issue of *The Saturday Review*, Cowley wrote about the young authors of the present age, members of the first generation to grow up with the automobile, radio, and talking pictures. Cowley pointed to one group, not inconsiderable in number, "that refused to conform and waged a dogged sort of rebellion," appeared "individual and nihilistic," and reveled in such "forbidden" delights as "heavy drinking, promiscuity, smoking marijuana." They drove fast, listened to cool jazz, considered themselves "cool" or withdrawn, and talked of existing "underground." Crediting Jack Kerouac with coining the phrase "the beat generation," Cowley referred to his yet-to-be published manuscript, *On the Road*, as "the best record of their lives." Cowley said this group was typical of a larger generation, exhibiting no concern for politics, but yearned for "something to believe, an essentially religious faith that would permit them to live in peace with their world."[39]

Moving to San Francisco in August 1954, Ginsberg, desirous of respectability, cut his hair, shaved his beard, and acquired a decently paying job with Towne-Oller, a market research firm. Shortly after settling in the city, Ginsberg also underwent psychiatric sessions at the Langley Porter Clinic, informing Dr. Philip Hicks at one point, "I really would like to stop working forever—never work again, never do anything like the kind of work I'm doing now—and do nothing but write poetry and have leisure to spend the day outdoors and go to museums and see friends." He also desired to live with someone, possibly "even a man." Ginsberg also wished, as he informed Hicks, to "cultivate the visionary thing in me," and just conduct "a literary and quiet city-hermit existence." Hicks responded, "Well, why don't you?" For a time, Ginsberg resided in the posh Nob Hill area with a pretty young woman, Sheila William Boucher, but the retriggering of an affair with Neal Cassady doomed that relationship. Ginsberg then met and fell in love with twenty-one-year-old Peter Orlovsky, with whom he soon shared an apartment in San Francisco.[40]

Antiheroic film protagonists like those played by Marlon Brando in *The Wild One* and James Dean in *Rebel without a Cause* appealed to Ginsberg, while speed, marijuana, and peyote provided the seeds for his most famous poem. In addition, as historian James J. Farrell indicates, the glimmerings "of a counterculture already existed in the writers' groups and poetry readings in Berkeley and the city; in coffee houses and clubs like the Black Cat, the Cellar, Café Trieste, and the Vesuvio Bar; and in little magazines like *City Lights*, *Goad*, *Inferno*, and *Golden Goose*."[41] Berkeley boasted listener-sponsored KPFA-FM radio, which Lawrence Ferlinghetti recalled as "a focal point for a lot of the 'underground.'"[42] KPFA regularly offered Alan Watts and Kenneth Rexroth, while a recent broadcast featured advocates for cannabis, leading to California attorney general's impounding of the radio broadcast.

Sporting a letter from his mentor William Carlos Williams, Ginsberg was allowed entrée into the San Francisco Renaissance circle headed by Rexroth. Subsequently, Ginsberg met the poets Gary Snyder, Philip

Whalen, Michael McClure, and Lawrence Ferlinghetti, among others. Ginsberg shared McClure's sensibility that the Academy was destroying poetry, and there existed a need to contest the deadening conformity and paranoia associated with the domestic Cold War. Allen agreed to participate in a poetry reading on October 7, 1955, at the Six Gallery in San Francisco, a converted auto repair shop containing about five hundred square feet, with white walls and dirt floors, which brought together important beat figures from both California and the Eastern seaboard. The occasion was designed, as Ginsberg put it, "to defy the system of academic poetry, official reviews, New York publishing machinery, national sobriety and generally accepted standards to good taste." Cassady and Orlovsky were among those in attendance, as the reading—what Snyder termed "a subterranean celebration"—took place. Fittingly too it occurred in San Francisco, long more receptive to bohemian types, possessing something of a radical political heritage, and the home of the nation's first long-lasting gay organization, the Mattachine Society.[43]

With Kenneth Rexroth serving as the master of ceremony, five young poets—Phillip Lamantia, Snyder, Whalen, McClure, and Ginsberg—participated in the reading, attended by an enthusiastic crowd of 150 people, encouraged by Jack Kerouac to purchase jugs of California wine. Kerouac captured the scene in his novel *The Dharma Bums*: "I followed the whole gang of howling poets to the reading . . . that night, which was, among other things, the night of the birth of the San Francisco Poetry Renaissance. Everyone was there."[44] Ferlinghetti later reflected, "Nobody had ever heard anything like that before. When you hear it for the first time, you say 'I never saw the world like that before.'"[45] Near the midnight hour, the twenty-nine-year-old Ginsberg, possibly drunk and certainly nervous, conducted his initial public recitation, reading from "Howl," composed earlier that year. Among the key influences for Ginsberg's epic poem were Rexroth's antipathy toward capitalism, Walt Whitman's *Leaves of Grass*, Kerouac's piece on "spontaneous prose," the jazz riffs of saxophonist Charlie "Bird" Parker, and the poet Robert Duncan's 1944 essay, "The Homosexual in Society." Biographer Bill Morgan claims that through the poem, Ginsberg "finally accepted his homosexuality and stopped trying to become 'straight.'" As Ginsberg continued his reading, which stood, Jonah Raskin contends, "as a testament to Allen's friendships and to his male friends . . . Kerouac . . . Burroughs . . .

Cassady, and Carl Solomon," Kerouac exhorted those in attendance with chants of "Go! Go!"[46]

A lyrical retort to the conservatism and conformity that seemingly afflicted the United States during the first half of the 1950s, "Howl" opened brilliantly with Ginsberg's woeful proclamation, "I saw the best minds of my generation destroyed by madness," referring to beat friends as well as himself. The beats, Ginsberg revealed, explored the black, mean streets of America, scouring for "an angry fix," notwithstanding the ferocity of drug laws. Ginsberg saw members of his now widened "small circle of friends" as "angelheaded hipsters" who aspired, in mystical fashion, for something beyond the crass materialism of modern, capitalist society. Self-imposed poverty enveloped them, as they listened to cool jazz and attempted to pass through "the Door in the Wall" that Aldous Huxley had pointed to, as various drugs enabled them to experience something of heaven in the manner of William Blake. American society hardly proved receptive, as Ginsberg's own experiences at Columbia demonstrated. The uptight, repressive nature of that society also produced stringent drug laws and proscriptions against homosexuality, turning the beats into outsiders at best, or even criminals. "Howl" was noteworthy for its universalistic qualities, as well as its depiction of those like Neal Cassady and Jack Kerouac who were taking to the road to seemingly experience all that life offered, no matter prevailing social mores, uptight cops, and punishment-inflicting courts.[47]

In the second section of his poem, influenced by a peyote trip and delivered during subsequent public readings, Ginsberg would assail Moloch, the ancient Semitic deity, but something that stood, in his telling, as a symbol of his own nation or contemporary society. Ginsberg associated Moloch with fearful children, young men forced to serve in the military, prisons, war, materialism, cultural blinders, polluting factories, soulless institutions, poverty, nuclear arms, sexual repression, suburbia, and the American dream. By contrast, members of a "mad generation" exulted, as seen in their "wild eyes" and "holy yells," in the manner they cavorted in the river or the street, Ginsberg revealed, again in prescient fashion.[48]

Ginsberg's initial, well-publicized public reading of part 1 of "Howl" reduced Rexroth to tears, and greatly excited Kerouac, who told his friend, "Ginsberg, this poem will make you famous in San Francisco." Rexroth responded, "No, this poem will make you famous from bridge to bridge."[49] By the end of the session, McClure, who believed that without the occasion "there would not have been an ongoing Beat Generation," thought "a body had been thrown against the barricades." As he recalled, "We had gone beyond a point of no return—and we were ready for it, for a point of no return. None of us wanted to go back to the gray, chill, militaristic silence, to the intellective void—to the land without poetry— to the spiritual drabness. We wanted to make it new and we wanted to invent it and the process of it as we went into it. We wanted voice and we wanted vision."[50] Snyder later declared that the Six Gallery reading provided a glimpse into an alternative culture involving community and vision. Gregory Corso acclaimed "Howl" as "the howl of the generation, the howl of black jackets, of James Dean, of hip beat angels, of mad saints, of cool Zen, the howl of the Withdrawn, of the crazy Sax-man, of the endless Vision whose visionary is Allen Ginsberg." He recommended the poem for "the hipsters, the angels, the Rimbauds." Following the Six Gallery readings, Ferlinghetti, who operated City Lights Bookstore in the North Beach section of San Francisco, sent Ginsberg a telegram that all but repeated Ralph Waldo Emerson's missive regarding Walt Whitman's publication of *Leaves of Grass*. "I greet you at the beginning of a great career. When do I get the manuscript?"[51]

Before Ferlinghetti published "Howl," Ginsberg crafted several additional poems, including "America," which he completed in mid-January 1956. In that poem, Ginsberg asked when the people of the United States would "end the human war," and then told his country, "Go fuck yourself with your atom bomb." He wondered when his nation would become angelic, get naked, and prove "worthy of your million Trotskyites," and then declared that it made him "want to be a saint." He decried the fact that Burroughs, residing in Tangiers, might not return. He confessed to smoking marijuana whenever he could, had read Marx, refused to spout the Lord's Prayer, had "mystical visions and cosmic vibrations," and was fixated on *Time* magazine. Ginsberg reflected about a number of figures, largely situated on the political left, victimized over the years inside or outside the United States, including Tom Mooney, the Spanish Loyalists, Sacco and Vanzetti, the Scottsboro Boys, and Scott Nearing. He mocked the Cold War, and admitted to not wanting to enter the military or work in a factory. After all, "I'm nearsighted and psychopathic anyway," Ginsberg acknowledged before concluding, "America I'm putting my queer shoulder to the wheel."[52]

City Lights/Pocket Poets published *Howl and Other Poems*, which included "America" and an introduction by William Carlos Williams that pointed to Ginsberg's demonstration that "the spirit of love survives to ennoble our lives if we have the wit and the courage and the faith—and the art! to persist." Williams also likened Ginsberg's personal passage into Golgotha to that of Jewish Holocaust victims, and warned, "Hold back the edges of your gowns, Ladies, we are going through hell," as a small black-and-white paperback appeared, with an initial printing of one thousand copies in England.[53] Ginsberg proudly informed his father on April 26, 1956, that Williams liked "Howl" and had written the introduction for his book, and he proclaimed himself ready to stand with other ostracized writers battling censorship. He mentioned Henry Miller's forbidden *Tropic of Cancer* and the French writer Jean Genet, whose work was also banned in the United States. Miller and Genet, Ginsberg wrote, were "such frank hip writers that the open expression of their perceptions and real beliefs are a threat to society." He concluded his note with the observation, "The wonder is that literature does have such power."[54] The American Civil Liberties Union (ACLU) promised to defend Ferlinghetti if prosecution resulted, a distinct possibility given the existing state of laws and court decisions involving obscenity. Following an initial seizure by a former member of the San Francisco Board of Supervisors, the federal collector of customs for the 18th District, Chester McPhee, deemed "Howl" obscene. Ginsberg's former mentor at Columbia, Lionel Trilling, also disliked Ginsberg's latest work, proclaiming his poems "quite dull" and lacking any music, in contrast to Walt Whitman's artistry.[55]

Responding to a charge by the poet Richard Eberhart, an English professor at Dartmouth College, that "you deal with the negative or horrible well but you have no positive program," Ginsberg denied that nihilism characterized *Howl*. Writing on May 18, 1956, he countered, "*Howl* is an 'affirmation' of individual experience of God, sex, drugs, absurdity, etc." He continued, "The title notwithstanding, the poem itself is an act of sympathy, not rejection. In it I am leaping *out* of a preconceived notion of social 'values,' following my own heart's instincts—*allowing* myself to follow my own heart's instincts, overturning any notion of propriety, moral 'value,' superficial 'maturity,' Trilling-esque sense of 'civilization,' and exposing my true feelings-of sympathy and identification with the rejected, mystical, individual even 'mad.'" He sought to propel those who read "Howl" to "the enlightenment of mystical experience," to empathy, and to a "starry spangled shock of MERCY." Furthermore, he was referring to the "*realization* of LOVE."[56] Already, Ginsberg was cultivating the art of self-promotion for beat writers. This offended Denise Levertov, the British-born poet, who informed William Carlos Williams that she accepted *Howl* "unconditionally," but worried that Ginsberg was "conducting a regular propaganda campaign" that would inevitably "damage his work."[57] Meanwhile, Ginsberg mailed copies of "Howl" to such distinguished writers as T. S. Eliot, Ezra Pound, William Faulkner, and Trilling.

The *New York Times* soon offered an essay titled "West Coast Rhythms," by Richard Eberhart. Only there, he noted on September 2, 1956, did "a radical group movement of young poets" exist, as "San Francisco teems with young poets." Among their mentors were San Francisco professor and poet Ruth Witt-Diamant, who had befriended the likes of W. H. Auden, Robert Lowell, Anais Nin, Theodore Roethke, Stephen Spender, Dylan Thomas, Rexroth, and Robinson Jeffers. Discussing the beats, Eberhart singled out the twenty-nine-year-old Ginsberg.

> The most remarkable poem of the young group is "Howl." . . . This poem has created a furor of praise or abuse whenever read or heard. It is a powerful work, cutting through to dynamic meaning. Ginsberg thinks he is going forward by going back to the methods of Whitman. My first impression was that it is based on destructive violence. It is profoundly Jewish in temper. It is Biblical in its repetitive grammatical build-up. It is a howl against everything in our mechanistic civilization which kills the spirit, assuming that the louder you shout the more likely you are to be heard. It lays bare the nerves of suffering and spiritual struggle. Its positive force and energy come from a redemptive quality of love, although it destructively catalogues evils of our time from physical deprivation to madness.

Poets like Ginsberg, Ferlinghetti, and Whalen, Eberhart concluded, were "finely alive . . . hostile to gloomy critics." They possessed "exuberance and a young will to kick down the doors of older consciousness and established practice in favor of what they think is vital and new."[58]

Back in California, Ferlinghetti defended "Howl," contending "it is not the poet but what he observed which is revealed as obscene. The great obscene wastes of "Howl" are the sad wastes of the mechanized world, lost among atom bombs and insane nationalisms. . . . Ginsberg chose to walk on the wild side of this world . . . mostly in the tradition of philosophical anarchism."[59] Charges were filed in mid-1957, following a second printing, that the book was obscene and indecent; police arrested both Ferlinghetti and the manager of City Lights Bookstore, Shigeyoshi Murao, a Japanese-American citizen whose family had been interned during World War II, although the charges against Murao were soon dismissed, thanks to attorneys associated with the ACLU. The controversy surrounding the bust ironically drew greater attention to both Ginsberg and "Howl," beyond his expanded circle of friends and like-minded individuals. As Ferlinghetti noted, "Allen was totally unknown until the book was busted."[60]

Meanwhile, Ginsberg undertook a series of excursions, both within the United States and outside of it, operating in the peripatetic fashion that would be associated with the beats. He also deliberately sought out well-known figures in the artistic realm, including the writer Anais Nin in Los Angeles, the artist Salvador Dali in Manhattan, and William Carlos Williams in New Jersey. After Ginsberg, Kerouac, Peter Orlovsky, and Gregory Corso visited Williams, the famed elder writer informed his fellow poet Theodore Roethke, "I think you've heard of Allen Ginsberg and his gang. . . . What does it mean? At least we live in an age where anything goes and I for one welcome it."[61] In March 1957, Ginsberg and Peter Orlovsky arrived in Morocco, traveling to Casablanca, where they partook of marijuana, hashish, and opium. Moving on to Paris, they discovered cheap, strong heroin, and smoked marijuana before heading over to the Louvre. They resided at a small establishment that Corso called the Beat Hotel.

The obscenity trial involving "Howl" proceeded in San Francisco's Municipal Court, during which the defense depicted both the author and his publisher as championing libertarianism, upholding First Amendment rights, and battling reactionary censorship. Defense witnesses praised *Howl*, terming it "prophetic" and "thoroughly honest," and attesting to its social merits. Mark Schorer, a professor of English at the University of California at Berkeley, declared that Ginsberg's poem served as "an indictment of those elements in modern society that, in the author's view, are destructive of the best qualities in human nature and of the best minds. Those elements are, I would say, predominantly materialism, conformity, and mechanization leading toward war." Ferlinghetti proclaimed "Howl," which he viewed as "apocalyptic" and Ginsberg's "first strike as the conscience of the nation and a provocateur for peace," the most significant long poem offered in the United States since the end of World War II, perhaps the most important one since T. S. Eliot's "Four Quartets."[62]

Judge Clayton W. Horn, operating without a jury, was compelled to issue a ruling on October 3, 1957, on the heels of a recent Supreme Court decision that proved burdensome to the prosecution. In *Roth v. United States*, Justice William Brennan delivered the High Court's ruling that "obscenity is not within the area of constitutionally protected speech or press." However, he went on to declare that obscenity involved material whose "dominant theme taken as a whole appeals to the prurient interest" to the "average person, applying contemporary community standards"; in other words, if such material exhibited "redeeming social importance," it would not be viewed as obscene. In addition to the Roth decision, San Francisco, along with other portions of the Bay Area, already possessed a well-established reputation by the mid-1950s as a haven for political and cultural outsiders. Thus, it should not have been surprising that Judge Horn found for the defendant, indicating that Ginsberg's book was not obscene. As Horn wrote, "The authors of the First Amendment knew that novel and unconventional ideas might disturb the complacent, but they chose to encourage a freedom which they believed essential if vigorous enlightenment was ever to triumph over slothful ignorance." Horn added,

> Would there be any freedom of the press or speech if one must reduce his vocabulary to vapid and innocuous euphemism? An author should be real in treating his subject and be allowed to express his thoughts and ideas in his own words. . . . If the material has the slightest redeeming social importance it is not obscene. . . . [Obscene words] must present a clear and present danger of inciting antisocial or immoral action. . . . [If words are] objectionable only because of coarse and vulgar language which is not erotic . . . in character, [they are] not obscene."[63]

As David Perlman of the *San Francisco Reporter* recognized, the trial helped to turn "Howl" into a bestseller throughout the city.[64]

Before the case of *The People of California v. Lawrence Ferlinghetti* was even decided, the beats and ideas associated with them, accurately or not, received additional publicity, both positive and negative. Writing in *Harper's Bazaar* in February 1957, Caroline Bird asserted that America's contemporary quest for rebels gravitated to the hipster, "an enfant terrible turned inside out." The hipster avoided society, and favored marijuana experiences that "squares" would never understand. He might be a jazz musician, but seldom was an artist or a writer. He was more likely to be "a hobo, a carnival roustabout" or a freelancer in Greenwich Village. James Dean, who excelled as the moody, brooding adolescent in cinematic roles before a horrific automobile crash took his life, stood as "a hipster hero."[65]

In the spring issue of the *Partisan Review*, the poet John Hollander, a former classmate of Ginsberg's at Columbia, referred to *Howl and Other Poems* as a "dreadful little volume," notwithstanding his belief that his friend possessed "real talent" and a "marvelous ear." Hollander claimed that Ginsberg's poems were "very tiresome."[66] Another blast came from the poet-critic James Dickey, writing in the *Sewanee Review*, who considered "Howl" inferior to the work of Henry Miller, Kenneth Patchen, and Kenneth Rexroth. Dickey effectively referred to Ginsberg's poem as "conventional," "adolescent," and exuding "an Attitude" hardly worth examining.[67] As Ginsberg later indicated in a lengthy letter to Hollander, he found reviewers' critiques to be off-kilter. "I get sick and tired I read 50 reviews of Howl and not one of them written by anyone with enough technical interests to notice the fucking construction of the poem, all the details besides," such as classical references.[68]

Charles I. Glicksberg, an English professor at Brooklyn College, discussed "The Lost Generation of College Youth" in the May 1957 issue of the *Journal of Higher Education*. Glicksberg focused on the intellectual elite on American campuses, where existentialist thought was in vogue. That philosophical strand, Glicksberg warned, "militantly" contested "all the values that have sustained civilized man," removing supernatural sanctions from morality, and enabling each individual to chart his own course. As Glicksberg saw it, existentialism as propounded by the French writers Jean-Paul Sartre and Albert Camus dissolved ties that bound man "to history and to humanity." Unfortunately, Glicksberg pointed out, skepticism could degenerate "into a militant cynicism" or nihilism. As earmarked by Camus, the few "rebels" within the college community might have garnered "a demoralizing glimpse of the possibility that all of life in which they once believed so passionately is foolish and futile."[69]

Following the lead of Caroline Bird, whom he quoted, Norman Mailer delivered an extended essay, "The White Negro: Superficial Reflections of the Hipster," in the summer 1957 issue of *Dissent*. Mailer referred to the psychologically disillusioning effects of World War II, with its concentration camps and atomic bombs, and the disinclination to dissent that took hold in early Cold War America. Rather, "a stench of fear" and "a collective failure of nerve" resulted, broken only by "the isolated courage of isolated people."[70]

In the midst of "this bleak scene," Mailer wrote, "the American existentialist-the hipster" appeared, ready "to divorce oneself from society, to exist without roots, to set out on that uncharted journey into the rebellious imperatives of the self." Mailer referred to "the unstated essence of Hip, its psychopathic brilliance," its association with rebellion and antipathy to "Square" America. He rooted hip in the African American, long compelled to live "on the margin," and jazz, which had undertaken a "knife-life entrance into culture." In various pockets around the country—New York, New Orleans, Chicago, San Francisco, and Los Angeles—an encounter took place involving bohemians, juvenile delinquents, and blacks. Subsequently, the hipster became embedded into American life, fueled by marijuana and a willingness to live on the edge. Having "absorbed the existentialist synapses of the Negro," the hipster became "a white Negro," Mailer declared. The hipster's world included "a muted cool religious revival," but also "exciting, disturbing," possibly "nightmarish" sensibilities. Nevertheless, Mailer saw the hipster striving "for the sweet" and devising a language in keeping with such a quest. He referred to "*man, go, put down, make, beat, cool, swing, with it, crazy, dig, flip, creep, hip, square.*" Those who were hip refused to stereotype individuals as good or bad, but instead believed that each individual remained an array of possibilities. Hipsters disliked societal restraints, favoring instead the liberated self, something the Lyrical Left had repeatedly emphasized. Hip morality, Mailer emphasized, involved a belief in the need "to do what one feels whenever and wherever it is possible," resulting in a clash with "the Square." Mailer considered the hip ethos to be immoderate, "child-like in its adoration of the present." He foresaw the fate of the hipster as intertwined with that of African Americans. The attainment of racial equality would rip away at "the psychology, the sexuality, and the moral imagination of every White alive," Mailer predicted. That in turn might enable hip to "erupt as a psychically armed rebellion" capable of challenging America's uptight sexual attitudes. [71]

After reading *The White Negro*, Ginsberg later applauded its "real grasp and kind of apocalyptic flip reality," calling it "the only good definitive article I've run into." Ginsberg continued, "I'd love to talk to him. I hope he takes to pure poetry and becomes an angel poet; he has a great grasp of the Goof." [72] Later, Ginsberg proved more critical still, viewing *The White Negro* as "well intentioned but poisonous." [73] By contrast, Jack Kerouac, as Ginsberg recalled, considered "the cool element, especially Mailer's interpretation as a psychopathic knifer, and John Clellon Holmes as a juvenile delinquent . . . an idiot misinterpretation of a yea-saying, Dostoyevskian, healthy colossus like Neal Cassady."

3

THE CONTINUED RECEPTION
OF THE BEATS

In the August 1957 issue of *The Saturday Review of Literature*, George Baker referred to the impending publication of Jack Kerouac's novel, *On the Road*; the devoting of the second issue of *The Evergreen Review*, a new publication, to the San Francisco beat writers; and the greater publicity attained by Kenneth Rexroth, soon, ironically, estranged from the beats. Rexroth saw the "dense crust of custom" enveloping American culture beginning to give way.[1] On September 5, 1957, the *New York Times* extolled *On the Road*, which Viking Press, following the advice of Malcolm Cowley, had just published. Completed half-a-dozen years earlier and delivered in a Joycean stream-of-consciousness manner Kerouac referred to as "spontaneous bop prosody," fueled by all sorts of intoxicants during a supposed twenty-one day marathon session, *On the Road* garnered mixed reviews but possessed the good fortune of avoiding coverage by the *Times*'s regular book reviewer, Orville Prescott. Gilbert Millstein opened his review by proclaiming publication of *On the Road* "a historic occasion," as well as "the most beautifully executed, the clearest and the most important utterance yet made by the generation Kerouac himself named years ago as 'beat,' and whose principal avatar he is." In the way that *The Sun Also Rises* by Ernest Hemingway represented the Lost Generation of the 1920s, *On the Road*, Millstein predicted, promised to do the same for the beat generation. The latter book engaged in "the frenzied pursuit of every possible sensory impression, an extreme exacerbation of the nerves, a constant outraging of the body, through alcohol, drugs, sex, driving frenetically, or adopting Zen Buddhism," the reviewer asserted.[2]

Such excesses were undertaken to foster spiritual growth, which remained "unfocused, still to be defined, unsystematic," distinguishing it from the cultural protest associated with the Lost Generation or the political engagement of the Depression Generation. Millstein suggested that the beat generation emerged disillusioned, viewing war as likely, politics as vacuous, and society as altogether hostile. That led its members to adopt the approach that the novelist John Clellon Holmes pointed to: the need to discover "*how* to live," rather "than *why*," and "a perfect craving to believe." That was the lesson *On the Road* imparted, Millstein wrote. He quoted from the novel's narrator, the Kerouac-like Sal Paradise, who revealed, "The only people for me are the mad ones, the ones who are mad to live, mad to talk, mad to be saved, desirous of everything at the same time, the ones who never yawn or say a commonplace thing, but burn, burn, burn like fabulous yellow roman candles." And then there was Paradise's sidekick, Dean Moriarty, patterned after Neal Cassady, who insisted that "Everything is fine, God exists. . . . God exists without qualms." To Sal, Dean, "the HOLY GOOF," was "a new American Saint" and had "the secret we are all trying to find." Thus for Millstein, Kerouac's new, "major novel," portions of it delivered with "a beauty almost breathtaking" of the tale of the beats, involved "this search for affirmation," which compelled them to take to the road.[3]

When Ginsberg, who was in Paris, read Millstein's review, he "almost cried, so fine and true." Ginsberg told Kerouac, "Well now you don't have to worry about existing only in my dedication [in "Howl"] & I will have to weep in your great shadow."[4] The journalist Bruce Cook later pointed to *On the Road*'s "liberating effect . . . on young people all over America." As Cook saw it, "There was a sort of instantaneous flash of recognition that seemed to send thousands of them out into the streets, proclaiming that Kerouac had written their story, that *On the Road* was their book."[5]

Some referred to Kerouac's standing at the cutting edge of a new literary generation. Kerouac, *The Village Voice*'s Arthur Oesterreicher declared, was "not just a writer, not just a talent, but a *voice*," in the manner of Hemingway, Henry Miller, and a young Ándre Gide. Most significant of all, Kerouac "offers a belief, a rallying point for the elusive spirit of the rebellion of these times," and thus *On the Road* was a crucial

part of American social history. No matter what academic reviewers contended, Oesterreicher wrote, "Kerouac's *got* it, really got it."[6] In *The
Saturday Review*, Ralph Gleason denied that *On the Road* and members
of Kerouac's generation lacked hope altogether, but insisted instead,
"they swing." Prophetically, Gleason suggested, "the jazz generation is
marking time, being cool, waiting, disengaged, if you must, looking for
somewhere to be," while Kerouac and jazz served as "its voice."[7] David
Boroff, writing in the *New York Post*, termed *On the Road* "a frightening
portrait" that contained "the core of truth," and captured a portion of the
new generation. Those individuals, Boroff indicated, were "bright, creative . . . and narcissistic." They were "religious without a God, insurgent
without a program; hell-bent on a self-transcendence which can find release only in speed and narcotics."[8] In a review published in *Commonweal*, Thomas F. Curley termed *On the Road* "a mirror of the American
roadway" and "a song of our restless soul" that recalled both the French
writer Louis-Ferdinand Celine and Walt Whitman. Kerouac was "a natural writer," whose only competition among young American authors appeared to be Saul Bellows and William Styron, although Curley disliked
the hollow pathos and dearth of seriousness displayed by his narrator. No
matter, Curley declared, "this is an exciting book to read."[9] American
studies' Professor Ray B. Browne of the University of Maryland delivered a review for the *Washington Post*, insisting that the characters in
On the Road contained "more than aimless haste in their movement,"
determined as they were to "LIVE," to "EXPERIENCE." Browne lauded
Kerouac's style, which he stated "never for a moment flags." Compari-
sons with Ernest Hemingway, Thomas Wolfe, Carl Sandburg, and F.
Scott Fitzgerald were inevitable, Browne wrote, but he insisted Kerouac
was "the junior version of none of them," providing the "voice of the
Frantic Fringe . . . himself."[10]

Others viewed *On the Road* far more critically, even disparagingly.
Author Truman Capote dismissed it out of hand. "That's not writing.
That's typing."[11] Carlos Baker, in *The Saturday Review*, assailed "this
dizzy travelogue," in which the author's "American landscape" was
"really sad and blank."[12] The *New York Times*' David Dempsey termed
On the Road "enormously readable and entertaining," containing "a de-
scriptive excitement unmatched since the days of Thomas Wolfe," but as
"plotless and themeless." In displaying a dysfunctional aspect of
American society, the book was a "stunning achievement," Dempsey

wrote, but one that "leads nowhere."[13] Ben Ray Redman told readers of the *Chicago Tribune* that Kerouac possessed "a powerful talent, but it is as yet completely uncontrolled."[14] *Time* magazine charged Kerouac with delivering "a rationale for the fevered young who twitch around the nation's jukeboxes and brawl pointlessly in the midnight streets."[15] *Newsweek* referred to Kerouac's Dean Moriarty as "a kind of T-shirted Ahab of the automobile," while declaring that only the author's "fast-tempoed, bop-beat prose" prevented the book "from careening headlong off into the trash heap."[16] Former beat champion Kenneth Rexroth dismissed *On the Road* as the product of a "furious square," with immature protagonists.[17] Rexroth had become estranged from the beat writers he had early championed, possibly owing to less than gracious statements made to him by both Kerouac and Ginsberg, and because of his failed marriage. At one point during a telephone conversation with Ginsberg, Rexroth roared, "I feel as if I walked into a candystore and got beaten up by a bunch of juvenile delinquents!"[18] As for the beats, the attention surrounding them would soon be "as dead as Davy Crockett caps," Rexroth, referring to a recent fad, predicted.[19]

In a similar vein, while reviewing *San Francisco Poets*, an album containing readings by ten writers, Thomas Lask took umbrage at Ginsberg's recording of "Howl." Readers must have considered "Howl . . . an honest reflection of the mind of one with no life lines to the world around him," notwithstanding the poem's "stridencies." However, Ginsberg's reading suggested the poem was "an enormous spoof." Lask now reflected, "Those who thought all along that 'Howl' was a fraud will have the strongest corroboration from Mr. Ginsberg himself."[20]

The November 16, 1957, issue of *The Nation* offered a lengthy examination of the hipster that also included another look at *On the Road*. In "Hip, Cool, Beat and Frantic," the novelist Herbert Gold, a former classmate of Ginsberg's at Columbia, explored "The American as Hipster." Readying for a television interview, Kerouac affirmed, "We're beat, man. Beat means beatific, it means you get the beat, it means something. I invented it." He also asserted, "We love everything, Billy Graham, the Big Ten, rock and roll, Zen, apple pie, Eisenhower." Moreover, the beat writer's pronouncement, "We're in the vanguard of the new religion," as Gold pointed out, had Charlie Parker playing the role of God, and Kerouac that of the Prophet.[21]

But Gold felt the need to draw a distinction between Kerouac and Allen Ginsberg and the hipsters, with thuggish, juvenile delinquent types, intellectuals, and jaded Upper Bohemians comprising "hipster society" in his estimation. The hipster desired a "flight from emotion," oblivion, silence, the "cool nothing." Gold likened the hipster to England's troubled Teddy Boys, Japan's "breaking-loose wild brats," and Paris' "existentialist zazous." The contemporary hipster, he continued, was "the true rebel without a cause" who suffered the "Passivity, Anxiety, Boredom" that beset American males, even those who idolized the Stanley Kowalski and Hal Carter characters in Tennessee Williams's *A Streetcar Named Desire* and William Inge's *Picnic*. The hipster was drawn to the "far-out religious camp," sweeping through St. John, St. Francis of Assisi, Dostoyevsky's Eastern Orthodoxy, and Zen Buddhism, while Kerouac delivered his claim regarding beats and religion. But dope and sex also came into play, leading Gold to wonder in the fashion of W. B. Yeats, "What rough beast, its hour come round at last, / Slouches toward Bethlehem to be born?"[22]

To Gold, Kerouac's exhortation, "WHOEE, I told my soul," served as an example of how the novelist made "such stuff hip, cool, beat, and frantic, all at once," enabling him to become "a Spokesman" for "a pack of unleashed zazous" who considered themselves "Zen Hipsters." At present, they possessed "a center in San Francisco, another in Greenwich Village, and claim outposts in Tangiers, on merchant vessels, in Chicago . . . in New Orleans . . . in Mexico City." These "Ivy League desperadoes" included Kerouac and Ginsberg, each a "hipster-writer" and "a perennial perverse bar mitzvah boy, proudly announcing: 'Today I am a madman. Now give me the fountain pen.'" Gold again differentiated Kerouac and Ginsberg from hipsters in general, because the two writers were "frantic. They care too much," albeit "mostly for themselves." Although exuding adolescence, this at least demonstrated that they cared "for something," while the hipster was "past caring." For Gold, Kerouac remained "the Columbia College boy," but one who possessed "a stubborn integrity" and who sought through his book "to do justice to his friends." Fondly but patronizingly, Gold declared the author of "Howl" and the writer of *On the Road* "typical of their little boys' town at its rare best, serious, convinced, and trying hard." Kerouac came across "as a wolf of the hotrod age," while *On the Road* "does nothing, thinks nothing, acts nothing, but yet manages to be a book after all, a loving portrait of hip Dean Moriarty and his beat, cool friends." The book's "frantic quality" indicated "there is hope for Jack Kerouac," Gold concluded.[23]

The furor, both positive and negative, that *On the Road* and "Howl" induced undoubtedly resulted, as their authors well recognized, from the timing of their publications. Those works appeared as the national ambiance underwent something of a shift away from the straightjacketed atmosphere of the early portion of the decade. Following his ill-advised attack on the U.S. military during the televised Army-McCarthy hearings, Senator Joe McCarthy lost political traction, although the vestiges of McCarthyism hardly disappeared altogether. American culture, and indeed, American society received a jolt of energy with the emergence of rock 'n' roll by the mid-1950s. Derived from hillbilly-country music, pop music, the blues, jazz, and rhythm and blues, rock 'n' roll exploded onto the music scene, charged with electricity and at least a hint of sexuality, making it doubly controversial and hence more attractive to young people. With white and black musical roots, and white and black stars such as Elvis Presley, Jerry Lee Lewis, Chuck Berry, and Little Richard, rock 'n' roll proved a catalytic, liberating force. Certainly during their rock 'n' roll heyday, each at times exhibited the antiheroic characteristics associated with the beats, whether that involved longer, unkempt hair; casual clothing; and a certain sensuality that made many Americans distinctly uncomfortable.[24]

Kerouac soon entered the realm of hipster celebrity, as Steven Watson indicates in his intriguing treatment, *The Birth of the Beat Generation: Visionaries, Rebels, and Hipsters, 1944–1960*. Journalists and television producers sought out Kerouac for interviews, as *On the Road* landed on the bestseller's list. Warner Brothers sought the film rights to the book, offering $110,000, and Marlon Brando expressed a readiness to play the part of the Neal Cassady–like figure, Dean Moriarty. The public appearances of Kerouac, still broodingly handsome, hardly failed to generate still greater interest.[25] Jerry Tallmer, one of the founders of *The Village Voice*, deemed Kerouac's "dark rakish face and glistening black hair more handsome than Cary Grant's or Wally Reid's."[26] *The Village Voice* reported on an event at the Village Vanguard jazz club, situated at 178 7th Avenue South in Greenwich Village, in which a full house greeted Kerouac, "the prince of the hips," with thunderous applause.[27]

Early in December 1957, with *Harper's* having recently indicated that "Howl" might "be *The Waste Land* of the younger generation," Ginsberg wrote to Paul Carroll, the poetry editor of the *Chicago Review*, suggesting that he consider the work of Philip Whalen and Gary Snyder, both "important poets" who had been "much underplayed with all the SF bullshit." He expressed appreciation for Carroll's interest in his work and that of his friends, and stated, "You know Time will get rid of all the trash and irrelevancy." Ginsberg then reaffirmed that the work of both Whalen and Snyder would stand. That left only William Burroughs, Ginsberg continued, who remained unpublished in the United States but was "Equal to Jack K. in prose strength" and should be "added to the Pantheon"; Ginsberg obviously "forgot" about *Junkie*. In follow-up correspondence, Ginsberg urged Carroll also to consider Gregory Corso's poem on H. G. Wells, and Kerouac's work. Acknowledging that Kerouac might appear to be writing "Zany," at least according to standard literary notions, Ginsberg insisted his poetry demonstrated that he was "a real EXPERIMENTALIST." Exhorting Carroll to "print everybody, madly!," Ginsberg again sought to reassure him. "Don't worry what people say if you turn out a screwey magazine full of idiotic poetry—so long as it's alive—do you want to die an old magazine editor in a furnished room who knew what was in every cup of Tea? Put some arsenic in the magazine! Death to Von Gough's [sic] Ear!"[28] At this point, Ginsberg was hanging out in Paris with Burroughs, newly arrived from Tangier. After an evening together, the two talked about the possibility of sharing "Love bliss" with others.[29]

John Clellon Holmes, writing in *Esquire* magazine in February 1958, discussed "The Philosophy of the Beat Generation," pointing to how many young people had existed vicariously through the antics of the late actor James Dean. They viewed him as one of their own, the "wistful, reticent" performer "looking over the abyss separating him from older people with a level, saddened eye; living intensely in alternate explosions of tenderness and violence; eager for love and a sense of purpose, but" on his terms. Dean "lived hard and without complaint; and he died as he lived, going fast." But Holmes also saw the beats, in the fashion of Jack Kerouac, engaged in a spiritual quest. "The Beat Generation," Holmes asserted, "is basically a religious generation."[30] The next month, Kerouac presented his own analysis of the beats' philosophy, for *Esquire*. He credited Holmes, Allen Ginsberg, and himself for envisioning "a generation of crazy illuminated hipsters suddenly rising and roaming America, serious, curious, bumming and hitchhiking everywhere, ragged, beatific, beautiful in an ugly graceful new way." Kerouac pointed to old hipsters who talked in "beat" fashion and "subterranean heroes" devoid, unlike members of the Lost Generation, of European influences. They dug drugs and bop, experiencing what some in postwar France were experiencing, influenced by Jean-Paul Sartre and Jean Genet. But a new phase of the domestic Cold War led beat characters "into jails and madhouses," or "shamed" them "into silent conformity." And yet, during that same period, with the Korean War as a backdrop, young people became drawn to "cool and jazz," their "gestures and the style," along with "the new look" that showed up in James Dean's films. The vernacular, the drugs, and the clothing of beat hipsters influenced "the new rock 'n' roll youth" and helped to resurrect the Beat Generation.[31]

Kerouac's latest book, *The Subterraneans*, appeared in early 1958 to decidedly mixed reviews. The *New York Post*'s David Boroff adjudged the book "a Baedeker of hipsterism—wild parties, Reichian analysis, existentialism, the literary idols, etc." Mixing what was genuinely poetic with incongruous slang, Kerouac was helping, Boroff indicated, to carve out "a new idiom, a new language of desperation," in a strange, transitional period.[32] Writing in the *San Francisco Chronicle*, Kenneth Rexroth reviewed Kerouac's latest book, *The Subterraneans*, insisting it featured "jazz and Negroes. . . . two things Jack knows nothing about." More damningly, Rexroth charged that Kerouac's sensibilities regarding blacks amounted to "Crow-Jimism, racism in reverse." Agreeing with Herbert Gold, Rexroth claimed that "Jack is a square, a Columbia boy who went slumming on Minetta Alley ten years ago and got hooked." But more important, Rexroth continued, Kerouac did convey "in a really heartbreaking fashion, the terror and exaltation of a world he never made." It was time to acknowledge, Rexroth concluded, "that we have another Thomas Wolfe on our hands, a great writer totally devoid of good sense."[33]

English Professor Esta Seaton of Spelman College later reviewed Kerouac's book, *The Subterraneans*, in *The Phylon Quarterly*, indicating that sociologists and psychologists should explore the appeal of the beat existence. She referred to "the leather-jacketed lost young and not so young men living disordered lives on the underside of society and passing their years drinking, taking dope, talking long into the night about jazz and Ezra Pound." The beat writers, Seaton stated, promised "intensity amidst chaos," which might well prove comforting to Americans beset by the dilemmas of the nuclear age.[34]

In the spring 1958 issue of *The Partisan Review*, literary critic Norman Podhoretz scathingly presented "The Know-Nothing Bohemians." Podhoretz, another former classmate of Ginsberg's at Columbia, expressed delight that Burroughs had been unable to find a publisher for his novel, *Naked Lunch*, and that Cassady's autobiography also remained unpublished. On the other hand, various reviewers delivered raves for "Howl" and *On the Road*, and Kerouac was considered the voice of a new batch "of rebels and Bohemians who called themselves the Beat Generation." The bohemianism displayed in *On the Road*, Podhoretz reluctantly admitted, exuded a certain charm, as energetic young men raced across America, attending wild gatherings, living frugally, acquiring odd jobs here and there, smoking marijuana, and bedding beautiful young women. The critic deemed the emotional intensity displayed by the protagonist Sal Paradise "the most desirable of all human conditions," and "the heart of the Beat Generation ethos," which separated it from previous bohemianisms. At the same time, Podhoretz compared the beats unfavorably with the Bohemianism of the 1920s, whose ideals, he asserted, "were intelligence, cultivation, spiritual refinement." The bohemianism of the following decade exuded "deep intellectual seriousness" and championed a more equitable distribution of civilization's fruits. These stood in sharp contrast to the current brand of bohemianism, Podhorertz continued, which was "hostile to civilization . . . worships primitivism, instinct, energy, 'blood.'" Its only intellectual interests involved mysticism, irrationality, "and left-wing Reichianism"; the latter referred to the school of thought associated with the Austrian-born psychoanalyst William Reich, who championed sexual freedom. As Podhoretz saw it, the new bohemians were drawn to jazz, particularly cool jazz, and bop language, disavowing articulateness. Additionally, the contemporary version of bohemianism included a fascination with "violence and criminality, main-line drug addiction and madness," as indicated in "Howl" and by the other protagonist in *On the Road*, Dean Moriarty. In a lengthy denouement, Podhoretz paired the beats' fascination with primitivism and spontaneity with their "pathetic poverty of feeling." Podhoretz exclaimed, "This is the revolt of the spiritually underprivileged and the crippled of soul—young men who can't think straight and so hate anyone who can." He likened the hipster spirit with that of juvenile delinquents, and wondered if Nor-

man Mailer reflected about a nine-year-old boy and a candy-store operator recently murdered by young hoodlums. Championing the beats, Podhoretz claimed, required a belief that incoherence, ignorance, and a lack
of intellectual discrimination superseded precision, knowledge, and "intelligence itself."[35]

In his column in the *San Francisco Chronicle*, dated April 2, 1958,
Herb Caen coined the phrase "beatniks" to refer to members of the beat
generation. He reported on "a party in a No. Beach house for 50 beatniks," and indicated that "by the time word got around the sour grapevine,
over 250 bearded cats and kits were on hand." In typically glib fashion,
Caen submitted, "There're only beat, y'know, when it comes to work."
Caen declared that the beats, in the fashion of the Soviet satellite Sputnik,
were way "out there." The following evening at El Matador, the renowned North Beach saloon-salon, he encountered an angry Jack Kerouac, who charged, "You're putting us down and making us sound like
jerks. I hate it. Stop using it."[36]

That summer, Ginsberg returned to the States, now viewed as the most
prominent figure within the burgeoning counterculture, although Kerouac
was referred to as "King of the Beats." The literary critic J. Donald
Adams, writing in the *New York Times*, proposed that "bleat" better en-
capsulated San Francisco writers like Ginsberg and Kerouac. "Bleating is
a monotonous sound," Adams wrote as he dismissed their work as "a
sleep-inducer." He considered their writing "baffling," as they supposedly engaged in a spiritual quest. Having examined Kerouac's novels, Adams thought "of nothing so much as an insistent and garrulous barroom
drunk, drooling into your ear."[37]

Conservative sociologist Ernest van den Haag, based at several educational institutions in New York City, contributed "Kerouac Was Here" to
Social Problems, issued by the University of California Press. Van den
Haag referred to "the inchoate grasping for Zen Buddhism or existentialism," and the success of beat writers Ginsberg and Kerouac. The "beat
hipsters," he wrote, were "unwilling or unable to accept discipline or
impose it upon themselves." Instead, they frenetically sought to imbue
their existence with meaning, while pretending that their rebellious
stances represented something. They deliberately attempted to place
themselves outside the mainstream and rejected social norms. They gravitated together, bound by "cultural anorexia" and "cultural starvation."
Supposed individualists, they resembled one another with their tight-fit-

ting jeans, just as businessmen in gray flannel suits did. They relied heavily on sex, booze, and drugs to break through "the 'blocks' that inhibit their 'true' personality." They traveled aimlessly across the country, with "the low brow types" opting for motorcycles. Affectations guided them, rather than feelings and passions. They exhibited a "frenetic desire, the will, the need to be excited, thrilled, impressed and impressive." They possessed literary precedents like Baudelaire and Rimbaud, but then those were poets, van den Haag damningly stated. Kerouac, by contrast, delivered "a counter language" lacking "differentiation, all subtlety, even meaning and grammar."[38]

During the spring of 1958, Citadel Press issued *The Beat Generation and the Angry Young Men*, a compilation of essays by Kerouac, Ginsberg, William Burroughs, Kenneth Rexroth, Carl Solomon, Norman Mailer, and John Clellon Holmes, among others. *Time* magazine deemed the volume useful to understand "the James Dean cult, the Elvis Presley and rock-'n'-roll crazes, and the gratuitous ferocity of juvenile delinquency." Without design, *Time* offered, the "central Beat character" represented "a model psychopath." The hipster proved fearful of both "family life and sustained relationships." At a minimum, the hipster was both "estranged from nature" and "a chronic manic-depressive," existing as "a kind of urban waif in the asphalt jungle." *Time* referred to the hipster as "a rebel without a cause who shirks responsibility on the ground that he has the H-bomb jitters." The magazine predicted the beat generation's future through its past—the early deaths of James Dean, Dylan Thomas, and jazz great Charlie "Bird" Parker, along with "the morbid speed with which its romantic heroes become its martyred legends."[39] Lawrence Lipton, in the midst of his own involved examination of the beats, offered an alternative analysis of the Citadel Press collection. Lipton viewed the East Coast and the West Coast beat scenes as distinctly different, clearly preferring the latter, which he saw as "fresher, less past-conscious" and able to draw "out the best in Ginsberg and Kerouac." The West Coast Beat scene, as Lipton called it, was less saddled with drug addiction, seemed "more dedicated," adopted a "more genuinely voluntary" brand of poverty, and comprised a younger, "better educated lot," overall, all the while proving more receptive to experimentation of various sorts. He virtually dismissed "the already tired and wilted Greenwich Village scene."[40]

Alan Watts, who had written *The Way of Zen* and taught at the American Academy of Asian Studies, presented a wholly different analysis of the beats and beat philosophy in the summer 1958 issue of the *Chicago Review*. In "Beat Zen, Square Zen, and Zen," Watts underscored "our vague discontent with the artificiality or 'anti-naturalness' of both Christianity . . . and technology," which separated man from nature and presented an "architect-God." Zen proved appealing, with its focus on both the spiritual and the secular, the mystical and the natural. Watts turned to "the 'beat' mentality," which he distinguished from hipster existence in both New York City and San Francisco. He considered this a means for the younger generation to revolt against "the American way of life," through no challenge to the prevailing order but rather by way of a subjective seeking of life's significance. The beat mentality refuted the "square," the socially conventional, the mutual hostility between capitalism and communism, and puritanism. [41]

In *Horizon* magazine, Robert Brustein, then lecturing at the School of Dramatic Arts at Columbia University, wrote about "The Cult of Unthink." Brustein pointed back to Stanley Kowalski, the lead character in Tennessee Williams's play *A Streetcar Named Desire*, whose "glowering, inarticulate" manner, as performed by Marlon Brando, "was to personify an entire postwar generation of troubled spirits" seeking an identity. The Brando-Kowalski figure stood as the Beat Generation's hero, Brustein offered. That hero also was represented by Kerouac, the action painter Franz Kline, or a rock 'n' roller. "He 'howls' when he has the energy, and when he doesn't, sits around 'beat' and detached in a funk. He is hostile to the mind, petulant toward tradition, and indifferent to order and coherence." He mainly sought to gratify himself, engaging in "'cool' kicks." At the same time, although purportedly an ardent individualist, he followed the pack. San Francisco writers, Brustein declared, were "the most striking examples of conformists masquerading as rebels," as they traveled, drank, doped, published, chased girls together, and even wore "a uniform costume": the ripped t-shirt, leather jacket, and tight blue jeans. While professing to stand apart from the masses and conformity, the beat authors proved to be "the Joiners of the new age," as they employed "extremely limited language" of the hip variety. Moreover, while Kerouac and his buddies professed to revere life, they exhibited "a disguised disgust and boredom with" it. Additionally, notwithstanding their supposed intellectuality, they were "persistently anti-intellectual." Their aggressiveness and passivity exemplified their rebellion's "adolescent" nature, as they accentuated youth while exalting juvenile delinquency, motorcycle gangs, and death. The individual beat appeared withdrawn from everyone, even his friends, and stood as "a man whom nobody understands and who understands nobody," as seen in films like *On the Waterfront* and *Rebel without a Cause*, starring Brando and James Dean, respectively. Brustein considered young people to be exhibiting "anarchic impulses," as demonstrated by a recent riot at a rock 'n' roll gathering in Boston. The "inarticulateness, obscurity, and self-isolation" of the beats exemplified a growing disinclination "to come to grips with life," Brustein concluded. The beats appeared to have abdicated the standard task of the avant-garde, to criticize society forthrightly, and instead seemed out "to slough off all responsibility whatsoever."[42]

On September 7, 1958, Father Bernard P. Donachie, a priest at St. Patrick's Cathedral in Manhattan, blasted the beats as "quitters in the game of life," evidently driven by "a terrifying fear of being ordinary." Donachie charged that the beats sought to be liberated "from the humdrum shell of sameness" that ensnared others, but were "unwilling to pay the price such greatness demands."[43] In the *San Francisco Examiner*, later that month, Michael Grieg wrote about the beats' appearing to have reached a dead end, fleeing in the face of police action, tourists, older bohemians, and inquiring journalists. The beats had scattered, with Allen Ginsberg, Gregory Corso, and Kenneth Rexroth in Europe, Gary Snyder residing in a Japanese Buddhist monastery, Lawrence Ferlinghetti on Potrero Hill in San Francisco, Philip Lamantia in Greenwich Village, and "Kerouac, handsome magus of the mindless," staying in a New York suburb with his mother.[44]

Interviewed by Marc D. Schleifer for *The Village Voice*'s edition of October 15, 1958, Ginsberg indicated that he had returned from overseas "to save America. I don't know what from." First, he praised Kerouac as "the greatest craftsman writing today," expressing appreciation for Schleifer's characterization of his friend's work as "Zen archery." Ginsberg countered Norman Podhoretz's criticism of beat writers, declaring "the novel is not an imaginary situation of imaginary truths—it is an expression of what one *feels*. . . . His criticism of Jack's spontaneous bop prosody shows that he can't tell the difference between words as rhythm and words as in diction." Then Ginsberg charged, "The bit about anti-intellectualism is a piece of vanity, we had the same education, went to the same school, you know there are 'Intellectuals' and there are intellectuals. Podhoretz is just out of touch with twentieth-century literature, he's writing for the eighteenth-century mind."[45]

In October 1958, Kerouac's novel, *The Dharma Bums* appeared, with a Gary Snyder inflected protagonist, Japhy Ryder, foreseeing "a great rucksack revolution thousands or even millions of young Americans wandering around with rucksacks, going up into the mountains to pray, making children laugh and old men glad, making young girls happy and old girls happier, all of 'em zen lunatics who go about writing poems that happen to appear in their heads for no reason and also by being kind and also by strange unexpected acts keep giving visions of eternal freedom to everybody and to all living creatures."[46] Later, Allen Ginsberg spoke of Kerouac's envisioning "a spiritual angelic generation that would ultimately take over with long hair and exquisite manners . . . wise as serpents and harmless as dogs."[47]

Charles Poore, a longtime book reviewer for *Harper's*, discussed Kerouac's latest for the *New York Times*. Referring to Kerouac as "the laureate of the Beat Generation," Poore asserted that *The Dharma Bums* would likely engender "jubilance among the Beejees" and fury by antagonists of the beat writers. The Beejees, Poore noted, were engaged in "intellectual imperialism," influenced by vagabondage and jazz, while "ruthlessly" contesting conformity, thereby shaping "a conformity of their own, as . . . nonconformists always do in the long run." According to Poore, Kerouac's characters proved only "deeply interested in Zen Buddhism," but could only engage in "its serenely contemplative disciplines precariously, because they are always on the go." At the close of his review, Poore referred to a recent *New Yorker* cartoon in which one intellectual informed two others he was conversing with in a café, "I'll be writing along, beat as you please, when suddenly this irresistible surge of optimism bubbles up inside me." Poore added, "When that happens the only thing to do is to rustle around and find some new conformities to confront with nonconformity."[48]

Also in the *Times*, the novelist Nancy Wilson Ross presented her own analysis of *The Dharma Bums*. As Ross saw it, Kerouac's latest cast of characters, led by the protagonist, Japhy Ryder, proved far "more respectable and articulate" than his earlier ones. While remaining "carefree wanderers," they sought enlightenment through Zen Buddhism. Ryder, for his part, envisioned a steady stream of youngsters "refusing to subscribe to the general demand that they consume production and therefore have to work for the privilege of consuming all that crap they didn't really want anyway, such as refrigerators, TV sets, cars, at least fancy new cars, certain hair oils and deodorants, etc." Ross praised Kerouac's "often brilliant descriptions of nature," and his depictions of spirited gatherings of beats. She reflected less happily on Kerouac's supposed "philosophical last statement" issued in the spring, when he intoned, "I DON'T KNOW. I DON'T CARE. AND IT DOESN'T MAKE ANY DIFFERENCE."[49]

Samuel I. Bellman, an English professor at Cal Poly Pomona, also examined Kerouac's most recent novel, declaring in *Chicago Review* that the author was once more "the restless wanderer, the disinherited outcast woefully seeking a family, an identity, a definition and localization on life's graph." Bellman referred to another Kerouac protagonist, Ray Smith, who ranged from freight-hopping to mountain-climbing, as "an aged child," whom he likened to "his begetter." Smith proved "artless, crude, emotionally overdependent, and an incorrigible hooky player," thereby providing ammunition for Kerouac's critics. Bellman nevertheless insisted that "Kerouac's rock 'n roll prose . . . is so well suited to his subject, which in turn is so well suited to the times." Furthermore, the beat writer, "with his Thoreau and Whitman genes tingling in his protoplasm," emphasized that which conventional authors too frequently exploited: "the world of physical sensation, of touchable and seeable matter." Consequently, Bellman asked why then did critics "persecute Kerouac?" He answered that it was because Kerouac's characters did not herald standard morality and because his fiction broke literary rules. [50]

Allen Ginsberg delivered his own review of *The Dharma Bums* in the November 12, 1958, edition of *The Village Voice*. He began by declaring the need "to clear up a lot of bullshit," pointing to the notion that Kerouac wrote *On the Road* in a burst of energy while on amphetamines and the fact that "presumptuous literary critics in publishing houses" tore apart the original brilliant version. To actually write Spontaneous Bop Prosody required "enormous art (being a genius and writing a lot)," as well as having faith in God. Kerouac's latest was an "extraordinary mystic testament" delivering "signposts on the road to understanding of the illusion of being." Terming Kerouac "the great master innovator" of American prose, Ginsberg wondered how his friend could be viewed "as anything but a gentle, intelligent, suffering prose saint." He deemed the abuse heaped on Kerouac "disgusting," and blasted "the technical ignorance" displayed by most reviewers, even favorable ones, as "scandalous." In closing, Ginsberg saluted the nation's "new visionary poet," and said it was time to "talk of Angels." Kerouac fired off a brief note to Ginsberg, proclaiming his review the "best I ever got," and urging him to begin his next article with "Now to put an end to all this cow-flop."[51]

At a seminar sponsored by Brandeis University titled "Is There a Beat Generation?" held at Hunter College Playhouse a few days before Ginsberg's review appeared, Kerouac, the only panelist attired in black jeans, boots, and a checkered shirt, read the following statement: "It is because I am Beat, that is, I believe in beatitude and that God so loved the world that He gave His only begotten son to it. . . . Who knows, but that the universe is not one vast sea of compassion actually, the veritable holy honey, beneath all this show of personality and cruelty." The beat generation, Kerouac said, amounted to "a revolution in manners . . . being a swinging group of American boys intent on life." This was in keeping with the antiheroic posture of first Humphrey Bogart and the private detectives, and then James Dean. As for "being beat," Kerouac said, that involved acting as did "the rebellious, the hungry, the weird, and the mad," with beat hipsters ranging from the Cool, dressed in black and offering few words, to the Hot, frenetically talking and moving, with "mad shining eyes."[52]

In the January 2, 1959, issue of *Commonweal*, the author and critic Seymour Krim discussed the "King of the Beats," focusing on "our so-called wild man," Jack Kerouac. Krim acknowledged that Kerouac was "often careless and slangy," with his language "dripping colorlessly into an undifferentiated puddle," a charge sometimes leveled at both "action painters" like Jackson Pollock and the avant-garde musical composer John Cage. The life featured in Kerouac's stories, Krim indicated, exhibited "confusion and waste," but that was in keeping with the American national scene. Moreover, many young people, including "quite gifted ones," sought to live in the fashion that Kerouac presented in his novels. Krim very tellingly noted that "what once was the inner circle of bohemia has expanded its values through modern jazz and the dissemination of avant garde art of all kinds to the very gates of the middle class." As could be seen in men's magazines, "so-called bohemian values have now become a part of American life." Notwithstanding "its comparative frailty and childishness," Kerouac's voice proved distinctive because he was brave enough to examine "the frantic modern scene" as he had experienced it.[53]

William Burroughs presented his own autobiographical examination of the beats in his 1959 novel, *Naked Lunch*, which became enormously controversial because of its highlighting of the ready use of drugs, including morphine and heroin, and the steady discussion of sex, both kinky and homosexual. Its publication resulted in a lengthy court battle that concluded only in the mid-1960s when *Naked Lunch* was deemed not to be obscene. Norman Mailer defended the author and his work, testifying, "Burroughs is in my opinion . . . a religious writer. There is a sense in *Naked Lunch* of the destruction of the soul, which is more intense than any I have encountered in any other modern novel."[54] Again, its controversial nature ensured notoriety and, undoubtedly, increased sales. On a less happy note, cultural critic Benjamin De Mott, a professor of English at Amherst College, referred to Burroughs as a pornographer.

While Burroughs awaited publication of *Naked Lunch*, his friend Allen Ginsberg took LSD for the first time during the spring of 1959, after agreeing to participate in a federally funded research experiment conducted at the Mental Research Institute in Palo Alto, California. Ginsberg had written a poem, "Laughing Gas," in which he related a different kind of hallucinatory experience. Referring to "the secret of the magic box," Ginsberg explored how nitrous oxide anesthetized "mind-consciousness." The poet had been introduced to the research team in Northern California by the anthropologist Gregory Bateson, the husband of Margaret Mead. Listening to Richard Wagner's opera, *Tristan and Isolde*, and a recording of Gertrude Stein, Ginsberg underwent a battery of psychological tests. In the midst of his initial LSD trip, Ginsberg wrote a poem, "Lysergic Acid," which indicated, "It is a multiple million eyed monster . . . it is a vast Spiderweb / and I am on the last millionth infinite tentacle of the spiderweb, a worrier / lost, separated, a worm, a thought, a self . . . / I allen Ginsberg a separate consciousness / I who want to be God."[55] In a letter to his father, Ginsberg discussed his experience, which he called "astounding," referring to Huxley's *Doors of Perception* and *Heaven and Hell*. Ginsberg likened the fantasy and trance-like state to the world explored by Samuel Taylor Coleridge in "Kubla Khan," the poem completed back in 1797. "I . . . saw a vision of that part of my consciousness which seemed to be permanent and transcendent and identical with the origin of the universe," Ginsberg explained. Lovely images "of Hindu-type gods dancing on themselves" also floated through his mind. LSD appeared necessarily to result in "a mystical experience," Ginsberg reported, but he also felt compelled to indicate, "It's a very safe drug," which he encouraged his father to try. Ginsberg soon traveled through Latin America, ingesting sizable doses of a strong hallucinogen used by Indians in the Amazon.[56]

That same spring, the *New York Times* explored another facet of the burgeoning counterculture, the socially conscious, politically charged comedians who appeared in nightclubs, television programs, and records, eventually garnering the title of "the sickniks." The May 3, 1959, edition of the nation's leading newspaper contained an examination of the thirty-three-year-old stand-up Jewish comedian Lenny Bruce, delivered by Gilbert Millstein, who had offered that initial rave review of *On the Road.* Bruce was known for his satirical orations on an array of topics including politics, big business, religion, the law, race, jazz, the Ku Klux Klan, and Jews. He performed frequently at the hungry I, the North Beach nightclub run by Enrico Banducci, appeared on national television programs like *Arthur Godfrey Talent Scouts* and the *Steve Allen Show*, and had recorded albums of his monologues. Millstein began his article by proclaiming Bruce "the newest, and in some ways, most scarifyingly funny proponent of significance, all social and some political," in contemporary American nightclubs. Referring to Bruce as "a sort of abstract-expressionist stand-up comedian," Millstein noted his "fidgety sense of moral indignation" that seemed to easily outdistance that of another performer, Mort Sahl. Bruce was presently pulling down $1,750 weekly for his stage show at the Den in the Duane, located on Madison Avenue. Delivering material he wrote himself, or which he tossed out extemporaneously, Bruce transmitted "nervous shards of hip talks," along with telling impersonations. One of his best known skits had Bruce as jazz musician respond to a radio interviewer with the following patter. "Man, it's like. Well, you know. I mean. Well, you *just blow.* Man don't *bug* me." Bruce acknowledged, "The kind of comedy I do isn't like going to change the world." At the same time, certain aspects of American society troubled him, and, as he put it, "satirizing them—aside from being lucrative—provides a release for me."[57]

San Francisco Chronicle columnist Herb Caen championed Bruce, during that period. "They call Lenny Bruce a sick comic, and sick he is. Sick of all the pretentious phoniness of a generation that makes his vicious humor meaningful. He is a rebel, but not without a cause, for there sure are shirts that need un-stuffing, egos that need deflating." Caen admitted that "sometimes you feel guilty laughing at some of Lenny's mordant jabs—but that disappears a second later when your inner voice tells you with pleased surprise, 'But that's true.'"[58]

Harry T. Moore, an English professor at Southern Illinois University, discussed Lawrence Lipton's new book, *The Holy Barbarians*, in the May 24, 1959, edition of the *New York Times*. In "Cool Cats Don't Dig the Squares," Moore called Lipton "a kind of Boswell of the Beatniks." As for Kerouac, Moore acknowledged that he possessed "the ability to transform attitude into myth." At the same time, Moore pointed out "that the cats lack humor," afflicted as they were by "their own determined ultra-bohemianism, their own grim conformities." Perhaps, as Lipton offered, the beats had "a holy-idiot quality," Moore stated. "Certainly they often behave as if they are playing an elaborate prank on society." But, in Moore's estimation, they lacked "the zany fun" that cropped up in the work of Saul Bellow, Truman Capote, and other non-beats.[59]

Among the most illuminating aspects of *The Holy Barbarians* was Lipton's analysis of Kerouac's writing. While attempting to capture the beat generation, Kerouac had, Lipton pointed out, "only scratched the surface," with *On the Road* more about the beats of the 1940s than the 1950s. *The Dharma Bums* concentrated on a small batch of writers and their lovers, who, along with jazz musicians, made up "a part of the scene, but only a small part," as did Kerouac's "rucksack revolution." These works paled by comparison with Ernest Hemingway's examination of the Lost Generation, John Dos Passos's look at the generation of the 1930s, and Norman Mailer's analysis of "the World War II and postwar Generation." Lipton also questioned whether hallucinatory drugs would result in "anything more than platitudes and cliches." At the same time, Lipton saw a place for the holy barbarians "in a society geared to the production of murderous hardware and commodities with built-in obsolescence for minimum use at maximum prices on an artificially stimulated mass consumption basis."[60]

Eugene Burdick, who taught political science at the University of California at Berkeley and who coauthored the bestselling novel, *The Ugly American*, regarding U.S. experiences in Southeast Asia, wrote about "The Politics of the Beat Generation" for the June 1959 issue of the *Western Political Quarterly*. Right up front, Burdick denied that a beat generation even existed, declaring rather that there existed "a small group of people with an intensely private vision." These included the writer John Clellon Holmes, Ginsberg, and Kerouac, who did indeed envision a "generation of crazy, illuminated hipsters suddenly rising and roaming America." San Francisco appeared to be the "natural home" of this movement, although many of its "originals" had departed from there. In the fashion of the existentialists, the hipster "disaffiliates," determining to exist "on the safe margins of society" while committing firmly to no organizations, including the family. Rather, the hipster sought to cultivate the self, as he "plays it cool and digs only those things which interest him personally," including sex, marijuana, and jazz. All the while, he believed "that as he grows more gentle and understanding he will take on a 'Christ-like' quality." Self-knowledge would allow him to transform society through the "power of example, like a young Mikhail Bakunin who propounded the gospel of spontaneous revolution and . . . the vivid example." Burdick doubted whether the hipster philosophy would dig deep roots in American society. [61]

Time magazine presented its own take on socially charged nightclub comedians in its July 13, 1959, issue. Referring to Mort Sahl, Lenny Bruce, Jonathan Winters, Shelley Berman, Elaine May, Mike Nichols, Tom Lehrer, and Don Adams, as "the Sickniks," *Time* noted that they dropped jokes about families, Sigmund Freud, masochism, sadism, drugs, even sainthood. The first of this breed, Sahl, pulling in $300,000 a year, appeared at top nightclubs around the country. Their patter, the magazine indicated, was "partly social criticism liberally laced with cyanide, partly a . . . kind of jolly ghoulishness, and partly a personal and highly disturbing hostility toward all the world." What distinguished the sickniks from earlier stand-up comedians was how closely they drew "to real horror and brutality that audiences wince even as they laugh." *Time* suggested that the sharpest barbs emanated from Bruce, via a "usually vicious barrage" that included a reputed defense of Nathan Leopold and Richard Loeb, two privileged young men accused back in 1924 of murdering a fourteen-year-old boy to commit the perfect crime. The magazine also acknowledged that Bruce was probably the most successful of the latest crop of sickniks. [62]

Time magazine included a blast against the beats in its September 7, 1959, issue. The magazine referred to "those unwashed minstrels of the West," the North Beach and Venice beats, who made "much of their loud vows of poverty. To be poor, yak the shirtless ones as they sit scratching in store-front espresso halls, is to be holy, man, holy." *Time* noted that Lawrence Ferlinghetti's *A Coney Island of the Mind* had sold 15,000 copies, while Allen Ginsberg's *Howl*, which it called "an effete epic," had forty thousand copies in print. Jack Kerouac's novel, *The Subterraneans*, had sold even more copies.[63]

During the fall of 1959, a new television program began, *The Many Loves of Dobie Gillis*, about a sensitive teenager, constantly fantasizing about beautiful girls, whose closest friend, Maynard G. Krebs, was a beatnik.[64] Maynard was best known for exclaiming in horror, "Work!" when the very notion of doing so occurred. At the same time, Maynard, exhibiting a degree of genuine hipness, continually referred to both Dizzy Gillespie and Thelonius Monk.

In an unpublished essay, dated November 4, 1959, Ginsberg urged, "Let's blow up America—a false America's been getting in the way of realization of beauty—let's all get high on the soul."[65] That same month, directors Robert Frank and Alfred Leslie released their short film, *Pull My Daisy*, about the beats. With a script and narration by Kerouac, the film starred Ginsberg, Peter Orlovsky, Corso, and the pop artist Larry Rivers, and was based on a dinner party hosted by Neal and Carolyn Cassady. Short-story writer Thalia Selz opened her review of *Pull My Daisy* for *Film Quarterly* by expressing bewilderment whether it was designed "in a mood of objective amusement or loving commitment." Selz suggested that the film's chief merit resided in its documentary quality, providing as it did "intimate shots of the new Bohemia and its conventions."[66] In his review of the third International Film Festival held in San Francisco, Paine Knickerbocker of the *San Francisco Chronicle* indicated that Kerouac's *Pull My Daisy* "glimmers with the author's delight at his own cleverness."[67]

On November 29, 1959, the poet Kenneth Rexroth scathingly reviewed Kerouac's latest novel, *Mexico City Blues*, while dismissing his earlier work as well. Kerouac flitted about the country "poorly" and in a "frightened" state, and knew little about either jazz or blacks, Rexroth charged. In fact, Rexforth now went so far as to accuse Kerouac as sharing the attitude of the Ku Klux Klan regarding blacks. Kerouac's latest work, a collection of poems, indicated a similar paucity of knowledge about Buddhism and drugs, Rexroth wrote. At the same time, he attested to Kerouac's "terrifyingly skillful use of verse . . . broad knowledge of life . . . profound judgments . . . almost unbearable sense of reality."[68] *Life* magazine, with a circulation greater than six hundred thousand, contained an article, "The Only Rebellion Around," in its November 30, 1959, issue. Paul O'Neil denigrated beats as "talkers, loafers, passive little con men, lonely eccentrics, mom-haters, cophaters, exhibitionists with abused smiles and mortgages on a bongo drum—writers who cannot write, painters who cannot paint, dancers with unfortunate malfunction of the fetlocks." O'Neil called the Beat Generation "a cult of the Pariah," seeking out as its adherents did, "the roach-guarded mores of the skid road, the flophouse, the hobo jungle and the slums, primarily to escape regimentation."[69]

In late January 1960, Lawrence E. Davies wrote about "'Beats' in Center of Coast Unrest," for the *New York Times*. Davies indicated that community tensions had heightened in North Beach, which he stated was often deemed "the national capital of the Beat Generation." A recent spate of drug busts had taken place, in "scantily furnished pads" that "were scenes of frequent orgies," Davies reported. However, he also referred to a report by a local minister, Pierre DeLattre, who decried the "week-end tourists" who visited North Beach, determined to encounter "something evil and orgiastic." The minister also bemoaned the presence of a growing number of kids, who arrived "after reading what a beatnik is and trying to dress and act like one." Moreover, DeLattre revealed, "the term beat" was received unhappily by many who favored "beatific, a search for a beautiful attitude." He considered the beats individuals who were seeking "a more direct insight into reality through emotional and intuitive forms of experience." They desired greater spontaneity, while "living for today" and believing "in nonattachment to material goods." Acknowledging that he sometimes found North Beach troubling, DeLattre also witnessed "tremendous life here." Additionally, he had never resided anywhere else with "such a sense of community." Many sought "spiritual vitality," although admittedly "a lot end up in disaster." The police hardly helped matters, piquing tensions.[70]

Bennett M. Berger, then teaching at the University of Illinois, explored "How Long Is a Generation?" in the March 1960 issue of the *British Journal of Sociology*, associated with the London School of Economics and Political Science. He noted the tendency of intellectuals to view generations as appearing and falling by the wayside more quickly than during, for instance, the Victorian age. In the United States, he indicated, a pronounced "extension of 'youthfulness'" suffused American culture. Consequently, "high school sub-bohemians mix with their 35-year-old mentors in the same cool coffee shop milieu." This very extension of youth, Berger emphasized, involved an era inclined "to cultural pronouncements, movements, 'statements,' rebellious outbursts, revolutionary flurries, and so on." He also pointed to the rapidly expanding number of intellectuals in the United States. But most intriguingly, Berger pointed out that *On the Road* suggested "a network of bohemian communities exists between San Francisco, Denver, Chicago, and New York, each ready to accept to its bosom the bohemian travellers of the Road."[71]

In the April 17, 1960, edition of the *New York Times*, Gilbert Millstein, that early champion of *On the Road* and Lenny Bruce, discussed the phenomenon of "Rent a Beatnik and Swing." The vogue of the beatnik, Millstein declared, could be seen in the recent advertisement by Fred W. McDarrah, a photographer for *The Village Voice*, in his paper: "add zest to your tuxedo park party . . . rent a beatnik. completely equipped: beard, eye shades, old army jacket, levis, frayed shirts, sneakers or sandals (optional). deductions allowed for no beard, baths, shoes, or haircuts. lady beatniks also available, usual garb: all black." McDarrah started such a service after receiving a call from a young woman from Scarsdale who wanted to know where she might rent a beatnik for a party she was hosting.[72]

Not quite a month later, Richard Schickel, then a New York editor, reviewed a collection of writings by Ginsberg, Kerouac, Ferlinghetti, Mailer, and several others, also for the *New York Times*. Schickel began by referring to Millstein's nearly three-year-old review of *On the Road*, stating that it compelled "the 'uptown' world" to pay attention to "a previously submerged style and viewpoint," thereby helping to usher in the Beat Generation. In the period ahead, the beats became "a subject of earnest debate, concern, study and emulation," along with "one of the major sociological phenomena of our time," Schickel stated. He also pointed to the recent report that beats were being rented out to "'squares" looking for "kicks." This occurred, Schickel noted, right around the time when Gold Medal Books, an uptown paperback publisher, asked both Madison Avenue squares and Beecker Street beats to attend a party celebrating the release of a new anthology, *The Beats*. Thus, as Schickel put it, "the customary avant-garde circle had been completed in less than three years." Schickel referred to the postwar hipsters as "the remote ancestors of the young beatniks." The former inhabited "the gray world of petty crime, drug addiction, gambling and of the jazz world. They were true causeless rebels, and they had a wonderfully colorful argot which attracted the attention of the Village-type intellectuals." By the close of the 1940s, "the pioneers of literary hipsterism" initiated an assault on American art and culture. [73]

Largely "refugees from the political wars of the Thirties and Forties," many of those smart and seasoned "revolutionaries" lost energy by the middle of the 1950s, having helped to shape "disciples" such as Kerouac, along the way. As "one of the survivors" recalled, "I remember him. We used to send him home because we thought he might get hurt playing with the big boys." Undaunted, Kerouac ploughed through rejection after rejection before making it. To Schickel, Kerouac succeeded "by softening and romanticizing the withdrawal of his intellectual predecessors." He furnished student intellectuals on college campuses the identity they needed, offering a justification "for silence and withdrawal." The world Kerouac created, Schickel asserted, was "anti-intelligent or non-intelligence." The Zen he delivered was "harmless, inoffensive," while being largely irrelevant to American society at present. Damningly, Schickel tossed out, "The Beats are so easily laughed off," along with their "mock protest," which explained their appeal to the mass media. [74]

The September 1960 issue of *Mad* magazine offered a spoof, "Beatnik: The Magazine for Hipsters," supposedly presented "by the Beat Generation which *really* defends the movement . . . the movement to abolish it." Fake ads included those for "Paint Smears For Beatnik Blue Jeans," "Oversize Sweaters for Beatnik Chicks," "Rent a 'Square' For Your Next Beatnik Party," and a solicitation for "A Beatnik Artist Scholarship." A column titled "The Inquiring Hipster" presented a half dozen responses to the query, "Like, how come you became a beatnik?" Those answering were labeled a "Free-Lance Philosopher," a "Poet and Push-Cart Peddler," a "Part-Time Intellectual," a "Full-Time Emotionalist," a "Metaphysician and Waiter," and a "Hanger-On and Part-Time Fink." The issue also contained a "Prize-Winning Beatnik Confession Story": "The Night 'Wild Harry' Flipped His Lid"; another column, "Dear Daddy-O," which provided "Advice to the Love-Bugged"; an explanation of "Wild New Beard Styles"; "A Glossary of Square Terms"; "The Beat Beat: Goings-on Around the Scene"; and "The Kick of the Month" to deflect entreaties regarding the most hip party to be found.[75]

Norman Mailer, by contrast, delivered a personal salute to one of the leading beat writers, in "Ode to Allen Ginsberg."

> I sometimes think
> that little Jew bastard
> that queer ugly kike
> is the bravest man
> in America.[76]

In his journal, Ginsberg fired back at those who assailed the beats, "Crap on all you Critics," then named Norman Podhoretz, Lionel Trilling, Nat Hentoff, Alfred Kazin, Robert Brustein, and James Wechsler, among others. He dismissed Podhoretz as "King of the Jews," Trilling as a "Mystic," and Kazin as "hypocritic," blasting the naysayers as "snoopers, creeps, hung up idiots, Incompetents, sneaks & dumbbells, quacks."[77]

A far more powerful critic of the beats expressed his opinion about them during the Republican Party's National Convention, held in Chicago during late July 1960. FBI director J. Edgar Hoover informed the gathered throng that the three greatest threats confronting the American nation were "Communists, eggheads and beatniks."[78]

4

FROM HARVARD TO MILLBROOK:
TIMOTHY LEARY

The man who considered himself America's leading beat, Allen Ginsberg, soon proved determined to spread the gospel of psychedelics, as did a new acquaintance, Timothy Leary, whom he referred to as "a hero of American consciousness," and Richard Alpert, a colleague of Leary's at Harvard.[1] In fact, Ginsberg and Leary considered one another allies in the psychedelic quest, although differing in how it should be conducted. Both wanted to target important intellectual, artistic, and even political figures, but Ginsberg initially favored a more free-flowing approach, while Leary championed a controlled, top-down dispensing of psilocybin, mescaline, and LSD.

Born in Springfield, Massachusetts, on October 22, 1920, Leary was the son of Timothy "Tote" Leary, an Army dentist and alcoholic stationed at the U.S. Military Academy in West Point, New York, and Abigail Ferris, a housewife. His father abandoned Abigail and him, when Leary was only thirteen. He nevertheless thrived at Springfield's Classical High School, serving as president of the school senate and editor of the school newspaper. Poor attendance during his senior year in high school prevented Leary from attending an Ivy League institution, but he enrolled at the U.S. Military Academy in the mid-1940s. Disciplinary problems, resulting from a drinking incident, led to his departure from West Point in August 1941, whereupon Leary subsequently enrolled at the University of Alabama, but he was expelled from there, after spending the night in a young woman's dormitory room. Eventually, following military service on the home front, Leary, now married to Marianne Busch, graduated from Tuscaloosa in 1945, with a bachelor's degree in psychology. Leary subsequently received his master's at Washington State University in 1946, and a PhD in psychology, four years later, from the University of California at Berkeley, where he studied under Erik Erikson, the famed child psychologist. In 1950 Leary, then teaching at Berkeley, helped to establish the Kaiser Foundation for Psychology Research in Oakland, California, subsequently garnering $500,000 in federal grants to conduct research into mental illness. In 1955, he became director of psychiatric research at the Kaiser Foundation Hospital. His wife Marianne, the mother of his two children, committed suicide that year; she was evidently disturbed by the fact that Timothy was breaking an agreement involving their open marriage in falling for his lover. Also in 1955, Leary married that lover, Mary Della Cioppa, but the marriage lasted only a year.

Leary began establishing an impressive academic reputation, particularly thanks to his writings on personality diagnosis. His book, *The Interpersonal Diagnosis of Personality*, published in 1957, garnered favorable reviews. In the *American Journal of Sociology*, Jeanne Watson of the University of Chicago deemed Leary's attempt to construct a methodology to evaluate personality "a major advance in the treatment of the interpersonal dimension of personality."[2] H. J. Eysenck of the University of London Institute of Psychiatry, reviewing Leary's book for the *British Medical Journal*, proved more critical but praised its "emphasis on the objective measurement of interpersonal relations . . . and the necessity for the dimensional analysis of such relationships."[3] In *American Anthropologist*, Bert Kaplan of the University of Kansas deemed it an "important volume," lauding its "honesty, rigor, and methodological sophistication"; Kaplan did express concerns about the too easy employment of the term "interpersonal" regarding "emotions, motives, fantasies, perceptions, roles, diagnoses, gestures, purposes."[4] Toshio Yatsushiro of McGill University offered a lengthy review in *Administrative Science Quarterly*, pointing to Leary's "comprehensive theory of personality based on interpersonal processes." Yatsushiro indicated that both clinicians and anyone genuinely exploring "conceptions of personality and interpersonal behavior" should examine Leary's book.[5]

In the June 10, 1957, issue of *Life* magazine, the New York banker Robert Gordon Wasson contributed a seventeen-page essay, "Seeking the Magic Mushroom," about the kind of psychedelic experiences soon associated with Leary. Wasson reported on the adventures he shared two summers earlier with his friend, the photographer Allan Richardson, when they supposedly became "the first white men in recorded history to eat the divine mushrooms." On ingesting several mushrooms, the men experienced visions, as Wasson reported, "whether our eyes were opened or closed. . . . They were in vivid color, always harmonious."[6] *Life* opened its pages to Wasson in this manner undoubtedly because both publisher Henry Luce and his wife Clare Booth Luce, along with English writers Aldous Huxley and Christopher Isherwood, were engaged in LSD sessions of their own.

In 1958, a thoroughly depressed Leary, drinking heavily and believing he was "practicing a profession that didn't seem to work," began residing in Europe with his children.[7] The following year, while the Learys were in Italy, Timothy's friend and colleague from Berkeley, Frank Barron, informed him about a religious experience he had while taking mushrooms in Mexico. Leary's initial response, ironically enough, was to express concern that Barron might lose professional credibility if word got out regarding his fascination with vision-inducing substances. While still in Europe, Leary spoke with David McClelland, director of the Center for Personality Research at Harvard, who had been quite impressed by his book, contending that the relationship involving patients and therapists needed to become more egalitarian. Leary emphasized the existential-transactional nature of the research he favored. Psychologists, Leary told McClelland, must "work with people in real-life situations" and become immersed in the subjects they studied. McClelland responded that Leary was calling for a dramatic recasting "of the role of the scientist, teacher, and therapist . . . an egalitarian or information-exchange approach."[8] When Leary agreed with that assessment, McClelland offered him a position at Harvard, stating, "There is no question that what you are advocating is going to be the future of American psychology. You're spelling out front-line tactics."[9] In words that must have returned to haunt him, McClelland exclaimed, "You're just what we need to shake things up at Harvard."[10] During the spring of 1960, Leary was employed as a lecturer at Harvard, soon offering a graduate course, "Existential Transactional Behavior Change." When McClelland asked for a recommendation for a one-year appointment, Leary suggested his friend Frank Barron, who was working at the Institute of Personality Assessment and Research at Berkeley. When Barron and Leary spoke about the prospective appointment, Barron suggested that the two take "magic mushrooms" that summer in Mexico, to help provide tools for tracking behavioral changes. Leary refused to commit himself.

A trip to Cuernavaca, Mexico, that summer altered Leary's life and, ultimately, as matters turned out, American culture as well. Temperate Cuernavaca had long served as a resort area for well-known Americans ranging from Hollywood actors to mobster Sam Giancana and heiress Barbara Hutton. Staying in a villa, Leary spoke to an anthropologist and linguist from the University of Mexico, Lothar Knauth, who helped find the kinds of mushrooms Barron had lauded. They chased down psilocybin mushrooms with cold Mexican beer, and Leary soon began to experience strange sensations. He recalled, "It was the classic visionary voyage and I came back a changed man. You are never the same after you've had that one flash glimpse down the cellular time tunnel. You are never the same after you've had the veil drawn."[11] Leary remembered, "I was whirled through an experience which could be described in many extravagant metaphors but which above all and without question was the deepest religious experience of my life."[12] He witnessed exotic images, ranging from Nile palaces to Moorish reptiles. He seemingly coursed down the evolutionary path, including "snake-time, fish-time, down-through-giant-jungle-palm-time, green lacy fern leaf-time."[13] Leary's academic sensibilities were shattered, never to be fully reconstituted.

On returning to Cambridge, Massachusetts, that fall, Leary, assisted by Barron—who was spending the year at Harvard—initiated the Harvard Psilocybin Project, whose founding board would include Huxley, Barron, McClelland, and the psychologist Ralph Metzner. First, Barron suggested that Leary read William James, the brilliant Harvard psychologist who underwent his own experiences using nitrous oxide, and Morton Prince, another Harvard psychologist, who explored altered states of consciousness. After Leary had read their works, Barron introduced him to Harry Murray, the Harvard psychologist and top OSS operative, who had launched brainwashing experiments for the CIA.

Leary also read Aldous Huxley's *The Doors of Perception* and *Heaven and Hell*. On receiving a letter from Leary, Huxley, who was offering a series of lectures at the Massachusetts Institute of Technology that semester, invited him to lunch and appeared highly supportive of the existentialist-transactional research approach. Working on his final novel, the utopian *Island*, where moksha served as "the reality revealer, the truth and beauty pill," Huxley saw Leary as the individual who could help to turn on important members of the intellectual, cultural, and economic elite to psychedelics.[14] "That's how everything of culture and beauty and philosophic freedom has been passed on," Huxley insisted.[15] At the same time, he warned that opposition, emanating from powerful individuals, would be forthcoming. As drugs arrived from Sandoz Laboratories, Huxley introduced French writer Theophile Gautier's analysis of the rituals conducted by the Hashish Club of Paris and the nineteenth-century poet Charles Baudelaire. Gautier underscored the importance of a tranquil mindset, along with a comfortable setting, to prevent nightmares, rather than ecstasy, from unfolding. After meeting Leary in the Harvard Faculty Club one day, Huxley suggested they take psilocybin that evening. As they did so, they discussed how to introduce mind expansion to American society. Referring to the knowledge gained through psychedelics as "this bloody philosopher's stone," Huxley emphasized how in the past such information had been closely held by scholars, mystics, and artists.[16] When Leary insisted that society required this information, Huxley countered, "These are evolutionary matters. They cannot be rushed." He suggested that Leary reach out to "artists, writers, poets, jazz musicians, elegant courtesans, painters, rich bohemians," who in turn would "initiate the intelligent rich."[17] Huxley indicated that Leary's role was very simple: he needed to proselytize for evolution, in the fashion he and his grandfather Thomas Henry Huxley, the acclaimed botanist who heralded Charles Darwin, had. "These brain-drugs, mass produced in the laboratories, will bring about vast changes in society. . . . All we can do is spread the word." The main "obstacle," Huxley noted, was the biblical admonition regarding eating from "the fruit of the Tree of Knowledge."[18]

Another important figure connected to psychedelic drugs that the architects of the Harvard Psilocybin Project encountered was Humphry Osmond. He and other early experimenters implored Leary and his gang to work within the existing system. They advised that drugs were designed to overcome disease, and that nonphysicians who doled out or took drugs themselves would be castigated. Consequently, Leary needed to influence physicians in the manner Sigmund Freud had. Stanford engineering Professor Willis Harman worried that prohibition would follow the use of psychedelics by nonmedical personnel.

Leary, who wanted to change the world, later informed his colleague Richard Alpert, an assistant professor of psychology, "We're going to take a whole new approach with this research. Everyone thinks these drugs cause psychosis, but that's because they've been controlled by psychiatrists. Of course they're going to view this as psychosis. That's all they know. But there is really something deeper going on here, Richard. Wait until you try them." The drugs, Leary insisted, "can revolutionize the way we conceptualize ourselves—not to mention the rest of the world. It'll be great. We'll give them to philosophers, poets, and musicians." Leary also planned to deliver specific dosages of psilocybin to participating graduate students and faculty members from throughout the Boston metropolitan area. [19]

While Alpert spent the fall semester teaching at Berkeley, Leary and a number of graduate students took doses of a synthetic brand of psilocybin, arrived from Sandoz Laboratories in Switzerland. Leary informed those taking the drug, "This is no field for the faint of heart. You are venturing out (like the Portuguese sailors, like the astronauts), on the uncharted margins. But be reassured—it's an old human custom."[20] The experiments were conducted at the large, three-story house Leary had rented in the affluent suburb of Newton, located on the side of the Charles River across from Harvard. By the fall of 1960, Leary knew that a small number of scientists were engaged in research involving psychedelic drugs and that a number of intellectuals had at least contemplated them. "We couldn't see ourselves as part of a secret priestly class following models that belonged to the Old World. We realized that we were approaching a crossroads. From the beginning the all-important question was going to be, *Who gets to go? Who gets to select this experience for themselves?*"[21]

Allen Ginsberg, whom Humphry Osmond had urged to consider joining the Harvard Psilocybin Project, had his own ideas about the spread of psychedelics. He contacted Leary through a handwritten note, expressing interest in Leary's research into altered states of consciousness. Soon after the initial correspondence, Leary met Ginsberg and Peter Orlovsky, with Allen sharing stories of his own hallucinogenic experiences. Ginsberg noted that gurus or shamans had long attempted, even in preindustrial societies, to foster visionary experiences.

In the midst of his first psilocybin experience, with music from Wagner and Beethoven wafting through the air, Ginsberg experienced contrasting emotions. Remaining all-too aware he had been unable to attain a state of perfection previously, Ginsberg recalled that Leary now "looked into my eyes, and said I was a great man." Experiencing a flash of light, Ginsberg heard Wagner's *Gotterdammerung* explode "like the horns of judgment calling from the ends of the cosmo," and "called on all human consciousness to declare itself into the consciousness." Ginsberg further felt there was a need for "someone to take on the responsibility of being the creative God and seize power over the universe." After deciding, "I might as well be the one to do so," Ginsberg soon informed Leary, "I'm the Messiah," and then indicated that he would "preach love to the world. We're going to walk through the streets and teach people to stop hating." Ginsberg called up Jack Kerouac, instructing him, "Take a plane up here immediately. The revolution is beginning. Gather all the dark angels of light at once. It's time to seize power over the universe and become the next consciousness!"[22] During a wide-ranging discussion regarding the world they hoped to shape, Ginsberg and Leary talked about peace, nuclear disarmament, ignorance, and conformity. They then began scheming to usher in a neurological revolution, with Ginsberg, "the quintessential egalitarian, want[ing] everyone to have the option of taking mind-expanding drugs."[23]

It was Ginsberg who helped to convince Leary that Huxley's approach was too inhibited, that the diffusion of drugs should become wider still. The growing friendship between the psychologist and the poet proved fruitful, as Ginsberg also helped to provide Leary entrée to important figures in the New York artistic and cultural world. As Ginsberg recalled, "The idea was to give [psychedelics] to respectable and notable people first, who could really articulate the experience, all while keeping it under the august auspices of Harvard. I could act as the go-between, keeping as much of a low profile as possible considering my visibility as America's most conspicuous beatnik." Ginsberg considered taking on the role of "Ambassador of Psilocybin."[24] At his behest, Leary began introducing— or reintroducing—the drug to various individuals, including Huxley, jazz musicians Maynard Ferguson, Dizzy Gillespie, and Thelonius Monk, the poet Charlie Olson, the artists Franz Kline and William de Kooning, the publisher Barney Rossett, Pulitzer Prize–winning poet Robert Lowell, Professor Huston Smith of MIT, Alan Watts, and Arthur Koestler, author of the anti-Stalinist novel *Darkness at Noon*. Ginsberg informed Neal Cassady, "We're starting a plot to get everyone in Power in America high."[25]

After Neal Cassady completed an all-but inevitable session with Leary involving mushrooms, he cried, "It's philosophical! I could write a book about the cosmic thoughts I had. This is the Rolls Royce of dope, the ultimate high."[26] When a drunken Jack Kerouac arrived, he asked, "So what are you up to, Doctor Leary, running around with this communist faggot Ginsberg and your bag of pills?"[27] Proclaiming himself "King of the Beatniks," Kerouac later indicated that on psilocybin he "felt like a floating Khan on a magic carpet with my interesting lieutenants and gods. . . . It was a definite Satori."[28] As Lowell underwent a trip on psilocybin, he informed Leary, "Now I know what Blake and St. John of the Cross were talking about. This experience is what I was seeking when I became a Catholic." Nevertheless, when Leary later suggested that perhaps Lowell should have been given a more powerful dose, Ginsberg replied, "That could have been risky for us. I wouldn't want to be known as the guy who put America's leading poet round the bend."[29]

Aldous Huxley's relationship with Leary proved complicated but both wanted it to continue. On March 3, 1961, Leary invited Huxley to participate in a symposium led by Alan Watts that would examine the effects of psychiatric drugs, to take place in Copenhagen that summer at the XIV International Congress of Applied Psychology. Still, unlike Leary, Huxley continued to believe that psychedelics should only be taken by intellectuals and elite members of society. By contrast, Leary saw psychedelics as having the potential to tackle such social ailments as alcoholism and juvenile delinquency, believing that mind-altering drugs compelled an individual to look at himself and the games he played.

That in turn placed Leary in opposition to the behaviorists at Harvard, such as B. F. Skinner, who believe in operant conditioning, the notion that behavior resulted from consequences, whether positive or negative; Skinner examined behavior, not internal mental development. Leary's relationship with Frank Barron also deteriorated, as his friend became concerned about Timothy's too easy consumption of psilocybin. Barron appeared to favor Huxley's sensibility regarding the spread of psychedelics, in contrast to that of Leary and Ginsberg. In the spring of 1961, Richard Alpert replaced Barron as a top advisor to the Harvard Psilocybin Project.

Just returned from California, Alpert arrived at Leary's home on the evening of March 6, 1961, to encounter Ginsberg, whom Timothy viewed as "the secretary-general of the world's poets, beatniks, anarchists, socialists, free-sex/love cultists"; the three took psilocybin pills.[30] Alpert later wrote, "A scream formed in my throat. I felt that I must be dying since there was nothing in my universe that led me to believe in life after leaving the body." As panic set in, Alpert nevertheless heard a voice asking him "rather jocularly . . . who's minding the store?" At that point, "I realized that although everything by which I knew myself, even my body and this life itself, was gone, still I was fully aware!" Consequently "a new kind of calmness—one of a profundity never experienced before" set in. "I had just found that 'I,' that scanning device—that point—that essence—that place beyond. A place where 'I' existed independent of social and physical identity. That which was I was beyond Life and Death." Moreover, that "'I' Knew—it really Knew. It was wise, rather than just knowledgable. It was a voice inside that spoke the truth."[31] The relationship between the handsome, charismatic, inveterate womanizer Leary, and the less out-spoken Alpert, compelled during that period to hide his homosexuality, proved important for the spread of the gospel of psychedelics.

By the spring of 1961, the Harvard Psilocybin Project—now referred to by Leary as the "Harvard Psychedelic Project"—had already resulted in "over 200 subjects" being administered the drug. Leary later recalled that "eighty-five percent of our subjects were reporting that the experience was the most educational of their lives," in contrast to the 33 percent success rate generally recorded for therapeutic treatment.[32] Still dissatisfied, Leary and Alpert wanted to expand their horizons and were, consequently, delighted on receiving an invitation to speak to prison officials about recidivism. In a controlled setting, Leary and various graduate students soon began administering psilocybin to various inmates at the Concord state prison; the hope was that the drug would help to reduce antisocial behavior. Leary wrote to Ginsberg about the latest experiment, whose initial half-dozen participants included a pair of murderers, two armed robbers, an embezzler, and an African American heroin dealer. "Big deal at the prison. Convicts love it. Hoodlums have satori, deciding to devote rest of life to keep JD's out of jail etc."[33] Helpful was the fact that the black prison psychiatrist, Dr. Madison Presnell, had, along with his wife, taken psilocybin at Leary's rental home at Newton Center.

That spring, Leary and the other architects of the Harvard Psilocybin Project received a call from Robert Gordon Wasson, who came to campus to talk about his own psychedelic experiences. Extolling the magic mushroom, Wasson declared that it allowed for many individuals to approach a visionary state and to do so without experiencing religious-styled mortification. But in contrast to Leary, Wasson was opposed to young people taking psychedelics for personal and spiritual growth.

At the XIV International Congress of Applied Psychology in mid-August, Aldous Huxley presented a lecture on the "visionary experience," referring, as Peter O. Whitmer indicates in *Aquarius Revisited: Seven Who Creates the Sixties Counterculture That Changed America*, to "the Bible, Blake, Milton, and Wordsworth." Aware that those in attendance were undoubtedly familiar with his books, *The Doors of Perception* and *Heaven and Hell*, Huxley refused to glorify drug experiments. Frank Barron followed with a discussion of the possibilities psilocybin and LSD afforded in restoring creative freedom.[34]

Then Leary delivered his fateful address at the conference. He related his views on "game-playing," criticizing American psychologists, who sought to quantify their experiments, for attempting to examine, manipulate, and control the actual behavior of their subjects, while ignoring the realm of consciousness. Referring to the studies of Huston Smith, Leary declared, "Tonight I speak to you from a point midway between the Western and Eastern hemispheres of the cortex presenting a theory and method which is Chinese in that behavior is seen as an intricate social game; Indian in its recognition of consciousness and the need to develop a more cosmic awareness; and finally Western in its concern to do good measurably well." In his speech, Leary publicly underscored the link between drugs and mysticism increasingly associated with the Harvard Psilocybin Project. He emphasized his belief in "game playing," and insisted that the West failed to acknowledge that life amounted to a series of games. Additionally, he emphasized, "The men who run the games think that they can't afford to have them seen as a game." Criticizing the psychotherapists who made up much of his audience, Leary warned that the "Judaic-Christian tradition" was manipulative and controlling, thereby "breeding helplessness." To overcome this, Leary suggested, "applied mysticism" was required, while psychedelic drugs—LSD, mescaline, and psilocybin—were most effective in contesting the games people played. They served to alter consciousness, and could result in "drug-induced satori." Among those in attendance was Leary's Harvard colleague Herbert Kelman, who shared his impression with others who heard the speech that it amounted to "incoherent rambling."[35] In Kelman's estimation, the talk was "basically a paean to the drug experience," lacked any substance, and proved "rather shocking."[36]

While Leary and Alpert viewed hallucinogenic drugs as consciousness-expanding devices, their research endeavors became increasingly controversial. Little helping matters were reports that undergraduate students began taking psilocybin, and that at least a pair landed in mental hospitals. By the fall of 1961, Harvard required Leary and Alpert to agree to exclude undergraduates from their experiments. The prohibition annoyed the two, while more students purchased drugs on their own. David McClelland expressed his own concerns about the Psilocybin Research Project in a memorandum delivered to the faculty, warning that it had "been marred by repeated casual ingestion of the drug," group decisions not being carried out, and a fixation "with the mystical East." McClelland hardly looked fondly at what he dismissively referred to as "undergraduate navel-gazing."[37]

That semester, William Burroughs expressed concerns of his own, after participating in the Harvard program, obviously less happily than some. Ginsberg had urged Leary, "You've got to write a big, enthusiastic letter to Burroughs, and get him interested in taking psilocybin. He knows more about drugs than anyone alive."[38] Burroughs appeared to undergo his own version of "Heaven and Hell," and complained about the presence of "many hostile territories in the cerebral hemispheres."[39] He soon wrote to Ginsberg about having broken off ties with Leary and the Harvard Psilocybin Project, which he deemed "completely ill-intentioned" and lacking "any serious scientific work."[40] Burroughs found it preposterous that Leary was pulling down $20,000 annually, along with expenses, for "pushing his pestiferous mushrooms."[41]

Other researchers continued their research into LSD as indicated by the publication in 1961 of *Exploring Inner Space*, by a scientist who employed the pseudonym Jane Dunlap. The author acknowledged taking the drug "in the hope of overcoming spiritual poverty," under the supervision of a psychologist. She experienced bouts of ecstasy, while spatial and temporal sensibilities dissolved. She did indeed undergo religious experiences, which included visions of God, and later reflected on her "stay in paradise," which required love of the divinity and humankind.[42]

As Leary and Alpert, along with cultural proselytizers like Ginsberg and Huxley, were seeking to transform American culture in dramatic fashion, another figure associated with challenges to the established order experienced both success and setbacks along the way. In September, Lenny Bruce was arrested in Philadelphia, for drug possession. The next month, he was busted on a charge of obscenity on October 4, 1961, after employing the word "cocksucker" at the Jazz Workshop in San Francisco. A number of cities banned him from performing. At an obscenity trial in San Francisco, presided over by Judge Clayton Horn, the jury refused to convict Bruce. He would soon suffer other arrests for drug possession and obscenity charges in Los Angeles, and yet another obscenity charge in Chicago.

In early 1962, Leary, who had undergone a large number of psilocybin trips, took LSD for the first time, along with Maynard and Flo Ferguson, and Michael Hollingshead, later indicating that this drug "was something different." It was "the most shattering experience of my life."[43] It was Hollingshead, executive secretary for the Institute of British-American Cultural Exchange, who introduced Leary to the drug. As Leary recalled, "Michael's heaping spoonful had flipped my consciousness into a dance of energy, where nothing existed except whirring vibrations and each illusory form was simply a different frequency."[44] Leary later wrote, "I have never forgotten it. Nor has it been possible for me to return to the life I was leading before that session. I have never recovered from that shattering ontological confrontation. I have never been able to take myself, my mind, and the social world around me as seriously."[45] Hollingshead, who had learned about LSD from Aldous Huxley, believed in a crusade to dole out the drug to trigger radical transformation.

As Leary delved more fully into the world of psychedelia, something he had already begun to recognize became more pronounced. His stay at Harvard proved increasingly controversial and tenuous. In late February 1962, the *Harvard Crimson* published an article by an undergraduate student, Andrew T. Weil, on psychedelics, likening psilocybin to Huxley's soma in *Brave New World*. Weil offered, "Ethical and philosophical questions raised by the availability of such a compound are staggering in complexity, yet they will have to be faced. The work going on now in Cambridge may force us to find answers to them in the very near future." Unable to restrain themselves, Leary and Alpert responded to the *Crimson*, emphatically denying that they were "unbounded in their enthusiasm" for the drug, but instead for "the many problems created by the consciousness expanding drugs." They defended the Psilocybin Project, affirming that the research adhered to strict standards, included university

guidelines, involved knowledgeable volunteers, and excluded both undergraduates and minors. Dr. Dana L. Farnsworth, who headed the University Health Services, soon warned that mescaline could induce "psychotic
reactions," severe depression, and "schizophrenic like reactions."[46] Opposition within the Department of Social Relations intensified, local
newspapers started publicizing the conflict, and a state inquiry began;
however, that led only to a requirement that a physician be present when
the drug was administered. Herb Kelman, a lecturer in social psychology,
urged David McClelland to act, insisting that the drugs were dangerous.
Huxley also began expressing greater reservations about Leary's campaign. Responding to Leary's question when he failed to highlight
psychoactive drugs' sexual component, Huxley declared, "Of course this
is true, Timothy, but we've stirred up enough trouble suggesting that
drugs can stimulate aesthetic and religious experiences. I strongly urge
you not to let the sexual cat out of the bag."[47]

A packed and contentious faculty meeting, called by McClelland, ensued in March 1962, with a number of Leary's colleagues expressing
misgivings about the project. McClelland warned Alpert, "Dick, we can't
save Timothy. He's too outrageous. But we can save you. So just shut up
at tomorrow's meeting." Alpert reflected on McClelland's advice, for
"being a Harvard professor gives you a lot of keys to the kingdom, to play
the way you want to play. Society is honoring you with that role."[48]
During the contentious session, Kelman asserted that the drug project
violated academic protocols and exuded anti-intellectualism. Also troubling to Kelman was his belief that the Psilocybin Project had seemingly
divided Harvard graduate students into those who had joined in Leary's
program and those who had not. Ensuring that his stay in Cambridge
would not be greatly prolonged, Alpert defended the project, while pointing out that Harvard had been involved in cutting-edge research before, as
exemplified by William James, the great psychologist who had himself
experimented with drugs and altered states of consciousness. The *Harvard Crimson* quickly published a story about the meeting, "Psychologists Disagree on Psilocybin Research," and the *Boston Herald* offered a
more incendiary take, "Hallucination Drug Fought at Harvard—350 Students Take Pills." Kelman indicated that he was not averse to the project,
but rather was worried about its "effects . . . on our graduate training."
Harvard lecturer Norman Zinberg, a physician teaching in the department

of social relations, expressed concerns about psilocybin's lasting impact on young people.[49]

On April 22, Leary gave a speech at Harvard, in which he contended that consciousness in the West remained underdeveloped. By contrast, "the pantheistic tradition of the East supports . . . mystical experience," Leary argued. Conveying concerns about monotheism, Leary expressed worries that "we are moving towards an anthill civilization." People were "mere puppets playing out roles in complex games," while "life is becoming mechanical." Leary was also troubled that sex in Western society had become "a game in which two rubber dolls sleep with each other." He spoke, more happily, of the "fifth Freedom, freedom of consciousness" and a new, nonmanipulative scientific approach.[50]

Unquestionably, the notoriety surrounding Leary and Alpert's drug experiments in Cambridge drew attention to psychedelics, including LSD, which previously were little known to the general public. LSD in particular had been well regarded inside the scientific community, most notably among psychiatrists, who considered the drug effective in dealing with sexual problems or alcoholism. However, opposition to its usage mounted in government circles and within the American Medical Association. The Food and Drug Administration attempted to restrict employment of LSD, deeming it an "experimental drug," available for research purposes alone. Oscar Janiger recalled how the perception of LSD research underwent a wholesale transformation during that period. As he put it, "The whole goddamn climate changed. Suddenly you were conspirators out to destroy people. I felt like Galileo. I closed my practice and went to Europe. I felt violated." Janiger clearly affixed the blame. "If you want to know, it was Leary and the others who were ruining what we had worked so hard to build."[51] Captain Al Hubbard also assailed Leary, whom he had warned several times to avoid controversies and remain academically respectable. "I gave stuff to Leary," Hubbard revealed, "and he turned out to be completely no good. . . . He seemed like a well-intentioned person, but then he went overboard."[52] Little helping matters were stories that LSD was cropping up at undergraduate parties. Growing restrictions regarding the purchase and use of LSD hardly affected CIA and military operatives, who continued with their own pharmacological experiments.

Other experiments in Cambridge involved Harvard divinity students, who took the drug on Good Friday in 1962 and reported what seemed to be authentic religious experiences. This demonstrated, Leary wrote later, "spiritual ecstasy, religious revelation and union with God were now directly accessible."[53] More and more, Leary studied stories of religious ecstasies experienced by individuals like William Wadsworth, Alfred Tennyson, and Virginia Woolf, along with Eastern mysticism. As Hollingshead reported, Leary, who considered LSD a religious sacrament, read widely from sacred Eastern texts and the Sermon on the Mount. Among those Leary introduced to LSD was Mary Pinchot Meyer, the former wife of top CIA official Cord Meyer, and a lover of President John F. Kennedy. Meyer, like a number of women in top Washington circles, believed that men in power should become familiar with mind-altering drugs. In fact she told Leary that important people in the nation's capital were taking psychedelics. Leary little worried about resistance within the academic community, but Ginsberg feared that a backlash could be forthcoming.

In May, Leary flew to Los Angeles, where he spoke with the psychiatrist Oscar Janiger, who had handed LSD to Cary Grant and a pair of young actors, James Coburn and Jack Nicholson, among others. Janiger revealed that the English writer Gerald Heard had introduced him to psychedelics. Heard indicated that LSD "was simply God's way of giving us the gift of consciousness," and a means "for saving humanity from Armageddon."[54] Leary met Grant, who stated, "LSD changed my life. I've lived more, felt more, enjoyed life more in the last few years than I had dreamed possible." At a Hollywood party, Marilyn Monroe implored Leary, "You've got to turn me on."[55] In mid-July, the *New York Times* headlined a story by Donald Janson, "Doctors Report a Black Market in Drug That Causes Delusions." LSD had recently become part of "underground traffic," Janson reported.[56]

That fall, Leary and his children settled into a large, three-story house that Alpert had bought, located in Newton Center, close to where the Learys previously resided. Twelve people lived there, including Ralph Metzner and, at times, the heiress Peggy Hitchcock, with whom Leary was having an affair. At one point, Leary informed David McClelland, "We're through playing the science game."[57] Along with Alpert, Leary established the International Foundation for Internal Freedom, to foster additional research into consciousness-expanding drugs. Leary set up camp at the Hotel Catalina in Zihuatanejo, Mexico, renaming the establishment Freedom Center. Thoroughly displeased, McClelland responded by stating, "It tears my heart out to see what's happened to them. They started out as good scientists. They've become cultists."[58]

Dean John Monro and Dr. Farnsworth submitted a letter to the *Harvard Crimson*, expressing concerns that LSD and psilocybin might produce "serious hazard to the mental health and stability even of apparently normal persons," resulting in depression and "other dangerous psychotic effects." The warning would be repeated in the pages of the *New York Times* on November 29, 1962. Dean Monro also spoke of drug experimentation as building on "the interest shown by Aldous Huxley and others." Those experimenting with consciousness-expanding drugs, Monro acknowledged, possessed a "deep conviction" they were shaping "a new frontier of the mind."[59]

As Monro warned against the promotion of mind-altering drugs, Leary and Alpert, who considered Monro's concern as amounting to "hysteria," declared that he was "ill-formed about the effects of these drugs." They denied that factual evidence existed to justify decrying drugs as "uniquely dangerous and considerable evidence that they are safe and beneficial." Leary and Alpert claimed "there is no reason to believe that consciousness-experiences are any more dangerous than psychoanalysis or a four-year enrollment in Harvard College." They also charged that efforts to restrict "competent and recognized scientists" from conducting research had led "for the first time in American history" to "a scientific underground." Leary and Alpert believed that the issue of consciousness expansion would pose a major civil liberties issue during the impending decade. They asked, "Who controls your vortex? Who decides on the range and limit of your awareness? If you want to research your own nervous system, expand your consciousness, who is to decide that you can't and why?"[60]

However, Aldous Huxley again became concerned about Leary's methodology, and his determination to mock conventionality and the Academy, as the great English writer expressed in a letter to Humphry Osmond.

> Yes, what about Tim Leary? I spent an evening with him here a few weeks ago—and he talked such nonsense . . . that I became quite concerned. Not about his sanity—because he is perfectly sane—but about his prospects in the world; for this nonsense-talking is just another device for annoying people in authority, flouting convention, cocking snooks at the academic world; to the headmaster of his school.

> One of these days the headmaster will lose patience. . . . I am very fond
> of Tim . . . but why, oh why, does he have to be such an ass?[61]

Notwithstanding the worries of erstwhile allies, Leary began to envision a day in the not-too-distant future when millions of Americans would have turned onto LSD. He declared that his ties to Harvard would conclude in the summer, but Alpert hoped to remain at Harvard.

President Nathan M. Pusey announced on May 27, 1963, that the Harvard Corporation had voted three weeks earlier to relieve Leary of his position at the university, for having been derelict in holding classes and remaining present in Cambridge. Alpert was also fired, purportedly for doling out psilocybin to an undergraduate student. Thus ended the Harvard Psilocybin Project; Alpert's firing involved the first such dismissal of a Harvard professor in several decades. Behind the scene, Andrew Weil had provided damning information to the Harvard administration regarding both Leary and Alpert, and on May 28 the *Harvard Crimson* featured an article by Weil and Joseph M. Russin about the firing. The authors declared, "It would be unfortunate if the firing of Richard Alpert led to the suppression of legitimate research into the effects of hallucinogenic compounds." However, they continued, it would have been "equally unfortunate" had Alpert "been allowed to continue his activities under the aegis of a University that he has misinformed about his purposes." Weil and Russin went on to charge that Leary and Alpert had delivered pronouncements of the sort "that one associates with quacks."[62]

The *Newsweek* issue of June 10, 1963, reported the dismissals of Leary and Alpert, while indicating that they had "pursued the ageless vision that drug-induced 'insights' can be used to make men wiser, kinder, more creative." Harvard had dumped the two men, *Newsweek* indicated, because each had "become a propagandist for drugs." Their former advocate, David C. McClelland, charged that the more frequently Leary and Alpert took drugs, "the less they were interested in science." *Newsweek* reported that Leary and Alpert had proven "embarrassing to other researchers," who believed in the scientific merits of "LSD and related compounds." Alpert denied that he had violated any agreement with Harvard, and claimed he and his associates had "safely" conducted drug experiments with more than four hundred individuals throughout Cambridge.[63]

The same day Pusey revealed the firings, the *Harvard Review* published its summer issue, titled *Drugs and the Mind*, featuring a lead article by the now former architects of the Harvard Psilocybin Project. Josiah Lee Auspitz, an editor with the *Review*, called Cambridge "the Drug Capital of the East Coast—at least for your better class of compounds," meaning "*hallucinogens* or *psychedelics*." Auspitz noted that "mescaline, psilocybin, and LSD" were "nowhere more hungrily consumed than in Harvard Square"; and nowhere were they debated more heatedly. There existed "the true believers, the scientists and the armchair commentators," with "the most evangelical" of the first group including Leary and Alpert. Another true believer was Robert Gordon Wasson, who declared that there existed individuals who had taken mushrooms and were "disqualified by our subjective experience and those who have not . . . and are disqualified by their total ignorance of the subject."[64]

Leary and Alpert delivered "The Politics of Consciousness Expansion," wondering if "we must continue to jail, execute, exile our ecstatic visionaries, and then enshrine them as tomorrow's heroes." LSD, they proclaimed, was "more frightening than the Bomb!" And now, in unprecedented, mass fashion, "mind-opening substances" were available and presented a "social-political" threat. Consciousness-enriching drugs promised to alter "our concepts of human nature, of human potentialities, of existence," Leary and Alpert wrote. "The game is about to be changed."[65] By contrast, Dr. Roy R. Grinker Sr., the editor of the *Archives of General Psychiatry*, published by the American Medical Association, warned that "latent psychotics are disintegrating under the influence of even a single dose," while sustained LSD use led to "a psychopathology." Sidney Cohen and Keith S. Ditman also pointed to adverse reactions ranging from psychosis to heightened depression and anxiety or "sociopathic behavior."[66]

Leary, Ralph Metzner, and Gunther Weil founded *The Psychedelic Review* in June 1963, offering a statement of purpose that referred to psychedelics as "powerful tools for the exploration of consciousness and the production of visionary experiences." The journal itself was published by the International Federation for Internal Freedom (IFIF), which was designed "to encourage, support and protect research on psychedelic substances." Most important, the IFIF intended to heighten the individual's ability to control "his own mind, thereby enlarging his internal freedom."[67]

The nonprofit IFIF became the centerpiece of Leary and Alpert's psychedelic endeavors. They hoped to create an atmosphere in keeping with Aldous Huxley's vision and his utopian novel, *Island*. Those who arrived at Freedom House in Zihuatanejo were informed that "the aim of the transpersonative community is to liberate members from their webs so they can soar, at will, through the infinite space/time of the energy fields surrounding them."[68] Leary referred to those at the Freedom House as thinkers, educators, and intellectuals determined to usher in greater liberation. He envisioned establishing other centers throughout the United States and elsewhere. Mexican newspapers, however, referred to "'beatniks' and 'queer people'" at Freedom House. Sensational newspaper accounts and government investigations led to the IFIF's being forced out of Mexico in mid-June 1963. Attempts to relocate to Dominica, where the CIA reported Leary and Alpert were seeking to establish "an alleged Happiness Hotel," and Antigua, both quickly foundered, with a corresponding $50,000 debt.[69]

In the midst of yet another move, Leary spoke on August 30, 1963, about "The Religious Experience, Its Production and Interpretation" to a group of Lutheran psychologists, among others, at the 71st Annual Convention of the American Psychological Association, held at the Stratford Hotel in Philadelphia. He discussed his initial encounters with mushrooms in Mexico three years earlier, stating that proved to be, unquestionably, "the deepest religious experience of my life." He had since repeated that "biochemical and . . . sacramental ritual" scores of times, almost always proving to be "awed by religious revelations as shattering as the first experience." At one point, Leary asked the psychologists if their own religious advisor were "talking from direct experience, or simply repeated clichés?" Did that advisor seek "answers to basic questions, or" was "he protecting . . . his own game investment?" Did he call for discovery of a collaborative sort? If opposed to "artificial methods of illumination," what did the advisor consider "the natural. Words? Rituals? Tribal customs? Alkaloids?" Leary asked, "If your advisor is against LSD, what is he for?"[70]

Dr. Dana Farnsworth of Harvard, in an editorial in *JAMA*, the *Journal of the American Medical Association*, warned that "mood drugs" like LSD could "damage the individual psyche, indeed cripple it for life." Farnsworth bemoaned the fact that students were drawn to "the siren song of expanded consciousness." He editorialized, "Our young people are being told that there is little hazard in the use of hallucinogens . . . and that the spiritual and intellectual rewards are vivid, wonderful, inexpressible. The case is made that men's minds are now 'imprisoned' . . . and that drugs offer an escape to a word free paradise."[71]

A different kind of paradise, which went on for nearly four years, awaited as Tommy and Billy Hitchcock opened up their four thousand acre estate in Dutchess County, New York, located less than one hundred miles from New York City, to Leary and Alpert. The estate featured a sixty-four room mansion, Millbrook, and several other houses, alongside lush grounds, stables, and tennis courts. Soon stationed in Millbrook, Leary and Alpert disbanded the IFIF in favor of another organization, the Castalia Foundation, modeled after the utopian colony explored in the final novel by the German Nobel Laureate Hermann Hesse. Millbrook regulars included Michael Hollingshead, and visitors ranged from famed musicians Maynard Ferguson and Charles Mingus to Alan Watts, Humphry Osmond, and the actress Viva, who appeared in a number of Andy Warhol's films.

The fall issue of *The Psychedelic Review* noted that Leary and Alpert had left the Board of Editors, which no longer included members of IFIF. An editorial pointed to three groups presently interested in psychedelics: psychologists and psychiatrists engaged in research, "artistic" sorts who included "young bohemians," and "psychologists, philosophers, psychiatrists, theologians, and others" desirous of employing the drugs to pique "experiences which transcend ordinary space-time, conceptual, and ego-oriented categories."[72]

Leary continued to garner attention in the national media, as indicated by a *Time* article on October 25, 1963, "Worship: Instant Mysticism." *Time* quoted Leary as contending that 75 percent of the "fulltime religious professionals" he had given psychedelics to during his Harvard research "had intense mystic-religious reactions, and more than half claimed that they had the deepest spiritual experience of their life." As *Time* noted, such experiences covered the gamut, with some undergoing "agonizing intimations of hell" and others believing they had been "reborn" and become aware that "oneness is all."[73]

Controversy continued to swirl about Leary and Alpert's operations. In its November 5, 1963, issue, *Look* published a lengthy article by Andrew Weil, titled "The Strange Case of the Harvard Drug Scandal." It discussed the developments that had led to the dismissal of Leary and

Alpert, including their conviction that "mystic insight" drawn from a psychedelic-like psilocybin "would be the solution to the emotional problems of Western man." Weil spoke of the growing popularity of psychedelics on the Harvard campus, including mescaline use by undergraduates and tales of hallucinogens being employed "for seductions, both heterosexual and homosexual."[74] That same month, *Cosmopolitan* presented an essay by Bob Gaines, "LSD: Hollywood's Status-Symbol Drug," in which Leary was quoted as predicting, "It's only a matter of time until the psychedelic experience will be accepted. We see ourselves as modest heroes, an educational tool to facilitate the development of new social forms. . . . We're simply trying to get back to man's sense of nearness to himself and others, the sense of social reality which civilized man has lost."[75]

Also in November 1963, *Playboy* magazine contained an interview with the writer Alan Harrington, in which he discussed his LSD experience, and a reflection by Huxley, "Hallucinogens: A Philosopher's Visionary Prediction." Huxley posed the question, "Which is better? To have Fun with Fungi or to have Idiocy with Ideology, to have Wars because of Words, to have Tomorrow's Misdeeds out of Yesterday's Miscreeds?"[76] Flying out to Los Angeles, Leary served as a guide for a dying Huxley, who wanted to take LSD one last time. "Be gentle with them, Timothy," Huxley urged on November 22, 1963, the same day John F. Kennedy was assassinated in Dallas, Texas. "They want to be free, but they don't know how. Teach them. Reassure them."[77]

The December 15, 1963, edition of the *New York Times* contained an extended essay on "Psychic-Drug Testers Living in Retreat." The community of Dutchess County, with 1,700 residents, appeared little knowledgeable about Leary and Alpert until *Look, Esquire, Time, The Saturday Evening Post*, and other national publications presented articles on the village's acclaimed pair of new inhabitants. The *Times* referred to the latest of Leary and Alpert's "'transcendental' multi-family communities," which coexisted with a bevy of dogs and cats. The previous week, Leary and Alpert indicated that their battle with psychiatrists regarding the use of psychedelics revolved around "the right, right now, of thoughtful Americans to change their own consciousness." They continued, "The LSD experience is so novel and so powerful that the more you think you know about the mind, the more astounded and even frightened you'll be when your consciousness starts to flip you out of your mind."[78]

Kay Parley, who trained in psychiatric nursing in Weyburn, Saskatchewan, delivered the first article exploring a nurse's role in LSD experiments, "Supporting the Patient," in the February 1964 issue of the *American Journal of Nursing*. Parley noted that LSD was mainly used to treat alcoholism, with consenting patients "tested physically and psychologically, and oriented to the treatment by a psychiatrist." As Parley explained, subject patients often proved highly sensitive, unveiling deep-seated emotional traumas. Likening the LSD experience to a space trip, she told her patients, "You are off on a trip with no baggage, no destination, and no compass. That's why I'm here. I can't go with you, but I can be your anchor." LSD, Parley affirmed, enabled one to come "closer to depths of human understanding and emotion than one has ever been."[79]

The editors of the *American Journal of Nursing* would only acknowledge that the psychotomimetics—mescaline, psilocybin, and LSD—"*may* offer hope as *aids* to psychotherapy for guiding behavior in healthier directions." At the same time, existing medical literature underscored that those drugs might result in "great harm," absent "thorough psychiatric and medical preparation of the patient." All three of the major psychedelics, the editors of the journal noted, produced similar "subjective effects," but it remained unknown how they altered consciousness. Drugs were inevitably controversial, the editors stated, for piquing responses ranging "from indescribable terror to evangelical enlightenment." They acknowledged that LSD might eventually be considered "as dangerous as heroin," once viewed "as *the* drug to cure morphine addicts."[80]

Joseph Havens, a psychologist at the University of Massachusetts, who had been involved with Leary's experiments in Cambridge, produced his own "Memo on the Religious Implications of the Consciousness-Changing Drugs" in early 1964. Drawing on reports presented by sixteen subjects in the Cambridge LSD or psilocybin trips, Havens indicated that emotions ranged "from terror, depression or loneliness to feelings of great strength, deep affection or Rabelaisian joy." Also calling on a lengthy questionnaire completed by eighty-two participants in Harvard's Psilocybin Project, Havens deemed "the subjective experiences . . . sometimes strikingly like those reported by mystics and visionaries of the past." He also pointed to both William James, who had acknowledged having undergone an "artificial mystic state of mind," and Aldous Huxley, who had contested the notion of "mere chemical religion." As for

Leary, Havens contended his major research focus involved "transcendental experiences."[81]

Back at Millbrook, Leary attempted to create a systematic approach to the use of psychedelics, soon relying on *The Tibetan Book of the Dead*, which Huxley had written about in *The Doors of Perception*. In 1964, Leary, Ralph Metzner, and Alpert published *The Psychedelic Experience*, dedicated to Huxley "with profound admiration and gratitude," and based on *The Tibetan Book of the Dead*. Their volume opened with the statement, "A psychedelic experience is a journey to new realms of consciousness. The scope and content of the experience is limitless, but its characteristic features are the transcendence of verbal concepts, of space-time dimensions, and of the ego or identity." Leary, Metzner, and Alpert indicated that expanded consciousness could be attained through "sensory deprivation, yoga exercises, disciplined meditation, religious or aesthetic ecstasies, or spontaneously." But "most recently they have become available to anyone through the ingestion of psychedelic drugs such as LSD, psilocybin, mescaline, DMT, etc." That, however, was "an ideal, not an actual situation" at present, the coauthors stated, because of federal restrictions regarding psychedelics. The drugs themselves, they wrote, did not induce "the transcendent experience," only providing "a chemical key" to liberate the mind and nervous system. The actual psychedelic experience, they contended, resulted from both "set and setting." Hence the need for a manual such as *The Psychedelic Experience*, Leary, Metzner, and Alpert asserted. They offered comforting advice, such as "whenever in doubt, turn off your mind, relax, float downstream."[82]

Leary also provided the introduction for *LSD: The Consciousness-Expanding Drug*, published in 1964 and containing essays by Humphry Osmond, Huxley, Dan Wakefield, Alan Harrington, Leary, Watts, Huston Smith, and William Burroughs, among others. Jazz critic David Solomon edited the volume, discussing his own initial psychedelic experience on mescaline, when, he wrote, "Instead of fleeing *from* reality, I flew more deeply *into* it. I had never before seen, touched, tasted, heard, smelled and *felt* so profound a personal unity and involvement with the concrete material world." Like William Blake, he could now see "the world in a grain of sand." In his introduction, completed in May 1964, Leary underscored the fact that "visionary plants" were in no way new, and that modern technology allowed for the production of "chemical synthetics of the active ingredients of these ancient and venerable concoctions." Such

drugs had always been controversial, Leary suggested, because they resulted in the most aspired to, yet feared, experience imaginable. "They
produce ecstasy. . . . They propel awareness out beyond normal modes of
consciousness." Hence, "they are properly called psychedelics—i.e.,
mind-opening substances." Both Western and Eastern philosophers had
long discussed altered states of consciousness, but change was now occurring at an unprecedented pace. Leary offered the kind of analysis that
garnered both fervent adherents and fierce critics: "It becomes necessary
for us to go out of our minds in order to use our heads." In the essay he
contributed to the volume, Leary related, as he had during the Harvard
Psilocybin Project, how drugs helped to make light of the games, or
socially determined roles, people play.[83]

In the August 1964 issue of *The Realist*, the politically charged sardonic magazine put out by Paul Krassner, the author Robert Anton Wilson wrote about "Timothy Leary and His Psychological H-Bomb." Wilson indicated that Albert Einstein and Leary might eventually be deemed
"the two greatest thinkers of the twentieth century." Einstein demonstrated "how to create atomic fission in the physical world"; Leary demonstrated how to do so "in the psychological world." The latter, Wilson
offered, might be considered more significant, and drew on Einstein's
discoveries. As the brilliant scientist suggested, his explorations set the
stage for Leary's, for atomic energy altered "everything but our habits of
thought." Now, Leary might have believed thought processes could similarly be transformed. Leary explained that his ouster and Richard Alpert's
from Harvard made sense. "Harvard had a verbal game, and we've got a
non-verbal game. Obviously, we had to find our own field." On departing
from Millbrook, Wilson's wife told him, "It used to bug me that I never
met Freud or Einstein. Well, now I can tell my grandchildren that I met
Timothy Leary."[84]

5

THE MERRY PRANKSTER: KEN KESEY

While Timothy Leary attempted to retain at least the façade of intellectual respectability, another psychedelic proselytizer had no intention or means of doing so. In mid-1964, novelist Ken Kesey and his Merry Pranksters roared onto the Hitchcock estate in Dutchess County only to be seemingly rejected by those gathered at Millbrook. Along with Allen Ginsberg and Leary, Kesey had become one of the greatest proponents of psychedelics in the United States. As in the case of Leary, Kesey's emergence as a countercultural icon could hardly have been predicted a relatively short time before.

Kenneth Elton Kesey was born in La Junta, Colorado, on September 17, 1935, the child of Frederick A. Kesey and Geneva Smith, whose ancestors included "hard shell Baptists" with Arkansas and Texas roots, and who ran a dairy farm in Springfield, Oregon, where they moved when Ken was a third-grader. Fred Kesey, his son Ken recalled, was a "kind of big, rebellious cowboy who never did fit in," yet became a highly successful businessman.[1] Encouraged by his father, Kesey became an avid hunter, fisherman, and swimmer, as well as a star wrestler, finishing third in the state championship tournament, and right guard on the football team in high school, when he was voted "most likely to succeed"; he also loved magic and devoured books by Zane Grey and Edgar Rice Burroughs, along with comic books featuring Captain Marvel, "The World's Mightiest Mortal." Kesey received a football scholarship at the University of Oregon, but the 177-pounder soon switched over to the wrestling squad. He became one of the top competitors in the Pacific Coast Conference, before suffering a shoulder injury near the close of his senior year. He studied speech and communications at the University of Oregon, joined the Beta Theta Pi fraternity, performed in university theatrical productions, including *Macbeth*, and went to Hollywood to try to break into the movies. While an undergraduate, he married Norma "Faye" Haxby, his high school sweetheart, with whom he would have three children. After graduating in 1957, and another venture to Hollywood, Kesey and Faye resided in Springfield, where Ken got a day job and worked on a novel in the evenings. He received a Woodrow Wilson Fellowship, which he applied to enter the creative writing program at Stanford University. Classmates included Robert Stone, Larry McMurtry, and Ken Babbs, while famed authors Malcolm Cowley and Wagner Stegner served as instructors in the graduate program. Kesey enrolled in a writing class of Cowley's in 1960. Cowley said of Kesey, "He had the build of a pluning halfback, with big shoulders and a neck like the stump of a Douglas fir." Cowley also recalled the response to chapters of a novel about a mental institution Kesey, whom he referred to as "an Oregon roughneck," was working on; they "were read aloud . . . and they aroused a mixed but generally admiring response." McMurtry recalled that Kesey, while in graduate school, "already had a court."[2]

The instructors at Stanford hardly viewed Kesey as Hemingway in the making. Stegner later reflected that Kesey was "crazy as a coot, and dangerous, and rather special in his charismatic qualities, and with what was once a fairly raw talent."[3] Dick Scowcroft, who also taught creative writing at Stanford, acknowledged, "Neither Wally nor I thought he had particularly important talent." Stegner told Scowcroft that Kesey "was sort of a fairly talented illiterate." Cowley seemingly agreed, noting that Kesey "hasn't ever learned how to spell, and didn't even begin reading for pleasure until he was an upper classman." At the same time, Cowley predicted that the book manuscript Kesey was working on "might just turn out to be something that would HAVE to be published."[4]

While attending Stanford, the blonde, blue-eyed, muscular Kesey, still hoping to make the 1960 U.S. Olympic squad, participated in the CIA-sponsored Project MKULTRA experiments conducted at the Menlo Park Veterans Hospital by Dr. Leo Hollister. After Stanford psychology graduate student Vic Lovell spotted an advertisement in 1959 involving drug testing experiments, Kesey became exposed to "psychomimetic" substances, including psilocybin, mescaline, LSD, morning glory seeds, the super amphetamine IT-290, MP-14 (Thioridazine), and JB-329 (Ditran). Lovell had introduced Richard Alpert to marijuana when Timothy Leary's future cohort was enrolled in a doctoral program at Stanford. Kesey, who had been writing an unpublished novel, *Zoo*, on the North Beach beat scene in San Francisco, joined Lovell for the initial, psilocybin experiment at Menlo Park, which paid participants anywhere from $20 to $75 per session. Some of the ensuing experiments proved troubling, but the ones on LSD and psilocybin were exhilarating. Later, Kesey revealed, "Before I took drugs, I didn't know why the guys in the psycho ward at the VA Hospital were there. I didn't understand them. After I took LSD, suddenly I saw it. I saw it all. I listened to them and watched them, and I saw that what they were saying and doing was not so crazy after all."[5]

Moreover, as Kesey recalled, "Suddenly I was shifted over to where I had been looking full front at a world; and by shifting over, I was seeing it from another position. It became dimensional."[6] To Kesey, it was as if he were "going to the nuthouse to take dope under official auspices," through which he could enter a "magic box." On first taking the drugs administered in the hospital, Kesey recalled, "It was like the books God keeps. You have heard about the Bible and the Akashic records, but suddenly you had a glimpse of them. These were the *real* books. These weren't kept in the school library, these were the real books." Consequently, "We wanted to see these books and took more and more drugs, until finally, at one point, God said, 'You want to see the books? I'll show you the fucking books,' and it was like this big hand grabbed us by the back of the neck and held us there for twelve hours. We were in absolute hell because we saw ourselves; we saw all the stuff we had done, mistakes we had made, our indulgences, our cruelties. That was hell."[7]

Eventually, Kesey obtained a job at the hospital, to both make money and acquire access to drugs at the psychiatric hospital. Working the graveyard shift, Kesey sometimes dealt with the staff and patients in a psychedelic-induced haze. Looking at the patients, Kesey determined that "Freud was full of shit. Something really dug deep in these people's minds, and it wasn't the way they were treated when they were toilet trained; it wasn't the way they were rejected when they were thirteen. It was something to do with the American Dream. How the American Dream gave us our daily energy and yet the dream was perverted and not allowed to develop fully."[8]

Kesey became a familiar figure in bohemian circles in Perry Lane, which boasted two-room cottages renting for $60 a month close to the Stanford golf course. Bestselling author Tom Wolfe later asserted that Kesey, with his "Oregon country drawl," could be likened to "Jack London Martin Eden Searching Hick, the hick with intellectual yearnings, written all over him."[9] All the while, Kesey read Hermann Hesse's books, Joseph Campbell's, and the Bhagavad Gita, among other Asian works.

Others began congregating at Kesey's home in Perry Lane, where friends ate his venison chili stew, laced with LSD, leading Malcolm Cowley to liken him to Ernest Hemingway among expatriates in Paris during the 1920s, as "the man whom the other young rebels tried to imitate."[10] As for the drink freely handed out at Kesey's, Cowley recalled "the sort of punch Satan would serve," which he declined. Willing recipients include fellow graduate students Robert Stone and Larry McMurtry, and Jerry Garcia, a young folk-blues musician. Garcia and his friends, including Robert Hunter, a fellow bluegrass performer and later acclaimed lyricist, Jerry later reflected, "were on the street. We just got high and went crazy, you know? . . . It was in Palo Alto, which is more bohemian than anything else. But we were definitely Dionysian."[11] Writer Ed McClanahan, a fellow resident of Perry Lane, remembered, "The commonplace would become marvelous, you could take the pulse of a rock, listen to the heartbeat of a tree . . . the ecstatic, ubiquitous 'far out!' rang oft upon the air."[12] McClanahan noted, "It wasn't something we did just to get wasted. It was a learning thing—we'd decide to take acid and prepare for it, set up games and things to do."[13] As Stone informed Martin Torgoff, "It was like we had found a bunch of people that we had always been looking for. We spent all our time talking, and when you have people that close, you wanted a sacrament to share." Furthermore, "The world was just beginning to be separated into the hip and the square, and we were firmly ensconced in the notion of being hip. Perry Lane was becoming a kind of wandering scene, a movable feast."[14] As Kesey would reflect, "All of the people that were hanging around together were already talking 'revolution' in kind of vague terms. We were educated enough to know that the beatnik kind of revolution just wouldn't work. It was going to take a revolution of consciousness. I don't think anybody *invented* this; I just think a bunch of people realized it at the same time and joined forces without even knowing that there was an enemy."[15]

Vic Lovell also reflected about Perry Lane. "We pioneered what have since become the hallmarks of hippy culture: LSD and other psychedelics too numerous to mention, body painting, light shows and mixed media presentations, total aestheticism, be-ins, exotic costumes, strobe lights, sexual mayhem, freakouts and the deification of psychoticism, eastern mysticism, and the rebirth of hair."[16] For Lovell, "it was like we had a magic lamp. The experience is not repeatable." Lovell stated, "I first felt love, sensuality, creativity, spontaneity, and the scenes of human community." However, "it was also there and thereafter that I first felt the possibility that total disaster could overtake mankind if something were not done, by each in his own way, if only to drop out."[17]

Kesey continued crafting a pair of novels that remained unpublished, as well as the book that catapulted him into the rungs of America's brightest young writers, *One Flew over the Cuckoo's Nest*, published in February 1962; Kesey soon received $20,000 for the movie rights to his novel, which he dedicated to Lovell, "who told me dragons did not exist, then led me to their lair."[18] Jack Kerouac saluted Kesey as "a great new American novelist," while the *New York Herald Tribune* exclaimed, "This is a first novel of special worth." The *Saturday Review* roundly praised Kesey: "His storytelling is so effective, his style is so impetuous, his grasp of characters so certain, that the reader is swept along." Kesey was referred to as "a large, robust talent," who had delivered "a large, robust book."[19] *Time* magazine extolled this "brilliant first novel" as "a strong, warm story about the nature of human good and evil, despite its macabre setting." *One Flew over the Cuckoo's Nest* contested "the reader's comfortable assumption about the nice normalities," serving as "a roar of protest against middlebrow society's Rules and the invisible Rulers who enforce them."[20] *Life* magazine declared the book contained "powerful, poetic realism" that "makes the tired old subject of life in a mental hospital into an absorbing Orwellian microcosm of all humanity." The *New York Times* book reviewer Martin Levin termed *One Flew over the Cuckoo's Nest* "a work of genuine literary merit," and indicated that Kesey's "unusual novel" had recast the existence of seemingly mentally ill patients "into a glittering parable of good and evil." The story, Levin wrote, "is so brilliantly illuminated that it is reward enough."[21]

Written somewhat in the vein of *On the Road*, *One Flew over the Cuckoo's Nest* also featured both intricately drawn characters and seemingly stream-of-consciousness-like language. The protagonist Randle

Patrick McMurphy, convicted of statutory rape, was being evaluated at a mental institution. There, on encountering the despotic Nurse Mildred Ratched, McMurphy had to scam his way into remaining at the psychiatric ward, to avoid being forced to toil on a prison farm. The two quickly became fierce antagonists, with Ratched pitted against McMurphy and his gang of mentally disturbed patients, including the six-foot-seven-inch tall Native American, "Chief" Bromden. In 1963 and 1964, Kirk Douglas starred as Randle McMurphy in a Broadway production of *One Flew over the Cuckoo's Nest*, which continued for eighty-two performances. Following a negative review of the play in the *New York Times*, Kesey referred to McMurphy as "a dream, a wild hope fabricated out of need in defeat," who was attempting to save "real, live human being (sic)." Douglas hoped to adapt the novel for Hollywood, but no film companies were willing to pick it up at that time.[22]

A developer purchased much of the Perry Lane property, seemingly ending that version of California bohemia. His commercial success enabled Kesey to buy a contemporary, six-room, paneled log cabin, boasting a large fireplace, on six acres of forested land, in La Honda, situated fifteen miles to the east of Palo Alto. The closest neighbor was a mile away. Kesey, Robert Stone later reported, "really seemed capable of making anything happen. It was beyond writing."[23] Indeed, as Stone saw it, "Kesey was, more than anyone else, in the grip of all the 1960s seemed to promise."[24] "We're on the verge of something very fantastic," Kesey predicted, "and I believe our generation will be the one to pull it off."[25] Ken Babbs, who had recently served as a marine lieutenant in Vietnam, soon arrived. Sometime during the summer of 1963, Neal Cassady, having read *One Flew over the Cuckoo's Nest*, showed up in La Honda to encounter the man he named "Chief." Books were passed around at La Honda, but instead of Hermann Hesse's German mystical tales, preferred by the Millbrook crowd, Robert Heinlein's *Stranger in a Strange Land*, Arthur C. Clarke's *Childhood's End*, and Theodore Sturgeon's *More Than Human*, all science fiction novels, proved among the most popular. At one point, Sturgeon's book, with its depiction of alienated youth who possessed paranormal capabilities, particular appealed to Kesey and his friends, who also enjoyed the *I Ching*, the ancient Chinese text containing a series of prophetic Confucian pronouncements.

Once again, Kesey kicked off the liberal employment of psychedelics, as trees on his property came to boast Day-Glo and amplifiers poured out rock 'n' roll, including music by the Beatles; this befitted what Kesey referred to as "The Neon Renaissance." La Honda, the writer Hunter S. Thompson reflected, became "the world capital of madness. There were no rules, fear was unknown and sleep was out of the question."[26] The regulars at La Honda came to be known as the Merry Pranksters, and included Cassady, Babbs, Ron Bevirt, Carolyn Adams, and Gretchen Fetchin. The Pranksters acquired additional names or titles, with Cassady called Speed Limit, Babbs referred to as the Intrepid Traveller, Bevirt turned into Hassler, Adams known as Mountain Girl, and Fetchin tagged as the Slime Queen. Kesey, for his part, took on the label of Chief or Swashbuckler. The Pranksters strove for Edge City, situated between one's ego and the Void.

As Stewart Brand, who later put out *The Whole Earth Catalog*, informed Martin Torgoff, "What made the Pranksters so different was that they were pursuing the recreational sports approach. . . . To be a Prankster was adventurous and dangerous and to be involved in real cultural electricity. It was also sloppy and slow and lazy, cheerily revolutionary and fiercely apolitical.[27] Kesey once declared that "the purpose of psychedelics is to learn the conditioned responses of people and then to prank them. That's the only way to get people to ask questions, and until they ask questions they're going to remain conditioned robots."[28] He also wanted to introduce more and more individuals to psychedelics, believing, "it only works if you bring other people into it."[29] Later, Kesey would be referred to as "the messiah of acid."[30]

Meanwhile, Kesey completed his second, sprawling novel, *Sometimes a Great Notion*, about a logging family from Oregon that battled against union labor. Kesey planned to drive to New York City to attend a party celebrating the publication of his latest book, and to visit the World's Fair. No more novels would be forthcoming from Kesey for an extended period. As his Stanford classmate and erstwhile neighbor Robert Stone stated, "There was no question of his limitless energy. But, in the long run, some people thought, the practice of novel writing would prove to be too sedentary an occupation for so quick an athlete—lonely, and incorporating long, silent periods between strokes."[31] Acid consciousness had altered Kesey, who felt, as did many of his compatriots, "like we were dealing with the end of time." Kesey noted, "It was a different consciousness than writing. I could not do the same kind of writing I had been doing. We got into what I would call Rosicrucian art. Tim Leary, Bobby

Dylan, John Lennon, Bill Burroughs—we were all reaching in to wrench the language apart. . . . The slate was ours. We wrote on it what we wanted. We felt like the consciousness revolution was going to take us off physically—like *Childhood's End*."[32] All of this was associated with the Neon Renaissance, which Kesey defined.

> It's a need to find a new way to look at the world, an attempt to locate a better reality, now the old reality is riddled with radioactive poison. I think a lot of people are working in a lot of different ways to locate this reality: Ornette Coleman in jazz, Ann Halprin in dance, the New Wave movies, Lenny Bruce in comedy, Wally Hedrick in art, Heller, Burroughs, Rechy, Gunter Grass in writing and those thousands of others whose names would be meaningless, either because they haven't made *it* yet, or aren't working in a medium that has an it to make. But all these people are trying to find out what is happening, why and what can be done with it.[33]

On April 24, 1964, eighteen police officers raided the La Honda compound, discovering marijuana, which Kesey purportedly attempted to flush down the toilet. Kesey was arrested for possession of the drug, and for socking a policeman in the face. Let out on bail, Kesey hardly slackened his pace. That summer, Kesey set off with several of the Pranksters aboard a quarter-century-old International Harvester school bus he had recently purchased for $1,500, loaded with a refrigerator, sink, and bunkbeds. The bus carried an intricate sound system, and the Pranksters intended to make a film of their journey, hoping to possibly sell it later. The Pranksters decked themselves out in all sorts of costumes, along with Day-Glo paint and pieces of the American flag. Driving the wildly colored bus was Cassady, the aging beat fixture who, wired on speed, invariably drove in frenetic fashion, going "Furthur," just as the sign on the front of the bus indicated; the one on the back, "Caution: Weird Load," undoubtedly elicited additional wonderment. Kesey often sat on top of the bus, able to do so because of a hole in the roof. He considered Cassady "the avatar" and "one of the great failures of all time," but tremendously influential.[34] Cassady operated, Kesey suggested, as "a man driven to the cliffedge by the grassfire of an entire nation's burning material madness." Jerry Garcia declared that "at his purest, Cassady was a tool of the cosmos." Sometime earlier, Allen Ginsberg had written to Cassady: "The Revolution Has Begun—Stop giving your authority to

Christ & the Void & the Imagination—you are it, now, the God . . . you are needed—stop hiding yr. light in a bushel."[35] Ginsberg later noted, "Neal Cassady drove Jack Kerouac to Mexico in a prophetic automobile . . . one decade later Cassady drove Ken Kesey's Kosmo-patterned school bus on a Kafka-circus tour over the roads of an awakening nation."[36] As Wavy Gravy, soon to head the Hog Farm Collective, indicated, "Neal was so far ahead of his time that he'd point for those of us who were just struggling to be with the moment."[37] At times, the Pranksters drove the bus backward through towns; they also expressed delight with the right-wing candidacy of Republican Party presidential nominee Barry Goldwater, the senator from Arizona, as they rode into that state. Ginsberg thought the Pranksters' trip signified that "the nation was on to the precipice of enormous awakening and change."[38] The perception took hold, as Robert Stone later noted, "that one was either on the bus or off the bus," which he considered "an insight of staggering profundity."[39]

America's cultural sensibilities may have been changing, but they were hardly altered altogether as exemplified by the most recent arrests of Lenny Bruce on charges of obscenity in Chicago, and drug possession. These followed additional arrests in Los Angeles and Greenwich Village that spring, on charges of obscenity, and the previous year in Los Angeles and Miami Beach on drug charges. Later that year, Bruce would be convicted of obscenity and sentenced to four months in a workhouse, notwithstanding outrage expressed by leading American intellectuals, including Bob Dylan, Allen Ginsberg, Lawrence Ferlinghetti, Norman Mailer, Henry Miller, James Baldwin, Joseph Heller, Reinhold Niebuhr, and Lionel Trilling. Ginsberg decried Bruce's latest arrest as connected to a concerted determination to reign in the avant-garde.

As for the poet, the *New York Times Magazine* presented a lengthy article on July 11, 1965, by Richard Kostelanetz, "Ginsberg Makes the World Scene." Kostelanetz began by declaring, "To university students all over the world today, Allen Ginsberg is a kind of cultural hero and sometimes a true prophet." This was true in both the West and the East, with Ginsberg recently having been selected as King of the May by university students in Prague. This followed earlier visits to Cuba, Prague, Russia, and Poland. In Prague a second time, Ginsberg was roughed up one night by someone calling him "'fairy' or 'queer,'" and then arrested, before being expelled from Czechoslovakia. Czech officials, Ginsberg acknowledged, might well have considered his talks subversive. He had spoken of "the greater values—the sense of new consciousness which seems to be going through the youth of all countries—the sexual revolution, the widening of the areas of consciousness, the abhorrence of ideology, direct contact (soul to soul), Dostoevskian tolerance, Blakean vision, Buddhist *mantras*." Responding to a query why he had become, as he put it, "a surrealist folk-hero" in Prague, Ginsberg responded, "Probably because everyone is sick of the politicians there." While drawing little income, Ginsberg managed to travel widely, resulting in "an occasion" wherever he went. Kostelanetz indicated, "As word spreads quickly, events are organized, hospitality arranged." By now, Ginsberg's poetry had been translated widely, including "into Italian, German, French, Spanish, Bengali, Russian, Czech, Japanese, Hindu." Worldwide, he had become "the most famous and admired of contemporary American poets." His popularity derived, in part, "from his commanding personality," the charisma he easily exuded. Ginsberg stood second only to John F. Kennedy, Kostelanetz suggested, as an "American cultural ambassador, hailed particularly by the young." He appeared to be both "a prophet not only of youth and disappointment—but also perhaps . . . [a] harbinger of a new kind of existence in an age of cybernation and increased leisure."[40]

In mid-July, the Pranksters arrived in Manhattan, staying at an apartment located on 86th Street on the Upper East Side. They held a party, and among those showing up were Kerouac, Ginsberg, and the writer Terry Southern; Kerouac, who had become more and more conservative, clearly felt out-of-place among the newest American bohemians, refusing to sit on a couch that had an American flag draped over it. Kesey, as Ginsberg later recalled, acted as the "respectful welcoming and silent, fatherly timid host."[41] Tom Wolfe discussed the meeting between the king of the beats and Swashbuckler: "It was like hail and farewell. Kerouac was the old star. Kesey was the wild new comet from the West heading Christ knew where."[42] Even Ginsberg recognized that "history was out of Jack's hands now."[43] Reviews of *Sometimes a Great Notion* began appearing, with kudos and brickbats both coming Kesey's way. Orville Prescott, in the *New York Times*, dismissed the book altogether as "monstrous . . . insufferably pretentious and the most totally tiresome novel" he had read in several years.[44] By contrast, freelance author and critic Conrad Knickerbocker, also writing in the *New York Times*, declared that *Sometimes a Great Notion* "captures the tenor of post-Korea

America as nothing I can remember reading," and praised its "extraordinary richness of event and character result."[45] Despite the paper's own conflicted reading of Kesey's latest novel, it eventually showed up on the paper's "Some of the Year's Best" list.

Kesey, hardly troubled by the mixed reviews, readied for the next leg of the Pranksters' journey: a visit to Millbrook to see Timothy Leary. When the Pranksters rolled up to the Hitchcock mansion, however, Richard Alpert, but not Leary, was one of the few to come out to initially greet the travelers from out West. Alpert informed Leary, "I feel like we're a pastoral Indian village invaded by a whooping cowboy band of Wild West saloon carousers."[46] Suffering from the flu, Leary did eventually meet Kesey and Ken Babbs, although the leader of the Pranksters considered the scene at Millbrook markedly uptight. As the Pranksters readied to depart, Alpert was unable or unwilling to deliver any LSD but he did hand over morningglory seeds. The trip, the thirty hours of film—*The Merry Pranksters Search for the Cool Place*—the Pranksters shot, and living expenses cost over $100,000, blowing through Kesey's royalties and the money he received for the Broadway play.

The Pranksters returned to La Honda, where they remained at the cutting edge of the budding counterculture. In August 1965, Kesey and the Pranksters met up with the group that rivaled them and the beats for achieving notoriety as outcasts or outlaws, seemingly hardly fit for decent society. The Hell's Angels, with their skulls and crossbones on denim or leather jackets, were the ultimate bad boys of postwar America, roaring through California cities and towns like Hollister, where they kicked off a riot in 1947 and provided the model for the motorcycle gangs portrayed in the Hollywood film starring Marlon Brando, *The Wild One*, which appeared six years later. The founder of the Oakland chapter, Ralph "Sonny" Barger received an invitation from Kesey to attend a party at the La Honda estate. A giant banner greeted the Angels, sporting swastikas as they raced into La Honda: "THE MERRY PRANKSTERS WELCOME THE HELL'S ANGELS." Thanks to the writer Hunter Thompson, who was drafting a book on the Angels, Kesey had met members of the motorcycle gang. As he informed them, "We're in the same business. You break people's bones, I break people's heads."[47] On hearing that Kesey planned to offer LSD to the Angels, Thompson was appalled. "You motherfucking, crazy bastard, you'll pay for this from Maine to here," Thompson, who "thought they would take the Pranksters apart like cooked chicken," warned Kesey. Thompson knew the Pranksters "were a gang of innocents playing with fire."[48] Arriving in La Honda, where several of the Perry Lane regulars were present, along with Allen Ginsberg and Richard Alpert, dozens of Angels first guzzled beer, then took LSD, which, as Thompson reported, made many of them "oddly peaceful . . . much easier to get along with."[49] Later that year, Ginsberg, who viewed the motorcyclists as "Angelic barbarians," crafted a poem, "First Party at Ken Kesey's with Hell's Angels," in which he referred to loudspeakers pouring out the music of the Rolling Stones, Ray Charles, and the Beatles at 3 in the morning, as a score of young people danced. Just outside Kesey's gate, four police cars stood guard, seemingly ready to pounce.[50]

Political radicals throughout the United States, but perhaps particularly in the Bay Area, hoped that the budding counterculture might provide new recruits for their causes, including opposition to the heightened war in Vietnam. The concern of some radicals that involvement in the counterculture could preclude political activism appeared justified when the most famous Prankster delivered a speech at the International Day of Protest and Vietnam Day Committee Teach-In on October 15, 1965, held on the University of California, Berkeley, campus. Kesey and several of the Merry Pranksters arrived in the old school bus, which now sported a gun turret, along with swastikas, American eagles, hammers and sickles, and skulls and bones, among other insignia. Singers Malvina Reynolds and Joe McDonald performed, and radical journalist I. F. Stone presented a blistering condemnation of U.S. involvement in Vietnam. Also speaking were Ginsberg, Lawrence Ferlinghetti, and Kesey, who informed the gathered throng of fifteen thousand, "You know, you're not gonna stop this war with this rally, by marching. . . . That's what they do. . . . They hold rallies and they march. . . . They're been having wars for ten thousand years and you're not gonna stop it this way. . . . You're playing . . . their game." Undoubtedly to the dismay of the teach-in organizers, Kesey, with his orange, Day-Glo, World War I helmet, began playing "Home on the Range" on his harmonica. He then bellowed, "Do you want to know how to stop the war! Just turn your backs on it, fuck it!"[51] The following day proved unsettling for antiwar activists in another manner, as protestors marched to the Oakland Army Base, where many soldiers departed for Vietnam. Hell's Angels, led by Sonny Barger, shredded antiwar banners and shouted, "Go back to Russia, you fucking communists." Kesey, Ginsberg, and Cassady went to Barger's home in Oakland, and convinced the Hell's Angel's leader not to attack another antiwar rally. As the discussion became heated, Ginsberg starting playing his harmonica and chanted the Prajnaparamita, the Buddhist mantra, leading one of the Angels to begin singing, "Om, Om, zoom, zoom, zoom, on!" The rest of the Angels joined in, as did Kesey and Cassady. Ginsberg remembered, "I was absolutely astounded. I knew it was history being made."[52]

In the *Berkeley Barb*, dated November 19, 1965, Ginsberg wrote about "Demonstration or Spectacle as Example, As Communication or How to Make a March/Spectacle." He called for imparting to the media "imaginative, pragmatic, fun, gay, happy, *secure* Propaganda" prior to demonstrations. He suggested the use of "masses of flowers" for "masses of marchers"; respectable figures placed at the front of rallies; the holding of crosses and Jewish stars; the carrying of American flags; the wielding of "harmonicas, flutes, recorders, guitars, banjos . . . violins. . . . Bongos and tambourines"; children's toys; the adoption of tactics from mass calisthenics to prayers of OM to the singing of "The Star Spangled Banner"; interesting Zen-tinged signs including those referring to "Hell's Angels Vietcong Birch Society"; candy bars and paper halos to be offered as gifts to potential adversaries; copies of the U.S. Constitution; white flags; movie cameras to document the events; student reporters; all kinds of floats, containing images of Jesus Christ, Buddha, other historic figures, American icons, the Hell's Angels, and the Birchers; the playing of Beatles' music; the Mime Troupe; Bay Area rock 'n' roll soundtracks; uniforms and signs from earlier wars; an invitation to Muslims and unions; continual interaction with the Hell's Angels; a flurry of information to the media; an urging that marchers remain "hip, calm and tranquil with a sense of humor"; and the possible deployment of women or gays to harass the Hell's Angels.[53]

Later that year, the Pranksters kicked off the Acid Tests along the California coast, the first held close to Santa Cruz, at the home of Ken Babbs, and in Portland. The initial Acid Test, with an admission price of one dollar, included Cassady's seemingly endless commentary, footage of the so-called Bus Movie from the trip back East, and the determination of both Kesey and Babbs to create as eccentric an atmosphere as possible. They intoned into a microphone, "The room is a spaceship and the captain has lost his mind."[54] Tape recordings filtered through the air, as

Pranksters played musical instruments and doled out LSD. The Acid Tests involved the free flowing use of psychedelics, often with music and light shows designed to further heighten sensations. Among the musicians regularly playing at the Acid Tests were members of the Grateful Dead—previously known as the Warlocks—led by Kesey's old buddy from the Perry Lane days, Jerry Garcia, who recalled that his band members "were younger than the Pranksters. We were wilder. . . . More bohemian than anything else. We were definitely Dionysian as opposed to Apollonian."[55] The Pranksters posed the question, "Can YOU Pass the Acid Test" and then proceeded to spike drinks with psychedelics. Garcia remembered thousands showing up, "all helplessly stoned . . . none . . . afraid. . . . It was magic, far out, beautiful magic." By contrast, Richard Alpert worried about the Acid Tests, claiming "they were attempts to engage people in their senses so totally as to make it a transformation experience through sensory overload. It was an attempt to overload one dimension so much that it forced people into another dimension. In many ways it was an attempt to find a collective unconscious in a Jungian sense."[56]

Providing LSD to both the Pranksters and the Grateful Dead was a thirty-year-old Air Force veteran, whose relatives included a pair of Kentucky governors, Augustus Stanley Owsley III. Tom Wolfe's book *The Electric Kool-Aid Acid Test* played up Owsley's prominent role in doling out pure doses of LSD for Kesey and the Acid Tests. Owsley and his apprentice Tim Scully determined to spread the gospel of acid widely. As Scully recalled, "Every time we'd make another batch and release it on the street, something beautiful would flower, and of course we believed it was because of what we were doing. We believed that we were the architects of social change, that our mission was to change the world substantially, and what was going on in the Haight was a sort of laboratory experiment, a microscopic sample of what would happen worldwide."[57] Nevertheless, Owsley determined to warn Kesey that the Pranksters were "messing around with ancient wisdom but without any of the maps." Owsley likened the Acid Tests to "a crash course in how to become a jet pilot when you had never seen a jet before. The way they did it was they dropped you in there, took you up, and said, '*The controls are yours!*' *Whoa! Barrel rolls! Immelmanns! Tailspins!*"[58] The Brotherhood of Eternal Love, founded in Laguna Beach, California, also provided LSD and hashish to members of the counterculture, setting up an international network that included drug trafficking in Pakistan and Afghanistan. The Brotherhood's ties to the Hell's Angels enabled members to acquire Owsley's acid and spread it throughout Southern California. They operated the nation's largest LSD distribution ring, and "the biggest marijuana and hashish smuggling network."[59]

As more and more people participated in the Acid Tests, showing up at the Fillmore on January 8, the folksinger Lou Gottlieb, who wrote a music column that appeared in the *San Francisco Chronicle*, lauded the events. But on January 17, Kesey was convicted of the marijuana charge dating back to the arrest at La Honda in April, resulting in the possibility of a jail sentence ranging from six months to three years. Admonishing Kesey, the judge ordered him to refrain from associating with the Pranksters and to stay away from the Trips Festival, scheduled over three days later in the month. Four days afterward, police, after supposedly watching him toss aside "a package of brownish plant material," again arrested Kesey, along with Mountain Girl, on the rooftop of the North Beach residence of Stewart Brand.[60] The second bust strengthened the likelihood that the famed author would have to serve considerable time behind bars. No matter, Kesey and his pals, attired in Prankster garb, headed for Union Square, smack in the heart of San Francisco, to trumpet the upcoming Trips Festival.

6

THE MAGIC ELIXIR OF SEX AND
A TOUCH OF ANARCHISM

Certainly heightened sexual opportunities proved to be among the greatest lures for many drawn to the counterculture, including Allen Ginsberg, Jack Kerouac, Timothy Leary, and Ken Kesey. All four participated in long-term intimate relationships, but that hardly precluded each from conducting trysts or affairs of various sorts. Ginsberg, of course, was drawn to both men and women, while usually preferring the former. Women fell easily for the thrice-married Kerouac, who hardly proved disinclined to engage in homosexual activity, when the opportunity took place. Leary acquired a reputation as a legendary lothario, while Kesey clearly did not adhere to monogamy with his wife Faye. This hardly dampened their reputations, as prevailing double standards regarding the sexual practices of the American male and the American female continued well into the 1960s.

The nation as a whole possessed highly conflicted attitudes regarding sexuality, with the postwar glorification of the nuclear home, monogamous sexual relations of married couples, and clearly defined gender roles, as well as general disapproval of both premarital and extramarital encounters. At the same time, artists and entrepreneurs alike employed sex to sell paintings, movies, books, magazines, and a vast array of other goods that American manufacturers produced in abundance immediately following World War II, when the federal government had mandated rationing and savings accounts surged. Philip Wylie's 1942 book, *Generation of Vipers*, had castigated the plague of "momism," the apparently self-centered, ineffectual, formerly Cinderella-like woman caught up in the glorification of motherhood that followed marriage. During the postwar period, another cult of domesticity did indeed emerge, with the expectation that the stay-at-home mother would attend to the needs of her growing flock of baby boomers and her hardworking husband. American popular culture abounded with images of that seemingly ideal woman, as exemplified by television's model mother-wives, Donna Reed in *The Donna Reed Show* and June Cleaver in *Leave It to Beaver*. Yet even early television programming offered a mixed message about gender roles, thanks to *The Honeymooners*' acerbic but ever-patient and wise Alice Kramden, having to take care of her blustering husband Ralph, and Lucy Ricardo, a stay-at-home wife and soon-to-be mother, who chafed at what she was allowed to do and aspire to become. And the most glamorous movie star of the 1950s was clearly the beautiful, busty Marilyn Monroe, who also served, however inadvertently on her part, as the original pinup for Hugh Hefner's new men's magazine, *Playboy*, which first appeared in December 1953. At the same time, Monroe's brilliant comedic and dramatic performances in films like *Gentlemen Prefer Blondes*, *The Seven Year Itch*, and *Bus Stop* refuted her characterization as a ditzy blonde bombshell, as did her intellectual pursuits among both the Hollywood set and New York intellectuals.

Even before those classic 1950s' television shows and Monroe challenged gender sensibilities, however subtly, *Sexual Behavior in the Human Male*, better known as the Kinsey Report, did likewise. Authored by Alfred Kinsey, Wardell Pomeroy, and Clyde E. Martin, the report, which appeared in 1948, proved a sensation, with *Time* magazine affirming, "Not since *Gone with the Wind* had booksellers seen anything like it."[1] Dr. Howard A. Rusk, who served as a columnist for the *New York Times*, delivered a book review in which he underscored the fact that "after decades of hush-hush," the Kinsey Report was certain to be explosive and become "bitterly controversial." Publishing the book and conducting the extensive research, involving twelve thousand interviews—one subject was Herbert Huncke, who then introduced Kinsey to Allen Ginsberg, Jack Kerouac, and William Burroughs—"took real courage, courage to fight taboos and prejudices," ignorant preconceptions and confusion, Rusk insisted. Kinsey revealed that male homosexual experiences were "much more common than" earlier believed, and that married men masturbated and conducted extramarital affairs.[2] One critic, the famed anthropologist Margaret Mead, expressed concern that the report omitted sex's "emotional meaning," depicted it "as an impersonal, meaningless act," and sustained puritanical notions already too prevalent in the United States.[3] Yale University anthropologist Ralph Linton took Kinsey to task for failing to cover the full range of human sexual behavior. By contrast, others charged that the Kinsey Report threatened familial relationships by questioning prevailing ethical standards.[4]

New York University philosophy professor William Barrett, who also served as editor of *Partisan Review*, discussed America's sexual practices as he explored Greenwich Village in the first years after the war. In an article that indicated the Village lacked both a crusade and "its avant-garde spirit," Barrett noted that the American nation first became cognizant of the existence of its own Bohemia during the 1920s, when a type "of great crusade" occurred that, in typical fashion for Bohemia, largely involved personal freedom, which meant "in practice, usually sexual freedom." But Barrett declared that sexual freedom presently could "hardly be a crusade in a nation that took the Kinsey Report so very much in its stride."[5]

Notwithstanding Barrett's analysis, Americans continued to remain conflicted, even perplexed about sex as demonstrated by the response to another landmark Kinsey study, *Sexual Behavior in the Human Female*, which was released in 1953 and led to the lead author's placement on the cover of *Time* magazine. Harvard anthropologist Clyde Kluckhohn actually opened his full book review by declaring that Americans were probably little interested in reading about many of the subjects the latest volume on sex discussed. Again drawn from thousands of interviews, the newest Kinsey study reported that women who had been aroused orgasmically before marriage were much more likely to become so during marriage, the experience of premarital petting might lead to dissatisfaction for married women who were not similarly attended to before sexual intercourse, and almost half of the women had intercourse before marriage. Acknowledging that this was an arena fraught with "frightening complexity," Kluckhohn admired the "courage, persistence . . . ambitious sweep of the total plan," and had "no patience with the prudery . . . and the anti-scientific, anti-rational attitudes" manifested by blanket condemnations of Kinsey.[6]

Nevertheless, that very prudery and the lingering double standard continued to affect Americans, with the vast majority expressing the belief that a woman should remain a virgin until she married. High schools dismissed pregnant girls, or sent them off to "continuation" programs, thereby segregating such "troubled" youngsters from their peers. Universities remained committed to the principle of *in loco parentis*, devising rules and regulations involving dating practices. Cities deemed cohabitation between unmarried couples unlawful, while various states also made extramarital sex and the use of contraceptives, even by a husband and wife, illegal. In 1953, the year that *Sexual Behavior in the Human Female* appeared, policemen in Detroit targeted stores that sold paperback copies of books by Ernest Hemingway, James T. Farrell, and John Dos Passos, historian David Allyn recounts. In Cleveland, they prevented Sigmund Freud's *General Introduction to Psychoanalysis*, John Steinbeck's *Wayward Bus*, and Mickey Spillane's *I, the Jury*, from being sold. The federal government continued to censor books viewed as lewd, affecting in the process John Cleland's eighteenth-century racy novel, *Memoirs of a Woman of Pleasure*, better known as *Fanny Hill*, along with modern classics like D. H. Lawrence's *Lady Chatterley's Lover* and Henry Miller's *Tropic of Cancer*.

The paired *Roth v. United States* and *Alberts v. California* decisions by the U.S. Supreme Court in 1957 reaffirmed the principle that the First Amendment afforded no protection against state and federal obscenity legislation. Justice William Brennan declared for the majority, "We hold that obscenity is not within the area of constitutionally protected speech or press." Justice William O. Douglas, with Justice Hugo Black concurring, dissented in the *Roth* and *Alberts* cases. Upholding the convictions, Douglas contended, made "the legality of a publication turn on the purity of thought which a book or tract instills in the mind of the reader," thereby violating both the First and the Fourteenth Amendments. Instead, Douglas wrote, "I would give the broad sweep of the First Amendment full support. I have the same confidence in the ability of our people to reject noxious literature as I have in their capacity to sort out the true from the false in theology, economics, politics, or any other field."[7]

Earlier in the decade, Barney Rosset, then married to the Abstract Expressionist artist Joan Mitchell, purchased the small publishing house, Grove Press, which under his direction in 1954 issued Samuel Beckett's play, *Waiting for Godot*. That same year, Mark Schorer, an English professor at the University of California at Berkeley, attempted to convince Rosset, whose favorite book, Henry Miller's *Tropic of Cancer*, was banned in the United States because of its depiction of sex and prostitution, to publish D. H. Lawrence's *Lady Chatterley's Lover*. Meanwhile, Rosset began putting out a literary journal, *Evergreen Review*, in 1957, including an article by Schorer in its first issue, and "Howl" in the next one. Those issues also contained work by Jean-Paul Sartre, Beckett, and a host of other beat writers like Lawrence Ferlinghetti, Jack Kerouac, Michael McClure, Gary Snyder, and Philip Whalen. Rosset proceeded to publish Lawrence's controversial novel, almost immediately resulting in the U.S. Post Office's holding of 164 copies and the easy dismissal of *Lady Chatterley's Lover* by Postmaster General Arthur Summerfield as "smutty . . . filthy, offensive and degrading."[8] No matter, the book sold over 160,000 copies within four months, landing near the top of the *New York Times'* best-seller list. In 1961, Rosset also published *Tropic of Cancer*, leading to arrests of booksellers, including nearly thirty in New Jersey alone. The book became largely unavailable, and Henry Miller himself suffered arrest in Brooklyn. Conspiracy charges were brought against Rosset and Miller, accused of conspiring "to depict and represent acts and scenes wherein the sexual organs of both male persons and female persons were to be portrayed and described in manners connoting sex degeneracy and sex perversion and were to be of such pornographic character as would tend to incite lecherous thoughts and desires."[9] Contrasting state decisions regarding whether Miller's novel was obscene ensured that the case would land before the U.S. Supreme Court. In the meantime, Rosset published other books with a sexual focus, such as John Rechy's 1963 novel, *City of Night*, about homosexual hustling. G.P. Putnam's Sons published another edition of *Fanny Hill*, leading to additional seizures and court cases. On June 22, 1964, the U.S. Supreme Court, in the case of *Grove Press, Inc. v. Gerstein*, affirmed that *Tropic of Cancer* "is entitled to the protection of the First Amendment and cannot be held to be obscene."[10] Twenty-five months later, the Supreme Judicial Court of Massachusetts, despite deeming it "grossly offensive," denied that William Burrough's novel, *Naked Lunch*, was obscene.[11]

The beats, for their part, defiantly contested American sexual mores during World War II and throughout the early postwar period, and did so deliberately, provocatively, courageously. They decried the sexual repressiveness that afflicted so many of their fellow Americans, celebrating instead the natural man. All the while, other legislation germane to several of the beats remained on the books, including those that attempted to preclude any kind of homosexual activity. But rather than link up with the small number of homosexual organizations that appeared by the 1950s, such as the Mattachine Society and the Daughters of Bilitis, the beats carried on through their small circle of friends before engaging in the frenetic behavior that helped to spread the beat gospel, part of which involved a direct assault on sexually restricted codes and lifestyles. Indeed, they at times operated in brazen fashion, albeit frequently in sanctuaries such as those found in North Beach, Greenwich Village, Venice, California, or bohemian-friendly enclaves overseas.

As the new decade began, technology and an alteration of judicial renderings also helped to set the stage for changes in sexual practices in the United States. On May 9, 1960, the Food and Drug Administration announced its impending approval of Envoid 10 or the combined oral contraceptive pill, better known simply as "the pill," thereby affording women the best means of birth control to date. In addition, federal courts began issuing more liberal rulings involving obscenity cases, loosening censorship in the process.

Serving as something of a bridge between the beats and the hippies who sprang forth during the 1960s, Timothy Leary and Ken Kesey continued and, at times, intensified their earlier determination to discard sexual barriers, at least involving monogamy. Both in Cambridge and then at Millbrook, Leary helped to usher in the sexual revolution, as Irwin and Debi Unger, astute chroniclers of the 1960s, note. Recognizing that he was not only a proselytizer for psychedelic drugs, Leary stood as the Dionysian apostle, refuting bourgeois sensibilities altogether.[12] While less of a philanderer than Leary, Kesey too engaged in sexual relationships with women other than his wife Faye, as in the case of Mountain Girl, who later married Jerry Garcia.

A small number of controversial thinkers also helped to set the stage for a change in sexual attitudes and practices in the United States, allowing for the sexual revolution that began to unfold in the 1960s and 1970s. As David Allyn puts it, this was a period "when utopianism and hedonism, idealism and opportunism" markedly altered the nation's sexual landscape.[13] Irwin and Debi Unger refer to "neo-Freudians" who helped to provide the intellectual justification "for instinctual liberation."[14] One was William Reich, the Austrian Jewish psychiatrist who had been a favorite student of Sigmund Freud at the University of Vienna, and attempted to meld Marxism and psychoanalysis, contending that neurosis resulted from the patient's total condition, taking into holistic account physical and sexual manifestations but also his or her economic and social situation. While still a medical student, Reich determined "that sexuality is the center around which revolves the whole of social life as well as the inner life of the individual."[15]

Ensuring that he proved controversial, Reich pointed to the importance of adolescent sexuality, contraception, abortion, divorce, and economic independence for women. Suppressing natural sexuality assured that the child was "obedient . . . good, and adjusted in the authoritarian sense," Reich asserted. At the same time, "it paralyzes the rebellious forces, because any rebellion is laden with anxiety."[16] In his book, *The Function of the Orgasm*, published in 1927, the thirty-year-old Reich stated that full and repeated orgasms were required by healthy individuals and to prevent neuroses. He began to set up a series of socialist sex-hygiene clinics, starting in 1928, and his book, *The Sexual Revolution*, appeared in 1930. Through several volumes, he attempted to bring about a synthesis of Marx and Freud, contending that psychoanalysis was itself revolutionary. *The Mass Psychology of Fascism*, appearing in 1933, dismissed the authoritarian patriarchal family, which purportedly suppressed genital sexuality by children and adolescents, in favor of the matriarchal family, which by contrast was wholly permissive. Moreover, Reich considered social and sexual liberation to be inextricably intertwined. He contended that sexual abstinence inflicted on adolescents resulted in juvenile delinquency, neuroses, perversions, and political apathy. In contrast to Freud, he also strongly defended sexual emancipation for women and condemned marital fidelity.

Compelled to flee Germany when Hitler took power, Reich, at the time a communist, moved first to Vienna and then Scandinavia, where he eventually ended up in Oslo. A flood of nasty newspaper articles targeting him soon poured forth, with such titles as "'Quackery of Psychoanalysis,' 'The Jewish Pornographer,' and 'God Reich Creates Life.'" In 1939, he headed for the United States, where the FBI began to accumulate a lengthy file on him, although he became strongly opposed to Joseph Stalin following the Soviet invasion of Finland. Reich believed more zealously than ever that a sexual revolution was required to emancipate individuals; moreover, he asserted that a sexual revolution was occurring, which nothing could thwart.

Despite recognizing that puritanical notions had long beset the United States, Reich, earlier expelled from the International Psychoanalytic Association, remained hopeful that a more receptive greeting awaited him than back in fascist-dominated Europe. He contested the Western propensity to dichotomize passion and reason, as his own explorations proved quirkier, with many wondering if his sanity had departed altogether. Challenging prevailing therapeutic practices, he touched patients during therapy, hoping to blunt their "body armor," posing questions all the while. He established the Orgone Institute in New York, later moving it to a large plot of land situated in Maine. His work, particularly *The Function of the Orgasm* (1942), was widely read in intellectual circles, attracting both Saul Bellow and Dwight Macdonald, among many others. Having determined to produce a biological examination of the psyche, Reich focused on the energy generated by orgasms, referring to that as orgone energy. Contending that inhibitions restricting orgastic potentialities precluded the individual from attaining "a normal psycho-physiological state," Reich soon devised Physical Orgonotherapy and Psychiatric Orgonotherapy. He even convinced Albert Einstein to try out his Orgone Energy Accumulator. Nevertheless, controversies continued to swirl about him, with both Stalinists and Trotskyists assailing him, but then so had his former mentor Freud and other leaders in the psychoanalytical movement. Increasingly isolated from within his profession, Reich nevertheless acquired a small band of devoted followers and allies, including the renowned cartoonist William Steig; A. S. Neill, founder of the progressive, coeducational Summerhill School in Suffolk, England; and Allen Ginsberg, who considered seeking treatment for his homosexual propensities from Reich. Increasingly, Reich believed that children were far more malleable, and he supported progressive child-rearing practices, home births, natural foods, and the nurturing of innate sensibilities.

During the spring of 1947, however, freelance journalist Mildred Edie Brady drew unwanted attention to Reich's work through a pair of articles, "The New Cult of Sex and Anarchy" and "The Strange Case of William Reich," which appeared in *Harper's Magazine* and *The New Republic*, respectively; the latter would be reprinted in full in the *Bulletin of the Menninger Clinic* the following March. Brady opened her *Harper's* essay by referring to the latest bohemia, which was emerging in Big Sur country, situated in northern California just south of Carmel. She pointed to early antecedents, including Henry Miller, who began living in a cabin in the Big Sur in 1943, as "pirated editions of his *Tropic of Cancer* and *Tropic of Capricorn*" were passed among inhabitants of the area. They also read his uncensored work that contained an amalgam "of mysticism, egoism, sexualism, surrealism, and anarchism." Among those inhabitants were several conscientious objectors, "men against the state," with their natural store of anarchism and desire for personal salvation. A small avant-garde weekly publication, *Pacifica Views*, actually ran an extended discussion about Reich's views on sexuality, "a sure come-on for the young." Up in San Francisco, the communist poet-turned pacifist anarchist Kenneth Rexroth also attracted literary adherents who explored the Russian anarcho-communist Peter Kropotkin and other anarchist thinkers, while delving into the writings of William Reich. Both groups, Brady noted, "reject rationalism, espouse mysticism, and belong to the select few who are orgastically potent." Setting themselves apart from the 1920s' bohemians, they also "prefer their women subdued—verbally and intellectually," while favoring a small number of female writers, including Anais Nin.[17]

Now residing in shacks and tents in the territory below Carmel, bearded and sandaled newcomers, with "corduroys and dark shirts," strove for isolation, featured abstract paintings on their rough walls, and held poetry sessions in nearby San Francisco and Berkeley. Some dwelled in San Francisco and others lived further north in Russian River territory. They seemed to share a philosophy that combined anarchist and psychoanalytical strands, which declared "you must abandon the church, the state, and family," and held aloft sex as the means to "individual salvation in a collective world that's going to hell." The creators "of the new Paris" were religious in their own fashion, referring to "'the outer reality,' 'the great oneness,' 'the life source,' or 'the vital core.'" But this was a religious sensibility through which love was depicted "as 'the ecstasy of the cosmos'" and "the sexual sacrament" was deemed "the acme of worship."[18]

Freud and Jung were out of vogue, Brady noted, replaced by the sexual evangelist William Reich, with his *Function of the Orgasm* regularly referred to by the new bohemians. Reich blamed physical and spiritual ailments on "orgastic impotence," and cast aspersions on "'the patriarchal family' and its 'compulsive morality.'" By contrast, the elite group of "orgastic potent" individuals could readily "surrender to love," exhibited "unusual aliveness and physical well being," proved exceptionally creative, and were "in tune with the great, cosmic, vital force that is the natural law of the universe." Popular too was the English poet and anarchist Herbert Read, who referred to religion as "a natural authority . . . the only force which can hold a people together." Brady noted that the California-based bohemians drew from both the irreligious Reich and the religiously rooted Read, but also favored Kropotkin, "D. H. Lawrence, Emma Goldman, Madame Blavatsky, Henri Bergson, William Blake, and even Ouspenski of *Tertium Organum*," among others. Some melded "vegetarianism, ballet dancing, co-operative handcrafts' anarchism, and sexual mysticism," while others engaged in "a co-operative search for orgastic potency" in the manner of "a primitive tribal group." Art appeared the only means to allow for "the fettered, mechanically burdened soul of man" to exhibit "his revolt against the dead hand of rationalism" and garner "that all but buried spark of natural life dying under the intolerable weight of modern man's sadistic super-ego," thereby attaining a means to return "to his spontaneous, natural creativeness."[19]

Brady spotted a lurking threat within the new bohemia, its mystical "mood and outlook" appearing to exhibit a decidedly antidemocratic twist. Those recalled for her "the glorification of instincts and urges, the subjective absolution of the famed Stefan George circle," of literary and academic figures, which appeared in Germany before the Nazis came to power. She was decidedly uncomfortable with Henry Miller's pronouncement: "A real man has no need of governments, of moral or ethical codes, to say nothing of battleships, police clubs, high powered bombs and such things. Of course, a real man is hard to find, but that's the only kind worth talking about. Why talk about trash? It is the great mass of mankind, the mob, the people, who create permanently bad times." Still, Brady admitted that it was difficult to ascertain "anything significantly sinister" currently emanating from Big Sur, where "anything goes" and where young bohemians believed they were experiencing "a cultural revival like that around Yeats in Dublin."[20]

In "The Strange Case of William Reich," Brady honed in more particularly on the controversial figure who was about to become far more controversial still, in part because of the attention her twinned articles induced. She began by declaring that a "cult of no little influence" surrounded her subject, who claimed that orgone was *the* cosmic energy." Reich remained influential in psychoanalytical circles, and only *Psychosomatic Medicine* spoke openly against him, calling his work involving orgone "a surrealistic creation." The lay press, from *The Nation* to *Science and Society*, Brady declared, had afforded Reich "almost entirely uncritical attention." Operating out of Forest Hills, New York, Reich stated that the vast majority of people were "endemically neurotic and sexually sick." Brady wrote about the six-sided orgone accumulator, a box that could accommodate a grown man, and whose organic material supposedly allowed for absorption of orgone from the air.[21]

In his final years, Reich became more misanthropic and paranoid, sometimes for good reason. Reich's own attempt to commercialize his orgone box resulted in an investigation in 1947 by the Food and Drug Administration, which later obtained an injunction to prevent shipment of his equipment and writings. William Burroughs was among those troubled by the assault on Reich, who he denied was crazy, calling him a genius instead. But violations of the injunction resulted in a charge of criminal contempt of court and a two-year prison sentence in 1956, along with the burning of tons of his works, including, ironically, his book *The Mass Psychology of Fascism*, in a bonfire; he suffered heart failure the following year. Shortly following his trial, Reich's friend A. S. Neil sent him a letter, stating,

> Reich I love you. I cannot bear to think of your being punished by an insane prison sentence. . . . The Tatsache [fact] that you are being crucified fundamentally because you are the first man in centuries who has preached pro-lifeness, because you are the one and only man to assert the right of adolescence to love completely. The majority in USA, Britain, Russia, in the whole world are anti-life. . . . In any court your defense should be in big letters I AM FOR LIFE AND FOR LOVE, not I am the victim.[22]

While behind bars at the Lewisburg Federal Penitentiary in Pennsylvania, Reich wrote a prison document in which he claimed, "I have disclosed to mankind the cosmic primordial mass-free energy which fills the universe. This energy rules all living processes and the lawful behavior of celestial functions. It determines our emotions, our first sense of orientation, judgment and balance. [It is] the basic force in nature which for millennia was called 'God.'"[23] As journalism professor Gerald Grow of Florida A&M University suggests, Reich's perspective approximated "the belief in natural innocence, sexuality, spontaneity, and the mating of physicality with spirituality" associated with the counterculture of the 1960s.[24] A number of figures linked to the counterculture were drawn to Reich, including Norman Mailer, Paul Goodman, Allen Ginsberg, Jack Kerouac, and William Burroughs.

Another highly influential figure who helped to shape attitudes regarding sexuality within both the counterculture and the movement of the 1960s was the German Jewish philosopher, sociologist, and political theorist Herbert Marcuse, who also became an expatriate escaping from German Nazism. A participant in the short-lived Spartacist uprising following World War I, during the brief lived heyday of Rosa Luxemburg and Karl Liebknecht, Marcuse went on to complete his PhD at the University of Freiburg, and then attempted to synthesize phenomenology, existentialism, and Marxism, believing that thought about the latter had ossified. Along with Theodore Adorno and Max Horkheimer, he cofounded the Frankfurt Institute for Social Research in 1933, and eventually helped to devise a model for critical social theory, another attempt to fuse Marxism with psychoanalysis and existentialism. He also came to view sexual repression as necessarily resulting from a repressive social order.

Marcuse decided to flee from Germany to Geneva in 1933, then emigrated to the United States the following year, while remaining one of the leading theoreticians associated with the Frankfurt School. Marcuse joined the Office of War Information during World War II, later moving over to the Office of Strategic Services, focusing in both instances on Nazi Germany. As explored in *Reason and Revolution* (1941) and in the fashion of Georg Lukas and Antonio Gramsci, Marcuse delved into Marx's early manuscripts, concentrating on issues pertaining to alienation, consciousness, and a new brand of individualism resulting from communism. Following the war, Marcuse worked for the State Department, heading its Central European section, then resumed his academic career, teaching at Columbia, Harvard, Brandeis, and the University of California at San Diego. He criticized neo-Freudians like Erich Fromm for lacking intellectual honor and theoretical depth, in their emphasis on the whole personality, which caused them to seemingly neglect how sexually repressive constraints impacted society. Unlike the neo-Freudians, Marcuse sought to fuse Marx and Freud in a sophisticated manner.

Two of Marcuse's books particularly helped to set the stage for the sexual revolution of the 1960s, along with the counterculture in general: *Eros and Civilization*, published in 1955, when Reich was encountering severe legal troubles, and *One-Dimensional Man*, issued in 1964. As Barbara Celarent astutely noted about the earlier work, several years after its publication, Marcuse posed the fundamental question: "How should we live?" He apparently took for granted that the core economic problem had been tackled, thanks to greater productivity and the advent of the welfare state. The conundrum to be tackled involved instead the quality of life, the very issue that the counterculture highlighted, in its own fashion. [25]

In *Eros and Civilization*, Marcuse examined Freudian theory, which deemed repression of both Eros and the death instinct essential for society's very existence. According to Freud, it was imperative to transform "the pleasure principle into the reality principle"; happiness itself, he said, "is not cultural value." Instead it needed to be subordinated to work discipline, "monogamic reproduction," and law and order. The libido had to be sacrificed, "rigidly" deflected "to socially useful activities and expressions." This had proven successful to a certain extent, allowing control over nature and the progress associated with Western civilization. However, it had led to heightened "unfreedom," with ever-more efficient "domination of man by man," along with "concentration camps, mass exterminations, world wars, and atom bombs." Ironically, these represented the "unrepressed" accomplishments of modern society, at the very point when "the creation of a truly free world" seemed most possible. Freud considered "civilization and barbarism, progress and suffering, freedom and unhappiness" to be joined, in the fashion of "Eros and Thanatos," a life instinct and one seeking respite or death. Marcuse called all of this into question, deeming a nonrepressive social order both possible and realistic, rather than utopian. Contesting Freudian analysis and culling from Marx's *Das Kapital*, he favored the lessening of sublimation or repression, pointing out that the bulk of it was unjustifiably employed to benefit dominant classes. Marcuse referred to this needless sublimation as "surplus repression," thereby combining Marx and Freud once more. He did so as well in pointing to the "performance principle," an alteration of Marx's concept of alienation. With that principle in place, individuals were unable to work for themselves, having to toil for others in unfree fashion. The economic efficiency of such a system resulted in productivity, improved working conditions, and leisure time, but permeated the society in which it prevailed. Ultimately, it took control of leisure and sexual practices too, which proved restricted and confined to monogamous relationships. Marcuse warned, "The individual pays by sacrificing his time, his consciousness, his dreams; civilization pays by sacrificing its own promises of liberty, justice, and peace for all."[26]

The final stages of *Eros and Civilization* did indeed highlight utopian possibilities, pointing to art's ability to foster freedom and imagination, the need to convert work into play, and the necessity of abandoning monogamous sexual relationships. In his epilogue, Marcuse called into question Freudian notions "that the human ideals of socialism were humanly unattainable." He pointed to early works of William Reich that underscored how fully "sexual repression is enforced by the interests of domination and exploitation, and the extent to which these interests are in turn reinforced and reproduced by sexual repression." Marcuse believed, however, that Reich set up sexual liberation as "a panacea for individual and social ills," minimized the issue of sublimation, failed to distinguish between sublimation of a repressive or nonrepressive variety, and suggested that freedom advances "as a mere release of sexuality." This led to "a sweeping primitivism." But Marcuse also took to task Neo-Freudians, particularly Fromm, who apparently accepted Freud's contention that love in Western society required "aim-inhibited sexuality," replete with restraints in keeping with "a monogamic-patriarchal society." This amounted, in Marcuse's estimation, to love effectively being declared out-of-bounds. "There is no longer any place in present-day civilized life for a simple natural love between two human beings." Thus the Neo-Freudian maintained "the disharmony between society and the individual." For his part, Marcuse saw the need for the "resexualization of the body," with mankind seeking a "return to the state of 'polymorphous perversity,' in which the entire body would once again become a source of sexual pleasure."[27]

Harvard's Clyde Kluckhohn termed *Eros and Civilization* a "remarkable book" wrestling "with 'the fatal dialectic of civilization.'" Marcuse questioned the work of both Freud and the Neo-Freudian revisionists, such as Fromm, who focused on the conscious and the cultural, thereby diminishing the significance of the instinctual "without questioning its origin and legitimacy." Kluckhohn noted that Marcuse's call to move "beyond the pleasure principle" involved a hoped for reinvigoration of esthetic possibilities, setting the stage for order becoming beautiful and work amounting to play. And the transformation of sexuality into Eros would result in a diffusion of sexual instincts into both private and public spheres that "bridges the gap maintained between them by a repressive reality principle."[28] The German-born sociologist Kurt H. Wolff, another Jew forced to flee from Nazi Germany, termed the scope of *Eros and Civilization* and the knowledge Marcuse displayed "magnificent," and its "sense of dedication inspiring." Wolff indicated that the necessary task Marcuse pointed to involved reconciling the reality and the pleasure principles, self-sublimating sexuality into Eros, and sensualizing reason to eroticize work and make morality "libidinous." Tellingly, Marcuse worried if civilization could even foster freedom for its lack had become "part and parcel of the mental apparatus."[29] The philosopher Herbert Fingarete stated that Marcuse had offered the first "systematic philosophy of Eros," while articulating a "concept of a non-repressive civilization" along with the "gradual abolition of repression."[30]

More digestible and hence more popular with the counterculture, *One-Dimensional Man* appeared nine years after *Eros and Civilization*, when the sexual revolution of the 1960s had certainly begun to simmer, at a bare minimum. In *One-Dimensional Man*, Marcuse warned that "The capabilities (intellectual and material) of contemporary society are immeasurably greater than before—which means that the scope of society's domination over the individual is immeasurably greater than ever before." He worried about the dissipating of "independence of thought, autonomy, and the right to political opposition," in the very period when they appeared stronger than they had for a good while. The media conditioned individuals "to behave and consume in accordance with the advertisements, to love and hate what others love and hate," stoking "false" needs while maintaining "toil, aggressiveness, misery and injustice." Goods helped to indoctrinate people, and the process of indoctrination "becomes a way of life," albeit seemingly "much better than before," while cultivating "*one dimensional thought.*" Meanwhile, American policymakers, in the manner that C. Wright Mills warned against, shaped the nation's agenda, producing a warfare state to extend American tentacles and a welfare state to mitigate against the possibility of a social or economic cataclysm. More troubling of all, Marcuse contended, "the totalitarian dimensions of the one-dimensional society" inhibited protest, while maintaining "the illusion of sovereignty."[31]

His writings, including *Repressive Tolerance* (1965), which seemingly assailed liberalism and termed "equality of tolerance . . . abstract, spurious," and his growing identification with the New Left, piqued new controversies regarding Marcuse and led to Brandeis's failing to renew his postretirement teaching contract.[32] In a new preface to *One-Dimensional Man*, Marcuse asserted, "Today the fight for life, the fight for Eros, is the *political* fight."[33] He went on to teach in La Jolla, acquiring greater renown and the title of "father of the New Left," a label he supposedly abhorred. However, later New Leftists were hardly pleased when Marcuse emphatically declared that revolution was "absolutely not" possible in the United States because no partnership existed between students and workers.[34] He also denied that students standing alone could become revolutionaries, which he believed they well appreciated. No matter, new calls occurred for his dismissal from his professorship at the University of California at San Diego, just as the *New York Times* referred to Marcuse as "the most important philosopher alive."[35]

Another celebrant of sexual liberation, the philosopher Norman O. Brown produced such bestselling works as *Life against Death* and *Love's Body*. Brown studied at Balliol College, Oxford, tutored by Isaiah Berlin, and received his doctorate in classics at the University of Wisconsin, Madison. Brown, who was drawn to Marxism in the 1930s and worked for the OSS during World War II, befriending Herbert Marcuse, became a professor of classics at Wesleyan University. Labeled by the *New York Times* "brilliant," *Life against Death* appeared in 1959, offering another radical examination of Sigmund Freud's work, particularly the theory of repression, which Brown considered to result in the failure of individuals to recognize their human potential. Urging "an erotic sense of reality," Brown instead presented a means to reconnect life and death instincts, Eros and Thanatos, to terminate repression, and to bring about "resurrection of the body" by exalting "the natural Dionysian body-ego." Contemporary society, however, was rooted in neuroses, while human history amounted to "the history of a mass neurosis." Brown dismissed attempted reforms by Neo-Freudians as insignificant, failing to address the core matter. Western society remained fixated on the denial of the body, repression, and the perversion of desire. Even "sex radicals" such as William Reich and D. H. Lawrence failed to eradicate sexual repression, emphasizing the orgasm's primacy and the psyche's connection to genitals. For his part, Brown favored a reinstilling of "polymorphous perversity," in which the full body was eroticized. Brown also condemned the concept of sublimation, which he saw as maintaining repression while crippling the body's potentialities. He favored "living in the moment," rather than dreading death as so many did, and reasoned that "the question confronting mankind is the abolition of repression."[36] The poet Francis Golffing called *Life against Death* "a complex and infinitely provocative work," with a utopian flavor that emphasized the need for "man's reconciliation with his own body." Brown's later *Love's Body* (1966) continued to urge that body and spirit be reconciled, "to recover the breath-soul . . . the life-soul instead of the ghost-soul or shadow," along with "body-consciousness instead of head-consciousness."[37]

Herbert Marcuse and Norman O. Brown proved enormously popular within the ranks of the counterculture, while the ideas of William Reich, far less appreciated, nevertheless resonated among many of the sexually adventurous during the 1960s. They influenced the human potential movement, which emerged during that turbulent period, and drew from many of the same figures as did the counterculture, like Aldous Huxley, Alan Watts, and Paul Goodman. They in turn had been influenced by the psychologist Abraham Maslow with his theories of self-actualization that would enable individuals to reach their full potential, and the German-born psychiatrist Fritz Perls. Goodman, along with Fritz and Laura Perls, helped to construct Gestalt Therapy, with its emphasis on sensations, perception, and personal responsibility. On the edges of the counterculture, the Esalen Institute operated out of Big Sur, seeking the realization of "human potential," as Huxley put it.[38] There, Huxley lectured at the start of the 1960s on human potentialities, and Perls conducted sessions in which he urged participants to strip and discard inhibitions, particularly sexual ones.

7

THE MAGIC IN THE MUSIC

Allen Ginsberg, Jack Kerouac, Timothy Leary, Ken Kesey, the late William Reich, a sometimes reluctant Herbert Marcuse, and Norman O. Brown were hardly the only proselytizers for the counterculture of the 1960s. Long-haired musicians, particularly from the United States and England, preached the gospel of alternative lifestyles, drugs, sex, and rebellion, in their own fashion. This was not altogether new, as musicians had frequently existed on the boundaries of respectability, during the first several decades of the twentieth century. Music wafting out of New Orleans and into Kansas City, St. Louis, Chicago, and New York City proved controversial because of its association with race and sex, well before youth-based rock 'n' roll exploded on the scene during the mid-1950s. Ragtime artists Scott Joplin and Jelly Roll Morton helped to set the stage for blues singers Mamie Smith, Bessie Smith, and Billie Holliday, and for jazz musicians on the order of Joe "King" Oliver, Louis "Satchmo" Armstrong, and Duke Ellington. Beside their artistic genius and sexually charged charisma, what distinguished those legendary performers was the fact that they were black. Certain lyrics, with their suggestive qualities and double entendres, and the passionate nature of the music, along with its appeal across racial borders, enraged or frightened some, who little desired that the nation's segregation practices come to an end. Hillbilly music of the 1920s and 1930s, which eventually gave way to country and western, hardly lacked its own dynamic figures, including Jimmie Rodgers and the Carter Family, who helped to establish a musical framework for Hank Williams, as notorious as blues and jazz performers for his fondness for drink, drugs, and the pleasures of the body. From the 1940s onward, rhythm and blues artists like Big Joe Turner, Sonny Boy Williamson, and Louis Jordan delivered hits, again some laced with sexual innuendos, with crossover appeal to white audiences.

Early 1950s stars Big Mama Thornton and Etta James witnessed white singers like Elvis Presley and Jerry Lee Lewis cover their songs, but Presley and Lewis joined with Chuck Berry and Little Richard to serve as the Original Holy Quartet of rock 'n' roll. This hardly lacked controversy, given that the latter two performers were black and all four were good-looking young men who exuded the sexuality that had made some leery of ragtime, blues, jazz, hillbilly music, pop, and rhythm and blues. But rock 'n' roll proved the most explosive because of how it drew from white and black roots; featured white and black musicians, sometimes appearing on the same card; and appealed to young people of all sorts. Like earlier genres, rock 'n' roll occasionally delivered lyrics of a provocative sort, whether involving romance, school, or work, as in Little Richard's "Long Tall Sally," Berry's "School Days," and the Coasters' "Yakety, Yak."

During the latter half of the 1950s, a new brand of folk music also garnered attention, along with the songs of Woody Guthrie, Pete Seeger, and Cisco Houston. The Kingston Trio's "M.T.A." and "Where Have All the Flowers Gone" contained social protest messages, but the most powerful indictments of contemporary society still lay ahead. By the beginning of the 1960s, a younger crop of singers appeared, led by folk's Madonna, Joan Baez, and Bob Dylan, described by Robert Shelton in the *New York Times* as "resembling a cross between a choir boy, and a beatnik."[1] Baez's angelic offerings were sometimes paired against Dylan's fiery lyrics as in renditions of "With God on Our Side" and "A Hard Rain's a Gonna Fall." Dylan's condemnations of domestic and international events also poured forth in songs like "Oxford Town," "Blowin' in the Wind," and "The Times They Are a-Changin." As Shelton suggested, Dylan, Baez, and other top young folk singers affected a beat-like image, in the opening stages of the decade.

Dylan, four young men from Liverpool, England, and a number of other musicians—several boasting folk roots, along with a fascination for early rock 'n' roll—helped to provide a musical backdrop to the budding American counterculture of the early 1960s. During the first several decades of the twentieth century, popular songs often contained rebellious undercurrents, again ranging from the provocative nature of the music itself to sexually drawn lyrics. That hardly changed as rock 'n' roll entered a more mature phase, following its first few years, but musicians displayed a new interest in other, less conventional topics, including those related to sex, drugs, and lifestyles. Among the first to do so was Dylan, in his typically cryptic fashion.

Already famous for protest songs dealing with civil rights, nuclear fallout, and generational strife, Dylan foreshadowed the growing involvement by many musicians with various aspects of the still budding counterculture. As early as the winter of 1964, Dylan, in the midst of reading the poetry of Arthur Rimbaud, was also crafting songs demonstrating, sometimes subtly and sometimes not, how drug usage, possibly including psychedelics, was affecting him. On a nearly month-long tour of the United States that February, he composed "Mr. Tambourine Man." Filled with pathos, the narrator asked Mr. Tambourine Man to perform a song for him, to help relieve loneliness, even numbness. The narrator hoped to be carried away, at least by the piquing of his senses, which might involve a "dancing spell," "a trip upon" Mr. Tambourine Man's "magic swirlin' ship." The song wove images that were almost ethereal in nature, in which the narrator might be "laughin', spinnin', swingin' madly across the sun," and was, at a minimum, "disappearin' through the smoke rings of" his mind. [2]

Also in 1964, Dylan produced the "My Back Pages," which appeared on his next album, *Another Side of Bob Dylan*. [3] The song opened by referring to "crimson flames," "flaming roads," and "using ideas as my maps," and by employing the refrain, "Ah, but I was so much older then / I'm younger than that now." At a minimum, it suggested that Dylan was wrestling with the celebrity he had acquired, but the surrealistic beginning offered the possibility of other influences, including pharmacological ones. [4] Dylan included "Chimes of Freedom" on the same album with "My Back Pages," referring to "the rebel," "the rake," "the luckless, the abandoned an' forsaked," "the outcast," and "the mad mystic." [5] By October 31, 1964, when he performed at New York's Philharmonic Hall, Dylan was playing new songs like "The Gates of Eden" and "It's Alright Ma, I'm Only Bleeding." Written as if in a dream, "The Gates of Eden" spoke of "the cowboy angel," the "savage soldier" with "his head in sand," Aladdin, "Utopian hermit monks," the Golden Calf, "promises of paradise," "the motorcycle black madonna,"and a "two-wheeled gypsy queen."[6] The phantasmagorical "It's Alright Ma, I'm Only Bleeding" elusively related life experiences from birth to death, underscoring the futility, the pain, of attempting to make sense of matters. It highlighted the absurdity of religion, education, politics, commercial pursuits, leaders, and society altogether. Ultimately, as the protagonist indicated, "I got nothing, Ma, to live up to." He acknowledged that his "thought-dreams" might lead to his demise, but then Dylan declared, "It's alright, Ma, it's life, and life only."[7]

Dylan's cutting-edge music continued in 1965, with the appearance of the albums *Bringing It All Back Home* and *Highway 61 Revisited. Bringing It All Back Home* included the recently released "Subterranean Homesick Blues" and "It's All Over Now, Baby Blue."[8] The first of those songs referred to police planting drugs, a wiretapped phone, the fact that you did not have to rely on a weatherman to find out "which way the wind blows" or leaders of any kinds, and the lengthy process of education resulting only in factory work.[9] "It's All Over Now, Baby Blue" presented its own kaleidoscopic picture of a gun-toting orphan, gamblers peopling the highway, "reindeer armies," a departing lover, the dead, and a vagabond dressed in one's own clothes.[10] *Highway 61 Revisited* contained "Ballad of a Thin Man," "Desolation Row," and, possibly Dylan's greatest masterpiece, "Like a Rolling Stone." "Ballad of a Thin Man" referred to "Mister Jones," who appeared incapable of understanding the changes occurring in contemporary life, let alone the America of the 1960s, but also to the existential realization that one was "all alone."[11] The imagery "Desolation Row" called on was sweeping, with references to Bette Davis, Genesis, *The Hunchback of Notre Dame*, Albert Einstein, Robin Hood, Nero, the *Titanic*, Ezra Pound, and T. S. Eliot.[12] "Like a Rolling Stone" featured a well-schooled young woman, who was now compelled to live "on the street," possessing nothing and having "nothing to lose." Dylan's haunting refrain asked "how does it feel" to be operating "like a rolling stone?"[13]

The influence of Dylan on American popular music proved enormous during the mid-sixties, as exemplified by folk rock and the British scene dominated by the Beatles. Coming out of Los Angeles, the Byrds, led by Jim McGuinn and including Gene Clark and David Crosby, helped to kick off the folk rock genre, with their first album, *Mr. Tambourine Man*, recorded in early 1965 and appearing in late June of that year.[14] Dylan covers included the title song, "Spanish Harlem Incident," "All I Really

Want to Do," and "The Chimes of Freedom." Beginning in June, the Byrds started putting together their second album, *Turn! Turn! Turn!*; it was released in December 1965, offering versions of Dylan's "Lay Down Your Weary Tune" and "The Times They Are a-Changin'," with the title song drawn from Pete Seeger's adaptation of the Book of Ecclesiastes.[15] In January 1966, the Byrds recorded "Eight Miles High," a conscious effort to move beyond Dylan and to offer their own paean to the counterculture. Written by McGuinn, Clark, and Crosby, the elusive sounding "Eight Miles High" related how strange one felt on touching down.[16]

Up north in the Bay Area, psychedelic drugs and rock 'n' roll, along with the region's long-existing bohemian and left-wing political scenes, provided the impetus for one of the clearest examples of the American counterculture of the 1960s. As early as January 1964, Dino Valenti recorded his anthem, "Let's Get Together," which talked about the need for people to "smile on" their brother, to "get together," to attempt "to love one another right now."[17] In October 1965, obviously influenced by antiwar protests in Berkeley, Country Joe McDonald and the Fish first recorded "I Feel Like I'm Fixin' to Die Rag," a seemingly whimsical but ultimately sardonic examination of U.S. involvement in the Vietnam War. McDonald urged "all you big strong men" to come to the rescue of Uncle Sam once more, as the United States was mired in a bitter conflagration in Southeast Asia. In the process, McDonald delivered scathing lyrics directed at the federal government, the military, Wall Street, jingoistic fathers, and anticommunism.[18] Country Joe and the Fish, like many psychedelic-based bands, desired far more, with rhythm guitarist Barry Melton later acknowledging, "We were setting up a new world that was going to run parallel to the old world but have as little to do with it as possible."[19] A month after Country Joe and the Fish's initial recording of "I Feel Like I'm Fixin' to Die Rag," the Warlocks, Ken Kesey's favorite band, went into a studio in San Francisco to cut "Can't Come Down." The Warlocks, led by Jerry Garcia, spoke of dreams "of forbidden treats" and insisted on not being able to come down. Garcia sang, "I've been set free," referred to Lewis Carroll's Cheshire cat, and mentioned "endless mirrors and infinite me's."[20]

Some later claimed that the Family Dog, four individuals determined to promote the counterculture, and music promoter Chet Helms all but spawned the San Francisco rock scene during this period by putting on a series of shows in the last months of 1965. In the process, they helped to promote bands like the Charlatans and The Great Society, with the exquisite lead singer Grace Slick, relying on silk-screened posters that were placed around the Bay Area for a concert at the Longshoreman's Hall close to Fisherman's Wharf. As Charles Perry, the author of a history of Haight-Ashbury, puts it, the two hundred or so people who showed up "came as if there might never be anything like it again. Arriving at the dance dedicated to Dr. Strange of Marvel Comics were individuals attired in Mod clothes, Victorian suits and granny gowns, Old West outfits, pirate costumes, and free-form costumes."[21] Even a pair of Hell's Angels arrived, as did the seemingly ubiquitous Allen Ginsberg. The next session hosted by the Family Dog again presented the Charlatans, along with the Loving Spoonful, with band members from Jefferson Airplane and the Warlocks in attendance. As Martin A. Lee and Bruce Shlain, authors of *Acid Dreams*, indicate, "Such performances amounted to a total assault on the senses: the electric sound washed in visceral waves over the dancers, unleashing intense psychic energies and driving the audience further and further toward public trance. Flashing strobes, light shows, body paint, outrageous getups—it was mass environmental theater, an oblivion of limbs and minds in motion."[22]

On November 6, rock impresario Bill Graham, who would have a decidedly mixed relationship with the same counterculture that he helped to promote, hosted a benefit for the San Francisco Mime Troupe, which performed political satire through a series of free shows in parks and had recently endured an obscenity bust. On December 10, Graham, who managed the Mime Troupe, put on the first of many shows at the Fillmore Auditorium, located at the cross section of Fillmore Street and Geary Boulevard in San Francisco, which featured Jefferson Airplane, The Great Society, and the Mystery Trend, among other groups. In January 1966, Jeff Blackburn and Sherry Snow, a San Francisco folk duo, along with their bandmates, recorded "Stranger in a Strange Land," written by David Crosby and drawn from Robert Heinlein's science-fiction novel.[23] That same month, Steward Brand introduced the Trips Festival at the Longshoreman's Hall in San Francisco; ten thousand showed up, with a light show offered and the Grateful Dead performing. On February 19, Chet Helms orchestrated a concert by Jefferson Airplane and Big Brother and the Holding Company, at the Fillmore.

Recorded on March 10, 1966, Bob Dylan's "Rainy Day Women No. 12 and 35" appeared the following month, with the singer repeatedly warning, "They'll stone you"—a double entendre, given the displeasure recently visited upon Dylan for supposedly abandoning the folk scene— in between refrains declaring "Everybody must get stoned."[24] In May, the double-album *Blonde on Blonde* appeared, with its cover featuring a wild-haired, stern looking Dylan, containing soon to be classics like "Rainy Day Women," "Visions of Johanna," "I Want You," "Just Like a Woman," "Absolutely Sweet Marie," which intoned that "to live outside the law you must be honest," and "Sad Eyed Lady of the Lowlands."[25]

Hardly innocents, the Beatles had begun taking amphetamines and other stimulants during an extended stay in Hamburg, Germany, in the first part of the 1960s, when they worked into the early morning hours, but Dylan is often credited with having turned them on to pot. Bob Dylan informed the Beatles that he had some good grass and they "smoked and laughed all night." John Lennon recalled the Beatles' "smoking marijuana for breakfast," as they slipped into their "own world."[26] The Beatles' music had already become more sophisticated, with the recording of their *A Hard Day's Night* album largely undertaken immediately following their initial, fantastically successful tour of the United States in February 1964. The title song of both the album and the first Beatles' movie, *A Hard Day's Night*, contained more sexually suggestive lyrics than the songs that initially captivated young American girls and boys, like "I Want to Hold Your Hand" and "I Should Have Known Better."[27] In April 1965, the Beatles recorded "Help," which served as the title of their album and second film, each released three months later.[28] Both "Help" and another song on that album, "Ticket to Ride," again moved the Beatles away from their earlier, more innocent lyrics.[29]

Nevertheless, the introduction to marijuana triggered something distinctly different for the Beatles, as evidenced by the bittersweet *Rubber Soul*, released in December 1965, which Lennon referred to as their "pot album."[30] The lyrics contained in this thematically connected work proved far more sophisticated than their earlier work, with songs like "Norwegian Wood" and "Nowhere Man," both recorded in October 1965, demonstrating a Dylanesque quality. With George Harrison playing a sitar, "Norwegian Wood" offered Lennon's somewhat sly recollection of an affair he was hiding from his wife. The song opened with Lennon's declaration that he "once had a girl," before his acknowledgment that perhaps "she once had me."[31] The still more cryptic "Nowhere Man" highlighted an individual who seemed vapid, lacked direction, and, consequently, was something of an everyman, able to see only "what he wants to see."[32] *Rubber Soul* also proved noteworthy, with the declaration in "The Word" that "love" made one free, needed to be spread, and could be heard everywhere, and amounted to "the light." The simple but elegant closing, repeated several times, "Say the word love," would serve as a generational touchstone for many who began looking to the Beatles, as they had Dylan, as pathfinders, beyond the musical realm. Shot by photographer Bob Freeman, the album jacket also proved cutting edge, displaying the four long-haired Beatles, with the title stretched out in quasi-psychedelic mode.[33]

Released in June 1966, *Yesterday and Today* contained several recent Beatles' singles, including "Nowhere Man," "Day Tripper," and "Doctor Robert."[34] Lennon later explained that "Day Tripper" was intended as something at a dig at the "weekend hippie," while McCartney acknowledged that it was indeed about drugs.[35] Recorded in April 1966, "Doctor Robert," a song about "a psychedelic medicine man," indicated that "if you are down he'll pick you up," and that one needed to "take a drink from his special cup."[36] *Yesterday and Today* proved more controversial still because of its initial album cover, which ended an impressive run when seemingly everything the Beatles touched turned golden. That cover almost inexplicably contained macabre images of the Beatles attired in blood-soaked butcher uniforms, with portions of their bodies covered in uncooked meat and decapitated baby dolls. As the Beatles readied for a concert tour in the United States, more criticism came their way following Lennon's pronouncement that "Christianity will go. It will vanish and shrink." Moreover, he asserted, "We're more popular than Jesus now."[37] As a firestorm of criticism resulted, Lennon quickly backtracked, apologizing for his statement. The controversy melted away as the Beatles began touring, and *Revolver* appeared in record stores across the United States.

If *Rubber Soul* exemplified the influence of marijuana on the world's most famous rock group, *Revolver*, recorded between early April and late June the following year, demonstrated how the Beatles had been drawn into the world of psychedelia.[38] Sometime earlier, John Riley, a "wicked dentist," as lead guitarist George Harrison referred to him, dosed Lennon, Harrison, and their wives with LSD in their coffee.[39] Harrison later recalled incredible sensations, including love, a feeling that all was perfect, and a fear that they were all going crazy. He likened the LSD trip to what an astronaut in space must encounter on examining the planet Earth, and to living a thousand years in only ten minutes.[40] In his typically sardonic but prescient manner, Lennon reflected, "We must always remember to thank the CIA and the army for LSD. . . . Everything is the opposite of what it is, isn't it? They brought out LSD to control people, and what they did was give us freedom."[41]

Revolver was the first psychedelic album of the Beatles, when they were in their heyday and during the very period that the counterculture was about to become a mass phenomenon in the United States and in parts of Europe. Two of Lennon's offerings—"She Said She Said" and "Tomorrow Never Knows"—particularly captured the LSD-spawned zeitgeist. Lennon began the first of those songs with the declaration, "She said I know what it's like to be dead."[42] This purportedly resulted from an incident that occurred in August 1965 at a house in Beverly Hills, California, rented by Beatles' manager Brian Epstein while they were undertaking another tour in the United States. Guests included the actress Peggy Lipton, actor Peter Fonda, folksinger Joan Baez, and the Byrds. All gathered there dropped acid, except for Beatles' rhythm guitar player and Lennon-writing partner Paul McCartney. As Fonda later indicated in an interview with *Rolling Stone* magazine, he talked about a childhood accident in which he shot himself, and thus had experienced a death trip. Lennon reportedly responded, "Listen mate, shut up about that stuff," before stating, "You're making me feel like I've never been born." He later admitted, "We didn't want to hear about that! We were on an acid trip and the sun was shining and the girls were dancing . . . and the whole thing was beautiful and Sixties." At the same time, Fonda, sporting sunglasses, kept declaring, "I know what it's like to be dead."[43] "Tomorrow Never Knows" clearly displayed the influence of *The Psychedelic Experience*, delivered by Timothy Leary, Richard Alpert, and Ralph Metzner. Lennon began by borrowing liberally from that text, which stated, "Turn off your mind, relax, float downstream," while referring to "being," "knowing," "believing," and "beginning." He also employed the sensibility that altered consciousness did not amount to death, that it was necessary to "surrender to the void," and, in the fashion of Leary, that life amounted to a game.[44] "Rain," recorded in April 1966 but not included on *Revolver*, also exuded a psychedelic flavor, while containing backward vocals, initiated by either Lennon or producer George Martin. Lennon wrote about hiding one's head, death, and the fact that it was all "just a state of mind."[45] Later, Lennon unhappily revealed, "I got the message on acid that I should destroy my ego and I did, you know. I was reading that stupid book of Leary's."[46] Also influencing the Beatles were Aldous Huxley's *The Doors of Perception* and the Swiss psychologist Carl Jung's *Man and His Symbols*, which explored revelations involving the unconscious mind.

Also proving popular in the United States during this period was the Scottish singer-songwriter Donovan Leitch, whom some dismissively referred to as a Dylan wannabe, but who produced memorable songs of his own, including several with clear psychedelic references or influences. His *Sunshine Superman* album, recorded between January and May 1966, included the title song, "Season of the Witch," and "The Trip."[47] Far more complex than many of the tunes associated with psychedelia, "Sunshine Superman" contained a kaleidoscope of images, with the offering that the narrator "could've tripped out easy" and the reference to blowing "your little mind."[48] With a shroud-like feel, "Season of the Witch" seemingly had Alice in Wonderland-shaped lyrics and the suggestion that "beatniks are out to make it rich."[49] More blatant still, "The Trip" indicated that a midnight trip through downtown Los Angeles "almost b-b-blew my mind," as a sign indicated "T-t-t-trip a t-trip, I trip trip." "The Trip" literally mentioned "Wonderland," the queen, a jester, Merlin, "the devil's white knights," Zen, and Bob Dylan.[50] Leitch also recorded his *Mellow Yellow* album in 1966, with its controversial title song said to be about the hallucinogenic impact of smoking dried banana peels, which he indicated had been reported by the American folksinger turned psychedelic rock star, Country Joe McDonald.[51]

As the Beatles continued recording *Revolver*, Country Joe and the Fish in June 1966 produced "Section 43," considered the first genuinely psychedelic song by a group from the Bay Area.[52] That same month, The Great Society recorded "Somebody to Love," with Grace Slick delivering the lyrics penned by her brother-in-law.[53] In November, Jefferson Airplane, with Slick, who had replaced female vocalist Signe Toly Anderson, providing the vocals for her new group, recorded yet another anthem for the counterculture, "White Rabbit." Written within the last several months by Slick, the song hearkened to Lewis Carroll's *Alice's Adventures in Wonderland* and *Through the Looking-Glass*, with obvious references to the psychedelic experience. Slick breathlessly sang about "chasing rabbits," "a hookah smoking caterpillar," "men on the chessboard" rising, the ingesting of a mushroom, and the Dormouse's infamous urging, "Feed your head."[54] That same month, band members based in Austin, Texas, became among the first to include a reference to psychedelics in the title of their premier album, *The Psychedelic Sounds of 13th Floor Elevators*.[55] British bands continued to influence the counterculture. The new supergroup, Cream, including lead guitarist Eric Clapton from the Yardbirds and the John Mayall and the Bluesbreakers band, bass player Jack Bruce from Manfred Mann, and Ginger Baker from Graham Bond's Organization, began to record an album in July 1966, which came out that December. The music and live performances, rather than the band's deliveries in *Fresh Cream*, which included covers of Willie Dixon's "Spoonful" and Skip James's "I'm So Glad," offered a psychedelic feel.[56]

On July 29, 1966, Bob Dylan, who had clearly pushed the Beatles to craft more sophisticated lyrics, suffered a serious motorcycle accident near his home in Woodstock, New York, resulting in an extended period of convalescence. Later, Dylan admitted using the accident as an excuse "to get out of the rat race." On August 29, the Beatles delivered what would prove to be their last live concert, at Candlestick Park in San Francisco, with only 25,000 tickets sold despite the stadium's 42,500 person seating capacity. As Ringo Starr recalled, "There was a big talk at Candlestick Park that this had got to end. At that San Francisco gig it seemed that this could possibly be the last time, but I never felt 100 percent certain til we got back to London. John wanted to give up more than the others. He said that he'd had enough."[57]

A Los Angeles–based band recorded an album in late August 1966 that was released on January 4 of the following year, containing an array of songs clearly influenced by band members' immersion in the world of psychedelia. The band took its own name from Aldous Huxley's book, *The Doors of Perception*, itself influenced by William Blake's "The Marriage of Heaven and Hell," and presented haunting lyrics delivered through the full-throated lungs of Jim Morrison. The initial album's offering was "Break on Through (to the Other Side)," which Huxley, in his own fashion, had called for, and which Allen Ginsberg, Timothy Leary, and Ken Kesey all sought to carry out through the use of psychedelics. Morrison's repeated refrain emphasized the need to "break on through to the other side," as he talked about his "baby" getting high.[58] Another possible reference to Huxley appeared in the second stanza, when Morrison sang about discovering "an island" in one's arms. "The Crystal Ship" spoke of slipping "into unconsciousness," while "Light My Fire" noted how false it would be to declare that "we couldn't get much higher."[59] The album's lengthy closing song, "The End," contained a seeming reference to Heinlein's *Stranger in a Strange Land*, and the vision of being "so limitless and free," but also "insane" children, danger lurking, a murderer, Oedipal fantasies, chants of "kill," and the haunted declaration, "This is the end."[60] The previous November, another Los Angeles group, the Electric Prunes released "I Had Too Much to Dream (Last Night)," with discussion of love and loss, and images racing through one's head.[61]

Also recorded during the fall of 1966, Jefferson Airplane's *Surrealistic Pillow* appeared a month following *The Doors*, and included both "Somebody to Love" and "White Rabbit."[62] With cascading vocals by Grace Slick and Marty Balin, along with swirling guitars and drums, *Surrealistic Pillow* possessed something of the unified feel, and attempt to replicate the psychedelic experience, that another album consciously offered a few months later. The Jimi Hendrix Experience, with an English drummer and an English bass player accompanying the Seattle-born lead guitar player and singer, put out its first album just before the Monterey Pop Festival that catapulted Hendrix to international acclaim.[63] Recorded in London, beginning in late October 1966, *Are You Experienced* included "Purple Haze," "Hey Joe," "Fire," "Foxey Lady," and the title song, all featuring Hendrix's psychedelically delivered guitar riffs and singing. "Purple Haze," with a soon-to-be legendary guitar track, referred to a confusing drug-induced state that led Hendrix to wonder if he were "comin' up or down," happy or miserable, and experiencing daytime or the night, as his mind was being blown.[64] As *Are You Experienced* exploded onto the pop charts, the Jim Hendrix Experience began recording *Axis: Bold as Love*, with a cover featuring the tri-headed group amid Hindu images, and songs like "Up from the Skies," "Spanish Castle Magic," and "If 6 Was 9."[65]

In November 1966, the Beatles began recording John Lennon's latest composition, "Strawberry Fields Forever." With a drug-like sensibility, Lennon sang about heading for "Strawberry Fields," where nothing was real and there was "nothing to get hung about," in a dream-inflected haze.[66] Beginning in early December 1966, the Beatles started putting together an album that Paul McCartney envisioned, with the group supposedly adopting a new identity, *Sgt. Pepper's Lonely Hearts Club Band*. The collage drawn cover included the Fab Four attired in colorful military-styled garb, and contained images of scores of such luminaries as Marlon Brando, William Burroughs, James Dean, Marlene Dietrich, Bob Dylan, Sigmund Freud, Aldous Huxley, Carl Jung, Karl Marx, Marilyn Monroe, Edgar Allan Poe, Elvis Presley, and Oscar Wilde. Lennon had hoped to also display pictures of Jesus Christ, Mahatma Gandhi, and Adolf Hitler, but commercial and artistic sensibilities failed to allow for that.[67] The album opened with a rendition of the title song, followed by "With a Little Help from My Friends."[68] The Beatles sang about "getting high" with such assistance, but also about wanting "somebody to love." The third song in the album, "Lucy in the Sky with Diamonds," at a minimum contained the initials LSD, while tracing a brilliant world with "tangerine trees and marmalade skies," "a girl with kaleidoscope eyes," flowers able to "grow so incredibly high," and train porters "with looking glass ties."[69] George Harrison's "Within You Without You" exemplified the Eastern influences affecting him, as he wrote about love capable of saving the world, and the need to appreciate "it's all within yourself" and that "we're all one."[70] Following a reprise of "Sgt. Pepper's Lonely Heart Club Band," the brilliant "A Day in the Life" closed the album. Lennon sang about a man who "blew his mind out in a car," a dream-like state, and the narrator's proclaimed desire: "I'd love to turn you on."[71]

Released on June 1, 1967, *Sgt. Pepper* proved tremendously influential both in the rock world and the growing counterculture. The Beatles hardly stopped there, continuing their studio work on their next album, *Magical Mystery Tour*, another thematically based work, directed by McCartney.[72] It contained Lennon's almost mournful—however ironically delivered—ode to the counterculture, "All You Need Is Love," and his brilliantly embittered "I Am the Walrus." Recorded in June 1967, "All You Need Is Love" seemingly captured the sentiments associated with the Summer of Love, as it was unfolding in the Bay Area in Northern California. The Beatles initially performed "All You Need Is Love," via live television, with several million viewers around the globe tuned in to *Our World*, largely broadcast by the British Broadcasting Corporation. Beatle friends Mick Jagger and Keith Moon, the drummer from The Who, among others, joined in the delivery of the song, which began with the soft chanting of "Love," repeated over and over. Then Lennon indicated that there was nothing that one did, sang, said, made, or saved, that someone else could not accomplish as well. But most important was to learn how to be oneself and about love.[73] "I Am the Walrus," with its obviously Lewis Carroll–influenced lyrics, became the first Beatles' song recorded following the death of longtime manager Brian Epstein in August 1967. Containing seemingly nonsensical verbiage, "I Am the Walrus" actually underscored the hippie ethos from the song's opening stanza with Lennon intoning, "I am he as you are he as you are me and we are all together." Lennon referred to himself as the apparently all-knowing walrus.[74] *Magical Mystery Tour*, which the Beatles recorded between late November 1966 and the following November, also featured Lennon's "Strawberry Fields Forever" and McCartney's "The Fool on the Hill," which alluded to the Beatles' recent acquaintanceship with the Maharishi Mahesh Yogi, the founder of Transcendental Meditation. At that point, McCartney, along with the other Beatles, remained enamored with the Indian guru, suggesting that "the fool on the hill," despite being ignored by many, was the genuinely perceptive one.[75]

Another British group that lacked the Beatles' enormous popularity but was also at the forefront of psychedelic music, Traffic issued its own first album in December 1967, *Mr. Fantasy*.[76] Powered by former Spencer Davis band member Steve Winwood and Dave Mason, Traffic was as upfront about drugs and the psychedelic aura as any musical group of the era. That initial album and the subsequent U.S. release (*Heaven Is in Your Mind/Mr. Fantasy*) included "Dear Mr. Fantasy," "Heaven Is in Your Mind," "Dealer," "Hole in My Shoe," "Paper Sun," and "Coloured Rain," all offering artistic renderings of pharmacology's impact.[77] As much as the lyrics, the music itself, like that of Jefferson Airplane, Country Joe and the Fish, and the Beatles, offered something of a psychedelic feel, with the band attempting to reproduce the experience of a psilocybin, mescaline, or LSD trip. "Dear Mr. Fantasy" referred to the evident discarding of "a straight mind," while "Heaven Is in Your Mind," in the manner of Aldous Huxley, discussed "guiding your vision to heaven and heaven is in your mind."[78]

8

CALIFORNIA DREAMING AND HAIGHT-ASHBURY

The American counterculture of the 1960s, drawing on the holy trinity of drugs, sex, and rock 'n' roll, looked westward as well as toward the East, with California again appearing for this latest version of bohemians as something of a new Mecca. At least from the onset of the Gold Rush, California seemed to offer the promise of unbounded riches and experiences, including those of a maverick variety. Walt Whitman recognized that California itself tilted in the direction of the East, where could be found "the God, the sage, and the hero." The native New Yorker Bret Harte, calling himself "The Bohemian," wrote about bohemian days in San Francisco and referred to an enchanted "fairy land" filled with flowers. Early movie producers headed out to Hollywood, a recently incorporated district of Los Angeles, in the 1910s, drawing on the area's rich and varied geographical makeup, to create images, such as those of the antihero, that at times proved subtly subversive and in keeping with the possibility of an American bohemia. Meanwhile, California's reputation as a place where one could start over or operate in a fashion deemed outside the pale in many communities back East waxed and waned, depending on economic and political climates. Nevertheless, pockets of American bohemians nestled into areas like Venice, Berkeley, and San Francisco, along with European transplants like Aldous Huxley and the Marxist-Freudian political theorist Herbert Marcuse, whose work would influence the counterculture of the 1960s. The beats particularly found the Bay Area accommodating, as did many artists and musicians, some of whom likewise played a role in the appearance of another group of American bohemians. In Los Angeles and San Francisco, early psychedelic pioneers, from Huxley to Ken Kesey, performed the role of pied pipers. By the mid-1960s, the groundwork for a thriving counterculture, including alternative institutions and the vision of an alternative lifestyle, was in place in pockets around the Golden State.

It was fitting that lush, libidinous California was home to some of the most seminal events associated with the American counterculture. It was there that an image of the American nation and the American character, however distorted, florid, or perverse, had long been shaped. The original forty-niners and the cinematic moguls had done their part, creating a veneer of infinite possibilities, at least of the material variety. But they had done far more than that, helping to craft the notion that one could be recast in the great American West. Those very ideals were transmitted across the nation and then globally, along with popular culture, conveying belief in the American Dream of limitless economic and personal achievements. The counterculture of the 1960s, of course, exemplified the enduring hold of such notions but also a means, however fleeting, to contest them. In November 1965, the Mamas and the Papas, the folk rock group led by John Phillips, presented "California Dreamin'," a song he had written some time earlier with his wife Michelle. The song conjured up images of relief from a wintry day to be found in California, albeit in a markedly less cheerful manner than the Beach Boys, Jan and Dean, and the Rivieras had raved about earlier in the decade. [1]

The counterculture challenged mainstream American culture through the establishment of new institutions, the carving out of seemingly liberated territory, and the holding of festivals designed to celebrate an alternative lifestyle. Notwithstanding his latest bust, Ken Kesey and the Merry Pranksters, along with Steward Brand, the Living Theatre, and Owsley Stanley, presented the Acid Trips, complete with accompanying music by the Grateful Dead or other Bay Area bands. Kesey strove to build up expectations: "The general tone of things has moved on from the self-conscious happenings to a more jubilant occasion where the audience participates because it's more fun to do so than not. Audience dancing is an assumed part of all the shows, and the audience is invited to wear ecstatic dress and to bring their own gadgets." [2] Lou Gottlieb promoted the event in his *San Francisco Chronicle* column, proclaiming it "of major significance in the history of religion." [3] The Trips Festival took place from January 21–23, 1966, at the Longshoreman's Hall in San Francisco, with some six thousand people attending. Promoters of the event heralded it in characteristic fashion: "america needs indians, sensorium 9—slides, movies, sound tracks, flowers, food, rock'n'roll, eagle lone whistle, indians . . . and anthropologists. 'the god box' by ben jacopetti. the endless explosion, the congress of wonders, liquid projections, the jazz mice, the loading zone rock'n'roll . . . and the unexpectable."[4] Big Brother and the Holding Company and the Grateful Dead performed on Saturday night, as the latest Acid Test unwound, with questions posed, "Can you die to your corpses? Can you metamorphose? Can you pass the twentieth century?"[5] Bill Graham and Kesey butted heads at one point, but the latter simply ignored the infuriated promoter, angered because Kesey had welcomed several Hell's Angels. At another moment, Kesey projected the following message: "Anyone who knows he is God please go up on stage."[6] Tom Wolfe referred to the Trips Festival as "the first national convention of an underground movement that had existed on a hush-hush cell-by-cell basis."[7]

The event clearly provided impetus for the already burgeoning countercultural scene in San Francisco. More and more, the dilapidated Haight-Ashbury district, alongside Golden Gate Park, and abutting the largely black Fillmore district, became a magnet for those attracted to the counterculture. Haight Street itself extended for about twenty blocks, while the park covered another fifty blocks or so, leading up to the Pacific Ocean. As the poet Allen Cohen later noted, Haight-Ashbury was yet "unknown to the world," but was "an artists' bohemia, and seed pod which was destined to catch the wind and blossom throughout the world."[8] Residing in Haight-Ashbury were African American and Chinese families, workers, students—despite San Francisco State's having relocated to South San Francisco—"beatnik refugees" from North Beach, hippies, and Bay Area musicians, including members of the Grateful Dead and Jefferson Airplane. Rents were cheap, including for large Victorians or Edwardians, many of which had been split into apartments. One great Victorian at 1090 Page Street, containing six bedrooms, offered rooms for as little as fifteen dollars a month. Any number of hippies moved into the area, living communally, making the grand old houses, whole or divided, still more affordable. Drugs were readily available, including the famous acid of Owsley, who became known as "the unofficial mayor of San Francisco," and sold his magic potion for two dollars a hit.[9] The Haight-Ashbury district thus became the latest in a series of utopian endeavors this country has experienced, albeit a somewhat unique one owing to its urban location.

Stores began catering to the hippies, with some of the owners becoming leading countercultural figures in their own right. Almost three weeks before the Trips Festival, brothers Ron and Jay Thelin opened the Psychedelic Shop on Haight Street, which became one of the focal points for hippies in the area. Flower children frequented the small store, which contained books by Hermann Hesse, Aldous Huxley, Alan Watts, and Timothy Leary and Richard Alpert, along with a number dealing with Eastern religion and the Western occult. As the Thelin brothers later reflected, "We went out and asked different friends of ours to compile books that they thought we should have. It was supposed to be information on dope. It was pro-LSD."[10] The Psychedelic Shop also offered Indian records, madrases, incense, necklaces, drug paraphernalia, advertisements for upcoming concerts, tickets for those shows, colorful fabrics, and a much visited community bulletin board. The very street on which the Psychedelic Shop resided, Ron Thelin hoped, would turn into "a world-famous dope center," with "fine tea shops" containing "big jars of fine marijuana, and chemist shops with the finest psychedelic chemicals."[11] More stores catering to the counterculture soon appeared nearby, including a health food store, Far Fetched Foods, also known as Blind Jerry's; In Gear, which featured Mod clothing; the Weed Patch; and the I/ Thou coffee shop. Golden Gate Park, one of the nation's finest, was itself a lure, with its lush, open spaces, gardens, and museums. Morri Moscowitz, the owner of Moe's Book Store on Telegraph Avenue in Berkeley, unsuccessfully sought to establish a large, used bookstore in the district.

The hip shops and stores proved controversial within the counterculture, because they involved commercial pursuits that many hippies were seemingly averse to altogether. On the one hand, hip entrepreneurs offered many of the accoutrements that those in the counterculture desired. And as historian Mark Hamilton Lytle explains, most hip capitalists confronted the same difficulties other merchants confronted: insufficient capital, too much competition, rapidly shifting fashions, and narrow profit margins. In addition, they faced hostility from non-hip merchants determined to pressure local officials to drive them out of business. But additionally, hip merchants suffered inherent contradictions in their workplaces, whether involving adherence to a business regimen or the disinclination of certain of their clientele to pay for goods at any price. [12]

Happiest of all, for many, as Allen Cohen recalled, "It wasn't difficult in 1966 to work occasionally, sell marijuana or LSD intermittently, and thereby earn a living for oneself and friends." Cohen explained, "One could devote most of one's time to art, writing or music, experience the enhanced and ecstatic states of mind accessible through the use of marijuana and LSD, interact with other artists, get high and talk until the sun's rays erased the night. In these years, and in these ways the particular styles of music, art, and the way of life identified with the Haight, the 60s and the Hippies developed." [13]

On February 6, 1966, the instigator of the Acid Trips, Ken Kesey, an iconic figure in the Haight, purportedly committed suicide, or at least police discovered an apparent suicide note on the front seat of a brightly colored bus located along a road outside of Eureka, California, and containing a sign, "Intrepid Traveler." The note, signed by Kesey, read:

> Last words. A vote for Barry is a vote for fun. Ah, the Fort Bragg sign and that means the ocean and that means time to drop the acid (not that I really need it, mind you; I've courage enough without chemical assistance. It's just that I'm scared. . . .) Driving along checking the abyss at my left like I'm shopping for real estate prospects. Ocean, ocean, ocean, I'll beat you in the end. I'll go through with my heels at your hungry ribs. I've lost the ocean again. Beautiful. I drive hundreds of miles looking for my particular cliff, get tripped behind acid. I can't find the ocean, end up slamming into a redwood just like I could have slammed into a home. Beautiful! So I Ken Kesey being of (ahem) sound mind and body do hereby leave the whole scene to [wife] Faye, corporation, cash, the works. And Babbs to run it. (And it occurs to me here that nobody is going to buy this prank and now it occurs to me that I like that even better.)" [14]

The police gave little credence to the note, and word soon got out that Kesey and several of the Pranksters had absconded to Mexico.

Back in San Francisco, Chet Helms, a native Californian but also a transplant from Austin, Texas, who had taken up residence in Haight-Ashbury, established Family Dog productions. In the process, he soon competed with the hard-driving Bill Graham, with the two becoming the area's most prominent music promoters. Both put on shows at the Fillmore Auditorium, before Helms began offering productions at the Avalon Ballroom on Sutter Street. The top Bay Area bands performed at both locations, including Jefferson Airplane, the Grateful Dead, Quicksilver Messenger Service, Country Joe and the Fish, Moby Grape, the Charlatans, the Steve Miller Band, the Beau Brummels, the Mystery Trend, and Big Brother and the Holding Company, soon featuring the electrifying Janis Joplin, another arrival from Austin. Several additional California groups, such as the Byrds, the Doors, Buffalo Springfield, Love, and the Seeds, also enlivened the scene.

As Charles Perry elucidates in his illuminating history of Haight-Ashbury, other artists influenced the scene, and helped to spread the word that something transformative was taking place in Northern California. A psychedelic art movement appeared in San Francisco, which included Alton Kelley, Wes Wilson, Stanley Mouse, Rick Griffin, and Victor Moscoso. Influenced by psychedelic experiences but also by Dada, the surrealists, and Pop Art, such artists and others produced brightly colored, swirling, fractal, kaleidoscopic images that appeared on concert posters, at lightshows, and in underground newspapers and comic books. Among the most well known of the images employed by psychedelic artists—in this instance, Mouse and Kelly—was Mr. Zig-Zag, whose omnipresent image could be found on packets of cigarette rolling papers. Elias Romero, Bill Ham, Ben Van Meter, and Roger Hilyard enriched the artistic scene too, through psychedelic light shows at the Fillmore Auditorium, the Avalon Ballroom, and additional spots where leading rock bands appeared.[15] Those attending added to the ambiance, attired as they were in colorful outfits, or, as Michael McClure put it, "We were all part of it—our clothes of Billy the Kid and Jean Harlow and Saint Francis and Pied Piper and Tom O'Bedlamn and Buddha and Daniel Boone and Robin Hood and Outlaw Cyclist were all ripples in the organism of the event, as well as expressions we'd longed for but feared to make." To McClure, "the costumes were not masks but were expressions," and demonstrated that "a new tribe was coming into being."[16]

As the counterculture expanded in the Bay Area and select locations across California and the nation, seeming hysteria regarding one of its touchstones and leading proselytisers mounted. *Time* bluntly charged, "If one man can be singled out as the father of the current epidemic of psychotic illness resulting from misuse of hallucinatory drugs, that man is Dr. Timothy Leary."[17] Dating back to an incident the previous December along the Mexican border, LSD's top promoter had recently been convicted under the Marijuana Tax Act, leading to a $40,000 fine, a maximum thirty-year jail sentence, and a court order to undergo psychiatric examination. Leary appealed his conviction, contending that the constitutional protection of religious freedom mandated in the First Amendment enabled him to employ marijuana and encourage others to do so. A *New York Times* editorial refuted Leary's argument, which it deemed filled with "speciousness and quackery"; the *Times* warned that for many young people, marijuana usage became "the first step down the fateful road to heroin."[18] The *Times'* edition of March 21, 1966, reported, "Drugs a Growing Campus Problem." John Corry pointed to more students leaving school to enter "the LSD cult, there to contemplate nature, induce periodic insanity and pursue a philosophy that is a curious melange of Zen, Aldous Huxley, existentialism and leftover Orientalism." He concluded that "drugs are, in a sense, the ultimate, as well as the hippest, student protest."[19]

The cover of the March 25, 1966, issue of *Life* magazine displayed an X-rayed hand with five colored squares attached to it, along with the headline, "LSD: The Exploding Threat of the Mind Drug That Got Out of Control."[20] *Life* indicated that a single dose of acid could "set off a mental riot of vivid colors and insights—or of terror and convulsions."[21] The reporter, Gerald Moore, encountered a unique subculture, as the *Life* team saw it. With accompanying photographs of Timothy Leary, a stoned young woman, and frenzied acid heads, Moore wrote about "the colorless, odorless, tasteless substance called LSD" that could induce "a 10-hour 'trip'—sometimes into a world of beatific serenity and shimmering insight, sometimes to frenzy and terror. In either case the person who has taken this remarkable drug never sees life quite the same way again." LSD had moved from being "a promising psychological research tool," and had been adopted "by a large underground cult" that began "in artistic, bohemian and intellectual circles" and "has now become a dangerous fad on the college campus." A government crackdown was in place, but "the genie of LSD, with all its tantalizing possibilities for good and evil, is out in the open," Moore asserted.[22] *Life*'s science editor, Albert Rosenfeld, warned that "a few pounds . . . dumped into the water supply of a major city would be enough to disorient millions."[23] The issue contained the tale of a teenager, who had undergone a bad trip close to Hollywood's Sunset Strip. On the other hand, Barry Farrell quoted Walter Clark, a psychology professor at the Andover Newton Theological School, who declared he experienced a vision that could be likened to one of Moses and "the burning bush," and insisted, "These drugs present us with a means of studying religious experience in the laboratory."[24] On April 13, 1966, an individual arrested for assault testified that federal agents had asked him "to 'set up'" Allen Ginsberg for a drug bust. Ginsberg, now heading a pro-marijuana legalization organization, Lemar, had recently declared, "I feel like the noose of the police state is closing in on me. I've had experiences of police states in Prague, and it's very similar."[25]

Out on bail, Leary got busted again, this time at the Hitchcock estate in Millbrook in late April. Leary decried the "intolerable violations of my rights," while accusing the Dutchess County Sheriff of harassing him and of "trampling on my civil liberties."[26] That same week, Leary informed an attentive crowd in New York's Town Hall, "I know lots of languages. I can talk to trees. And I do pretty well talking Holyman. You must be able to speak first to an amoeba, your father, a madman, Buddha, your lover." Delivering an address titled "The Politics and Ethics of Ecstasy," Leary proclaimed that the "psychedelic battle" was successfully completed, with approximately one million Americans having undertaken psychedelic experiences. He declared, "It is perhaps indicative that LSD was invented in the same decade as the atomic bomb. Maybe the deepest and most basic chords of all human life, the DNA codes deep within each cell of all living organisms, saw that man now had the capacity to destroy all life, and decided that it was time to mutate." After all, "I look around us," Leary continued, "and I see metal—all living things and all my cells hate metal—and I see the pollution of the air and the poisoning of the rivers and the concrete over the earth, and I have to say, 'Baby, it's time to mutate.'"[27]

In mid-June 1966, Sir Aubrey Lewis, professor of psychiatry at the Institute of Psychiatry in London, reviewed a book by Richard Blum and associates, many working for the University of California at Berkeley or Stanford, titled *Utopiates: The Use and Users of LSD 25*. One article presented what Lewis called an "unbiased account" of the Psychedelic Training Center in Zihuatanego, and proved revelatory regarding "the non-medical aspects of the lysergic acid cult . . . in the United States." Aldous Huxley initially piqued interest, Lewis stated, culminating in "group activities intended to be educational and mystical." Lewis worried that "much uncontrolled and irresponsible administration of the drug" resulted, producing "alarming social consequences." Nevertheless, Lewis considered Blum's book to be refreshing and enriching. Blum himself indicated that "the drug movement" offered "a framework for the intellectual apolitical rebel who cannot control himself and events as he would" and thus was inclined to LSD.[28]

On June 14, 1966, Allen Ginsberg testified before a U.S. Senate Special Subcommittee of the Committee on the Judiciary, hoping to prevent passage of federal legislation generally banning the use of LSD. He introduced himself as a poet, the present recipient of a Guggenheim fellowship, a graduate of Columbia University, and a former market researcher. Ginsberg referred to his visionary experience at the age of twenty-two, and extolled the nation's "most loved thinkers—Thoreau, Emerson, and Whitman," for propounding the gospel that "each man is a great universe in himself." This was "the great value of America that we call freedom," Ginsberg declared. He likened various drug experiments to the one he had undergone earlier, again emphasizing their "personal" nature, and spoke about the time when the Merry Pranksters and the Hell's Angels simultaneously took LSD, shattering "the fear barrier" in the process. He denied hysterical tales about LSD use, and pointed to several "very legitimate proper studies," including those done by the Rand Corporation and by Timothy Leary.[29]

In late August, Ginsberg urged that the National Student Association conduct a survey of college students regarding the use of marijuana and hallucinogenics. He admitted, "I wrote part of my poem 'Howl' on peyote. . . . I have written other poems entitled 'LSD,' 'Mescaline,' 'N20' and 'Ether'—so you see I specialize in this area." Speaking at the organization's convention attended by student body presidents, Ginsberg also hollered at his audience, in Kesey-like fashion, "I declare the end of the war." In mid-September, Leary revealed that he was initiating a new religion revolving around LSD, peyote, and marijuana, called League of Spiritual Discovery. "Like every great religion of the past," he declared, "we seek to find the divinity within and to express this revelation in a life of glorification and worship of God. These ancient goals we define in the metaphor of the present—turn-on, tune-in and drop-out." Speaking at the New York Advertising Club on Park Avenue, Leary explained, "Turn-on means to go beyond your secular tribal mind to contact the many levels of divine energy which lie within your consciousness; tune in means to express and to communicate your new revelations in visible acts of glorification, gratitude and beauty; drop out means to detach yourself harmoniously, tenderly and gracefully from worldly commitments until your entire life is dedicated to worship and search."[30]

The September 1966 issue of *Playboy* contained an interview with Leary conducted by freelancer Bernard Gravzer, who referred to him as "not only the messiah but the martyr of the psychedelic movement." Declaring psychedelics "the medium of the young," Leary contended they signified to young Americans "ecstasy, sensual unfolding, religious experience, revelation, illumination, contact with nature." He argued that "the breakthrough" had already taken place. "The psychedelic battle is won." He did advise having a guide for one's first several trips. Leary went on to talk about the dramatic nature of LSD's sensorial effects: on vision, hearing, taste, smelling, and touch. As for sex, he referred to the experience under LSD as transcendental rapture, as "miraculously enhanced and intensified." He was both "Irish and revolutionary," as Dr. Humphry Osmond suggested, but Leary denied that he was "careless about anything that's important." The most important lesson he had learned from using LSD involved keeping "the life game going."[31]

For many, like Ginsberg, Leary, Kesey, and the Merry Pranksters, the growing stigma attached to psychedelic drugs, and the increased calls for their criminalization, undoubtedly served as another source of appeal but also ensured they would acquire something more of an outlaw reputation. At the same time, risks became greater for acid heads in general, along with the recognition that other substances, such as marijuana and hashish, were already banned, making users subject to criminal prosecution. Meanwhile, the new acid rock bands, in keeping with the counterculture, flaunted existing drug laws, while celebrating psychedelics through their music and lifestyles. Others in the hip community similarly remained determined to partake of whatever drugs they desired, particularly believing that marijuana and psychedelics offered rewards that outweighed the risks that many, but certainly not all, recognized existed in partaking of them. In fact, by early June, the governors of both California and Nevada signed laws mandating fines topping out at $1,000 and one-year jail sentences for LSD possession. By contrast, Dr. James L. Goddard, the U.S. Food and Drug Commissioner, warned that outlawing LSD would turn perhaps a tenth of college students into criminals and force users underground, making treatment of psychotic conditions more difficult.

On September 16, 1966, residents of Haight-Ashbury conducted an "Anti-Fascist Rally and March," to condemn a recent drug bust at 1090 Haight Street. Intended to help link the hip community, San Francisco's *Oracle*, among the first of a soon-to-be mushrooming number of underground newspapers, initially appeared four days later. This followed a series of meetings in Haight-Ashbury that summer, triggered by the poet Allen Cohen, who dealt dope for Stanley Owsley, and the Thelin brothers, who put up around $500. After a more politically oriented production, *P.O. Frisco*, proved displeasing to the Thelins, Cohen became editor of the short-lived *Oracle*. Cohen intended to "judo the tabloid lowprice anguish propaganda and profit form to confront its readers with a rainbow of beauty and words ringing with truth and transcendence." Initial *Oracle* editorials pointed to the "turn on, tune in, drop out" slogan of Timothy Leary's, and his "attempt to create an open voice for those involved in a 'life of art.'"[32] John Brownson's article, "Anarchy 66 Provo," highlighted the Dutch anarchists who had proven inspirational for the Merry Pranksters and would for another group just about to appear on the scene: the Diggers.[33]

On September 27, 1966, the Hunters Point Riot occurred in a black neighborhood of San Francisco, following the killing by a white police officer of Matthew "Peanut" Johnson, a sixteen-year-old African American, who had fled from a stolen vehicle. Riots went on for several days, spilling over into the Fillmore district. San Francisco Mayor John Shelley mandated a curfew for two neighborhoods, including the Haight-Ashbury district, and Governor Pat Brown called on the National Guard, which arrived with tanks.

Concern about conditions in San Francisco, and particularly the plight of the poor and destitute, led to the formation of the Diggers, who identified with their seventeenth-century English namesakes. Responding to political upheaval and economic distress, the English Diggers, guided by Gerrard Winstanley and William Everard, had practiced a form of nonviolent, agrarian communalism before mob violence and legal assaults destroyed their colony. The modern version of the Diggers also contested the holding of private property and money, while distrusting the New Left, hip store owners, and the counterculture that revered them. An offshoot of the guerrilla theater group, the Mime Troupe, the Diggers included Emmett Grogan, Peter (Cohon) Coyote, Peter Berg, Kent Minnault, Bill Fritsch, and Billy Murcott, who tended to be older than many hippies. They too performed guerrilla theater, as when they orchestrated "The Death of Money and the Birth of Free," passing along Haight Street in funeral procession, with a trio of hooded figures holding aloft a "silver dollar sign on a stick," Martin A. Lee and Bruce Shlain recall. Twice that number of pallbearers, their faces covered by large animal masks, carried "a black-draped coffin."[34] Rather than protests and demonstrations, the Diggers believed individuals should seize the moment to challenge hierarchy involving private possessions and power. They determined to make a difference in the alternative community, seeking to provide free meals, goods, money, and medical care. Operating out of Golden Gate Park, the Diggers gave away food each afternoon at four o'clock, and they set up a series of free stores in the area, with "liberated goods," and a Free Medical Clinic. They also issued the *Digger Papers*, the first appearing on or around September 30, 1966, titled "A-Political Or, Criminal Or Victim Or Or Or . . ."[35] Mark Hamilton Lytle suggests that the Diggers never believed that reform of the existing system was possible, desiring instead "to subvert the money game that dominated straight society."[36]

On October 6, 1966, LSD, notwithstanding FDA Commissioner Goddard's admonition, became illegal, ironically enough, in California, the first state where that occurred. Some considered the date particularly ominous, as 6/66 signified the Beast of the Apocalypse, according to Revelation. John Starr Cooke—earlier involved with L. Ron Hubbard's Scientology cult—and his Psychedelic Rangers, who included Cohen and the Beat artist Michael Bowen, issued "A Prophecy of a Declaration of Independence."

> When in the flow of human events it becomes necessary for the people to cease to recognize the obsolete social patterns which have isolated man from his consciousness and to create with the youthful energies of the world revolutionary communities of harmonious relations to which the two-billion-year-old life process entitles them, a decent respect to the opinions of mankind should declare the causes which impel them to this creation.
> * We hold these experiences to be self-evident, that all is equal, that the creation endows us with certain inalienable rights, that among these are: the freedom of body, the pursuit of joy, and the expansion of consciousness * and that to secure these rights, we the citizens of the earth declare our love and compassion for all conflicting hate-carrying men and women of the world.

We declare the identity of flesh and consciousness; all reason and law must respect and protect this holy identity. [37]

The Oracle staff determined to protest the occasion peacefully, with Cohen recalling, "We were not guilty of using illegal substances. We were celebrating transcendental consciousness, the beauty of the universe, the beauty of being." [38] Thus, *The Oracle*, led by Cohen and Michael Bowen, who was involved with the San Francisco Renaissance and had acquired a certain notoriety following his drug bust in Millbrook the previous year—conducted by Assistant District Attorney G. Gordon Liddy, later of Watergate infamy—sponsored the Love Pageant Rally in Golden Gate Park. Posters advertising the rally urged interested parties, "Bring the color gold . . . Bring photos of personal saints and gurus and heroes of the underground . . . Bring children . . . Flowers . . . Flutes . . . Drums . . . Feathers . . . Bands . . . Beads . . . Banners, flags, incense, chimes, gongs, cymbals, symbols, costumes, joy." As many as two thousand people showed up at Golden Gate Park's Panhandle sector, covering eight lengthy blocks, while organizers proclaimed that the event was designed "to affirm our identity, community and innocence from influence of the fear of addiction of the general public as symbolized in this law," referring to the new drug legislation. [39] Members of the Merry Pranksters were present, and Big Brother and the Holding Company was one of the bands providing music. The *Sunday Ramparts*, put out by Editor Warren Hinckle, predicted that the new movement could prove enormously subversive. The *San Francisco Examiner* wondered about an LSD revolution being spawned in the city.

The underground press, including the *Berkeley Barb*, soon featured the Diggers, talking about their free food program. The *Barb* particularly played up the Diggers, beginning with the issue of October 21, 1966, which referred to the first appearance of *The Digger Papers*, and a determination to demonstrate a chasm between the new counterculture and radical political ideology. That same issue of the *Barb* contained an article, "Delving the Diggers," purportedly written by George Metevsky, the so-called Mad Bomber, a former Marine angered by the denial of a claim for workers' compensation, who had planted a series of bombs in New York City during the 1940s and 1950s. The presiding judge committed him to the Matteawan Hospital for the Criminally Insane, where he resided for over half a decade. "Delving the Diggers" referred to a group of individuals, ranging from teenagers to those approaching forty, who were wide-eyed and tattered. When the article's author, probably Billy Murcott, who wrote many of the initial *Digger Papers*, asked one kid where the free food came from, the response was, "It's free because it's yours." A variety of food was available, much of it good and all of it healthy. Some of the Diggers offered a song condemning "Evil Auto . . . the noise it makes and the accidents it involves and the war it supports and the air it pollutes and the monopolies it feeds."[40]

Meanwhile, the Pranksters planned the Acid Test Graduation for October 31 at the large Winterland auditorium in San Francisco, with Bill Graham attending to commercial operations and the Grateful Dead performing. Ken Kesey had been telling reporters, "Taking acid is not the thing that's happening anymore."[41] Then plans fell through, with Graham worried that Kesey and Owsley planned to spike the water at Winterland with LSD, the Dead honoring a previous commitment, and only approximately two hundred people showing up for a private party at the Calliope Company warehouse, situated on Harriet Street. Kesey asserted the need "to move on," but denied this meant abandoning acid. With television cameras filming, he declared, "I believe that man is changing . . . in a radical basic way. . . . The waves are building, and every time they build, they're stronger. Our concept of reality is changing. It's been happening here in San Francisco." He referred to an entirely "new generation of kids," who "walk different." The music was different too, emphasizing life, rather than death. For the past year, Kesey said, "We've been in the Garden of Eden," thanks to acid, which "was the Garden of Eden and Innocence and a ball. Acid opens that door and you enter and you stay awhile." Police began pushing through a group of Hell's Angels, seeking the renegade Kesey, who continued orating. "We've been going through that door and staying awhile and then going back out through that same door. But until we start going that far . . . and then going beyond . . . we're not going to get anywhere, we're not going to experience anything new."[42]

As music critic Barney Hoskyns indicates, the countercultural scene in the Bay Area, including even the Merry Prankster's old musical partners, members of the Grateful Dead, had started to distrust Kesey and his call for moving beyond LSD. Chet Helms, who had told Graham that Kesey probably did plan to dose Winterland, acknowledged the Merry Prankster's considerable belief in his "ability to transform people" and that of "acid to transform them." But he worried about "a very military tone to Kesey's trips. . . . It even extended to their affection for the Angels and wearing of colors and uniforms. A kind of militancy in collective action."[43] Hoskyns contends that the Haight betrayed Kesey, with Bill Graham and the "more efficient marketing of Flower Power" prevailing over Kesey's chaotic Acid Tests.[44]

Another article in the *Barb*, containing George Metevsky's supposed signature, dated November 18, 1966, and titled "The Ideology of Failure," blasted the "wearing [of] hipsterism on our sleeves." The article ridiculed the hip merchants who were such a part of the Haight-Ashbury scene. "We make music with mercenary groups who bleed money from any fools on the street, or we carve leather into sandals for twenty dollars a pair, or shape forms into art while a psychiatrist whispers formulae for a healthy life-style into our ear." In the same manner, "We focus everything towards the transcendence of daily consciousness: macrobiotic diets, hallucinogens, eastern and western aesthetics, philosophies, etc." Security derived from "our salaried hipness," as "we . . . grab whatever pleasures we might in the name of Love, always quick to contrast ourselves with middle-class man." By contrast, some established "peace centers . . . and contribute to the cause of freedom," or "drop out all over again and go back to the woods." As for the Diggers, "We stay dropped-out. We won't, simply won't play the game any longer. . . . We do our thing for nothing. In truth, we live our protest." They would not be taken in any longer "by the romantic trappings of the marketers of expanded consciousness. Love isn't a dance concert with a light show at $3 a head." Rather, it was free shows delivered in Golden Gate Park by the San Francisco Mime Troupe, the handing out of free food in the Panhandle, and love.[45]

Yet another offering by the Diggers, "In Search of a Frame," appearing in the *Barb*'s November 25, 1966, issue, questioned the willingness of such local bands as Big Brother and Holding Company and the Charlatans to appear side-by-side with advertisements or on commercials. This amounted to the same "old story again" once more of "the fame/power/money trip," the article asserted. Again, the Diggers questioned why it cost $2.50 to attend a dance, asking, "What's revolutionary about that?" They called for compelling the city administration to hold "block dances, parking lot dances, FREE dances," and wondered if Chet Helms and Bill Graham would be averse to that, which "would be a revolution; something joyous and free in America." As for bands like Jefferson Airplane and the Grateful Dead, the Diggers predicted, they would likely go on "to bigger gigs, better publicity, managers . . . until they are ***STARS***." But "where's the revolution? Long-hair? Beautiful clothes?" Would mod attired soldiers behave differently? The Diggers predicted a possible future: "John Wayne in Carnaby St. clothes," and expressed dismay at the street scene, which appeared to replicate capitalism, proving to be "egocentric, competitive, and material."[46]

Ralph Gleason, the jazz and music critic who closely followed the counterculture in his column for the *San Francisco Chronicle*, wrote about the Diggers as he spoke of "the New Youth." Gleason contended that the Diggers, like the Provos in Berkeley and Los Angeles and the Prunes in Cleveland, were engaged in an "assault against the money culture." Perhaps, Gleason suggested, they would drive "the money changers out of the temple." Yet the Diggers indicated it was futile to battle or join the system, thereby adopting a different mode of dropping out than advocated by Timothy Leary.[47]

Later reflecting on the Diggers, Peter Coyote insisted that they strove for anonymity and autonomy. He recalled the impact of "Power," the poem by Gregory Corso, which declared, "Power is standing on a street corner doing nothing." As Coyote remembered, "What we were about was autonomy, finding what authentic, autonomous impulses were. And then being responsive to them, and not making excuses, not waiting for the revolution." Rather, "you create a post-revolutionary society by saying, 'We won. It's over. Now let's do what we want.' And you do it." The Diggers strove "to create the conditions they described. And the condition we described was eternity is now, if you have a fantasy, take responsibility for it and actualize it, build or imply a society around it. And if it's nice, people will join you." Diggers like Coyote distrusted political revolutionaries, many of whom he considered to be "bullshitters." As he stated, "You scratch a revolutionary, I'll show you a guy who thinks that he should be in charge." He often joked that it wouldn't be the FBI that would gun him down, but rather Jerry Rubin, Abbie Hoffman, the Communist Party, "the Tom Haydens of the world . . . because we stood for the sanctity of the individual and the irreplacibility of the individual."[48]

The Free Food Program involved "something that needed to be done," thanks to the presence of young people that the media had helped to lure to the city. "Our feeling," Coyote noted, "was that they were our kids.

You know? This was America; these were our kids." And the Haight-Ashbury district at the time "was really free turf," but there existed a need for food, shelter, and medical clinics. "Truly great women," who were "resourceful, cunning, tough-minded, street-wise, beautiful," took the lead in acquiring food from "old Italian and Chinese green-grocers" at the market and preparing it for the Free Food Program. They did this "day after day. No vacations. No overtime." Meanwhile, the men were "scoring building materials, lumber," keeping old trucks running, and engaging in "the visionary, metaphysical end of things." Many Digger houses possessed free banks, "where you threw everything into a central pot," then signed out to indicate how much had been taken for toothpaste or truck repairs. "It was anarchic, it was cooperative, and it was collaborative."[49]

In their "Trip without a Ticket" manifesto, the Diggers celebrated guerrilla theater, which they contended fostered "a cast of freed beings. . . . Its aim is to liberate ground held by consumer wardens and establish territory without walls. Its plays are glass cutters for empire windows." All property, in the fashion of free stores, they asserted, should be free "to liberate human nature." In the same manner, street events were "rituals of release. Reclaiming of territory (sundown, traffic, public joy) through spirit." The Diggers called for infiltrating great corporations "with life-actors as nymphomaniacal secretaries, clumsy repairmen, berserk executives, sloppy security guards, clerks with animals in their clothes," including "goldfish, rabbits, pigeons, cats on leashes, loose dogs." The Diggers urged all to "give up jobs. Be with people. Defend against property."[50] Not surprisingly, given that many had been involved with the San Francisco Mime Troupe, the Diggers began to engage in street theater. On December 16, 1966, they orchestrated their Death of Money Parade, with over one thousand people, including two members of the Hell's Angels, participating.

Not all proved enamored with the growing number of countercultural participants in Haight-Ashbury, whether hip merchants, bands, Diggers, or young runaways. The police arrested five Diggers, including Emmet Grogan and Peter Berg, claiming that their setting up of a Halloween puppet show and Intersection Game created a public nuisance. The Thelins and other hip entrepreneurs received eviction notices, as well as being denied membership in the Haight Street Merchants' Association, leading to the creation of the Haight Independent Proprietors (HIP). A police raid of the Psychedelic Shop and the arrest of Allen Cohen in November 1966 also followed his selling of Lenore Kandel's *The Love Book*, on obscenity charges. The resounding victory by former Hollywood actor Ronald Reagan, who ran as a hardline conservative, over incumbent governor Pat Brown, even more clearly reflected a rightward tilt among the California electorate. In late December, building inspectors boarded up the Diggers' garage, declaring that it violated sections of the Health and Safety Code pertaining to lighting, ventilation, and sanitation.

9

SPREADING THE WORD: ALTERNATIVE MEDIA

Alternative media, including the underground press, comix, and radio, helped to spread the gospel of the counterculture, through its heralding of Dylan, the Beatles, the Doors, Jefferson Airplane, and sundry musicians, as well as iconic events in the Bay Area and elsewhere. The nation's latest cultural radicals thereby continued a tradition established by earlier American rebels, including members of the Revolutionary generation, abolitionists, transcendentalists, antebellum feminists, and labor activists. During the early twentieth century, the Socialist Party of America, the Industrial Workers of the World, and the Lyrical Left employed their own newspapers and journals, such as *Appeal to Reason*, *Industrial Worker*, *Mother Earth*, and *The Masses*, to propound radical messages championing socialism, anarchism, communism, feminism, or free love. The Old Left of the interwar years and following World War II relied on left-wing and left-liberal publications to champion or denounce Holy Mother Russia, pacifism or interventionism, and revolution or the gradual transformation of well-entrenched societies in the age of rival ideologies, particularly those of a totalitarian cast. Among the most influential were *The Nation*, *The New Republic*, *The New Masses*, the *Daily Worker*, the *National Guardian*, *Politics*, and *PM*, spanning the left side of the political spectrum. During the 1950s, new independent publications on the order of *I. F. Stone's Weekly*, *Dissent*, *Liberation*, and *The Village Voice* appeared, not attached to any political organization. One of the founders of *The Village Voice*, Norman Mailer, later remarked, "They wanted it to be successful, I wanted it to be outrageous. . . . I had the feeling of an underground revolution on its way, and I do not know that I was wrong."[1]

None of the celebrated publications established in the 1950s, including *The Village Voice*, however, fully captured shifting cultural currents that allowed for the planting of the seeds for an American counterculture. Rather, a pair of publications, at one point joined by the sharing of an office in New York City, more directly foreshadowed the underground publications that proliferated in the United States during the last half of the 1960s. First appearing in comic book fashion in August 1952, *Mad* was largely the creation of cartoonist Harvey Kurtzman, later credited by underground artist Robert Crumb with having altered his perspectives altogether. Kurtzman drew the soon-to-be iconic impish cartoon character Alfred E. Neuman, perennially young, gap-toothed, with a tousled, less groomed batch of John F. Kennedy–styled hair, and like JFK, ever ready to run for political office. Unlike Kennedy, Neuman was prone to less than brilliant statements such as "It takes one to know one—and vice versa!" and "What, me worry?" Following *Mad*'s irreverent lead, Paul Krassner first published *The Realist* in the summer of 1958, immediately promising a critical examination of organized religion and "the tragicomic currents of our time," while extolling individual freedom.[2] It contained early impolite interviews with Lenny Bruce, Alan Watts, Dr. Albert Ellis, Jean Shepherd, Dick Gregory, Norman Mailer, Timothy Leary, and many others. *The Realist* delivered sharp-edged social commentary of the sort that the so-called Sickniks—like Mort Sahl and Bruce—presented in their nightclub acts.

More promising still, the Los Angeles *Free Press*, patterned after *The Village Voice*, began operations in May 1964 under the tutelage of thirty-seven-year-old Art Kunkin. *Freep* soon offered stories such as "The Psychedelic Viewpoint" about an art show in Topanga Canyon, with references to "Hieronymous (sic) Bosch-like orgiastic scenes," defrocked Harvard professor Richard Alpert, and elderly teachers who saw LSD as a panacea for physical ailments. That piece, appearing in the September 24, 1965, issue of *Freep*, insisted that "psychedelics liberate energy, and that all it craves to become excitingly creative is POSSIBILITIES."[3] The month before, another underground paper first appeared, the *Berkeley Barb*, put out by Max Scheer, who had owned a bar in Berkeley called *Steppenwolf*, after the novel by German author Hermann Hesse. Scheer promised his publication would "nettle that amorphous but thickhided

[sic] establishment that so often nettles us."⁴ The *Barb* clearly reflected its owner, as artist Tom Weller recalled: "Max always wore a filthy gray cap and a scraggly beard. The paper was a sloppy, smudgy designer's nightmare, and the ink was so cheap that reading it turned your fingers black. Max addressed the radical agenda with all the taste and intelligence of the *National Enquirer*. I recall one headline that shrieked, INFANT RIPPED FROM MOTHER'S ARMS BY NARCS!"⁵ Starting operations two months after the *Barb*, New York City's *East Village Other* ((EVO) was founded by Walter Bowart, the poet Ishmael Reed, Allen Katzman, Dan Rattiner, Sherry Needham, and John Wilcox. Particularly influenced by Bowart and Katzman, the staff of the *East Village Other* strove to present an artistic, innovative newspaper. Brilliant cartoonists were particularly drawn to the *East Village Other*, including Art Spiegelman and Robert Crumb. Nineteen-year-old Harvey Ovshinsky established Detroit's *Fifth Estate* in November 1965, later explaining that standard journalism comprised the Fourth Estate and indicating, "We hope to fill a void . . . created by party newspapers and the cutting of those articles which express the more liberal viewpoint. That's what we really are—the voice of the liberal element. . . . We want to be a truly free press." While likely to be tagged with labels ranging from "radical" to "socialist" or "communist," the *Fifth Estate*'s staff members just strove to be "honest."⁶ In December 1965, *The Paper* appeared, established by Michael Kindman, a student at Michigan State University, who quickly focused on expanded U.S. military operations in Vietnam.

In mid-1966, Walter Bowart, Allen Katzman, and John Wilcox of *EVO* helped to found the Underground Press Syndicate (UPS), whose initial members included the *East Village Other*, *Los Angeles Free Press*, *Berkeley Barb*, San Francisco *Oracle*, and *The Paper*. Allen's twin brother Donald delivered an editorial in *EVO* for the July 1–15 edition, calling for such an organization to unite and promote underground newspapers. The UPS, as Bowart referred to it, would provide teletype service across the United States and to England; pool resources; serve as a clearinghouse allowing for the general use of bylines, columns, and comic strips; produce advertising; and represent members to the communications industry. UPS's founding statement stated its intention "to warn the civilized world of its impending collapse. . . . To offer as many alternatives to current problems as the mind can bear. . . . To consciously lay the foundations for the 21st century." Writing in *EVO* in early August, Katzman claimed there were "literally thousands of young people . . . who have, in one form or another, dropped out of the system" in the manner "of just barely existing on its borders." Those associated with underground papers already seemed to be existing "in another country" in "the Underground States of America."[7]

During the fall of 1966, at least two other important underground papers initially appeared: the San Francisco *Oracle* and *The Rag*, published in Austin, Texas. Frequently offering stunning graphics, *The Oracle* also contained essays or advice from such countercultural heavyweights as Allen Ginsberg, Timothy Leary, Ken Kesey, Michael McClure, Gary Snyder, and John Sinclair, manager of the MC-5 rock band and later head of the White Panther Party. The vibrancy of *The Rag*, with its support for both radical politics and alternative lifestyles, demonstrated that the allure of the counterculture was hardly limited to the two coasts and was resonating across the American landscape, at least where large numbers of college-age young people congregated. Eventually, additional seminal underground publications soon appeared, including *Helix* (Seattle), the *Seed* (Chicago), *Avatar* (Boston), *Rat* (New York City), *The Great Speckled Bird* (Atlanta), *The Kudzi* (Jackson, Mississippi), *Old Mole* (Cambridge, Massachusetts), *San Francisco Express-Times*, the *Berkeley Tribe*, *Kaleidoscope* (Milwaukee), and *Space City* (Houston).

Following the selection of a new editor for the *Daily Texan*, the campus newspaper at the University of Texas, who was strongly supportive of the U.S. war effort in Vietnam, several members of the Students for a Democratic Society (SDS) chapter in Austin decided to create an alternative publication, which they named *The Rag*. These included Thorne Dreyer, Carol Neiman, Jeff Shero, Gary Thither, George Vizard, and Marilyn Vizard. At the time, only a handful of underground papers existed in the United States, none in the former Confederacy—thus, the significance of *The Rag*'s appearing when and where it did. *The Rag*, like the New Left during this period, relied on consensus, allowing all who helped to put out the paper to determine editorial positions. Later, however, charges arose that *The Rag*, again in the manner of movement organizations in general, exuded male chauvinism, with men holding positions of prominence and women relegated to grunt work.

Given its location in Austin, one of the epicenters for both the Movement and the counterculture, *The Rag* and its history remain of considerable import in understanding the era's zeitgeist. As indicated, many of

The Rag's staffers also belonged to SDS, even if only in spirit, and, as historian Doug Rossinow indicates, helped deliver "the primary source of information for both freaks and leftists in Austin."[8] In the process, they birthed "one of the few legendary undergrounds," as Laurence Leamer puts it in his book, *Paper Revolutionaries: The Rise of the Underground Press*. *The Rag*, Leamer writes, was "singularly successful in creating a politically and culturally radical community in Austin."[9] Abe Peck, who for several years edited *The Seed*, a leading underground paper in Chicago, and then became a journalism professor at Northwestern University, asserts that "the *Rag* was the first independent undergrounder to represent, even in a small way, the participatory democracy, community organizing, and synthesis of politics and culture that the New Left of the midsixties was trying to develop."[10]

Thorne Dreyer, who served as "funnel" for *The Rag*, which functioned without an actual editor, fired off a letter on October 3, 1966, to the small band of existing underground newspapers. He explained, "From deep in the bowels of reaction, from the home land of Superlbj, yes, from Austin, Texas, friends, arises—(doodley-doo-de-doo)—*THE RAG*." This latest underground publication, Dreyer declared, would perform several roles, necessary because most students at the University of Texas made up "the soggy greedy masses. Apathy and dullness thrive." Still, a sizable number of university students were "completely disassociated from the Machine," Texas's capital city had long housed "a very active and vocal underground," with "Austinites . . . gobbling down peyote most of our present crop of hippies discovered atop their shoulders and between their legs." In addition, Austin served as "the capital of radical political activity in the South-Southwest," with its greater than 150-person strong SDS chapter one of the nation's largest and a key instigator in that organization's recent tilt toward anarchism. Dreyer stated bluntly, "The Austin radical scene has the strongest sense of community of any I have come in contact with; hippies and politics merge." Moreover, the University of Texas's student newspaper, *The Daily Texan*, long possessed "a 'liberal' editorial policy," but "a veritable fascist" had recently been elected editor. As Dreyer saw it, the campaign platform of John Economidy "was essentially to kill commies and uncover all that dope on campus." This turn of events ensured "a great demand for *THE RAG*." Dreyer expressed *The Rag*'s determination to join the UPS, and signed off, "Up the Revolution."[11]

Run collectively, *The Rag* nevertheless contained a staff, called "Rag-staff" or "Ragamuffins," that included Dreyer as "funnel," Carol Neiman as "funnella," "supersalesman" and SDS leader George Vizard, artists, and "shitteworkers," among them SDS national figure Jeff Shero. Robert Pardun, who helped to establish Austin's SDS chapter, later recalled, "*The Rag* was embedded in a community that provided support and a place to relax and have fun. The staff made collective decisions, and volunteers from the growing movement did much of the layout and paste-up in preparation for printing."[12]

When *The Rag* delivered its first issue on October 10, 1966, there existed only a handful of underground papers in the country, and none other in the region. That initial offering of *The Rag* contained a front-page article by Neiman, bemoaning, as Dreyer did, the fact that "most people seemed to remain turned off, unplugged, and militantly apathetic members of the soggy green masses."[13] The first issue included an essay by Shero, "Playboy's Tinseled Seductress," indicating that "the liberated standards" associated with the sexual revolution "offer people the chance to express their deepest feelings to one another in a natural way." Shero found offensive the "expert" analysis characterized by "pseudo-sophisticated dribble" attempting to shape how men and women viewed sexuality.[14] In what proved to be characteristic fashion, *The Rag* also featured artistic sketches with a psychedelic feel, as did the cartoonishly drawn title of the paper, positioned at the head of every issue. Page five of the first issue offered more sketches tied to psychedelia, including a tousled-haired young man, with a mustache, a legion of arms, and a circle in the midsection of his body with the caption, "I AM THE LIGHT"; coming out of his head was a stop sign-styled symbol, with a dove carrying an olive branch sporting the inscription, "Peace Thou Shalt Not KILL."[15]

The lead article in *The Rag*'s second issue on October 17, "Sexual Freedom League: The Naked Truth," was intentionally provocative, referring to a state senator's castigation of league participants as a "bunch of queer-minded social misfits," while he threatened to reduce public funding unless the league were disassociated from the University of Texas. Proponents of the Sexual Freedom League sought to pique discussion regarding "various taboos and archaic laws involving sexual activity," *The Rag* reported. The league's members believed "any consensual sex act between adults which did not involve force or physical harm should not be illegal."[16] National publications, including *Time* magazine, picked up the story, while parents of UT students orchestrated a campaign to fire two professors who had served as faculty sponsors. *The Rag* itself immediately encountered difficulties, with efforts to restrict its sale on campus, despite the fact that other publications, including the mainstream *Austin Statesman*, suffered no such prohibition. As he attempted to sell copies of *The Rag* on campus, George Vizard met up with a formally attired elderly man from the office of the Dean of Student Life, who told him to stop doing so. Vizard indicated he wasn't a student, and blurted out, "So you can go to hell."[17] *Rag* vendors sold one thousand copies of the newspaper in four hours. That second issue contained a box, "Super-Scoop," by the paper's "funnel," Thorne Dreyer, on Austin's contribution to psychedelic rock, 13th Floor Elevators. Dreyer indicated that several of the songs on the Elevators' first album were original, "hallucinated by Roky Erickson and the crew."[18]

In the next issue of *The Rag*, Allen Pasternak referred to the death by heroin overdose of sicknik comedian Lenny Bruce, following the recent passing of New York School poet Frank O'Hara, hit by a dune buggy on the beach at Fire Island, and the motorcycle accident that had apparently incapacitated Bob Dylan. For Pasternak, "these tragedies" compelled one to again consider "the absurdity of human existence." The nation's "lost youth," Pasternak declared, "are groping for answers, for truth, for someone that they can look up to." Instead, they were saddled with politicians like Lyndon B. Johnson, theologians on the order of Billy Graham, and cultural guides of the cast of *Time* and *Life* magazines. Bruce, Pasternak noted, "had both the talent and the balls to fill the void" produced by such "leaders." But "where now can American youth find inspiration?" Pasternak revealed that they were starting "to look to the underground movement" burgeoning in America, as exemplified by Tuli Kupferberg of the Fugs "folk-rock-shock" band, a poet residing on New York City's Lower East Side, who spoke of the need to "FUCK FOR PEACE."[19]

The paper, on October 31, 1966, publicized an event or "circus for everyone" that the local chapter of SDS, led by Jeff Shero, supported but denied controlling, the festival-like "Gentle Thursday." A full-page announcement in *The Rag* indicated this would involve "the celebration of our belief that there is nothing wrong with having fun." Thus, "We are asking that on this particular Thursday everybody do exactly what they want on Gentle Thursday." This might involve bringing a dog, or a baby, or red balloons to campus. Poets and musicians would likely appear, with the latter "leading merry bands of celebrants." Moreover, "maybe you would like to wade in a fountain . . . you might even take flowers to your Math Professor . . . at the very least wear brightly coloured clothing."[20]

As Shero later informed Glenn W. Jones, who helped to organize Gentle Thursday, "Part of the image I had . . . was a socialist revolution in Germany in the 1840s where they wouldn't walk on the grass. They were trying to make a revolution but they still obeyed the signs that said 'keep off the grass.'" Shero believed that "mental boundaries" existed, with individuals refusing to walk on the grass and classrooms retaining "rigid hierarchies." Approximately two hundred people showed up, congregating on the grass that covered the West Mall at the University of Texas, with several times that number watching the goings-on. Participants played music, held aloft flowers, played with soap bubbles and colored chalk, or drew graffiti, "Fly in peace, gentle plane," on a warplane that fronted the building housing the Reserve Training Corps program on campus.[21] The following edition of *The Rag* contained a montage of photographs of "Gentle Thursday," including a blonde child, flute players, a bubble blower, balloons, a lounging dog, and people simply milling about.[22] Susan Olan, at the time an undergraduate at the University of Texas, later recalled participating in Gentle Thursday. "You have to understand that until that moment, people just didn't do things like sit down on the West Mall and talk to other people." She joined with others in heading toward the campus ROTC building. They danced around the ROTC site, while some intoned "Make love, not war," "Peace Now," or "Fly Gently Sweet Plane."[23]

Perhaps appropriately, Larry Freudiger offered an essay on Ken Kesey and his Merry Pranksters, in the paper's October 31, 1966, issue. After acquiring literary fame and a certain amount of money, Kesey desired "to lead a psychedelic movement on the west coast," Freudiger noted. Kesey did so during the period when most Americans considered marijuana addictive, little was known about LSD, "and the would-be-hip" were compelled to follow "the morbid hopeless productions" associated with the likes of William Burroughs. Freudiger continued, "There were no proponents of joy—to be hip was to be lost." Barely two years before, Kesey and his pals were holed up at his ranch in La Honda, California, before deciding "to harness all [the] energy into some expression of the ecstasy in which all were living." Freudiger highlighted the cross-country road trip by Kesey's "brightly colored apostles of joy . . . through darkest

America," with "forty-year-old madman" Neal Cassady driving the bus, followed by the bust that led to Kesey's becoming a fugitive in Mexico. An accompanying cartoon sketch displayed three Mexicans staring at the Pranksters' psychedelically etched bus, with one stating, "Heer comes dees crazy Americanos dronk on these LSD." Freudiger wrote about federal agents pouring onto Kesey's ranch, only to discover "cannabis satava (sic)." Soon arrested a second time, Kesey opted to take off after being released on bond. "And then the fun began," Freudiger recounted. Reports ensued that Kesey had committed suicide along an ocean cliff surfaced, but Freudiger asked, "We know better don't we?" In fact, Kesey and the Pranksters had apparently "been generally raising hell in Mexico all this time," before popping up at a "pro-LSD 'Love Pageant Rally'" in San Francisco. While Kesey was away, "the psychedelic movement . . . he had envisioned had become a real and established social force in the Bay Area." Still a fugitive, Kesey kept appearing "like a modern-day Zorro," even delivering a classroom lecture at Stanford. Kesey spoke of initiating a new movement that involved "turning on without drugs," and intended to join in a "commencement exercise" on Halloween, when "those who believe in joy and ecstasy as a way of life" would receive "psychedelic diplomas."[24]

The early issues of *The Rag* demonstrated how the budding underground press catered to more than just the still burgeoning counterculture. Given the escalation of the war in Vietnam and the emergence of black power within the civil rights movement, it was hardly surprising that *The Rag* featured numerous essays on those twin-fold developments that tore at the liberal consensus President Johnson, a native Texan, represented. Furthermore, *The Rag* immediately identified with and championed the antiwar movement and the New Left, although sometimes questioning tactics associated with either. The newspaper's staff fully supported disgruntled soldiers, including several stationed at nearby Fort Hood, a stepping stone for many on their way to Vietnam. A front-page story by a private first class based at Fort Hood but awaiting orders to head overseas likened a soldier's predicament to that of a caged animal. "Existing only as a number, another dumb animal who must be trained, as a leashed dog, as a mindless vegetable, you find yourself subjected to the war-monger's training schedule." Continuously fed propaganda, this soldier was supposed to chant, "I wanta go to Viet Nam; I wanta kill a Viet Cong." Meanwhile, he could look forward to "the fun, the travel, the adventure, the good feeling," as well as the "contentment that comes from killing a Viet Cong for Mother."[25] The October 31, 1966, issue contained a front-page article, "All-Woman Sit-In at S.S. Office," which involved several top *Rag* and SDS activists.[26] The issue also included a full-length letter, signed by Alice Embree, Marilyn Vizard, Carol Neiman, and seven others, to the state Selective Service director, deeming the draft "an affront to democracy and to the freedom of the individual." The letter stated, "If a war is just, men will fight, but if they as individuals feel that a war is unjust, they must have the right to refuse military service without fear of imprisonment or intimidation." Most important, the signatories condemned "the brutalizing effect of compulsory military" on American society, pointing to the recent mass murders committed by Charles Whitman, an ex-Marine turned sniper who had been perched on the tower atop the graduate library at the University of Texas during the rampage. The women declared that they did "not want our husbands, brothers, and sons turned to killing machines," championing instead the Nuremberg principles that indicate "a man has a higher duty than that to his superiors. We believe that murder remains murder no matter how it is cloaked."[27] *The Rag* also reported that several young men had recently been convicted in federal court for refusing military service or the alternative civilian service demanded of conscientious objectors.

In somewhat typical fashion for the early underground press, Paul Deglau expressed reservations regarding the New Left. In an open letter, he began by stating, "Student radicals, I have lost my faith in you. You seem to have degenerated into some dull, repetitious, yet serious group of people" favoring progressive causes but demonstrating cynicism and a holier-than-thou attitude regarding "the new arrival" who was still seeking to effectuate change. Damningly, Deglau wrote, "Most of you behave like 20-year old professors reciting your lessons at meetings." Deglau asked why New Leftists didn't form a new political party, or run for political office.[28] Robert Pardun refuted Deglau's analysis, pointing out that political campaigns required a good deal of money and manpower. At the same time, Pardun insisted that administration decisions guided policy in Vietnam, thus requiring the antiwar movement to convince the American people how destructive that conflict, conscription, and resulting inflation were. The civil rights conundrum was equally complex, demanding attitudinal changes.

In the November 7, 1966, issue of *The Rag*, Larry Freudiger, who printed the underground newspaper, defended the concept of black power, which he believed had been unfairly attacked by both the right "and establishment liberals." Freudiger dismissed criticism emanating from "the tired old white liberals," who had previously been a bulwark of the civil rights campaign. He referred to a recent gathering at the University of California at Berkeley, where fourteen thousand students happily received Stokely Carmichael, chair of the newly revised Students for a Nonviolent Coordinating Committee (SNCC), and a leading proponent of black power. SNCC activists, Freudiger reported, had heroically conducted voter registration efforts in the Deep South during the past five years, confronting epithets of "nigger," guns, and beatings. And yet, he pointed out, "the liberal mystique of two-party politics persisted," despite the South's having long been a one-party region. That had led to recent attempts to create the Mississippi Freedom Democratic Party, supported by SNCC and civil rights activists. As for black power, Freudiger insisted, it was "very much in keeping with American democratic principles."[29] In the same issue, Gary Thither wrote about "Malcolm X; Wretched of the Earth: Black Men Speak Out." Like black militants, Thither dismissed condemnations of "the open enmity of angry blacks" by fearful whites, who had failed to condemn slavery, the near extermination of Native Americans, European colonialism, and present-day dealings with apartheid South Africa. As Malcolm X had suggested, nonwhites around the globe demanded "their due." Fanon too, in *The Wretched of the Earth*, emphasized "the developing consciousness of the colonial people," and warned that "decolonization is always a violent phenomenon." Indeed, Fanon went so far as to insist that "only unrestrained violence" directed "against the oppressor" would enable "the native [to] regain his humanity, and begin the task of nation-building." To Thither, Fanon's analysis was still more telling than that of Malcolm X, who had been impressed by the Saudi Arabian regime and expressed little concern about economic justice at home other than that visited on blacks.[30] The November 14, 1966, edition of *The Rag* reprinted SDS's statement in support of black power, which it deemed "not a magic charm or a promised land," but rather "a strategy and a mode of organization" called for because the United States remained beset by "an essentially racist culture." Moreover, "racism and economic exploitation" afflicted black Americans.[31] That issue also pointed to the Lowndes County Freedom Organization in Alabama, which was referring to itself as the Black Panther Party.[32]

In the next edition of *The Rag*, Freudiger discussed recent regressive U.S. Supreme Court decisions, including one in which the justices refused to even hear an Iowa case that involved California photographer Harold W. Painter being denied child custody due to the fact that "he was a 'Bohemian.'" Freudiger suggested that the justices seemingly felt that the First Amendment compelled them "to sanction some things they don't like in the political realm, but feel no guilt at all about punishing those whose lives are unconventional" and lacked "the sanctity of 'political protest.'" This appeared evident in the upholding of an obscenity conviction against *Eros* publisher Ralph Ginzburg. Both Painter and Ginzburg, Freudiger underscored, were "participating in a social revolution in" America, but the High Court was clearly indicating that constitutional rights "do not hold for those whose moral and social values differ from those of the existing order." Apparently, it was "allright [*sic*] to be a Communist, but not a 'Bohemian.'" A new constitutional amendment might be required, Freudiger concluded, to prevent government attacks on "the unalienable rights to sex, song, and consciousness-expansion."[33]

Regarding consciousness-expansion, Bruce Schmiechen described a recent visit by Timothy Leary to Chicago, in which the high priest of LSD seemingly referred to it as "the mere sacrament, the chemical symbol, in the scientific metaphor that must clothe modern spiritual discovery." Leary unhappily noted "his own impressive arrest record," which was in keeping with "the expected persecution that all prophets and new spiritual movements encounter." He had been targeted, Leary indicated, not simply due to LSD's dangerous possibilities, but largely because of his contention that "LSD 'works,'" that it convinced people to depart from "the plastic jungle" and enter a new spiritual realm. Schmiechen nevertheless believed that Leary, no matter how "intelligent and attractive," was devising nothing more "than a cult based on LSD." He insisted that Leary might "show us the best, the most pleasurable kind of trip, but he can't show us The Way." Leary had become a celebrity, drawing large fees for public performances. This was "not bad," Schmiechen suggested, "but it makes the holy man appear a little less incandescent." In addition, as one individual asked, on hearing Leary speak, "What can he give us that we don't have already?"[34]

Responding to a request by *The Rag* that he contribute an article, Tuli Kupferberg presented "The Uses and Fuses of Education," in the paper's November 28, 1966, edition. School, the Fugs' musician asserted, served as "nursemaid, castrator and keeper of young men out of the draft," while also producing "cogs for the war-peace machine." A child, Kupferberg continued, could pick up more knowledge on the streets of New York City than from having been "incarcerated for a year in edcell, tied rest-lessly to a desk. Pushed about, counted, lectured upon, tested, trained, mindfeebled and brainwashed." Students should take control of univer-sities, hire teachers, choose courses to be taught, refuse to dole out de-grees or grades, and offer lectures themselves. Classes should be present-ed away from schools, whether in parks, jails, hospitals, insane asylums, or dumps. All of this would be in keeping, Kupferberg wrote, with "some sort of primitive-hysterical communism."[35]

Larry Freudiger maintained his examination of the "social revolution" taking place in America, which, he indicated, "has struck most violently against the values and taboos that are religious in origin." Young people in particular, Freudiger suggested, "are becoming the children of Camus, seeing death as meaningless, absurd, sometimes cruel, but never a relig-ious occasion." To such "drop-outs," efforts "to sanctify death become feeble at best, macabre at worst." Freudiger had recently received a funer-al announcement of the death of a friend from high school and college, which contained a picture of a transformed Jesus, who was "very un-Jewish, so very blonde and blue-eyed, so very beautiful and Anglo-Sax-on." He recalled when the two had studied at Stanford together, and encountered a religious bookstore that contained buttons with that very image. They proceeded to dole them out to friends "with great levity." Clearly, his deceased friend "would have been horrified" at "the disre-spect this shows for who he really was."

Continuing his series in the next edition of *The Rag*, Freudiger now asked, "Who Are the Brain Police?" He opened by acknowledging that the paper had yet to articulate its philosophy, but had obviously displayed support for "free speech, black liberation, sex, the Beatles, student power, consciousness expansion, children, cats, and all the other good things in life." These clearly comprised "a part of the Rag Philosophy," Freudiger acknowledged. He referred to the previous issue that contained a head-line, "Censorship," and revealed that staffers first intended to indicate, "Fuck Censorship," but then engaged in self-censorship, in part to placate

Gary Thither, who authored the article. They designed the original head-line to garner student attention, regarding a clash pitting the university administration against student organizations like SDS. Various under-ground publications confronted "the exact opposite problem," with print-ers engaging in censorship. More troubling to Freudiger was the fearful response of certain *Rag* staffers, who appeared concerned about getting into trouble or disturbing their parents. Thus he likened them to Vice President Hubert Humphrey or California Governor Pat Brown, rather than "the presumably courageous Austin underground." Freudiger won-dered what *The Rag* readership desired, "whether we should keep the brain police within ourselves, or . . . become impervious to the moralities we've argued against all along."[36]

The December 12, 1966, issue of *The Rag* opened with the headline, "Merry Christmas: Buy a War Toy." The accompanying article by Alan Locklear indicated that Christmas mail-order catalogues contained "every imaginable device for a child to 'pretend' kill his companions. Tanks that shoot; machine guns that chatter and spark and smoke; G.I. dolls that do everything but bleed; intercontinental ballistic missiles complete with warheads; complete guerrilla outfits with camouflage suits, throat-cutting knives, the latest army rifles, fragmentation grenades, and land mines." As Locklear noted, "Nothing is too good (or too macabre) for the American boy or girl." And for older, more sophisticated children, stores boasted "BB guns, pellet guns, .22's." Locklear wondered "what kind of respect for human life" was engendered by such "toys," and asked if a military officer who ordered artillery strikes against "the enemy" could appreciate the enormity of what he was doing.[37]

The Rag resumed operations on January 2, 1967, following the Christ-mas break, presenting an article on Austin High School's attempt to quash the sale of "that trash"—*The Rag*—on campus, Soviet dissident writers Yuli M. Daniel and Andrei D. Sinyavasky who were condemned to a labor camp, draft advice, physical threats confronting "Texas hip-pies," a full-page advertisement for 13th Floor Elevators and the Conque-roo, a report on antiwar protestors gathered "outside Himself's ranch" who faced off with Nazis from Dallas, and another regarding the "moral indignation" expressed by church leaders on the bombing of Hanoi.[38] Under the heading "The Artful Dodger," Chet Briggs indicated that *The Rag* would initiate a series certain to appeal to many, but "especially the FBI," with the newspaper determined to "play games with the Justice

Department." *The Rag* intended to dissect the operations of the Selective Service System, including information on conscientious objector classification.[39]

On a different note, one writer in *The Rag* warned that "the most immediate hostile force the Austin hippy faces is, of course, that obnoxious product of Instant Social Life, The Frat Rat." Long-hairs encountered "threats, insults, and beer bottles thrown from The Speeding G.T.O." Operating as "herd animals with herd mentalities," frat boys sought to "yell 'queer' the loudest and lowest and with the greatest degree of Texas accent," but generally refrained from violence, as they did in failing to sign up to fight in the war they "hawkishly" backed. By contrast, everyday Texans operated "on hate and violence, having been raised to hate queers, niggers, commies." It was less socially acceptable to attack Jews and less safe to target blacks, with "all the BAD NIGGERS" having organized and discarded nonviolence, so hippies were left. "You, you dirty, queer, drug-eating consymp that any REAL MAN hates." Six "REAL MEN" had recently attacked several *Rag* staffers at Zilker Park, with Freudiger's head split open by a billy club, leading to a forty-dollar fine against his assailant. Other likely victims included those who might be considered "a BAD NIGGER or even worse a MEXican or a drifter or just poor."[40]

The last of the first dozen *Rag* issues appeared on January 9, 1967, containing a lengthy account by Timothy Leary; new questions about the Warren Report, which indicated that a lone gunman, himself shot by the now recently deceased Jack Ruby, had assassinated President Kennedy; reflections about the New Left's stance on draft resistance; the determined ferreting out of marijuana users at Fort Hood; and the paper's own financial woes. *Rag* staffers sought financial assistance from those who received succor from its operation "in this capital of enlightened communications."[41]

Among the most popular features to be found in *The Rag* and other underground publications were the sometimes long-running cartoon sketches offered by brilliant artists like Robert Crumb, Gilbert Shelton, and Ron Cobb. Arguably following in the tradition of Jules Feiffer, the syndicated cartoonist for *The Village Voice*, with his politically motivated drawings, but also *Mad* magazine, Crumb, Shelton, Cobb, and other cartoonists added flair to underground publications. As former *Berkeley Barb* editor David Armstrong indicates, Crumb, who helped to found *Zap*

Comix, with its initial issue headlining, "Fair Warning: For Adult Intellectuals Only," created several easily recognizable figures.[42] The best known were Fritz the Cat, with his existential flair and supposed attraction to the ladies; bald-headed Mr. Natural, with his lengthy white beard and zestful personality, who held himself out as a guru but was more a con artist; and the wholly uptight Whiteman, but Crumb probably became most acclaimed for his aphorism, "Keep on Truckin'." Gilbert Shelton, who served as art director of the Vulcan Gas Company, Austin's first psychedelic music venue, created "The Fabulous Furry Freak Brothers," initially published by Berkeley's Print Mint and subsequently by San Francisco's Rip Off Press. The pursuit of drugs, especially pot, drove the Freak Brothers, who often had to ward off establishment and right-wing figures of various sorts.

10

PEOPLE OF THE BOOK

Ironically, given the insistence by critics that the counterculture was profoundly anti-intellectual, many of the leading figures associated with it were writers themselves—and not just on underground newspapers—including some, like Aldous Huxley, Allen Ginsberg, and Ken Kesey, possessing well-deserved international reputations. Some of their own work, such as *Doors of Perceptions, Heaven and Hell*, "Howl," and *One Flew over the Cuckoo's Nest*, extolled consciousness-raising experiments in different fashions, just as those three noted authors did. Although increasingly known for his celebrity rather than the academic prowess and a much acclaimed book of his own that landed him at Harvard, however briefly, Timothy Leary exemplified the reliance on written texts that linked both well-known figures and hippie foot soldiers. It was Leary, after all, who hearkened back to *The Tibetan Book of the Dead*, and his publicizing of that work came to the attention of John Lennon, among many others. Musicians ranging from Lennon and Bob Dylan to Tommy Hall and Roky Erikson of 13th Floor Elevators painted crystalline images of psychedelic experiences through poetically drawn lyrics. And more and more, messages connected to the counterculture were transmitted to young people around the country by the rapidly expanding underground press.

While accused, as a group, of discarding intellectuality and disregarding rational thought altogether, many hippies were literate, some strikingly so. As Helen Perry acknowledges in her early examination of the counterculture, *The Human Be-In*, she was surprised to discover that many authors she had pored over as an undergraduate more than three decades earlier, were still popular, including D. H. Lawrence, Sigmund Freud, James Joyce, and Aldous Huxley, as well as Melford E. Spiro, whose *Children of the Kibbutz*, examined the attempt to nourish alternative lifestyles in Israel.[1] In a curious manner, a good number of hippies were people of the book, devouring the writings of Zen Buddhists; Hermann Hesse, the 1946 Nobel Prize winner for literature; Lewis Carroll, the English creator of *Alice's Adventures in Wonderland* and *Through the Looking-Glass* fame; English author A. A. Milne, who contributed Christopher Robin, Winnie the Pooh, and the Hundred Acre Wood to the world of children's literature; the Lebanese-American poet Kahlil Gibran; Oxford don J. R. Tolkein; the English socialist George Orwell; sci-fi favorites Robert Heinlein and Arthur C. Clarke; satirist-fantasist Kurt Vonnegut; beat writers Allen Ginsberg, Jack Kerouac, Gary Snyder, and Michael McClure; Sigmund Freud; and sexologists William Reich, Alfred Kinsey, William H. Masters, and Virginia E. Johnson. Thus, the range of literary interest was sweeping, including Oriental religion, coming-of-age tales, children's stories, sweetly delivered poetry, fantasies, accounts of traipsing through America, and psychoanalytical treatises. The more politically inclined among the counterculture, like members of SDS and SNCC, also explored, intensively or not, the writings of Karl Marx, Friedrich Engels, Vladimir Lenin, Che Guevara, Mao Zedong, Franz Fanon, C. Wright Mills, Herbert Marcuse, I. F. Stone, Albert Camus, Bertrand Russell, Albert Einstein, and countless others. Along with copies of their local underground newspaper, they picked up *I. F. Stone's Weekly*; *Ramparts*, after it shifted leftward in the mid-sixties; and the *New York Review of Books*.

Admittedly, far more participants in the counterculture were likely to have read *Siddhartha*, *The Prophet*, *The Lord of the Rings*, *Animal Farm*, *A Stranger in a Strange Land*, *Childhood's End*, Richard Farina's *Been Down So Long It Looks Like Up to Me*, and *Cat's Cradle*, than *Capital* or *"Left-Wing" Communism: An Infantile Disorder*, or probably even *The Stranger*, *1984*, or *The Power Elite*. In the manner of the beats, any number of American hippies looked beyond their country and Europe, with some conducting their own "journey to the east," traveling to ashrams in India, while avoiding military service in former French Indochina. Many more made that journey in their own minds, delving into the writings of D. T. Suzuki, the Japanese author of *An Introduction to Zen*

Buddhism, which emphasized self-realization by way of meditation and divinely ordained propriety over the acquiring of theoretical knowledge alone. Suzuki sought to convey how individuals could strive for total enlightenment, which the British philosopher Alan Watts also attempted to transmit through his lectures and writings such as "This Is It."[2] For two decades, beginning in 1953, Watts delivered a weekly radio program on Pacifica Radio, the nation's oldest public radio channel, with a longstanding pacifist orientation.

The all-but-forgotten German novelist Hermann Hesse particularly became a beneficiary of the looking eastward by many of the nation's young, as his novels began to be read by Americans in large numbers for the first time. Again, this proved at least somewhat ironic given the charges of anti-intellectuality repeatedly hurled at proponents of the counterculture, as Hesse's writing, although elegantly presented, was filled with challenging stories, tales, and analyses of young and not-so-young protagonists engaged in various quests. Probably most popular among hippies were *Siddhartha*, *The Journey to the East*, *Demian*, *Narcissus and Goldmund*, and *Steppenwolf*, although the last of these was probably the least read, owing to its very complexity. Undoubtedly pleasing to them would have been a letter Hesse wrote to Gerhard Friedrich of Guilfor College after the start of WWII.

> Your faith in humanity I share completely, although I am no longer expecting anything for myself. Man is capable of much that is good and much that is evil, and when he had acquired the central view and experienced the tragical-beautiful aspect of life (which, to be sure, happens only through suffering), he is indeed capable of most sublime things. And this capacity never ceases to exist—not even today. It is, however, the business of only a few; yet these form, across the centuries, a continuous quiet unity and tradition. Nothing can make me doubt that this is true.[3]

In 1946, shortly following Hesse's receipt of the Nobel Prize for Literature, one Swedish critic had decried the selection as "inscrutable," insisting the writer was "too obscure" to merit such an honor. Another Swede defended the choice, claiming that Hesse vied with Thomas Mann for the title of "the greatest contemporary German author."[4] In an editorial titled "For Service to Mankind," dated November 16, 1946, the *New York Times* indicated that the choice of Hesse "creates an international fame where none existed before." At the same time, the *Times* editorial staff applauded the decision if it were intended to acknowledge "an early revolt against German anti-humanism."[5] Felix E. Hirsch of Bard College refuted the contention that Hesse remained largely unknown, writing instead that "he ranks as one of the most widely read novelists of the European continent." For approximately forty years, each of his books garnered "large audiences . . . sometimes going up to six figures, despite the absence of mass book clubs in Europe." In addition, most Hesse books had been translated into various languages, in both Europe and Japan. Hirsch continued praising Hesse, whom he called "not only a remarkable novelist but" an individual who "symbolizes in his person also many traits of a truly good European." Widely traveled, Hesse "does not belong to just one country or one language," Hirsch offered. "May it be added here that he never left any doubt about his feelings in regard to the outrages committed in Nazi Germany." Hirsch lauded the Nobel committee "for its judicious and courageous choice."[6]

In an extended essay in the *New York Times*, the Austrian journalist and literary critic Alfred Werner noted that Hesse was "remarkably prolific," publishing around fifty books in Germany. On the other hand, only *Gertrude and I*, *Demian*, *Steppenwolf*, and *Death and the Lover* (*Narcissus and Goldmund*) had been translated into English, but were presently out of print. By contrast, in the German-speaking sectors of Europe, it was difficult "to find any book lover . . . who has never read at least of one of Hesse's books." This included college graduates, laborers, and housewives, alike. Hesse's earliest novels, "romantic and slightly effeminate"—*Peter Camenzind*, *Under the Wheel*, *Gertrude and I*, and *Rosshalde*—were delivered "in a lucid, simple, easy-flowing and well-tempered prose," Werner noted. But "an entirely different Hesse" emerged following World War I through the publication of *Demian*, with Hesse's earlier "relative meekness" discarded and "the taboos of the bourgeois world . . . more scathingly satirized." This continued through subsequent novels: *Siddhartha*, *Steppenwolf*, and *Death and the Lover*. Werner particularly pointed to "the amazing and disturbing" *Steppenwolf*, which proved a bestseller in 1920s Weimar Germany, and foreshadowed *Civilization and Its Discontents*, Sigmund Freud's later "devastating analysis of contemporary life." Both "the Viennese soul doctor and his Swiss disciple, Jung," particularly influenced Hesse. As Werner saw it, Hesse left behind the romanticism of his earlier work to enter "the realm of universal humanity, emulating the wide-ranging love of Saint Francis, the mysticism of Buddhism, the psychological insight of Dostoevsky, the world-embracing striving of Goethe, and the Europeanism of Nietzche." Refusing to collaborate with the Nazis, Hesse was dismissed "as a diseased and spineless traitor to his race who had permitted himself to be poisoned by the alien science of psychoanalysis." Dwelling in "the oasis of Switzerland," which was ringed by fascist states, Hesse, "that modern Job," maintained his determination "to write independently," while "sorrowfully raising that unanswerable question: 'Why does God afflict the righteous ones?'" As the dramatist Gerhart Hauptmann, winner of the 1912 Nobel Prize for Literature, abandoned his earlier pacifism to accede to Nazism, Hesse chose to remain "faithful to his humanitarian ideals." While Heinrich Mann might have deserved the Nobel Prize even more, Werner concluded, one should hardly regret it had been awarded "to a writer who has devoted his efforts toward the redemption of humanity through analysis of the self."[7]

Claude Hill, who taught German at Rutgers University, reviewed the recently reissued *Steppenwolf* in the March 16, 1947, edition of the *New York Times*. Also calling Hesse one of Germany's best-known authors, Hill proclaimed him "an exquisite novelist and one of the greatest lyric poets since Goethe," who had captured the neurosis of contemporary life. Thomas Mann, the 1929 recipient of the Nobel Prize for Literature, had long insisted Hesse should similarly be honored. Mann declared that *Steppenwolf* was as experimentally bold as James Joyce's *Ulysses* and Andre Gide's *Faux-Monnayeurs*. While "deserving of a wide audience, *Steppenwolf* is not likely to become widely read," as it might come across "as too 'European,' too mystical and possibly too shocking in its brutal honesty," Hill conjectured. Instead, the novel "will most likely remain fare for the knowing few."[8] *Time* magazine viewed *Steppenwolf* differently, calling it "a repellent example of that beery old thing, German Romanticism, being sick in the last ditch before Nazism."[9] The following February, Alice S. Morris, a regular reviewer for the *Times*, more favorably examined *Demian*, which she called a "brief, bewitching and bewitched novel" that piqued "a deep stir among young" European and American intellectuals, because of "its revolutionary attitude toward good and evil; its prophetic insight . . . its repudiation of the accepted forms of thought and behavior as" antithetical to human nature. Those same intellectuals also were drawn "by the heroic demands of its *mystique*, of self above society and destiny above dicta."[10]

On October 30, 1949, the *Times* featured a review of Hesse's magnum opus, *Magister Ludi* or *The Glass Bead Game*, by Richard Plant, a German writer who left his native country following the Nazis' accession to power. Plant lauded the novel for being "as original as it is profound," and as "standing beside those few rare achievements of modern German writing which belong to world literature."[11] The *Times* presented a review of *Siddhartha*, in its December 2, 1951, edition. The art historian and editor Christopher Lazare considered Hesse's renewed popularity eminently logical, given the great writer's longstanding concerns regarding "the regimentation of youth, by the unnatural powers of the authoritarian state." Following World War I, Hesse was so out of favor in Germany that he not only went into exile but felt compelled to publish *Demian* pseudonymously. Lazare stated that Hesse had subsequently won the Nobel Prize "as much for his unfaltering belief in the freedom of man's spirit as for his services to German letters." Postwar German youth, Lazare revealed, presently accorded *Siddhartha* the acclaim, albeit more tempered, that *Demian* now received.[12] Writing in the *New Yorker* on January 23, 1954, Dwight Macdonald, by contrast dismissed Hesse as a "pretentious minor writer."[13] New York University's Seymour L. Flaxman treated Hesse far more respectfully in a lengthy article on *Steppenwolf* that appeared in the December 1954 issue of the *Modern Language Quarterly*. Flaxman praised Hesse as "a master of style," whose "work invites comparison with" Thomas Mann's.[14]

In *The Outsider: The Seminal Book on the Alienation of Modern Man*, published in 1956, the young English writer Colin Wilson also proved troubled that "the magnitude of Hesse's achievement is hardly recognized in the English-speaking countries, where the translations of most of his works are difficult to come by." Hesse's earliest novels revolved around *Bildungsroman*, allowing for a wrestling with the question, "What shall we do with our lives?" But by the time Hesse wrote *Steppenwolf*, he seemed to suggest "the irrelevancy of youth," Wilson noted.[15]

Richard Plant delivered a review of the latest book of Hesse's to be translated into English, *The Journey to the East*. In the July 21, 1957, edition of the *New York Times*, Plant discussed "Mystical Pilgrims," while indicating that "the community of Hesse readers . . . led by T. S. Eliot . . . has been growing steadily."[16] That same summer, *Books Abroad* included a recollection by Rutgers University professor Claude Hill, "Hermann Hesse at Eighty." Hill bemoaned the fact that eleven years following his receipt of the Nobel Prize for Literature, Hesse still "left no imprint whatever on either the reading public or the creative forces in" the United States. This saddened Hill, who considered Hesse "one of the wisest and subtlest writers of our time, one of the last remaining 'grand men of European letters' . . . but utterly ignored in America." Hill pointed to that which distinguished Hesse from most Europeans, while demonstrating his "greater spiritualization": his "effort to infuse the individual with the wisdom of the East, strengthening and widening the European soul in the face of the imminent decline of the West." Proclaiming Hesse "a conservative at heart," Hill noted that the great author sought to protect humankind's "great heritage . . . which he finds threatened by technology, material comfort, bourgeois arteriosclerosis." He feared for "the European soul, equally endangered by Russian collectivism and American mechanization." Hesse posited "a new man who will revitalize his personality by fusing the intellectual traditions of the West with the therapeutic methods of the East." Hill predicted, "The spiritualizing effect of his work will be felt for some time to come."[17]

With other academicians like Ralph Freedman, Ralph Mannheim, and Theodore Ziolkowski calling attention to Hesse's work, Brooklyn College professor Gisela Stein discussed "Hermann Hesse at 85," in the July 1, 1962, edition of the *New York Times*. She mentioned that during the past decade-and-a-half, Hesse's books had attained "a growing appeal for readers—especially those of college and university age—throughout the world, including the United States." This resulted from Hesse's concern "with the crisis of the individual in our time," notwithstanding his disinclination to offer easy solutions. Stein noted that Hesse had received the Goethe Prize, the prestigious German literary award, in 1946; she deemed no one alive at present to be as deserving as he, operating as a "'Weltbuerger' (world citizen) and poet."[18] The following month, Hesse died at his home in southeastern Switzerland. The *New York Times* again suggested that "to American readers he remained largely unapproachable," possibly because he emphasized "profound spiritual themes" or due to his "deep disdain for a world represented by bestial wars and the conflicts of a modern industrial society, and for a life marked by loud machines, money grubbing and the quest for material comfort."[19] While remaining largely ignored in North America, he had acquired something of a cult following in Europe, including among many young people.

In the fall 1963 issue of *The Psychedelic Review*, Timothy Leary and Ralph Metzner presented a lengthy essay, "Hermann Hesse: Poet of the Interior Journey," discussing the writer's "'unpatriotic' anti-war attitude" during World War I and his tracing of "the progress of the soul through the stages of life." Referring to Hesse as "a trickster," who employed "mental acrobatics," Leary and Metzner wondered if Hesse attained a visionary state and if so, how. "By meditation? Spontaneously? Did H. H. . . . use the chemical path to enlightenment?" They considered *Steppenwolf* to involve "a psychedelic experience, a drug-induced loss of self, a journey to the inner world." While referring to Hesse as "esoteric," Leary and Metzner again insisted that the German author had to have been involved in "a real-life psychedelic brotherhood." They urged that prior to taking LSD, one should "read *Siddhartha* and *Steppenwolf*."[20]

Hesse's U.S. publisher, Harper and Row, expressed a determination in mid-1965 to offer his major works in translation, and, as *Time* magazine put it, "to persuade U.S. readers that Hesse is essential to their ethos." *Time* predicted that "will not be easy," for "Hesse is relentlessly esoteric." At the same time, "he is one of the purest lyric poets since Moerike, and among the most profound of the many novelists who elaborate the drama of modern man in search of his soul." Reviewing *Demian*, *Time* stated that as in his other important novels, Hesse wrote subtly, albeit with the "mocking simplicity of an oracle," and at his finest, "with diamantine clarity—not about the psychological self in current fashion, but about the metaphysical self of traditional contemplation."[21] Within a matter of months, the critic and novelist Robin White reexamined *Siddhartha* for the *New York Times*, dismissively terming it "all talk, a child's guide to naval-contemplation," nothing more than "a placebo." White wrapped up the review, stating that *Siddhartha*'s new-found popularity was "scarcely distinguishable from the popularity of the pill as a solution to the dilemmas of the individual and the anguish of existence. Drugs, easy-outs and now books on superficial self-analysis would appear to have become the play-it-cool Holy Trinity in a nascent religion of rank cowardice and pampered non-thinking."[22]

Enormously appealing to hippies, *Siddhartha*, originally published in 1922, offered the story of "the handsome Brahmin's son," already conversant with both how "to pronounce Om silently," and "to recognize

Atman within the depth of his being . . . at one with the universe." Having read holy books, particularly the Upanishads, the philosophical texts association with Hinduism, he understood the concept, "Your soul is the whole world." Along with his friend Govinda, he decided to join the monastic Samanas, aspiring "to become empty of thirst, desire, dreams, pleasure and sorrow—to let the Self die." However, he found insufficient meditation, self-abnegation, fasting, that very "flight from the Self," which served only as a "temporary palliative against the pain and folly of life." He determined that "one can learn nothing." The ways of the Buddha," the Illustrious One," proved no more enlightening. Siddhartha "learned the art of loving" from the beautiful Kamala, while recognizing that neither was genuinely capable of love. He became rich, with a house, a garden, and servants, but felt no "glorious, exalted awakening" as he had in his youth.[23]

After several years, he departed, having heard the following message, "A path lies before you which you are called to follow. The gods await you." He saw Govinda and a ferryman, Vasudeva, who had taken him across the river two decades earlier. Siddhartha agreed to work as a ferryman, and soon informed his new friend that the river possessed many voices, but the two agreed on the single word it pronounced when one could hear "all its ten thousand voices" simultaneously: "Om." He encountered Kamala, who informed him that she had borne his son, "little Siddhartha." Following the death of Kamala, Siddhartha was left with the "defiant and angry" eleven-year-old; for the first time, Siddhartha experienced "blind love," for his son, who was "full of rage and misery" and soon ran away from his father. The pained Siddhartha now appreciated the sensibilities of "ordinary people," and came to appreciate how he had caused his own father to grieve his disappearance.[24]

Later, the aged Siddhartha ferried a group of monks, who included Govinda, across the river. Expressing appreciation for how kindly Siddhartha treated monks and pilgrims, Govinda asked, "Are you not also a seeker of the right path?" Siddhartha gently admonished his old friend that seeking resulted in becoming obsessed with a goal, whereas "finding means . . . to be free, to be receptive, to have no goal." Vasudeva, Siddhartha pointed out, was "a simple man," no thinker, "but he realized the essential as well as Gotama. He was a holy man, a saint." As for himself, Siddhartha indicated that it was difficult to explain his thoughts, but appreciated most of all that "wisdom is not communicable." Siddhartha did explain that just as "the Illustrious Buddha" felt compelled to divide the world "into Samsara and Nirvana, into illusion and truth, into suffering and salvation," a man and a deed were never "wholly Samsara or wholly Nirvana; never is a man wholly a saint or a sinner." Given that time was not real, that which separated "this world and eternity . . . suffering and bliss . . . good and evil, is also an illusion." Both Siddhartha and Govinda were themselves sinners, "but someday the sinner will be Brahma again, will someday attain Nirvana, will someday become a Buddha," Siddhartha revealed. Moreover, "the potential Buddha already exists in the sinner; his future is already there." Siddhartha continued, "The potential hidden Buddha must be recognized in him, in you, in everybody." Refuting Govinda, Siddhartha offered that Gotama too had to "know love, he who has recognized all humanity's vanity and transitoriness, yet loves humanity so much that he has devoted a long life solely to help and teach people."[25]

The American author and critic John Simon presented a detailed review of *Narcissus and Goldmund* and a brief one of *The Journey to the East* for the *New York Times'* edition of May 19, 1968. Simon opened his essay by referring to a review delivered at the tail end of the nineteenth century by the then twenty-four-year-old poet Rainer Maria Rilke of the first book by the twenty-two-year-old Hermann Hesse. "In its best passages, it is necessary and unique," Rilke had reported. Some authors were unique and a few were necessary, Simon offered. But "to be both highly personal, eccentric, extraordinary . . . and penetrating, humane, universal . . . is given only to a very few." To exemplify both qualities that Rilke highlighted was contradictory, Simon continued, but then Hesse's story was riddled with contradictions involving the religious and the secular, "poetic, nature-loving realism and rarefied, mysticizing grapplings with the transcendental." As for *Narcissus and Goldmund*, Simon praised its "body-and-soul-shaking debate," which remained unresolved, as "so limitlessly vast: that pitting flesh against spirit, art against scientific or religious speculation, action against contemplation."[26]

Narcissus and Goldmund also proved especially popular with those attracted to the counterculture. Initially published in 1930, and translated into English two years later as *Death and the Lover*, this novel spun the story of two young men, engaged in individual quests for meaning during the Middle Ages. The blond "budding beauty" Goldmund attended a Catholic monastic school, Mariabronn, where the dark, handsome, arrogant Narcissus taught. Initially, Goldmund considered remaining in the cloister school, as his father envisioned, devoting himself to God. A dreamer, Goldmund greatly admired the gifted young teacher, while the thinker, Narcissus, in turn viewed the pupil as "a kindred soul." Each "bore the special mark of fate." After falling in love with a beautiful young woman, Lise, Goldmund decided to leave the school, while displaying wanderlust. "Everywhere women desired him and made him happy," but none stayed with him, nor had he asked any to do so. Women proved attracted to "his childlike openness, the inquisitive innocence of his desire, his absolute readiness for anything a woman might wish of him." He quickly learned "many kinds of love, many arts of love."[27]

Enamored with a wooden Madonna in a church, Goldmund met the artist who sculpted her, Master Niklaus, then sought to become his apprentice, before declining an offer to become a master himself. As he explained to Niklaus, Goldmund declared, "I must leave, I must travel, I must be free." With a traveling companion, a pilgrim named Robert, Goldmund discovered disfigured corpses, as the Black Death swept through Germany. Passing through a small town, Goldmund picked up a pretty girl, Lene, who indicated how horrible things were, with "everybody . . . dying." But eventually, Lene, for whom he killed a man who was assaulting her, also died, saddening him terribly. Goldmund recognized how the entire region was afflicted with death, with anarchy unleashed and everybody seeking a scapegoat. "The rich blamed the poor, or vice versa; both blamed the Jews, or the French, or the doctors." Goldmund sadly watched as the residents of one town burned a whole ghetto, torturing and murdering innocent people. Enraged, Goldmund saw the world as "destroyed and poisoned; there seemed to be no more joy, no more innocence, no more love on earth." He sought to protect a beautiful young Jewish girl, Rebekka, but she rejected his suggestion that they remain together, after her father and several other Jews "had been burned to ash . . . by order of the town's authorities." Approaching Master Niklaus's town, Goldmund delivered a confession, in which he declared, "I've become an evil, useless man. I have squandered my youth . . . and little remains. I have killed, I have stolen, I have whored." He acknowledged doubting the very existence of God, who had "ill-created the world," which was filled with corpses, Jews being slaughtered "like cattle"; the suffering and death of many innocents; the prospering of many wicked individuals. Goldmund became involved with another "delicate, sickly young girl," Marie, but was fascinated by Agnes, the mistress of the governor and "the most beautiful woman he had ever seen."[28]

Jailed, he discovered that the priest who visited him was Narcissus, his former teacher. Narcissus freed him, and they rode away, conversing all the while. When Goldmund asked if Narcissus would "be capable of burning Jews," Narcissus responded, "No, why should I? Do you take me for a fanatic?" Yet the two agreed that they had stood aside as Jews were torched, and Goldmund angrily exclaimed, "What is this world in which we are made to live? Is it not hell? Is it not revolting and disgusting?" Narcissus insisted, nevertheless, that those who resided in the cloister "constantly set the idea of justice against original sin," and worked "to correct evil and put ourselves in everlasting relationship with God."[29]

On November 1, 1968, *New York Times* book critic Eliot Fremont-Smith reviewed *The Journey to the East*, first released in 1932, which had acquired its own following among those drawn to the counterculture. Fremont-Smith began by discussing what young people were presently reading, other than required college textbooks and underground publications. Young people appeared drawn, Fremont-Smith wrote, "to a kind of intimate, individual-crisis romanticism," a trend that dated back a decade or longer, to the writings of Albert Camus, Allen Ginsberg, William Golding, William Burroughs, and Norman O. Brown. Also popular were J. R. R. Tolkien's *Lord of the Rings* trilogy and such lesser known works as *Beautiful Losers* by Leonard Cohen, and *Sheeper* by Irving Rosenthal. While some considered such a trend "anti-intellectual and confessional," Fremont-Smith suggested that it bespoke instead "intellectualism fiercely concentrated in isolated and quasi-religious contexts." This was best exemplified by the current attraction of Hermann Hesse. *The Journey to the East*, Fremont-Smith concluded, was "probably the most accessible of Hesse's mature ponderings. And an at least analogous relationship between its theme and the hang-ups and hopes of its youthful admirers is plain to see."[30]

Briefer still than *Siddhartha*, *The Journey to the East* began with the narrator's declaration regarding his participation in the League—"It was my destiny to join in a great experience"—which had to appeal to those enamored with Tolkien's story of hobbits and the other creatures of Middle Earth. As if foreshadowing what later would be said about the 1960s, Hesse wrote, "What wonder it had at the time! How radiant and comet-like it seemed, and how quickly it has been forgotten and allowed to fall into disrepute." The league, despite having renounced modern transportation devices, had conducted a Journey to the East that proved "heroic and magical." This occurred following the World War, when defeated nations, such as Hesse's native Germany, experienced "an extraordinary state of unreality." Agreeing with Siddhartha that "words do not express thoughts very well," the narrator nevertheless quoted from a verse crafted by a league member, "He who travels far will often see things / Far removed from what he believed was Truth."[31]

The narrator, "a violinist and story-teller," entered the league after the World War, when his country was replete with "saviors, prophets and disciples," warning about the impending "end of the world" or envisioning the start "of a Third Empire." Phantoms attracted many, but "many real spiritual advances" also occurred, including "a widespread leaning towards Indian, ancient Persian and other Eastern mysteries and religions." As for the league, its members conducted their pilgrimage to the East, to "the Home of Light." This was part of "a wave in the eternal stream of human beings, of the eternal strivings of the human spirit towards the East." The pilgrims also headed "into the Middle Ages and the Golden Ages," spending time "with the patriarchs or the fairies." They bested "the war-shattered world by our faith and transformed it into Paradise," melding the past, present, and future. Joining in the quest were the artists Paul Klee and Klingsor (a mythological figure, but also a protagonist devised by Hesse); the poet Hermann Lauscher; Sancho Panza; Hesse's own Goldmund; and the composer Hugo Wolf. And "Zoraster, Lao Tse, Plato, Xenophon, Pythagoras, Albertus Magnus, Don Quixote, Tristram Shandy, Novalis and Baudelaire were co-founders and brothers of our League," the narrator explained.[32]

Published shortly after World War I, *Demian* proved to be one of Hesse's most beloved novels, and a classic example of *Bildungsroman*, with its examination of the enormously sensitive youth Emil Sinclair and his childhood friend Max Demian. In the prologue, Emil underscored the fact that "every man's story is important, eternal, sacred." His new friend Demian, several years older than he, reworked the tale of Cain and Abel, evidently identifying with the accursed one. Demian suggested killing Kormer, who continually tormented Emil. At one point, Emil looked at Demian, whose face was a man's but appeared somewhat feminine, and "somehow a thousand years old, sometimes timeless, bearing the scars of an entirely different history than we knew." He was simply "different, unimaginably different from the rest of us," Emil recalled. On another occasion, Demian denied being able to compel someone to think what he wanted him to, but he insisted he frequently knew precisely what that individual thought, felt, or intended to do. In discussing religion, Demian deemed "this God of both Old and Testaments . . . certainly an extraordinary figure but not what he purports to represent." Yes, "he is all that is good, noble, fatherly, beautiful, elevated, sentimental." However, the world included "something else besides," which was blamed on the devil, including sexuality. Emil too believed that the world was split "into two halves—the light and the dark." Demian denied that anything was acceptable, but declared that each individual had to discover "for himself what it permitted and what is forbidden—forbidden for him." During a Confirmation class, Demian once told Emil, "You can achieve anything you desire passionately enough." Later, Emil encountered an organist, who asserted, "We consist of everything the world consists of," including "every god and devil that ever existed." His friend Pistorius also pointed to the fact that their god "Abraxas . . . is God and Satan and he contains both the luminous and the dark world." Pistorius warned the precocious Emil, "He will leave you once you've become blameless and normal." Insisting that he would have had to lie to become a minister, Pistorius referred to Jesus as "a hero, a myth, an extraordinary shadow image in which humanity has painted itself on the wall of eternity." As for himself, Emil came to believe that he had "the mark of Cain" on his forehead.[33]

Later encountering Demian for the first time in several years, Emil listened as his childhood friend bemoaned "the herd instinct" that prevailed. Individuals were fearful, Demian indicated, because they failed to understand themselves. "A whole society composed of men afraid of the unknown within them!" he exclaimed. Contemporary religion and morality lacked validity, and individuals distrusted one another and those with new ideals. War appeared likely, but would be beneficial in one regard: it would underscore "the bankruptcy of present-day ideals," and usher in "a sweeping away of Stone Age gods." They too might be victimized, Demian acknowledged, but he prophesied that "the will of the future will gather" around "those of us who will survive." For "what Nature wants of man stands indelibly written in the individual, in you, me," as "it stood written in Jesus, it stood written in Nietzsche." After meeting Frau Demian, whom he viewed as "a universal mother," Emil joined Demian and others, who aspired to "power and greatness." Such individuals were "marked," considering themselves to represent "the will of Nature, to something new, to the individualism of the future." Among those in the circle were "astrologers and cabalists . . . followers of new sects, devotees of Indian asceticism, vegetarians, and so forth." There was also a Tolstoy disciple, who "preached nonresistance to evil."[34]

Demian warned that "the soul of Europe is a beast that has lain fettered for an infinitely long time," and when unleashed would hardly prove gentle. Nevertheless, "our day will come, then we will be needed . . . as men who are ready to go forth and stand prepared wherever fate may need them." They were indeed marked, like Cain, to pique trepidation and hatred, and to compel others to aspire to something more perilous. Such had been "true of Moses and Buddha, of Napoleon and Bismarck." Later, Demian acknowledged that the world sought renewal, but there existed "a smell of death in the air." Moreover, Demian indicated, "nothing can be born without first dying," but what was portended "is far more terrible than I had thought." As the novel neared its close, Demian informed Sinclair that he was now a lieutenant, ready to participate in what might well be a "gigantic" war. And yet, Demian stated, "That, too, will only be the beginning. The new world has begun and the new world will be terrible for those clinging to the old." A "sacred" intoxicating spirit took hold, as Emil also went to the front. The soldiers appeared to be "the clay of which the future could be shaped," and "a new humanity" formed. War enabled them to eradicate "the soul divided," filling "them with the lust to rage and kill, annihilate and die so that they might be born anew."[35]

Hesse's masterpiece, *Steppenwolf*, which originally appeared in 1927, offered a still more complex examination of postwar Europe, but one that resonated with some attracted to the counterculture. This was the story of a middle-aged writer, Harry Haller, whose home in a small rural German town at different points held images of a Siamese Buddha, Michelangelo's *Night*, or Mahatma Gandhi, and the works of Goethe and Dostoyevsky. Harry authored works about "art . . . genius . . . tragedy and humanity." Hesse's novel presented the records of Harry Haller, the Steppenwolf. During a walk in town one day, Harry encountered a door on which was posted, "MAGIC THEATER ENTRANCE NOT FOR EVERYBODY." Unable to pass through the door, Harry then spotted a message on the asphalt, "FOR MADMEN ONLY!" Returning to the town's old quarter, Harry met up with an individual holding a placard that stated,

"ANARCHIST EVENING ENTERTAINMENT MAGIC THEATER
ENTRANCE NOT FOR EVERYBODY." The man handed Harry a
booklet, before disappearing. [36]

Back home, Harry read the booklet, which was titled "Treatise on the
Steppenwolf. Not for Everybody." The story was about a man named
Harry, also known as the Steppenwolf, who possessed "two natures, a
human and a wolfish one," which "were in continual and deadly enmity."
At times, the Steppenwolf lived as a human, and at other points, as a wolf.
The treatise indicated that the Steppenwolf was hardly singular, that
many individuals had "two souls, two beings within them. There is God
and the devil in them." While such people might consider life "but a bad
joke," they could also believe that man was "a child of the gods and
destined to immortality." Seeking independence above all else, the Steppenwolf then became troubled by solitude. True, he possessed many
friends, but no one was close to him. Notwithstanding his own bourgeois
proclivities, the Steppenwolf could love "the political criminal, the revolutionary or intellectual seducer, the outlaw of state and society, as his
brother." In the same fashion, an individual could adopt a saint-like posture, or give way to profligacy and "the martyrdom of the flesh." One
could never return fully "to the wolf or to the child," with "the return into
the All . . . the reunion with God" requiring the necessary "expansion of
the soul." But for now, Harry became depressed on hearing a professor
call him "a traitor to his country." [37]

Later, Harry discussed his love of Goethe, Stephen, and St. Francis,
with a young woman, Hermine, at a public house called "The Black
Eagle." She, in turn, soon pointed to a write-up in a newspaper that
castigated Harry's antiwar stance, portraying him as "a noxious insect
and a man who disowned his native land." The newspaper called for the
suppression of Harry's dangerous and "sentimental ideas of humanity."
Denying that he was troubled by such an attack, Harry discussed the
belief held by the Kaiser, generals, economic leaders, politicians, and
newspaper editors that they were "all guiltless," notwithstanding the millions killed in the war. As his countrymen read such drivel, the likelihood
of another war loomed larger. "And it will be a good deal more horrible
than the last," Harry offered. As for Harry, he had "no country and no
ideals left. All that comes to nothing but decorations for the gentlemen by
whom the next slaughter is ushered in." Hermine agreed with his prediction, while stating that "the war against death . . . is always a beautiful,

noble and wonderful and glorious thing, and so, it follows, is the war against war." And yet "it is always hopeless and quixotic too." Harry had indeed condemned "the barbarity of the war," yet "he had not let himself be stood against a wall and shot," which should have resulted from his way of thinking.[38]

Hermine introduced Harry to his soon-to-be lover, the beautiful Maria, and to the handsome saxophonist Pablo, who took drugs, including cocaine, "for stilling pain, for inducing sleep, for begetting beautiful dreams, lively spirits and the passion of love." Harry turned down a suggestion by Pablo that they carry out a ménage-à-trois, somewhat to Maria's evident disappointment. Meanwhile, Hermine spoke to Harry of "the kingdom on the other side of time and appearances," declaring, "It is there we belong." There, Harry would meet Goethe and Mozart, once more. Eventually, Harry entered the Magic Theater, which was designed "for madmen only," with the "PRICE OF ADMISSION YOUR MIND" and an indication that "HERMINE IS IN HELL." In the theater, Harry witnessed "the long-prepared, long-awaited and long-feared war between men and machines," resulting in "dead and decomposing bodies" but also a campaign to prevent "fat and well-dressed and perfumed plutocrats" from using "machines to squeeze the fat from other men's bodies." He entered a door reading "ALL GIRLS ARE YOURS," and met several girls from his youth, whom he could now "inspire . . . with love." As he conversed with Mozart about impending death, the two saw Richard Wagner. Returning from his reverie, Harry spotted the naked Hermine and Pablo, and, as she had predicted earlier, he plunged a knife into her breast, then saw a notice, "HARRY's EXECUTION." Nevertheless, Mozart offered the possibility of restoring Hermine to life, thereby enabling Harry to marry her. Harry declined, stating, "No, I should not be ready for that. It would bring unhappiness." As Pablo placed a shrunken Hermine in his pocket, Harry became "determined to begin the game afresh," to "sample its tortures once more and shudder again at its senselessness." Thus, "I would traverse not once more, but often, the hell of my inner being," Harry reflected.[39]

In "Saint Hesse among the Hippies," published in the *American-German Review* in 1969, Theodore Ziolkowski wrote, "If young American readers, in their enthusiasm, sometimes go too far in their sanctification of Hesse, it is equally certain that the sneering critics of the literary Establishment reveal little but their own provincialism in their failure to

understand the forces that move the post-modern generation and the reasons for Hesse's appeal."[40]

By 1970, several of Hesse's works had been reissued or retranslated.
Princeton University professor Ralph Freedman, working on a biography
of Hesse, reviewed *The Glass Bead Game* in the January 4, 1970, edition
of the *New York Times*. Freedman referred to Hesse's "surprising revival
in America," resulting from his appealing "both to young people and to
adults, to an underground and to an establishment, to a comfortable middle-class and to the disenchanted young sharing his contempt for our
industrial civilization." As Freedman saw it, "Hesse suddenly caught on
in America several years following his death . . . when his off-beat,
mystical, highly subjective vision struck responsive chords in a fresh
generation who seemed to reenact the enthusiasm generated for him
among German youth half a century before." Now, Hesse's "revival here
has turned into a vogue, the vogue into a torrent," as exemplified by both
a rock group and a nightclub in San Francisco named after *Steppenwolf*.
Presently, young people were devouring his novels. Freedman posed the
question of why such an "ethereal, bookish, highly lyrical writer" would
be "such an enormous attraction for two generations of youth living in
two different countries half a century apart." Calling Hesse a "rather
limited novelist," Freedman acknowledged that the German author,
nevertheless, "expresses the alienation of youth who identify with his
descriptions of the sensitive outsider."[41] The critic John Leonard, in the
February 17, 1970, edition of the *New York Times*, declared that "Hesse
was admired by his betters—Rilke, Gide, Thomas Mann, T. S. Eliot."
Hesse's seeking of mysticism, Leonard wrote, explained his appeal to
"the Now Generation."[42]

Egon Schwartz, a professor of Germanic languages and literature at
Washington University, St. Louis, published "Hermann Hesse, the
American Youth Movement, and Problems of Literary Evaluation" in the
October 1970 issue of *PMLA*. As Schwartz noted, Hesse was "suddenly
popular in America," with *Siddhartha* having "sold 100,000 copies in one
year (1967)." Hesse's *Steppenwolf* was "enjoying a veneration reserved
for major works of literature," while Farrar, Straus and Giroux planned "a
400,000 pocketbook edition of *Narcissus and Goldmund*." This was an
astonishing turn of events, given that barely a decade earlier Hesse was
little known even by "the reading public or the creative forces in the
country." Now, Schwartz asserted, "the Hesse cult in America . . . is

carried by the Hippies, the alienated, and the young radicals." He suggested that Colin Wilson's *The Outsider*, with its extended treatment of Hesse, had served as "the Bible of a whole segment of British youth," whose "enthusiasm may well have been carried over here." However, Timothy Leary, with his proclaiming of "*Steppenwolf* his favorite work of literature," proved "much more directly influential."[43]

Several additional books by Hesse appeared in English translation in the latter stages of the 1960s or the beginning of the following decade. Some connected to the counterculture eagerly awaited each of the latest publications of the German Nobel Laureate. They had other favorite authors, including Kahlil Gibran, Robert Heinlein, Arthur C. Clarke, Kurt Vonnegut, and Richard Brautigan, along with older masters Lewis Carroll, J. M. Barrie, A. A. Milne, and J. R. R. Tolkien. The English mathematician and Anglican clergyman Carroll published *Alice's Adventures in Wonderland* and *Through the Looking-Glass and What Alice Found There* in 1865 and 1871, respectively. Hippies, in the manner of both children and adults, proved enamored with the adventures of Alice, who chased a white rabbit down a rabbit hole, followed the instruction, "DRINK ME," attached to a bottle, only to find herself reduced to ten inches, then partook of a small cake that contained the words, "EAT ME," resulting in a growth spurt causing her head to butt against a ceiling; soon, however, she shrank again. Finding all this "curiouser and curiouser," Alice spoke to Mouse, before other creatures, including "a Duck and a Dodo, a Lory and an Eaglet," met up with them. As her adventures continued, Alice received advice from a large, hookah-smoking blue caterpillar, about a mushroom: "One side will make you grow taller, and the other side will make you grow shorter." On taking bites from the mushroom, Alice felt her body becoming disoriented. She encountered a large Cheshire cat, who was sitting in a tree and told her about the Hatter and the Hare. As they were conversing, the cat slowly disappeared, leaving behind his grin. Alice saw the March Hare and the Mad Hatter having a tea party, with a sleeping Dormouse perched between the two of them. She introduced herself to the King and the Queen of Hearts, but when Alice was unable to explain who three gardeners were, the Queen roared, "Off with her head!" Unfazed, Alice responded, "Nonsense!" and the King stated, "Consider, my dear; she is only a child!" Following additional adventures, Alice was awakened by her sister and began dreaming once again about "little Alice," the White Rabbit, the Queen, and other characters in Wonderland. She also envisioned her-self as a grown woman, who would possibly tell her own children about "the dream of Wonderland." In *Through the Looking-Glass*, Alice en-countered Tiger Lily, a talking flower; the twins Tweedledum and Twee-dledee, who spoke about the Walrus and the Carpenter; Humpty Dumpty; the Lion and the Unicorn; and the White Knight. That story concluded with a poem that asked, "Life, what is it but a dream?"[44]

Popular too among the hippies were the lovely stories of Winnie-the-Pooh and his band of friends—Piglet, Tigger, Eeyore, Rabbit, Owl, Kan-ga, and Baby Roo, who lived in the Hundred Acre Wood. Cambridge-educated A. A. Milne created the world of Pooh and the boy Christopher Robin, patterned after his own young son. Jefferson Airplane drew from both Lewis Carroll and Milne in devising two of the band's most iconic works: "White Rabbit" and "The House at Pooneil Corner," which ended with the refrain, "Cows are almost cooing / turtle doves are mooing; / Which is why a Pooh is poohing in the sun."[45] Still more popular was the whole story of Middle Earth, of Bilbo Baggins and the hobbits, presented by Oxford don J. R. R. Tolkien. *The Hobbit* and *The Lord of the Rings* trilogy, published between 1937 and 1949, cast a spell that drew in read-ers to Tolkien's high fantasy epic, replete with magic, wonderment, and adventures. That was in keeping with Scottish author J. M. Barrie's *Peter Pan; or, the Boy Who Wouldn't Grow Up*, which first appeared near the turn of the century.

The national media began reporting that *The Lord of the Rings* and *Siddhartha* were among the bestsellers at college and university book-stores across the country. Writing in the *Saturday Evening Post* on July 2, 1966, Henry Resnik discussed "The Hobbit-Forming World of J. R. R. Tolkien." Resnik attempted to separate the more numerous "Tolkien peo-ple," as he fondly referred to them, from the more "noisy . . . LSD-heads" who had piqued a "melodramatic scandal" during the previous twelve months. He considered "the Tolkien movement" surprising, the byprod-uct of the creation of Middle-Earth by an Oxford don. The Yale Co-Op reported selling more copies of Tolkien's 1,300-page trilogy than it had of William Golding's *Lord of the Flies*, popular among undergraduates since its publication in 1954. The Ballantine Books trilogy was also out-selling John Knowles's *A Separate Peace* and J. D. Salinger's *The Catch-er in the Rye*, other mainstays on campuses.[46]

Robert Sklar, a history professor at the University of Michigan, discussed "Tolkien and Hesse: Top of the Pops" in the May 8, 1967, issue of *The Nation* magazine. Sklar stated forthrightly, "Tolkien and Hesse's visions of life accord with the contemporary visions of youth," in the same way that *Lord of the Flies* and *The Catcher in the Rye* had. The latter two works reflected, Sklar indicated, the "helplessness . . . hopelessness" young people felt during the period when Joseph McCarthy rampaged and the bomb loomed over humanity. As Sklar noted, the move from Ayn Rand's *The Fountainhead*, the 1943 novel popular during the immediate postwar era, with its celebration of unfettered individualism, to William Golding and J. D. Salinger had been a step forward. He continued, "With Tolkien and Hesse we have attained an astonishing goal," with young people selecting great literary works as their particular favorites. To Sklar, the hobbits well reflected American youth's "concern . . . with the power that resides in simple lives and everyday people." Moreover, Tolkien's fantasy established "a paradigm for action," Sklar indicated. In a "strikingly similar" manner, Hesse offered fantasy involving "new mysteries for our normal state of consciousness and [this] creates new possibilities in the quotidian world." Hesse's popularity, Sklar noted, rested largely on *Siddhartha*, which "any seeker of self who has looked into Zen or Oriental mysticism" had probably read. Also popular was *Demian*, which like both *Siddhartha* and *The Lord of the Rings*, was a "quest" book, Sklar continued. Rather than Middle Earth, Hesse's protagonists "turn and tunnel deep down into 'the innermost, the Self.'" Appealing too was Hesse's "nonviolent humanism" and his declaration through Siddhartha that "love is the most important thing in the world." It was essential, Siddhartha asserted, "to be able to regard the world and ourselves and all beings with love, admiration, and respect." *Demian* and *Siddhartha* appealed to young people, Sklar declared, who were seeking "personal authenticity, separate from, yet expressed through, common action." Elegantly, Sklar concluded, "Delight in Tolkien and Hesse signifies a new delight in human mysteries, in life's possibilities, in the power of will and the pleasures of imagination. Life imitates art, may the taste of the young, and our luck, hold."[47]

Countercultural participants proved drawn to more recent fantasies too, such as those offered by Robert Heinlein, Arthur C. Clarke, and Kurt Vonnegut. Heinlein attracted many fans during the 1960s, who would never have approved of his deeply conservative political views, through books like *Starship Troopers* and *Stranger in a Strange Land*. The latter work, published in 1961 and the first science fiction work to land on the best-seller list of the *New York Times* notwithstanding a blistering review by Orville Prescott, recounted the story of Valentine Michael Smith, the son of astronauts who had been raised by Martians before coming to the planet Earth. Prescott dismissed Heinlein's novel as a "disastrous mish-mash of science fiction, laborious humor, dreary social satire and cheap eroticism." Prescott appeared particularly put off by what he referred to as Heinlein's "sophomoric (high school, not college) enthusiasm for sex."[48] *Stranger in a Strange Land* extolled mind expansion and free love, with Smith serving as a Messiah-like figure, but one hardly disinclined to mete out violence when he considered that necessary. As Smith explained at one point, "I *am* God. Thou art God. Any jerk I remove is God too." On another occasion, he stated, "Look at me. I am a Son of Man." Smith employed the technique of grokking, which allowed for the sharing of intelligence intuitively or empathetically.[49]

The best-known books, *Childhood's End* (1953) and *2001: A Space Odyssey* (1968), by Arthur C. Clarke, a fellow of the Royal Astronomical Society, also fitted easily into the countercultural grab-bag. *Childhood's End* began with the alien overlords, who, initially all but entirely unknown, helped to spawn a utopia on Earth, with racial discrimination and national rivalries eradicated, just as the United States and the Soviet Union readied for nuclear war. During a second stage, a so-called Golden Age, a leisure-driven society prevailed. However, some worried that human instincts were being thwarted and thus determined to establish "New Athens." Then, the Last Generation emerged, with children possessing telekinetic powers, readying to merge with the Overmind, which would result in the extinction of the human species.[50] An early review of *Childhood's End*, which appeared in the *New York Times* and was written by William Du Bois, indicated that "the noblest theme in all our literature is the destiny of man." Those who constructed empires fixated on some idea involving a "master" or altered race, but humanitarians "foundered just as fatally."[51] Published fifteen years later, *2001* presented another dystopian examination of the potential future of humanity. In that book, soon turned into a Hollywood blockbuster directed by Stanley Kubrick, the issues of nuclear war, evolution, space travel, and technology run amok came to the forefront.[52]

In more whimsical, yet frequently sardonic fashion, Kurt Vonnegut Jr. offered readers artfully drawn stories of characters, who also partook of extraterrestrial explorations and mind games, deliberately or not. He did so in a series of easily digestible novels such as *Player Piano*, *The Sirens of Titan*, *Mother Night*, *Cat's Cradle*, *God Bless You, Mr. Rosewater*, and *Slaughterhouse-Five*. These again offered dystopian treatments of technology, capitalism, and humanity itself, while revisiting the horrors of World War II; the world of Tralfamadore; and granfalloons, individuals who falsely considered themselves to share connections. The poet-novelist Richard Brautigan likewise delivered bittersweet accounts of America and the counterculture itself in such books as *A Confederate General from Big Sur* (1964), *Trout Fishing in America* (1967), and *In Watermelon Sugar* (1968), which featured a commune, purportedly based on Brautigan's real-life experiences in the Bay Area. More classically etched, the poetry, essays, stories, and drawings of Lebanese-born Kahlil Gibran, a Maronite Christian, nevertheless resonated markedly with many young people during the 1960s. Most popular, of course, was *The Prophet*, originally published in 1923, which offered the thought of Al-Mustafa, who discussed issues ranging from love, marriage, and children, to eating, drinking, work, laws, freedom, self-knowledge, and friendship.[53]

The writings of Carlos Castaneda, a Peruvian-born anthropologist, also proved enormously popular, both within and outside the counterculture. He wrote his first book, *The Teachings of Don Juan: A Yaqui Way of Knowledge*, while a doctoral student at the University of California at Los Angeles. The novelist Charles Simmons reviewed the book for the *New York Times*, beginning with an extended quote from Castaneda discussing his trips to the Southwest to acquire information about medicinal plants employed by Indians in the region. He encountered "a white-haired old Indian," Don Juan, who proved quite knowledgeable about those plants, particularly peyote. Eventually, Don Juan introduced Castaneda to peyote, what he called "*Mescalito*." Following Don Juan's instructions, Castaneda ingested seven mescalitos, producing hallucinogenic effects. Subsequently, Don Juan determined to teach Castaneda "the secrets that make up the lot of a man of knowledge." Don Juan explained that such an individual had to overcome four enemies: fear, clarity, power, and old age. As further drug experiences occurred involving "Mescalito, Jimson weed and . . . probably *Psilocybe Mexicana*," Castaneda suffered repeated "spontaneous states of nonreality," including the seeming loss of a sense of one's soul. Tellingly concluding his essays, Simmons admitted to lacking the anthropological background to evaluate Castaneda on that basis, but praised the book as "an extraordinary spiritual and psychological document."[54] Also writing in the *Times*, Dudley Young of the University of Essex discussed Castaneda's quest "to gain power over the demonic world" by way of hallucinogenics, adjudging his descriptions of "both terror and ecstasy" as "interesting and moving." Young admitted his inability to ascertain if Don Juan were a genuine sorcerer, a crank, or a dangerous authoritarian figure.[55] Others would soon more directly question Castaneda's veracity, deeming that first book and subsequent ones works of fiction, but for a period his influence proved considerable.

Peter Marin, who coauthored *Understanding Drug Use* with Allan Y. Cohen, delivered an account of the favorite books of the young as of early 1971, by which time a new image had emerged. Marin envisioned an image, which he admitted was absurd: "a longhaired hermaphrodite striding through the suburbs with a prayer-wheel in one hand and a rifle in the other." He then listed what young people appeared to be reading: Vonnegut's *Cat's Cradle*, Heinlein's *Stranger in a Strange Land*, Frank Herbert's *Dune*, and Tolkien's *Rings* trilogy, but *Do It!*, *Revolution for the Hell of It*, and *Soul on Ice*, by Jerry Rubin, Abbie Hoffman, and Eldridge Cleaver, respectively, as well. He also tossed in *The Autobiography of Malcolm X* and *Quotations from Chairman Mao Tse-tung*. The books, Marin offered, included heroes with "marvelous or occult talents, the magical tantric and yogic powers of self-control and perception," in dream-like states, similar to that induced by the usage of psychedelics and delving into "Eastern cosmologies."[56]

FROM THE HUMAN BE-IN TO
THE SUMMER OF LOVE

Throughout 1967, as various seminal essays and books on the counter-culture appeared or neared publication, the grand spectacle characterized the latest rendition of American bohemia. These ranged from the Human Be-In, the Monterey Pop Festival, and the Death of Hippie, all intimately identified with the carving out of new lifestyles on the West Coast, to the March on the Pentagon. The impact of such events proved mixed, garnering far greater attention for both the still germinating counterculture and the continually metamorphosing movement. That, in turn, led to greater media attention—of both the underground and mainstream variety—and the determination of countless young people to participate in the cultural and political flowerings that appeared to be taking place in the Bay Area, but also in New York City and Austin, Texas, among other fronts. This was, after all, the year of massive antiwar rallies, the marching side-by-side of Benjamin Spock and Martin Luther King Jr., the iconic placing of a flower in the barrel of a soldier's rifle in front of the Pentagon, but also of the Diggers, Sgt. Pepper, and the Summer of Love.

It all began so propitiously with the seemingly apt declaration by *Time* magazine in its January 6, 1967, issue that "The Man of the Year 1966 is a generation: the man—and woman—of 25 and under." *Time* referred to young people as "well-educated, affluent, rebellious, responsible, pragmatic, idealistic, brave, alienated, and hopeful."[1] Equally appropriate, "A Gathering of the Tribes" or "A Human Be-In," as Michael Bowen referred to it, occurred on January 14, 1967, at the Polo Field in Golden

Gate's Park Stadium. The driving forces behind the Be-In were Allen Cohen, editor of the San Francisco *Oracle*, and Bowen, who was close to beat poets and had befriended both Timothy Leary and Allen Ginsberg. Troubled by the apparent chasm between hippies and antiwar activists, Cohen and Bowen sought "a powwow," and spoke to a number of Berkeley radicals, including Jerry Rubin and the *Berkeley Barb*'s editor, Max Scheer. They built on the ideas of the philosopher-historian Lewis Mumford and a peyote shaman, Charlie Brown, who broached the notion of eliciting magical energy to exorcise the Pentagon.

Among the speakers at a press conference conducted at the Park Mint two days earlier was Rubin, a political radical recently turned on to LSD and the counterculture. A dropout from graduate school at the University of California at Berkeley, who had just managed Robert Scheer's unsuccessful congressional campaign, Rubin predicted the Be-In would demonstrate that political and cultural radicals could come together; both wanted, he believed, to leave behind "games and institutions that oppress and dehumanize" and help cultivate "new values and new human relations."[2] Cohen predicted that "Berkeley political activists and [its] hip community and San Francisco's spiritual contingent and contingents from the emerging revolutionary generation all over California" would engage in "a Gathering of the Tribes for a Human Be-In."[3] The *Berkeley Barb* quickly prophesied, "The spiritual revolution will be manifest and proven. In unity we shall shower the country with waves of ecstasy and purification," quashing fear, ignorance, capitalism, empire, and violence.[4] The fifth issue of *The Oracle*, with a decidedly more psychedelic twist, heralded the event.

Cohen fired off a message to Art Kunkin, editor of the *Los Angeles Free Press*, affirming that "the days of fear and separation are over," as demonstrated by the forthcoming Be-In. He wrote, "Now that a new race is evolving in the midst of the old, we can join together to affirm our unity, and generate waves of joy and conscious penetration of the veil of ignorance and fear that hides the original face of humankind." To that end, the Be-In and similar events, Cohen continued, could produce a sea change in thought that would lead to an end of the Vietnam War "and revitalize many dead hearts." Cohen hoped Kunkin and other underground press editors would "help the echoes of this event reverberate throughout the world," enabling all of them to "move closer to the revolution." Other promotions of the Be-In appeared in the hip shops, on bulletin boards, and in other underground publications. One press release asserted, "For ten years, a new nation has grown inside the robot flesh of the old. Before your eyes a new free vital soul is reconnecting the living centers of the American body." The note declared that "Berkeley political activists and the love generation of the Haight-Ashbury will join together . . . to powwow, celebrate, and prophesy the epoch of liberation, love, peace, compassion, and unity of mankind." It urged all to "hang your fear at the door and join the future. If you do not believe, please wipe your eyes and see."[5]

Somewhere between twenty and thirty thousand people congregated at Park Stadium on January 14, most of them hippies attired in the garb of the counterculture, which included simple trousers, T-shirts, jackets, long skirts, and blouses. As Jay Stevens writes, they appeared "in serapes and desert robes and Victorian petticoats and paisley bodystockings, bedecked with bells and flowers, young boys with nasturtiums wagging from their ears and at least one gray-haired grandmother with a rose tied to her cane."[6] Dogs and children were in abundance, along with flowers, incense, marijuana, tambourines, bells, wine, and food. Poets were also in attendance, including Allen Ginsberg, Gary Snyder, Michael McClure, Lawrence Ferlinghetti, Lew Welch, and Lenore Kandel. Present too were Timothy Leary, stoned on acid, Richard Alpert, the comedian and social critic Dick Gregory, and jazz musician Dizzy Gillespie. Ginsberg delivered a series of chants, while Leary offered his "Turn on, tune in, drop out" mantra and Snyder could be seen blowing on a conch shell. The Diggers handed out turkey sandwiches, thanks to Stanley Owsley, who also contributed White Lightning, his newest LSD concoction. The Diggers broke up the LSD, mixing it into the sandwiches. The Grateful Dead, Jefferson Airplane, Quicksilver Messenger Service, Moby Grape, Sopwith Camel, Big Brother and the Holding Company, and Sir Douglas Quintet were among the bands providing music, as those who desired to danced or cavorted. The Hell's Angels delivered announcements regarding lost children. During mid-afternoon, a parachuter hovered over the crowd, before descending.

Also, during the Be-In, Chester Anderson, a beat writer and editor who was working for the *Sunday Ramparts*, and Claude Hayward presented themselves as the Communication Company, declaring their policy to be a belief that "love is communication." They intended to make cheap, quick printing available to the hip community, and more particularly to put out anything the Diggers wanted published. They hoped to assist *The Oracle* with daily offerings, whenever necessary, and to function as the satirical North Beach magazine, *The Underhound*, had, in contesting police harassment. Simply put, Anderson and Hayward intended to operate "as a Haight-Ashbury propaganda ministry," and "to do what we damn well please."[7] They asserted that the hip community in the Haight was merely part of a global revolution involving young people determined to foster spiritual unity throughout the universe. At the same time, the Haight-Ashbury community represented "a cultural renaissance and creative force that is changing the bruted face of America."[8]

United Press International offered an account of the Be-In by Richard M. Harnett, which appeared under the headline, "All Kinds of 'Kooks' Gather for 'Happening.'" Harnett referred to the coming together of Bay Area "beatniks, hippies, beardies, and LSD 'saints,'" along with many "tourists and other square people who happened by and were dumbfounded at the sight." The event, Harnett reported, involved a gathering of "the love-cultists and leftists," with arrests resulting.[9] Writing in the San Francisco *Oracle*, Steve Levine referred to the seeming "reincarnation of the American Indian" appearing in "this brand-new Aquarian Age." He noted the food, including turkeys, bread, and oranges, provided by the Diggers, who affirmed, "It's free because it's yours." Levine mentioned political activist Jerry Rubin, who exclaimed to the crowd, "The police, like the soldiers in Vietnam, are victims and agents!"[10]

At Studio A in Los Angeles, the Grateful Dead recorded the bulk of their first album, which included renditions of Sonny Boy Williamson's rhythm and blues song "Good Morning Little School Girl," the folk-blues song "Sitting on Top of the World," Bonnie Dobson's "Morning Dew," and an intended jam, "Viola Lee Blues." The cover, which included Jerry Garcia sporting an Uncle Sam hat, included indecipherable lyrics shaded by Stanley Mouse.

Luminaries from various aspects of the political spectrum worried about the growth of the counterculture. On January 24, 1967, San Francisco police chief Thomas Cahill, meeting with representatives of the Haight Independent Proprietors, asked, "You're sort of the Love Generation, aren't you?"[11] Mayor John F. Shelley quickly expressed his concerns about "a summer influx of indigent young people who are apparently being led to believe by a certain element of society their vagrant presence will be tolerated in this city." Worrying about public health issues and the general well-being of the community of San Francisco, Shelley feared that "a chaotic condition" might well result, which would prove "detrimental" to the new migrants and city residents alike.[12] The Communication Company soon offered a broadside, signed by the Psychedelic Rangers, urging the people to remain "calm and gentle in the face of harassment."[13] But another broadside soon reported on a "news flash" indicating that the federal government was readying concentration camps for "dangerous elements of the population."[14]

Back on New York's Lower East Side, an anarchist group, self-named Up Against the Wall Motherfuckers, emerged out of an art group with a Dada focus, Black Mask, and Angry Arts Week, held to protest the Vietnam War. Key figures included Alan Hoffman, Tom Neumann, whose stepfather was Herbert Marcuse, and John Sundstrom, while among the close acquaintances was the radical feminist Valerie Solanas. Like the Diggers out West, the Motherfuckers established crash pads, offered free food, began a free store, and established links between political radicals, physicians, and attorneys.

At the behest of the San Francisco *Oracle*, countercultural heavyweights Leary, Ginsberg, Snyder, and Alan Watts met on the houseboat Watts owned in Sausalito Bay. *The Oracle* presented a lengthy account of "the Houseboat Summit" in its February 1967 issue. Watts posed the question that had to be confronted: "whether to drop out or take over." Ginsberg referred to having recently turned on with Free Speech Movement leader Mario Savio, who indicated that large crowds were moved by "righteousness, moral outrage, and *anger* . . . righteous anger." Taking immediate umbrage at that, Leary declared he wanted nothing to do with a mass movement, and referred to leftist activists as "young men with menopausal minds, who were duplicating the doctrinal squabbles of the Old Left." A "completely incompatible difference" separated political and cultural radicals, Leary insisted. Ginsberg, in turn, viewed Leary's perspective as riddled with stereotypes about political activists and hippies. For his part, Snyder suggested that the historical roots of revolutionary movements and the present spiritual movement were "identical," emanating "from a utopian and essentially religious drive." Watts pointed to "a secularization of mysticism." Contesting Leary's admonition "to drop out, turn on, and tune in," Ginsberg indicated that concerned young people like Savio were perplexed by this conundrum: "how do you have a community and a community movement, and cooperation within the community to make life more pleasing for everybody . . . without a fascist leadership"? They were clear about one thing—"they don't want to be messiahs—political messiahs." But Ginsberg, in contrast to Watts and Leary, recognized that "organized leadership" pulled off happenings like the Be-In. [15]

Snyder pointed to the emergence of "a new social structure" patterned after "historically known tribal models." Already, he said, "we're in the seeds of a new society." This was different from what the beats experienced, because no community had existed for them, Snyder remarked. "You were really completely on your own." That required accepting a minimal standard of living, and a willingness to carry out "any kind of work. Strawberry picking, carpenter, laborer, longshore[man]." It also demanded patience. By contrast, "a huge community" now existed, and countercultural proponents possessed "a subculture to go fall into." Responding to Snyder's question of what he was building, Leary predicted that "thousands of groups" would help guide individuals "into the garden of Eden." Somewhat slyly but wisely, Snyder responded, "But that garden of Eden is full of old rubber truck tires and tin cans, right now, you know." He insisted that individuals had to "learn new structures and new techniques." Again challenging Leary's assertions, this time the notion that "the tribal people" demonstrated "the evolution of mankind is not over," Snyder stated bluntly, "C'mon, Tim, they're humans and they're gonna be here." Nevertheless, he believed that within three generations countercultural proponents would "get the kids," as family structures altered and clan-like developments ensued. And Snyder asserted, "If we change America we are changing the planet." [16]

The February 6, 1967, issue of *Newsweek* contained an article, "Dropouts with a Mission." It indicated that hippies referred to themselves as "a new race," and sought to transform the nation "from within—by means of a vague regimen of all-embracing love." Hippies were "nonviolent, mystical, bizarre," employing psychedelics as an "instant passport to Nirvana" and euphorically dismissing anything considered "square." *Newsweek* deemed the Human Be-In "a love feast, a psychedelic picnic, a hippie happening," and called San Francisco "the hub of the hippie world." Hippies possessed a global network, as they traveled from Amsterdam to Afghanistan, *Newsweek* noted. The magazine pinpointed the Haight-Ashbury district, declaring that hippies appeared "to float" there, "serene, smiling, detached," while attired in "probably the most clownish array of clothing" found in a single community. [17]

Newsweek reporter Hendrik Hertzberg delivered his own report on Michael Bowen's apartment in the Haight. Hertzberg quoted from twenty-one-year-old Laurie Baxer, who stated, "For the first time, men and women are becoming friends again. Just friends. . . . Certain external things, such as short hair, long hair or manner of dress, no longer make the difference." Sex was not a matter of debate to the hippies, who believed the sexual revolution was already present. An Englishman, a former journalist residing in the Haight-Ashbury district named Gary Goldhill, noted, "Sex is psychedelic. And in all psychedelic things, sex is important." At the same time, Hertzberg pointed out, the hippies operated in a manner in which women agreed to take on traditional feminine tasks. Twenty-four-year-old Martine stated, "More chicks are now getting into sewing, making their own clothes, and getting into leatherwork, so they can make moccasins and sandals." And she revealed, "I spend all day cooking, sewing, straightening the house." Whereas previously she wanted to be an artist, "Now, I am," she said. Hertzberg also explained how hippies were drawn to macrobiotic food, as "an offshoot of Buddhism," and to new, extended family structures. As Goldhill explained, "It's a cooperative and not a competitive thing." The U.S. Postal Service, Hertzberg indicated, was the largest employer of hippies. Others sold dope, and worked in the creative realm, creating posters, acting, dancing, or playing rock music. Material possessions did not guide Goldhill and his compatriots, who, unless they were doing something creative, would rather earn enough to get by and then "live joyously and creatively . . . close to God." The most introspective members of the counterculture, Hertzberg contended, were seeking religion, but religion of a "firsthand, personal and immediate variety" as revealed through LSD trips. That distinguished the Haight-Ashbury hippies from the North Beach beats. The latter, Hertzberg wrote, were "worldly and secular," while the hippies were "religious and ethereal." Some hippies possessed a "messianic" determination to transform "the square world."[18]

Michael Bowen of the San Francisco *Oracle* deemed himself a member of the Psychedelic Rangers, who, he explained, "are for everything good. It's very supersecret. They range around and straighten out the rot wherever they find it." Bowen went on, "The psychedelic baby is what is occurring here in the United States, with people taking LSD, dropping out, making these communities and so forth." The psychedelic baby would devour the cybernetic monster, fueled by "the strength of the electronic civilization." This did not suggest a return to savagery or the end of computer systems, but rather "a question of the mind being turned enough, so that it's involved in making things better. All this will result in a civilization that is super-beautiful. We're out to build an electric Tibet."[19]

At the close of his extended essay, Hertzberg acknowledged there was another aspect "to the hippie phenomenon." A good number of deeply troubled individuals and young runaways could be found in the Haight. Also disturbing were "the incipient anti-intellectualism" and the damage caused by drugs. As Hertzberg put it, "the hippie's euphoria is too often bought at the price of his intellectual and critical faculties." At a minimum, "overpowering boredom" loomed ahead for many hippies. Still, he applauded their "spontaneity, honesty and appreciation for the wonder of life."[20]

By contrast, *New York Times* reporter Gladwin Hill reported on February 23, 1967, that "LSD Spread in U.S. Alarms Doctors and Police." Both psychiatrists and police expressed a growing sense of helplessness regarding how to deal "with the nation's newest scourge," LSD. Dr. Keith Ditman, a psychiatrist at UCLA, opposed "making criminals out of LSD users" for that would dissuade them from obtaining treatment. California Attorney General Thomas Lynch blasted the drug trip as "a flight from reality." On a more positive note, the poet Leonard Wolf, a professor at San Francisco State University, established Happening House, intended to offer alternative courses and programs. In the same period, a Haight-Ashbury resident, Al Rinker, envisioned a "Switchboard" to provide information for the local hip community.[21]

Editor Warren Hinckle of *Ramparts*, now a leading fount for the New Left and the antiwar movement, presented a caustic article, "The Social History of the Hippies," in the March 1967 issue of his magazine. A welter of photographs accompanied the lengthy piece, including photographs of Timothy Leary, Allen Ginsberg, Ken Kesey, Jay Thelin, Ron Thelin, Emmett Grogan, Allen Cohen, Jerry Garcia, Bill Graham, Stanley Mouse, Alton Kelley, Jerry Rubin, and Mario Savio. Hinckle opened by writing about "the Summit Meeting" involving "leaders of the new hippie subculture," who had gathered at the base of the California High Sierras in early February. He referred to the Day-Glo inflected school bus of the

Merry Pranksters, calling Kesey a "novelist turned psychedelic Hotspur" and Neal Cassady, the driver of the bus, "the Tristam Shandy of the Beat Generation" who abandoned Jack Kerouac after "the beat scene became menopausal." But Allen Ginsberg and Timothy Leary were not present at the summit. To Hinckle, "the absence of the elder statesmen of America's synthetic gypsy movement," who might well "be Pied Pipers," was revealing. It suggested that Ginsberg and Leary were basically "playing old tunes," while the younger men involved with "the booming psychedelic bohemia" in the Bay Area "were their own men." Hinckle saw the Haight-Ashbury district as "a little psychedelic city-state edging Golden Gate Park," where as many as "15,000 unbonded girls and boys" were conducting "a tribal, love-seeking, free-swinging, acid-based type of society." In one remarkable moment, Hinckle reflected on the long-haired, paisley-dressed young men of the Haight, who otherwise "sounded for all the world like Young Republicans." After all, Hinckle noted, "they talked about reducing government controls, the sanctity of the individual, the need for equality among men." They envisioned the kind of society they aspired to, and believed that they would have to create it, recognizing that government would never do so. [22]

At the same time, Hinckle refused to dismiss the utopian sensibilities of the hippies. They possessed, he wrote, "a clear vision of the ideal community—a psychedelic community . . . where everybody is turned on and beautiful and loving and happy and floating free." Notwithstanding its "Alice in Wonderland phraseology," Hinckle continued, that vision exuded "a radical political philosophy: communal life, drastic restriction of private property, rejection of violence, creativity before consumption, freedom before authority, de-emphasis of government and traditional forms of leadership." While the hippies exhibited a troubling propensity to "quietism," they conveyed a political stance involving "unremitting opposition to the Establishment" that deemed them criminals and social misfits because of their drug use, sexual practices, communal ways, and readiness to "raise healthy children in dirty clothes." The hippies appeared ready "to love the Establishment to death rather than protest it or blow it up." Taking the hippies seriously, Hinckle believed they might well create "the first utopian collectivist community since Brook Farm." Meanwhile, the Diggers were attempting to convince Kesey to attend the conclave. Kesey, Hinckle suggested, had "abdicated his role as Scoutmaster to fledgling acid heads," while engaging in "the one mortal sin in the hippie ethos: *telling* people what to do." That made him, in Hinckle's words, "a hippie has-been." Kesey would still have "his hippie memories," because he "did for acid roughly what Johnny Appleseed did for trees, and probably more," through the Acid Tests. [23]

Tracing the history of the counterculture, Hinckle looked back to "two distinct strains in the underground movement of the '50s." Jack Kerouac, in his estimation, exemplified "a distinctly fascist trend . . . recognized by a totalitarian insistence on action and in nihilism, and usually accompanied by a Superman concept." Such a strain coursed "deeper and less silent, through the hippie scene today," Hinckle warned. He placed Kesey and the Hell's Angels, along with Leary, somewhat more subtly, "into this fascist bag." By contrast, the dominant strain associated with the beats, as exemplified by Ginsberg and Lawrence Ferlinghetti, involved adopting "the role of conscience for the machine," rejecting all values, and telling "America to 'go fuck itself.'" The introduction of psychedelics, initially peyote, then mescaline, and later LSD, altered the countercultural scene in first Greenwich Village and later North Beach and Haight-Ashbury. [24]

Hinckle ridiculed the "merchant princes," figures like Leary and rock impresario Bill Graham, who were financially benefiting from the "little psychedelic city-state" emerging in the Haight-Ashbury district. While Leary claimed to have birthed America's first native religion, Hinckle described Dr. Leary as "Aimee Semple McPherson in drag," while acknowledging that he had contributed mightily "to the psychedelic scene" by helping spread the gospel of LSD. As for rock promoter Bill Graham, Hinckle saw him as "the biggest Robber Baron" who controlled "the hippie bread and circuses concession." [25]

After proclaiming that *The Lord of the Rings* was "absolutely the favorite book of every hippie," and pointing to Frodo Baggins as the hero of J. R. R. Tolkien's trilogy, Hinckle indicated that the Diggers' Emmett Grogan was "the closest thing" Haight-Ashbury hippies had "to a real live hero." Grogan was repeatedly in and out of jail, including for having belted a policeman. He was equally troubling to hip entrepreneurs, believing they had no right to charge hippies "for their daily needs." For his part, Grogan dismissed hippie merchants as "nothing but goddamn shopkeepers with beards." Everybody in the Haight-Ashbury district, Hinckle said, feared Grogan, "a one-man crusade for purity of purpose" and "the conscience of the hippie community." Hinckle also called him something "of a daredevil and a madman," likening Grogan to Randle McMurphy, the protagonist of Kesey's *One Flew over the Cuckoo's Nest*. Grogan and the Diggers appeared to impress Hinckle the most, along with their determination to seed "a wholly cooperative subculture." Freedom most mattered to Grogan, who considered New York City's Mad Bomber and Gary Snyder his heroes because they did their own thing.[26]

Such an ethos, however, was problematic, Hinckle offered, who predicted that few would participate in Grogan's utopia. Meanwhile, the hip merchants would keep making money, as more young people came to the Haight. Grogan recognized that a gap existed "between the radical political philosophy of Jerry Rubin and Mario Savio and psychedelic love philosophy." Because he recognized that simply sniffing flowers would not suffice, Grogan was infuriated by the hip storekeepers. "They created the myth of this utopia; now they aren't going to do anything about it." He worried about the impending summer, when "a psychedelic 'Grapes of Wrath'" beckoned. Hinckle additionally warned that if more young people adopted "the hippie political posture of unrelenting quietism, the future of activist, serious politics is bound to be affected." Yes, the hippies had demonstrated "it can be pleasant to drop out of the arduous task of attempting to steer a difficult, unrewarding society." However, "when that is done, you leave the driving to the Hell's Angels."[27] Hinckle's diatribe induced contributing editor Ralph J. Gleason to resign from *Ramparts*.[28] It also resulted in a broadsheet from the Communication Camp that termed Hinckle a "FANTASY PROFIT SHIT-EATING BASTARD," whose piece on the hippies was riddled with "LIES," defended Kesey, and indicated that if one required a leader to show the way, "that's your hangup."[29]

During this period, Allen Ginsberg again attempted to create a bridge between the counterculture and the movement. As he saw it, "the hippies have deeper insight into consciousness, the radicals more information about the workings and nature of consciousness in the world." He believed in the necessity of returning "to magic, to psychic life," viewing power as "a hallucination." Ginsberg recognized that "whoever controls the language, the images, controls the race." In the April 1967 issue of *Liberation*, he declared, "America's political need is orgies in the park."[30]

On April 5, the Council for the Summer of Love held a press conference regarding the anticipated flood of scores of thousands of young people who would soon arrive in San Francisco. Participants included the

Diggers, the Family Dog, the Straight Theater, and *The Oracle*. Along with Dr. David Smith, they helped to bring about the establishment of the Haight-Ashbury Free Clinic. They also assisted the Reverend Larry Beggs, who set up the Huckleberry House for Runaways. The council joined with the Diggers to ensure that people had food and shelter.

Associated with the Diggers, Chester Anderson of the Communication Company delivered a warning on April 6, 1967, about those who supposedly were guiding the counterculture. "Beware of leaders, heroes, organizers: watch that stuff. Beware of structure-freaks. They do not understand." In a devastating opening, the manifesto, titled "Uncle Tim's Children," stated bluntly, "Pretty little 16-year-old middle-class chick comes to the Haight to see what it's all about and gets picked up by a 17-year-old street dealers who spends all day shooting her full of speed again and again, then feeds her 3,000 mikes and raffles her off temporarily unemployed body for the biggest Haight Street gang bang since the night before last."[31]

Anderson dismissed "the politics and ethics of ecstasy," declaring, "Rape is as common as bullshit on Haight Street." As for the hip merchants, they, who had "sold our lovely little psychedelic community to the mass media, the world," appeared "blithely and sincerely unaware of what they have done." Somehow, they ignored the "hunger, hip brutality, rape, gangbangs, gonorrhea, syphilis, theft, hunger filth." Haight Street had devolved into "uglyshitdeath," while Alan Watts called for "more elegant attire." In another brutally honest pronouncement, Anderson asserted that the hip merchants failed to understand how "they and Uncle Timothy have lured an army of children into a ghastly trap from which there is no visible escape. They do not see that they are destroying a whole generation of American youth." But then, after all, "they are what they are: businessmen, salesmen, money counters." Meanwhile, "the HIP merchants" had drawn "a million children here recklessly and irresponsibly," with more arriving daily. By contrast, only the Diggers, so little appreciated by the merchants, were behaving responsibly, attempting to feed and nurture those children. The hip merchants, on the other hand, "are The System, playing The System's games in The System's way, and they don't give a flaccid fuck about you or me or any of their sheep," Anderson exclaimed.[32]

In a follow-up memo, the Communication Company acknowledged that the Thelin brothers, who operated the Psychedelic Shop, were "most unusual people." Yes, they had been fully "indoctrinated in the U.S. business ethic," but "they really *are* turned-on people, steeped in the love of love, incredibly eager to fill the world with love, genuinely good people." The Communication Company expressed delight that the brothers were converting their store into a cooperative; consequently, the Communication Company would no longer consider Ron and Jay Thelin merchants to be damned in the manner "of so picayune a class."[33]

The Communication Company's Claude Hayward and Anderson also took to task the UPS, of which it was a member, for failing to report that members of the Loving Spoonful, the beloved folk-rock group, had helped the police bust Bill Loughborough, manager of the improvisational theater group, the Committee. Hayward and Anderson claimed that Loughborough had been set up, then charged with having delivered drugs to the Spoonful's bass guitarist Steve Boone and lead guitarist Zal Yasinski. Now, Hayward and Anderson exclaimed, "TO KNOW WHAT IS THIS FUCKING BULLSHIT SILENCE THAT COMES FROM THE UNDERGROUND PRESS!" They declared that the UPS either stood for something, which demanded that the Spoonful story be told, "or else the Underground Press Syndicate is nothing more than the same old America shit in a bright new polyethylene extruded psychedelic wrapper."[34]

The Bay Area countercultural scene continued to receive extensive coverage, some of it bordering on the positive, from the establishment press. The April 27 edition of *The Wall Street Journal* contained an article, "Offbeat 'Diggers' Aid Drifters in Bohemian Area of San Francisco." The Diggers, the newspaper pointed out, were providing housing for "as many as 300 youngsters a night" and "free hot meals to nearly 500 hippies a day." The Diggers also handed out free clothing, covered legal and medical costs, bailed young people out of jail, and provided counseling for those experiencing bad LSD trips. One sociologist praised the Diggers as "the only meaningful social agency" operating in the Haight-Ashbury district. Moreover, "the Digger movement" appeared ready to spread beyond San Francisco, into Los Angeles and New York City's Lower East Side. When asked why the Diggers offered the services they did, the part-time poet Tobacco answered, "Somebody has to take responsibility of these kids." Presently, the Diggers planned "to raise carrots, beans, apples and chickens" on 31 acres of farmland in Northern California.[35]

Also that spring, disc jockey Tom Donahue began his program on KMPX, pledging "no jingles, no talkovers, no time and temp, no pop singles," thereby kicking off underground commercial rock radio.[36] As Donahue indicated later that year, the all-hits formula that dominated rock stations strove for "the lowest common denominator," with disc jockeys serving as "robots performing their inanities at the direction of programmers who have succeeded in totally squeezing the human element out of their sound, reducing it to a series of blips and bleeps and happy, yes, always happy, sounding cretins who are poured from bottles every three hours."[37] By contrast, listeners could hear full albums on KMPX, rather than the two-to-three-minute slices of pop music on virtually every other radio station featuring rock 'n' roll.[38]

The May 1967 issue of the *New York Times Magazine* contained an article by the iconoclastic journalist Hunter S. Thompson, "The 'Hashbury' Is the Capital of the Hippies." Thompson contended that "the hot center of revolutionary action on the Coast began moving across the bay to San Francisco's Haight-Ashbury district" the previous year. He referred to the district as the "Hashbury," and said it was "the new capital of what is rapidly becoming the drug culture." Its inhabitants included hippies, among them many "refugees from Berkeley and the old North Beach scene." The latter, Thompson indicated, were far less "provincial" than the young people frequenting Haight-Ashbury. They were well read, well traveled, and possessed "friends all over the globe." Thompson attempted to explain the denizens of the new hip scene. "Hippies despise phoniness; they want to be open, honest, loving and free. They reject the plastic pretense of 20th-century America, preferring to go back to the 'natural life,' like Adam and Eve." They failed to identify with the beats, considering them too negative, or with politics, which they saw as "just another game." They disliked money and aggressiveness of any sort. Veterans of the beat era in turn worried that Haight-Ashbury, like North Beach and Greenwich Village earlier, would be enveloped by publicity and commercialism. In the manner of the Diggers, Thompson jabbed at hip merchants, stating that few genuine hippies, in contrast to weekend "borderline" ones, could afford the expensive sandals and mod apparel being sold, or the $3.50 entrance fee at the Fillmore and the Avalon. Thompson particularly underscored the presence and ubiquity of drugs. He also warned that there were simply too many "penniless heads," who were overwhelming even "the mass sharing" ethos of the Diggers.

Thompson predicted an influx of as many as "200,000 indigent young people," which, he noted, "appalled" the Diggers. They wondered where those young people would stay and what they would do, with one young woman affirming that the Diggers would keep attending to "the casualties of the love generation." At the same time, Police Chief Cahill warned, "Law and order will prevail," and insisted that no sleeping would be allowed in Golden Gate Park. [39]

Concluding his write-up, Thompson blasted "the vicious excesses of our drug laws," which precluded a genuine account of the hippie phenomenon. That required, he stated bluntly, taking psychedelics, or else one was "a fool and a fraud." He likened the situation to Prohibition when journalists drank freely, declaring that many journalists were "unregenerate heads." As a recent ten-day trip to San Francisco revealed, professional journalists doped regularly. If he were able to write about this, Thompson continued, he would deem Haight-Ashbury "little more than a freak show and a soft-sell advertisement for what is happening all around . . . that drugs, orgies and freak-outs are almost as common" throughout comfortable sections of San Francisco as in the city's "new Bohemia." Underscoring his point, Thompson asserted, "The current Haight-Ashbury scene is only the orgiastic tip of a great psychedelic iceberg." Thompson saw political activism waning, with more seeking "merely to escape, to live on the far perimeter of a world that might have been—perhaps should have been." [40]

New York Times reporter Martin Arnold discussed the fact that hippies in Haight-Ashbury were becoming more organized, and threatening to transform the "the hippie capital . . . into just another Bohemia or East Village." He dismissively declared that "hippies stand for nothing," offering a quote from one, "Why can't I stand on a street corner and wait for nobody? Why can't everyone?" He acknowledged that "old-line hippies" were "definitely religious," believing that "God is Love." However, younger hippies appeared to operate somewhat distinctly, exuding more of an anarchistic quality provided that doing so didn't impinge on others. No matter such differences, Arnold bluntly wrote, "all pure hippies, both boys and girls, have long and dirty hair," which came about from their failure to pay bills and the inevitable resulting turning off of the water "in their pads." Arnold thought that what distinguished the Haight-Ashbury hippies from other bohemians was their "strong communal sense," as exemplified by the Diggers. The hippies professed love for all, but "nobody here loves the hippies," Arnold wrote from San Francisco.[41]

Also in May, the Los Angeles band, Strawberry Alarm Clock, reissued a single, with "Incense and Peppermints" converted to the A-side. With kaleidoscopic lyrics, the song referred to innocence, "Dead kings," "Cajun spice," "games we choose," "beatniks and politics," and "a yardstick for lunatics," among other matters. After a quick dash up the pop charts, it would do even better later in the year, following the Summer of Love.[42]

Meanwhile, momentum continued building toward that Summer of Love, with discussions regarding a pop festival in Monterey, south of San Francisco and San Jose. Monterey, with its breathtaking view of the Pacific Ocean, had hosted a jazz festival since 1958, and a folk festival five years later. Following the 1966 Monterey Jazz Festival, Alan Pariser, heir to the Dixie Lily Sweetpaper Cup Company fortune, spearheaded the CAFF concert after the Sunset Strip riots that induced Buffalo Springfield's Stephen Stills to write "For What It's Worth." The song opened with the ominous refrain, "There's something happening here / What it is ain't exactly clear," and the pointing to a gun-wielding man. Stills sang about "battle lines being drawn," and opinionated young people facing resistance, as a thousand people ended up in the street. He talked about paranoia digging deep roots, overwhelming the individual, who worried that "the man" would bust him.[43] The Byrds, the Doors, the Springfield, and Peter, Paul, and Mary were among the headliners who appeared at that benefit, designed to assist those arrested. Pariser then envisioned a larger pop festival, soon hooking up with Benny Shapiro, well connected within the music industry. In early 1967, Pariser and Shapiro created a partnership to carry out a pop festival in Monterey.

During the spring, Pariser talked to John Phillips of the Mamas and Papas, the folk-rock group that had seemingly carved out a comfortable niche at the top of the pop charts, about performing at the festival. Instead, Phillips and his producer, Lou Adler, pushed Shapiro aside and sharply curtailed Pariser's role. Using their connections, Phillips and Adler set up a board of directors for the festival, which included Paul McCartney, Mick Jagger, the Rolling Stones' manager Andrew Loog Oldham, Donovan, Brian Wilson of the Beach Boys, Jim McGuinn of the Byrds, and Smokey Robinson. They also garnered a $250,000 contract with ABC, and agreed to allow independent filmmaker D. A. Pennebaker, who had recently completed *Don't Look Back*, which traced Bob Dylan's concert tour of the United Kingdom in 1965, to shoot the festival. The producers met with the *San Francisco Chronicle*'s Ralph J. Gleason, who initially proved noncommittal; Danny Rifkin, co-manager of the Grateful Dead; and the Diggers' Emmett Grogan. To placate the Diggers, Phillips pledged that "no money will go to a hippie organization."[44]

To help promote the festival and at Adler's behest, Phillips carved out a song, "San Francisco (Be Sure to Wear Some Flowers in Your Hair)," which Scott McKenzie recorded. Released on May 13, 1967, the song shot up the pop charts in both the United States and Europe. Although later panned by many critics, the Phillips's hopeful but wistful tune captured something of the atmosphere surrounding the anticipated Summer of Love. It urged those coming to the city to sport flowers and be prepared to encounter "some gentle people there." The summer of 1967 in San Francisco, Phillips wrote, would "be a love-in there." This, moreover, merely replicated something that was occurring across the United States. Seemingly, an entire generation was "in motion," possessing "a new explanation."[45]

The Communication Company parodied Phillips's song, talking about "rioting in the ghettos (sic)," employing the refrain "Hair a Krishna," charging that Phillips and other artists were triggering the Summer of Love, warning that gentle people might be "raging in the streets," and concluding that if things didn't pan out in San Francisco, then hippies could try it in London.[46] Despite the scathing attack, the song's commercial success served to promote both the Monterey Pop Festival and the Summer of Love, the latter at least to the chagrin of the Diggers and many established residents of the Bay Area. Also flying high on the Billboard Hot 100 was Jefferson Airplane's "Somebody to Love," with Darby Slick's poignant lyrics and Grace Slick's haunting vocals, which proved another lure to thousands of young people. Soon appearing was *Sgt. Pepper's Lonely Hearts Club Band*, which many saw as an anthem to the counterculture.

The same day that Scott McKenzie's rendition of "San Francisco" was released, the Council for the Summer of Love delivered an announcement asserting that "this summer, the youth of the world are making a holy pilgrimage to our city, to affirm and celebrate a new spiritual dawn."[47] This was but "a small part of a worldwide spiritual awakening." San Francisco was the temporary "focus of this awakening," which was "a gift from God." In preparation for the large number of young people expected to arrive, the council planned to put up a mammoth tent that would "contain a field kitchen, sleeping facilities, educational programs, concerts, art shows, lectures and similar activities." Also planned were "a Summer Solstice Festival, a Tolkien Festival of Elves and Hobbits, festivals of Christ, of Krishna, of the young and of the old."[48] The esteemed British historian Arnold Toynbee, who was seventy years old, offered his analysis of the Haight-Ashbury district for the *London Observer.* "The leaders of the Establishment will be making the mistake of their lives if they discount and ignore the revolt of the hippies and many of the hippies' non hippie contemporaries on the grounds that these are either disgraceful wastrels or traitors, or else just silly kids who are sowing their wild oats."[49] On a more ominous note, the Communication Company, still associated with Chester Anderson and the Diggers, put out a flyer declaring, "An Armed Man Is a Free Man," and word got out that the Diggers, like several others in the district, were packing guns.[50] The greater availability of amphetamines and the growing number of speed freaks on the street little helped matters. Partially in response to the heightened concern about bad trips and mounting cases of venereal disease, the Haight-Ashbury Free Medical Clinic opened in early June, founded by Dr. David Smith, an intern at San Francisco General Hospital. Smith also established *The Journal of Psychedelic Drugs* that summer.

Back on the East Coast, two hundred young people referred to as "hippies" in the *New York Times* waged a battle with police in Tompkins Square Park, on New York City's Lower East Side. The New East Village Area and Steps for Community, formed by "hippie businessmen," was hosting a series of art performances and concerts. The confrontation occurred after police demanded a halt to the pounding of bongo drums and the chanting of "Hare Krishna." Cries of "Heil!" and "Fascist!" rang out, and "a human chain" appeared, soon broken up by police wielding night-sticks. Thirty-eight arrests followed, with one individual calling out, "Where is this happening? This is America. Everything is free," but several women shouted at the police, "We know we love you." Later, at the courthouse, a group marched outside, chanting, "Police brutality must go," along with "Flower power, not Fascist power." One neighborhood resident warned, "They'll have to have thousands of cops this summer if they're going to try and keep us off the grass."[51]

Stephen A. O. Golden wrote about a commune of "diggers" in the East Village, who resided on 11th Street between Avenue B and Avenue C, and included young people he profiled such as Galahad, Groovy, Runaway, Kitty, and Kelly. Twenty-one-year-old Galahad, a transplant from Kansas City, decried the fact that police had raided his "digger" apartment "about 30 times" within the past two-and-a-half months. While other hippies in the East Village spoke of "Love as the be-all and end-all," Galahad talked about God. While the police disliked his compatriots, Galahad insisted that "J. C. guards this place and us. He won't let anything bad happen. It's got to work. We have a beautiful thing here—something I don't want to see disappear."[52] Another confrontation occurred in Tompkins Square Park, as someone threw a bottle at a policeman and a nearly nude, twenty-nine-year-old woman was arrested. By June 3, 1967, the *New York Times* was warning in a headline, "Hippies Heighten East Side Tensions," with the accompanying article discussing racial and ethnic tensions in the neighborhood around Tompkins Square Park. Out-of-state tourists began congregating to the area to check out "the Lower East Side's new hippies haven." Later that summer, a Criminal Court judge dismissed the charges against the defendants arrested following the clash with police in Tompkins Square Park, although he blasted them as "unwashed, unshod, unkempt and uninhibited."[53]

The Monterey Pop Festival took place from June 16–18 at the Monterey County Fairgrounds, with each of five shows costing between $3.00 and $6.50, and as many as ninety thousand in attendance by festival's end. The Rolling Stones' Brian Jones and Nico, the actress and singer for the Velvet Underground, were present. Performers included Eric Burdon and the Animals, Simon and Garfunkel, Big Brother and the Holding Company with Janis Joplin, Country Joe and the Fish, Quicksilver Messenger Service, the Steve Miller Band, Moby Grape, the Byrds, Jefferson Airplane, Otis Redding, Buffalo Springfield, The Who, the Grateful Dead, the Jimi Hendrix Experience, and the Mamas and the Papas. The performances by Joplin, Redding, and Hendrix catapulted each into the national limelight. Joplin's renditions of "Down on Me" and "Ball and Chain," Redding's offerings of "Shake" and "Try a Little Tenderness," and Hendrix's "Foxy Lady," "Hey Joe," and "Wild Thing" proved especially electrifying.

With the Summer of Love playing out in the Haight-Ashbury district, the Diggers announced they were conducting "Feed-Ins" daily at two in the afternoon, and providing housing for those in need of it.[54] They considered their offering of food, shelter, and clothing a mere starting point,

and consequently intended to conduct a series of workshops to help cultivate skills from sewing to automobile repair. The Diggers wanted to help
empower those who were presently powerless, while not acting like the
Establishment individuals were escaping. The Diggers also sought to cultivate "talk-ins" that would allow for discussions of "new philosophies,
ideas or values." Admittedly, "We don't profess to know the answers, but
we hope together we will find some," the Diggers stated. They aspired to
nurture tolerance, in keeping with seemingly "consciously aware" and
"enlightened" individuals. "Among the restless and wandering breed,"
the Diggers believed, "a vast wasteland of intellectual" existed, which
was too often blunted. Youth appeared to lack anything in the way of a
future. The Diggers sought to assist those who were alienated. The Diggers' philosophy involved "love, tolerance and understanding of the
young, the old and the helpless and those with different views." Such an
approach, the Diggers hoped, would prove "contagious."

Writing in the June 26, 1967, issue of *The Nation*, Jack Newfield of
The Village Voice delivered "One Cheer for the Hippies." To Newfield,
"individually, the hippies are beautiful." They recognized that pot was
"mildly pleasant"; that Bob Dylan, John Lennon, and Leonard Cohen
offered "authentic poetic voices"; that making love was better than waging war; that spontaneity, communal ways, and tolerance were healthier
than repression, materialism, and bigotry; "and that it is groovy to read
Hermann Hesse, Snoopy and Allen Ginsberg." At the same time, Newfield declared "that the hippies have been overrated," with their vision "in
no way superior to that of the New Left, of Mailer, Camus or Pynchon."
Also back on the East Coast at the Newport Folk Festival, Arlo Guthrie
delivered "Alice's Restaurant," his extended riff on having been busted
for tossing out trash and subsequently compelled to go to the induction
center at 39 Whitehall Street in Manhattan. The long-haired son of the
radical folk musician Woody Guthrie presented a humorous but scathing
indictment of the draft process, with Arlo supposedly tossed into the
group of unsavory sorts that included "Mother rapers. Father stabbers.
Father rapers!"[55]

The cover of the July 7, 1967, issue of *Time* displayed the rendering
by the Group Image, a cooperative of hippie artists in New York City's
East Village, of a long-haired rock group, with the headline, "The Hippies: Philosophy of a Subculture." The magazine's lead story quoted from
a sociologist, who referred to the hippies as "the Freudian proletariat."

Episcopalian bishop James Pike likened them to the first followers of Jesus Christ: "There is something about the temper and quality of these people, a gentleness, a quietness, an interest—something good." *Time* delivered its own analysis, stating that the hippie phenomenon constituted "a wholly new subculture, a bizarre permutation of the middle-class American ethos from which it evolved." Hippies were said to "preach altruism and mysticism, honesty, joy and nonviolence," and to be seeking "nothing less than the subversion of Western society by 'flower power' and force of example." The nation's leading mass circulation magazine suggested that such "unreality" characterized "hippiedom, a cult whose mystique derives essentially from the influence of hallucinogenic drugs." And yet *Time* acknowledged that the counterculture's largely young adherents were "generally thoughtful," but had turned into "internal emigres, seeking individual liberation" by way of drugs, the rejection of capitalism, and a quest for personal identity. The hippies no longer appeared to be as faddish as had been predicted just a year earlier, with enclaves cropping up in all large metropolitan centers in the United States, with "a 50-member cabal in, of all places, Austin, Texas." There were also international way stations in Europe, the Near East, and Asia, as pilgrims sought drugs and "Buddhist lore." The Haight-Ashbury district, *Time* declared, was "the vibrant epicenter of the hippie movement."[56]

Time quoted New York Senator Robert F. Kennedy, who stated, "They want to be recognized as individuals, but individuals play a smaller and smaller role in society. This is a formidable and forbidding arrangement." Consequently, hippies sought to carve out "an entirely new society, one rich in spiritual grace that will revive the old virtues of agape and reverence." The hippies demonstrated, Professor Martin E. Marty of the University of Chicago Divinity School suggested, "the exhaustion of a tradition: Western, production-directed, problem-solving, goal-oriented, and compulsive in its way of thinking." Smartly, *Time* recognized that rising utopianism suffused "the hippie philosophy," but was "purely Arcadian: pastoral and primordial, emphasizing oneness with physical and psychic nature." Professor Northrop Frye of the University of Toronto considered the hippies to be following the "outlawed and furtive social ideal known as the 'Land of the Cockaigne,' the fairyland where all desires can be instantly gratified." The hippies also drew from Henry David Thoreau, with communards attempting to carve out a "Waldenesque good life on the bare essentials," such as "a diet of turnips and brown rice, fish and bean curd." They seemingly harked back as well to Jesus, Rabbi Hillel, Buddha, and St. Francis, all of whom were icons for various members of the counterculture. More recent heroes included Gandhi, Aldous Huxley, and the hobbits created by J. R. R. Tolkien. The dominant ethical component of the hippies, *Time* offered, was "love— indiscriminate and all-embracing, fluid and changeable, directed at friend and foe alike." Like their immediate predecessors, the beats, hippies contested sexual norms, partook of drugs, engaged in wanderlust, and proved interested in Oriental mysticism. But the hippies were far more colorful, more white, seemingly lacked leaders, favored psychedelic drugs, particularly LSD, and gravitated to rural communes. Somewhat remarkably, *Time* concluded its extended essay by acknowledging that in rejecting materialism and exalting "peacefulness and honesty," the hippies might well be conducting "considerably more virtuous lives than the great majority of their fellow citizens." On the other hand, *Time* soon warned about LSD causing possible damages to chromosomes. [57]

12

THE DEATH OF HIPPIE AND
EARLY POSTMORTEMS

The Summer of Love 1967 continued in San Francisco, with "All You Need Is Love," the Beatles' anthem to the counterculture, released on the very day imprinted on the issue of *Time* exploring the hippie phenomenon. The anticipated crush of new arrivals in the Haight-Ashbury district proved less overwhelming than had been feared, and yet a host of social pathologies soon became apparent. Young people milled about, with any number homeless and directionless, targets for abuse of all sorts. The police continued conducting drug raids, as new drugs appeared on the scene, most ominous of all, STP, supposedly standing for "Serenity, Tranquility, Peace," and a byproduct of Dow Chemical experiments; the U.S. Army Chemical Corps and the CIA both employed the drug in carrying out "behavior modification studies." As STP arrived on the streets of the Haight, bad trips proliferated. Physicians passed out Thorazine to alleviate unfortunate LSD experiences, but it only exacerbated STP's impact. Another drug coursing through the district was PCP, referred to as "angel dust," employed by the CIA during Operation MKULTRA, and used as an animal tranquilizer. Heroin also became more available.

Then in early August, two well-known acid dealers in the Haight, John Kent Carter, called Shob, and William Thomas, known as Superspade, were killed. *Time* magazine wrote about the "End of the Dance," discussing Eric Dahlstrom's statement that a bad trip had compelled him to murder Shob Carter. Speculation grew that Dahlstrom had actually been on speed, and Dr. David E. Smith warned, "Amphetamines are the biggest drug problem now in the Haight."[1] The August 22 issue of *The Oracle* included Allen Cohen's "In Memoriam for Superspade and John Carter," charging that a "state of mind called Mafia" resulted in the killings, and insisted that drugs be free.[2] On August 23, CBS News presented a program, *The Hippie Temptation*, hosted by Harry Reasoner, which contended that hallucinations guided the hippies.[3] The next day a purported "band of hippies," spearheaded by James Fourrat and Abbie Hoffman, tossed dollar bills onto the New York Stock Exchange. Fourrat forecast, "It's the death of money."[4]

In September, the Grateful Dead started work on their second album, *Anthem of the Sun*, eventually recorded in North Hollywood, New York City, and San Francisco. This time, the Dead largely featured only their own songs, including those on which their longtime lyricist Robert C. Hunter, one of the early volunteers in the same psychedelic experiments at Stanford involving Ken Kesey, contributed.[5]

In the September 1967 issue of *Evergreen Review*, *San Francisco Chronicle* columnist Ralph J. Gleason declared that members of the Love Generation made up "the most powerful single social movement in the country amongst Caucasians." Moreover, "they generate psychic forces; they accomplish things and" had fostered a community capable of overcoming "guerrilla attacks" meted out by the Establishment and mainstream society. They were turning aside Timothy Leary's admonition to "turn on, tune in and drop out," but opted instead for something far more constructive and creative. They were shaping "a new set of values, a new structure, a new society . . . horizontal to the old but in it." Through "communes, handcrafts, survival in the wilderness, farming," they were seeking to demonstrate "*how* to live *now*." Gleason referred to the Diggers as "the self-appointed conscience of the community," and the practitioners of doing "your thing." Perhaps the Diggers would be unable to "change the world," he admitted. But they had fostered a new sensibility regarding material possessions, particularly money, and conformity.[6]

The September 23, 1967, issue of the *Saturday Evening Post* offered an editorial on "Our Mysterious Children," and an involved essay by Joan Didion, "Slouching towards Bethlehem." The one-page commentary deemed San Francisco hippies "worthy successors to the beatniks, the goldfish swallowers, and the marathon dancers of yesteryear," while questioning how seriously they should be viewed. The middle-aged, the magazine acknowledged, proved inclined "to moralize about the wild wickedness of the young." At the same time, "sociological soothsayers" invariably examined current fads for signs of what the future portended. As if engaging in yin and yang itself, the *Saturday Evening Post* admitted that the determination of so many young people to withdraw from society suggested something was wrong with it. However, it remained questionable, the *Post* indicated, "how many do drop out." For each hippie wandering through San Francisco, there were numerous young people involved "in the competitive grind" of attending school, working, "and all the rest." The latter appeared "much more ordinary," but also "much more important," the magazine offered. "Our Mysterious Children" noted that the examination of the hippies was merely part of an "obsessive fashion with young people." Myths existed that they made up a huge cohort, and were economically and culturally potent, but the editorial refuted those notions. After all, the median age would rise as the baby boomers aged. Additionally, their purported affluence appeared as yet another myth, as did the theory that the young would prove culturally influential. Extended education explained something of the youth phenomenon, as students possessed seemingly "endless time for endless chatter and self-contemplation," the editorial argued. "In trying to protect our children so long, we let them remain overgrown children, restless and basically helpless. It is this life that the hippies, far from dropping out, pathetically cling to." Eventually, however, the *Saturday Evening Post* concluded, "even the wildest teenagers usually abandon the false independence of Bohemia" and enter the workforce.[7]

Didion indicated that she had gone to San Francisco because that "was where the social hemorrhaging was showing up." In one of the more telling moments in her lengthy essay, Didion quoted from a psychiatrist in San Francisco, who denied that the experience in the Haight was simply about drugs. "It's a social movement, quintessentially romantic, the kind that recurs in times of real social crisis. The themes are always the same. A return to innocence. The invocation of an earlier authority and control. The mysteries of the blood. An itch for the transcendental, for purification." That way led to "trouble . . . to authoritarianism," the psychiatrist warned. At the same time, Didion noted that while many young people in the Haight appeared apolitical, the Diggers were "imaginatively anarchic," and recognized that "something important" was tak-

ing place. "We were seeing the desperate attempt of a handful of pathetically unequipped children to create a community in a social vacuum."[8]

In a type of postmortem, Nicholas von Hoffman of the *Washington
Post*, who had spent a good deal of time in the Haight-Ashbury district
during the summer of 1967, subsequently published a book, *We Are the
People Our Parents Warned Us Against*. In a brief preface, von Hoffman
discussed the gathering together of young people in large cities across the
country, who violated drug laws without compunction, "proudly, publicly, and defiantly." In the process, they articulated "a different social philosophy and a new politics," while possibly creating "a subculture . . .
new to America." Von Hoffman chose to focus particularly on the
Haight, which had garnered so much attention, while quoting liberally
from both well-known figures in the counterculture and others as well.
Rock Scully, who helped to manage the Grateful Dead, referred to the
group's initial turn to LSD three years earlier, and how members of the
band discovered "what it was like to feel community and take care of our
brothers." But now, Scully acknowledged, "We just can't keep up with
these kids." The members of the Grateful Dead had been "pioneers in
LSD," but "took it very sparingly" in comfortable surroundings. Young
people, by contrast, dropped acid "two and three times a week and go a
little crazy." During the Summer of Love, "every kind of freak" showed
up at the doorstep of the Dead in Haight-Ashbury, which Scully considered unfortunate. The Dead had "one cardinal rule" previously: "Do not
impose your trip on anyone else." However, "that's what these people are
doing, and we don't want to go on their trip," which amounted to "a
sidewalk freak show."[9]

The Haight, von Hoffman indicated, exhibited illuminating possibilities, with "plenty of elucidating philosophy" offered: "Zen, anarchism,
nihilism, Taoism, Jesus, astrology, visions of new social rectitudes." No
matter, what "people of the street" did was "deal dope." The Haight had
become "the acid center of the world," where it had initially been produced in bulk, was least expensive, and most readily acquired. But other
drugs were also sold, ranging from grass to heroin. All of this took place,
von Hoffman wrote, in an area that had become "a runaway scene" too.
As the summer moved along, graffiti on a coffeehouse wall indicated,
"WE ARE THE PEOPLE OUR PARENTS WARNED US AGAINST."
Von Hoffman noted that "every day the scene got a little heavier, a little
crazier." As marijuana became less available, and because LSD could

only be taken "every other day or so," more people turned to alcohol and speed. Consequently, "more freaky people appeared on the streets."[10]

Among those who attempted to make sense out of all of this, and to care for those on the street, were the poet Richard Brautigan, and Emmett Grogan and Peter Coyote of the Diggers. Astutely, von Hoffman referred to the Diggers as "members of the unorganized group of politically aware people in the Haight," who were "acting out the demonetized, communal society of their dreams." Regarding what compelled him to act as he did, Coyote stated, "I want to lay life. I want to taste it, beat it, feel it, kill it, fuck it, and I want to have all these things done to me." On a broader scale, he wanted to "take this system apart," to avoid the guilt feelings that beset college students. "I'd like to live a life that is free, so I begin living that way. I don't do it to teach or propagandize, but because I want to. To live an alternative that is totally outside the alternatives of this culture is a profoundly political act."[11]

Coyote and the Diggers, von Hoffman suggested, actually existed "on the fringes of the dope world of the Haight-Ashbury," despite the fact that "it was they who coined and popularized the love slogans" that became so popular. As von Hoffman saw it, the ideas that led the Diggers to invite newcomers to the Haight became enmeshed "in a flash-fire of a social movement that got completely out of their control." In the process, the Diggers became "irrelevant to the dope peddling, the avarice, and the human exploitation that" supplanted "their fraternal communitarian dream." And yet von Hoffman believed this "eclipse" was merely "temporary," as the Diggers represented "a current" bound to reemerge elsewhere. This involved "emotive, affective politics . . . of the gut, of feeling, of unqualified conviction," which insisted on "a perfect consistency between private and public life," and an absence of artifice. Von Hoffman saw this as emanating from "the affective politics of the left."[12]

We Are the People Our Parents Warned Us Against also quoted from hip entrepreneur Ron Thelin, who referred favorably to the Diggers' perspective. Thelin indicated that it was most difficult to overcome monetary relationships, and engage in "doing things for free instead of for money." It was important, Thelin indicated, to accept "new relationships . . . new styles . . . [a] new metaphor," to "turn on to Hare Krishna chants . . . Zen Buddhism . . . dancing." Individuals had been programmed since childhood, and to overcome that might require psychedelic experiences.[13]

In the *Atlantic Monthly* in September 1967, San Francisco resident Mark Harris, author of an acclaimed trilogy of baseball novels, including *Bang the Drum Slowly*, discussed at length "the Flowering of the Hippies" in the Haight-Ashbury district. As Harris indicated, "the best of the hippies . . . hoped to reclaim and distill the best promise of a movement which might yet invigorate American movement everywhere. It might, by resurrecting the word 'love,' and giving it a refreshened definition, open the national mind, as if by the chemical LSD, to the hypocrisy of violence and prejudice in a nation dedicated to peace and accord." The hippies aspired to love and sharing, Harris reflected, but their eyes frequently appeared "sorrowful and frightened," as they had engaged "in an experiment they were uncertain they could carry through." They sought community, but the question arose as what type of community. They were largely white boys and girls, "middle-class American children to the bone." They appeared drawn to the Orient, as demonstrated by their fondness for the *I Ching*, *The Prophet*, and *Siddhartha*. They were fascinated by "the occult, the astrological, the mystical, the horoscopic, and the Ouija." Harris placed Gibran's classic in the pantheon "of American self-help subliterature," declaring that "no sillier book exists." The attraction to Hermann Hesse hardly appeared to impress Harris more, for it replicated that by German youth generations earlier. Damningly, Harris noted that the hippies "were going through all these things twice, unaware of things gone through before." While satirizing American culture, they devised their own platitudes. More difficult was the attempt to carve out meaningful work, which the hippie aspired to "from the outset." Dealing with the straight community also entailed more effort, whether that involved acquiring housing, food, or telephone service. Acknowledging their "unwavering adherence to the ideal of nonviolence," Harris considered that miraculous and a valuable challenge to American practices at home and overseas.[14]

Lawrence Swaim wrote about "Hippies: The Love Thing" in the September 1967 issue of *The North American Review*. He indicated that large numbers were apolitical, equally cynical about both protest and the war in Vietnam. Many appeared to be replicating the perception, widely shared among lower-middle-class Americans, that because "politics stink . . . you might as well forget about" them. Swaim saw younger hippies as disinclined toward "existentialism and related literary, artistic, and social styles," dismissing them as products of the previous decade. He considered a "weariness," a "burning desire to stop disbelieving, to stop fighting, to get off the political and emotional limb," as integral "to the new bohemianism."[15]

The drug usage that characterized the hippie flowering and the recent Summer of Love resulted in a review by Stanford University's Richard Blum of *The Varieties of Psychedelic Experience*, delivered by sexologists R. E. L. Masters and Jean Houston. The authors argued that "the present alarm of LSD risks" was "exaggerated" provided a guide were carefully selected, that psychedelics could prove beneficial in the treatment of various social pathologies, and that normal individuals could receive "insight, integration, religiosity, joy" with the assistance of various drugs. Consequently, they believed that present legal restrictions on LSD research should be altered. At the same time, they admitted hallucinogens could prove dangerous, and that some individuals should avoid them. Blum continued to express belief in "a chemically expandable, complex, potentially religious and necessarily beautiful Unconscious."[16]

As the Summer of Love petered out, the Diggers proclaimed "The Death of Hippie" and the "birth of free man" in a broadside appearing in early October.[17] The manifesto opened with the declaration, "MEDIA CREATED THE HIPPIE WITH YOUR HUNGRY CONSENT. BE SOMEBODY. CAREERS ARE TO BE HAD FOR THE ENTERPRISING HIPPIE."[18] Invitations were posted, regarding the death of "Hippie, devoted son of Mass Media."[19] On October 6, residents of the Haight conducted a mock ceremony, but the *Berkeley Barb* charged this was "the same kind of media crap as the Be-In, the Summer of Love and all that, and the same people dishing it out."[20] Nevertheless, two hundred people followed behind a fifteen-foot-long coffin and ten pallbearers. Digger Arthur Lisch bemoaned how badly things had ended up.

The Psychedelic Shop closed its doors, with the announcement by the Thelin brothers on October 6, 1967, that they had attempted to transform the world and had succeeded. The Thelins prepared to head for Washington, D.C., where an attempt would be made to "exorcise" the Pentagon. One sign in the store indicated "BE FREE," while another exhorted, "NEBRASKA NEEDS YOU MORE THAN THE HAIGHT."[21] Publicity, Ron Thelin, charged, destroyed the Haight. "The mass media made us into hippies. We wanted to be free men and build a free community. The word hippy turned everybody off. . . . Well, the hippies are dead." Teddybear, who dealt pot and acid in the district, insisted, "There were never any flower children. It was the biggest fraud ever perpetrated on the American public." There had been no Summer of Love, he continued, but instead one "of bullshit," which the press constructed. "The so-called flower children came here to find something" the media built up, "and there was nothing to find," Teddybear declared. In reality, the Haight was "based on dope, not love."[22] Word was heard about the death of a curious icon for both the movement and the counterculture, Ernesto "Che" Guevara, the Argentine physician turned communist revolutionary, killed by Bolivian troops trained by the CIA.

In a brief essay, "Hippies: Where Have All the Flowers Gone?," *Time* explored "the most frolicsome funeral in memory." It recalled the shout that rang out during the procession, "Hippies are dead: now the Free Men will come through!" In dismissive fashion, *Time* stated that it was probably inevitable that "in the mecca (sic) of mindlessness," hippies announced their own demise. San Francisco hippies, the magazine reported, believed that "hip is no longer a fun trip," because of the constant media coverage, the appearance of "thousands of 'plastic' or part-time hippies, and the adoption by mainstream society of hippie language and practices." *Time* did see the funeral as an effort "to purify the Movement." It also reported that veteran hippies in the Haight-Ashbury district were displeased about the attention they had received, but also due to the appearance of speed freaks and venereal disease in the community. Because San Francisco had served as a pacesetter for hippies, *Time* considered it likely that other hippie enclaves in Los Angeles, Chicago, and New York City would experience similar disillusionment.[23]

A report from Martin Arnold in the *New York Times*, on October 15, hardly indicated that things looked better for the counterculture on the other side of the country. In an article titled "The East Village Today: Hippies Far from Happy as Slum Problems Grow," Arnold referred to the seemingly innocent summer days when rock 'n' roll music and the smell of pot wafted through the air, as hippies "lolled on the grass." That promising "adventure in freedom" had given way to "life in a slum, with all the attendant problems of violence, robbery, cold, hunger and dirt." Most tragic of all, someone had murdered eighteen-year-old Linda Rae Fitzpatrick and her twenty-one-year-old boyfriend James L. "Groovy" Hutchinson, earlier profiled in a *New York Times* article on a Diggers' commune in the East Village. A police commander worried that hippies had turned into "bait," with many "undesirables" determined "to prey on the ignorance and naiveté of a lot of these love kids." Twenty-four-year-old Richie, a recent transplant from Haight-Ashbury who operated the Diggers Free Store on 10th Street, acknowledged, "A young girl who just ran away from home is not going to report being raped to the police and be sent home, in disgrace." Additionally, he continued, "a lot of kids here now have guns and knives. If someone hits me, I don't give him a flower."[24]

The Village Voice's rock critic Richard Goldstein delivered his own ode to the hippie ethos, "Love: A Groovy Idea While He Lasted." The killings of "Linda" and "Groovy," a pair of "beautiful people," garnered attention, Goldstein wrote, because of who they were and what they represented. Groovy was "a speed-saint, guru-clown, lover-dealer," now turned into "a true martyr," seemingly personifying "the love ethic." Linda, who had also been raped several times, came across as "a pretty fair-skinned aspiring artist who clung to the fringes of hippiedom, terrified of the denizens of that accursed land, but fascinated by them." Fear now enveloped the East Village, with other recent murders recalled, while the death of Groovy resulted in the realization that the area around Tompkins Square, where the hippies hung out, was a slum. Also appreciated was the fact that hippies had become "the new niggers," opposed by "every corner." Some indicated that "flower power was a summer vacation." While the San Francisco counterculture staged the death of hippie, "Here, we got the real thing." Goldstein was most struck by the fact that it had taken this long to appreciate "flower power began and ended as a cruel joke," shaped by "media-men." Thousands of young people on both coasts proved "the real victims of flower hype," notwithstanding warnings by hippies to "their suburban following." Even "Groovy's legacy . . . a new slum-hippie" acknowledged that "the mystique has worn off. People are beginning to admit the ugliness of it now. The myths are peeling away, like bad paint, man. Take the drug thing. This is an amphetamine scene here. Part of your flower power survival kit is meth. It's ugly, and it's real, man. And it was here all along, for anyone to see who felt like it." Talk was in the air that some Diggers on both the East and West Coasts now had "guns—and intend to use them."[25]

The San Francisco novelist Earl Shorris contributed an essay, "Love Is Dead," for the October 29, 1967, issue of the *New York Times Magazine*. It opened with a declaration by a nineteen-year-old young man that "Leary is a fake. The underground newspapers are fake. Lots of the young kids are fake. Maybe the Diggers aren't fake—maybe." Having spent a troubled several months, at a minimum, in the Haight-Ashbury district, he was ready to depart. Plunging ahead, Shorris pronounced unequivocally, "The hippie movement is over." While the Human Be-In had attracted a crowd of several thousand, the recent Death of Hippie funeral attracted less than a hundred. Shorris contended, "The alternative to the 'computerized society' has proved to be as unsatisfactory to its adherents as the society that gave birth to it." Continuing, Shorris wrote, "The hippie philosophy, in which Buddha reads Tarot cards, Confucius is an astrologer and Hesse peddles acid, was incapable of sustaining a mass movement." The resort to drugs resulted in a turning inward, thereby precluding "the possibility of a hippie community." Lacking "a viable, unifying philosophy," members of the counterculture fell victim "to disease, commercialism, publicity, teeny-boppers, boredom, one another and the psychopathic criminals who found them the easy underbelly of the white middle class." Now it was clear, to Shorris at least, that it was "not easy for a hippie to be filled with love." After all, macrobiotic diets resulted in one becoming "more susceptible to disease." Then, there were the bad trips, which led "to suicide, murder or madness," while the good ones produced "a mushy brain." Still, it was boredom, possibly most of all, Shorris suggested, that produced the movement's "moribund state." Little helpful too was the fact that "the promises of the hippie life were illusory," whether involving sex, materialism, or notoriety. Clear too was a racial divide, with hippies viewing blacks "as intruders." Shorris wrapped up his analysis, claiming that most hippies were "plastic," and easily returned to straight society. A few remained "outside, marked by venereal disease, life-shattering experiences, felony convictions, or with their minds jellied by LSD and Methedrine, the victims of a failed adventure in search of the perfect, ineffable groovy."[26]

By contrast, David Crosby of the Byrds explained his continued affinity for drugs, ranging from pot to LSD, in *The Oracle of Southern California*. An acid trip, which he undertook four to six times a year, Crosby explained, "clears the deck and shakes everything up and loosens up the whole thing and keeps it from getting too static." He also got high from playing music or making love, and realizing that "you ARE love, and thou art God . . . and everything is IT, and if you get into it the whole universe is yours: playground, playpen, universe!" Drugs alone did not produce the desired result. Instead, "YOU MUST WANT TO EXPAND

YOUR CONSCIOUSNESS. THAT'S THE REAL EXPANDER . . . THE
WANTING TO / AND BEING UNAFRAID TO . . . ya gotta dig change.
As a matter of fact, CHANGE IS WHAT'S HAPPENING!"[27]

Also in October, the Off-Broadway debut of *Hair: The American
Tribal Love-Rock Musical* took place, with its cast of politically engaged
hippies residing in New York City and avoiding the draft. Within months,
Hair opened on Broadway, triggering a long run, which was duplicated in
other cities throughout the United States and in Europe. Songs extolling
"Aquarius," "Hashish," "Sodomy," "Hair," and "Good Morning Star-
shine," captured something of the zeitgeist. In the initial review in the
New York Times, Clive Barnes stated that "if only good intentions were
golden, *Hair* . . . would be great." Instead, he wrote, "it is merely pretty
good; an honest attempt to jolt the American musical into the nineteen-
sixties." Lacking a story, *Hair* was "a mood picture of a generation,"
shaped "by drugs, sex and the two wars, the one about color and the one
about Vietnam," and "the likeability and honesty of its cast."[28]

In November, Eric Burdon and the Animals released "Monterey,"
about the pop festival. Written by Burdon and his mates, "Monterey"
talked about people coming to listen or play, with some giving away
flowers. "Young gods" seemingly "smiled upon the crowd," where a
music "born of love" was created and "religion was being born." The
song referred to the Byrds, Jefferson Airplane, The Who, the Grateful
Dead, Jimi Hendrix, and "Prince" Brian Jones, among others.[29] Cream
issued *Disraeli Gears*, complete with psychedelic cover and songs on the
order of "Strange Brew," "Tales of Brave Ulysses," and "Sunshine of
Your Love," all highly elliptical.[30] "Strange Brew" pointed to a woman
or a mad potion "killin' what's inside of you," and "Tales of Brave
Ulysses" seemingly recreated the story of the ancient Greek warrior-king
and sirens.[31] Cream's most commercially successful single, "Sunshine of
Your Love," again painted images of a love affair or a psychedelic trip,
with references to "the light's shinin' through on you" and having "been
waitin' so long / To be where I'm going / In the sunshine of your love."[32]

On November 9, Jann Wenner, a twenty-one-year-old dropout from
the University of California at Berkeley, released the first issue of *Rolling
Stone* magazine. Wenner indicated that his new publication was "not just
about the music, but about the things and attitudes that music embraces."[33] The lead article on page one asked, "The High Cost of Music
and Love: Where's the Money from Monterey?"[34] Just under the mast-

head was a photograph of John Lennon, decked out in military garb with wire-rimmed glasses, his hair shorn for his role as Musketeer Gripweed in Richard Lester's black comedy, *How I Won the War*.

Speaking at California State University, Long Beach, on November 13, 1967, barefooted Timothy Leary, sporting a white tunic and love beads, put on a show alongside John Griggs of the Brotherhood of Eternal Love, which *Rolling Stone* magazine would call "the Hippie Mafia." "Pretend that John and I are agents of God sent here in answer to your questions," Leary told the crowd. He then asked those in attendance to meditate for two minutes, before fielding questions. When asked why contemporary man required LSD, Leary responded, "Because it's the twentieth century." He continued, "You under 30 are a new breed. A new race. Your generation is going to pull the human race out of the mess. . . . The message is love. . . . That's the word, the goal, the purpose, the essence. There's nothing else."[35] On December 1, the Jimi Hendrix Experience released *Axis: Bold as Love*.[36]

The December 4, 1967, issue of *The Nation* offered the "Last Word on the Hippies: Anatomy of a Hangup," by Hans Toch, a psychology professor at Michigan State University. The American press, during the past year, Toch wrote, had experienced "its Discovery of the Hippie," with reports by *Look*, *Saturday Evening Post*, and *Time*, among other mass circulation publications. As public interest mounted, however, the hippie was mythologized. Hippies were allowed to express contempt, alongside purported offerings of "solicitous affection." They were viewed as society's vanguard, and said to exemplify "Our Values Come Home to Roost." Some attempted to turn "hippies into Noble Dissenters," whose "open-mindedness, love of freedom and . . . tolerance of deviation" contrasted favorably with the attitudes and behavior of reactionary politicians, police officers, and general members of the American public. Even academicians propounded "the myth of the Hippie Revolt against Soul Enslavement." In reality, Toch charged, hippies failed to become politically engaged, engaged in a hostile relationship with blacks, and demanded services desperately required by others, while refusing to make an economic contribution. Ultimately, the hippie subculture, Toch wrote, covered "our own infantile impulses with a pretense of respectability."[37]

On December 7, the Beatles, who had poured 100,000 British pounds into the operation, opened Apple Shop on Baker Street in London. Paul McCartney called it "a beautiful place where beautiful people can buy beautiful things."[38] Released on December 8, the Rolling Stones' album, *Their Satanic Majesties Request*, attempted, not terribly successfully, to compete with *Sgt. Pepper's Lonely Hearts Club Band*.[39] The Rolling Stones' latest included "She's a Rainbow," and a fairy land–like cover with the band members decked in medieval garb; Mick Jagger sported a long wizard's hat.[40] By contrast, the next pair of Stones' albums would prove cutting edge and demonstrate their conflicted relationship with the counterculture.

13

ALTERNATIVE LIVING

Both Timothy Leary and Ken Kesey pioneered another venue associated with the counterculture, communal living, through various endeavors including those at Millbrook and La Honda. Altogether, during the latter part of the 1960s and the decade of the 1970s, thousands of communes appeared in the United States. As Timothy Miller, author of *The 60s Communes: Hippies and Beyond*, notes, eventually several hundred thousand individuals belonged to communes at one point or another, with typical memberships of twenty to fifty people, and high turnover rates. Communes cropped up in both urban centers and rural sectors, with a small number becoming quite well known. Religious sensibilities drove many, thanks to the Jesus movement, a few Jewish communes, and several rooted in Asian religious sensibilities, including Hare Krishna, Zen, and Tibetan Buddhism. Some communes were politically oriented, while others used psychedelics as sacraments in some fashion, and dozens, at a minimum, extolled homosexuality or radical heterosexuality in the form of group marriages. Musicians like the Grateful Dead and Jefferson Airplane had their own communes, while several concentrated on "medicine, therapy, or personal growth," Miller reports. [1]

In *Getting Back Together*, Robert Houriet, himself an earlier communard, examines the communal movement of the 1960s, declaring that as in the case of twenty-five individuals who "fled Minneapolis," they possessed no time to explore historical antecedents or carefully devise an agenda. Instead, "their flight was desperate," as they recognized their country was catapulting in the direction of "*1984*, *Brave New World*, and ecocatastrophe." They considered resistance futile, believing that neither nonviolent protest nor revolutionary action would dissuade the police from crushing their urban communes, would alter the stultifying existence of American city life, or could transform established institutions from churches to corporations. They acted, Houriet contends, in the fashion of their ancestors fleeing urban grit in the Northeast or the exploitation, persecution, and warfare in Europe. "They went back to the land; but this time, they went together," in "spontaneous, simultaneous" fashion. Beginning in cities across the country, from Massachusetts to California, they sought a new beginning in open spaces, going "to the redwood region of the Pacific Northwest, the mesas of the vast Southwest, the rocky abandoned farms of New England."[2]

Houriet argues that the communal movement of the 1960s involved "the gut reaction of a generation. Hippie groups living a few country miles apart were unaware of each other's existence and equally unaware of the other utopian experiments in American history. They thought theirs were unique and unprecedented." Some called their endeavors "tribes; others nests, affinity groups, collectives, intentional communities or simply families," but most spoke of communes. They desired something different, while demonstrating a readiness to reexamine and experiment. In the process they shaped "a micro culture—a synthesis of forms, ideas, art and technology," constructing smaller, self-sufficient enclaves that strove for harmonious relationships with the planet. They adopted shifting familial and child-rearing patterns. They began schools that appeared more open and flexible. They birthed home industries rooted in old-styled craftsmanship. They set up "churches, ashrams and lay orders," revitalized seemingly decaying religions, and established their own creeds. Most of all, Houriet writes, "they infused their rediscovered awareness of immanent divinity into every action of daily life, seeking rituals and traditions with which to pass on to their children the timeless vision."[3]

The civil rights movement served as a spur, through the Freedom Houses in the South. Individuals gathered together, hoping to rekindle the movement's "broader community." Disintegration of the urban hippie ideal was yet another goad, as many, in the way Canned Heat sang about "Going up the Country," fled metropolitan areas.[4] New Left activism provided another impetus, a good number seeking to escape the growing contention exemplified by the Democratic National Convention in Chicago and the impending fracturing of SDS.

The communal tradition dated back to the antebellum period, when the Shakers, New Harmony, Brook Farm, Oneida, the Icarians, and the Mormons thrived, briefly or for more extended periods. Communitarianism hardly died out following the Civil War, as Robert S. Fogart indicates in *All Things New: American Communes and Utopian Movements, 1860–1914*. Fogart discusses commune-founders who were "charismatic-perfectionists, cooperative colonists, and political pragmatists." New Odessa, the Kaweah Cooperative Colony, and Ruskin Colony were among the most intriguing of the communes appearing during the last half of the nineteenth century. Young Jews, who referred to themselves as Friends of New Odessa, established a colony in Oregon, led by William Frey, which initially attempted to follow his tenets "of altruism, self-perfection, common property, and moral cooperation." A utopian socialist undertaking, the Kaweah Colony, appeared in the Sierra Nevada range in central California, its members spurred by the writings of Laurence Gronlund and Edward Bellamy. Another utopian socialist colony, Ruskin, was founded close to Tennessee City, located in Dickson County, Tennessee, by Julius Augustus Wayland, publisher of the leading socialist journal, *Appeal to Reason*. Followers of Henry George, who propounded the idea of a "single tax" on the "unearned increment" from inflated land values, and of Edward Bellamy, whose novel *Looking Backward* led to the formation of Bellamy clubs, established experimental communities by the latter stages of the nineteenth century. "Small back-to-the-land farms" appeared in early twentieth century, such as the Little Landers community in the San Ysidro sector of San Diego, California. The motto of the egalitarian community, established by the journalist William Ellsworth Smythe, was "a little land and a living surely is better than desperate struggle and wealth possibly."[5]

Failed mayoral candidate Jeb Harriman set up the Llano Del Rio colony east of Palmdale, located in Los Angeles County's Antelope Valley. A longtime leading figure in the Socialist Party, Harriman attempted to attract idealistic, hardworking, and sober colonists to create a socialist community that would serve as a model for American society. Llano sought, not always successfully, to obtain conscientious objector status for its young men during World War I. A number of anarcho-pacifist communities emerged during the interwar period, and as World War II unfolded, when pacifist cooperatives proved especially popular. The Catholic Worker Movement, founded by Dorothy Day and Peter Maurin in 1933 to "live in accordance with the justice and clarity of Jesus Christ," ministered toward the less fortunate, while propounding the gospel of nonviolence and communitarianism; the Catholic Worker Movement soon set up a number of farm communes. Morris Randolph Mitchell established the Macedonia Cooperative Community as an educational laboratory in northern Georgia in 1937, offering "communal living, spiritual searching, and pacifism."

Fellow students at the Union Theological Seminary, David Dellinger, Meredith Dallas, and Don Benedict formed the Newark Ashram, which Dellinger called the Newark Christian Colony and was patterned after Mahatma Gandhi's Ashram and the very idea of "Christian colony" spawned by the Catholic Worker Movement. Interracial co-ops focused on race relations, such as the Harlem Ashram, established by Jay Holmes Smith, which included Bayard Rustin among its supporters, and Koinonia Farm, set up in Americus, Georgia. Considerable attention was paid to Ahimsa Farm, established by Antioch College students, who read pacifist authors and sought to nurture "a fellowship farm dedicated to the ideals of a non-violent Christian life." Its champions included A. J. Muste and James Farmer. The interracial Koinonia Farm first appeared in 1942, designed by Clarence and Florence Jordan, working with Martin and Mabel England, to provide a "demonstration plot for the Kingdom of God" with a commitment to human dignity, justice, nonviolence, communal living, and stewardship of the land. Influenced by their involvement in Civilian Public Service camps during the war, a number of conscientious objectors attempted to engage in communal living. In 1947, anarcho-pacifists, led by David Dellinger, formed the Glen Gardner Cooperative Community in New Jersey, whose members ran a publishing house, which eventually put out *The Liberator*; a preschool; and a farm, while professing belief in God-inspired communitarianism.

Also in 1947, the young anarchist writer Paul Goodman and his brother, Percival Goodman, an architect and urban planner, published *Communitas: Means of Livelihood and Ways of Life*, which focused on three types of possible unstructured communities that fostered equality: one based on consumption, another rooted in artistic and creative possibilities, and the third centered on maximizing human liberty.[6] Charles K. Agle, writing in the *New York Times*, praised the book for usefully summarizing the ideas associated with Frank Lloyd Wright, Le Corbusier, Buckminster Fuller, the Tennessee Valley Authority, and Greenbelt communities constructed by Franklin D. Roosevelt's New Deal administration during the Great Depression. Agle underscored the Goodmans' contention that "only a seventh of the population" needed to be employed, conjuring up all sorts of seeming utopian possibilities. [7]

In the *Yale Law Journal*, David Riesman, then serving as associate professor of social sciences at the University of Chicago, referred to the Goodman brothers as utopians, who saw "man as fundamentally good," but considered the American people to be largely unhappy and passive. At the same time, influenced by "optimistic Enlightenment traditions," as exemplified by the English anarchist William Godwin, Robert Owen, Peter Kropotkin, and John Dewey, who believed in the malleability of the individual learner, the Goodmans deemed their fellow citizens capable of greater spontaneity and democratic cooperative behavior. As for the Goodmans, in Riesman's estimation, they envisioned utopian planning as "an exploration of alternative possibilities." While favoring the architectural designs of Frank Lloyd Wright, they leaned toward Kropotkin in the social and political realms, believing "each producer must have a say in the distribution of 'his' product." They also looked "to regionalist and syndicalist writers" rather than authoritarian-nationalists like Edward Bellamy, with his image of an industrial army. That only conjured up nightmares presently, Riesman wrote. Yet both Bellamy's futuristic city and the Goodmans' "New Commune" promised considerable leisure; ample goods to take care of "genuine needs"; urbane domestic life; the possibility of a life of study or the arts; friendly, nonexploitative human relations; gender equality; the nurturing of children; "quiet happiness"; peace; and an absence of economic competition. [8]

Behavioral psychologist B. F. Skinner published *Walden Two* in 1948, a novel about a utopian community in Indiana, led by a psychological genius, Frazier, and shaped by experimental control. The book resulted from a conversation the author participated in at a dinner party during the summer of 1945, when Skinner expressed concerns that returning veterans would be forced into "old ruts." A woman convinced Skinner to offer his ideas regarding "an experimental attitude toward life," and within seven weeks, he completed *Walden Two*. A number of rejections followed, however, and the book was not published until three years passed. Skinner later explained that he wanted to demonstrate how conditioning could result in "a world in which there is food, clothing, and shelter for all, where everyone chooses his own work and works on the average only

four hours a day, where music and the arts flourish, where personal relationship develop under the most favorable circumstances, where education prepares every child for the social and intellectual life before him,
where-in short—people are truly happy, secure, productive, creative, and
forward-looking."[9]

Reviewing *Walden Two* in the *New York Times*, Orville Prescott
deemed "life in Mr. Skinner's land of milk and honey . . . just as intolerable as in any of its renowned predecessors." Skinner's ideas, Prescott
warned, were "alluring in a sinister way, and appalling, too," with cultural and behavioral engineering, directed by elite planners, supplanting
religion and families.[10] Also in the *New York Times*, Charles Poore began
by stating that "man dreams forever of the Almost Perfect State." As
Poore noted, Skinner recognized that the quest for utopia could be undertaken by "a despot or an evangelist. Or both." It could also simply be the
byproduct of an individual's "fits of useful absent-mindedness." It could
range from the "complex and terrifying" to the "simple and beguiling," in
the manner of Thoreau's Walden Pond.[11] In *The Philosophical Review*,
Donald C. Williams of Harvard University discussed "The Social Scientist as Philosopher and King," labeling Skinner "an illustrious psychologist" who had also produced utopian fiction with a look at "the brave new
world" psychology could produce. Williams viewed the protagonist Frazier as one whose social philosophy effectively amounted to totalitarianism, dismissing political democracy, competition, and democratic socialism, while heralding the state, control, and "having my own way."[12]

In 1954, Helen and Scott Nearing published *Living the Good Life*,
which traced their seeking of a simple, self-sufficient lifestyle, as they
began dwelling in an old home in rural Vermont. They became known as
"back-to-the-landers," striving for "the good life" and aspiring to live "as
decently, kindly, justly, orderly and efficiently as possible."[13] They were
quite accomplished individuals, she a trained musician, and he at one
point a distinguished economist and university professor, who had lost his
academic post during World War I because of his antiwar stance. Unsuccessfully prosecuted under the Espionage Act, Nearing taught at the Rand
School of Social Science, joined the Communist Party, conducted speaking tours, and broke with the party, while remaining an important figure
on the American left, despite the communists' easy dismissal of him as
one who "should be deposited on the scrap heap of the revolution." During the 1930s and 1940s, he lived with Helen Knothe, who became his

second wife, on a farm in Winhall, a small community in Bennington County, Vermont. They grew their own food, and erected a series of buildings on their large forest tract. As for American society, Nearing considered it "a competitive, acquisitive, aggressive, war-making social order, which butchers for food and murders for sport and for power."[14]

Thirty-three-year-old John Peltz "Bro Jud" Presmont, a World War II veteran and bohemian, founded what became known as Kerista Commune in 1956, featuring the practice of group marriage based on polyamory, rooted in gender equality, free choice, mutual trust, respect, and love. The Voice spoke to Presmont, amid an extended period of smoking marijuana and reading the Koran, which followed his earlier exploration of Eastern religions. The Voice purportedly informed him, "THERE IS NOTHING YOU CAN DO TO PREVENT THIS THING FROM HAPPENING. HAVE A BALL, ENJOY YOURSELF TO THE UTMOST. FIND THE MOUNTAIN BESIDE THE SEA. THE PIED PIPER WILL PULL OUT THE SWINGING PEOPLE." For the next five years, the religion of Kerista, as it was eventually called, was referred to as "our thing" by its adherents.

As Timothy Miller points out, dozens and possibly hundreds of communes, such as Koinoinia Farm, still existed as the 1960s began. A number of established communes like San Francisco's East-West House, with a Buddhist emphasis, and Vermont's Quarry Hill, designed as a retreat for artists and other creative individuals, welcomed new arrivals as the decade unfolded. Many new communards were already familiar with communal approaches, including individuals associated with the Catholic Worker Movement, left-wing politics, peace churches, radical relatives, and artists' colonies. That, however, was of course not true for all those attracted to the era's communes, longstanding or new. Circumstances, including financial exigencies and concerns regarding the law, drove others into the communal lifestyle. Miller suggests that the communal movement became a force, around 1968, as alienated young people poured into urban and rural locales, often spurred by media coverage in underground publications and mass circulation magazines and newspapers. In addition, new "specialized publications," like the *Modern Utopian* and Alice Bay Laurel's *Living on the Earth*, heralded the Movement and countercultural lifestyles.[15]

Perry Lane, located in Stanford's bohemian district, served as a focal point for Ken Kesey and other young writers, artists, and musicians who created a free-flowing atmosphere where important seeds of the 1960s counterculture were planted. Along with Kesey, Neal Cassady, Larry McMurtry, Ed McClanahan, Robert Stone, Carl Lehmann-Haupt, Vic Lovell, Jerry Garcia, and Richard Alpert were among those helping to create, as Tom Wolfe later put it, something of an *"underground* sensation . . . in Hip California." Many partook of Kesey's LSD-laced Venison Chili. Wolfe writes, "The Lane was too good to be true. It was Walden Pond, only without any Thoreau misanthropes around. Instead, a community of intelligent, very open, out-front people . . . who cared deeply for one another, and *shared* . . . in incredible ways, even, and were embarked on some kind of . . . *well*, adventure in living. Christ, you could see them trying to put their finger on it and . . . then . . . gradually figuring out there was something here they weren't *in on*." [16]

Once again, Aldous Huxley influenced the early counterculture, this time through the publication in 1962 of his utopian novel, *Island.* Charles Poore reviewed this work for the *New York Times*, discussing the determination of intellectuals to proselytize about "the almost-perfect state." Dystopian novels, such as Huxley's *Brave New World* and George Orwell's *1984*, proved wildly popular, in their own fashion. This time around, Poore revealed, Huxley had adopted a "cheerier" tone regarding utopianism, and yet the author continued to assail modern society. In his latest book, Huxley depicted the island of Pala, benevolently ruled for more than a hundred years by "very wise Palanese and an even wiser Scot or two." It had become "a tranquility of dutiful permissiveness, thrifty abundance and selective Buddhism." Love prevailed throughout the island among its inhabitants, who appeared smug regarding how they had it so much better than those who dwelled elsewhere. Helping to maintain tranquility on Pala was a wonder drug, moksha, but the dictator of a nearby island threatened harm. [17] Also in the *New York Times*, Beloit College English Professor Chad Walsh reviewed *Island*, discussing the protagonist's acceptance of "the intelligent pursuit of man's Final End, the unitive knowledge of the immanent Tao of Logos, the transcendent Godhead or Brahman." On Pala, Mahayana Buddhism and science appeared to have been happily melded, while the mushroom moksha provided "an opening wedge into ultimate consciousness." [18]

Various groups focused on the need for open land in the first half of the 1960s, including Amelia Newell's Gorda Mountain, situated close to Big Sur, along the California coast. By the middle of the decade, Newell's land was "a center for drug trading and a convenient stopping-off-place and crashpad." In 1963, Tolstoy Farm, located in eastern Washington state, began operations, thanks to a veteran peace activist, Huw "Piper" Williams, who had been deeded eighty acres of land from his mother. He advertised in peace publications, seeking others to join him; among those who responded was the woman who became his wife. Williams determined to establish a community rooted in "the anarchist principle of voluntary cooperation: no rules, no structure, people helping each other because they saw a need and wanted to be of service." Familiar with the writings of Tolstoy and Gandhi, Williams desired to foster their principles through "a simple living kind of alternative Christian lifestyle, cooperation, self-reliance." He welcomed anyone who chose to participate, including other peace proponents, such as members of the Catholic Worker Movement, to "attempt to live in a way that would not require violent acts, being in the military, courts, jail, or police." Lacking regulations, Tolstoy Farm impeded neither sexual experimentation nor drug usage. With few economic resources, the commune virtually operated in subsistence fashion, as Williams reflected. "We were pretty poor, trying to grow our own food, build our own shelter, use old tools and equipment. It occupied us and challenged us."[19] Timothy Leary and Richard Alpert, the defrocked Harvard faculty members, carried on their own communal endeavors, initially under the heading of the Castalia Foundation, at the expansive Millbrook estate of Tommy and Billy Hitchcock, starting in August 1963. Twenty-five to thirty people comprised the core of the Millbrook crowd, which included Leary, his wife and children, Alpert, the psychologist Art Kleps, and other academics and spiritual seekers. The commune operated for about four years, featuring the use of psychedelics, in a controlled setting, to undergo religious experiences. Group LSD sessions took place, with numerous well-known artists, philosophers, and musicians participating during visits to Millbrook.

The year after both Tolstoy Farm and the Castalia Foundation initiated operations, John Sinclair, his lover Leni Arndt, the filmmaker and poet Robin Eichele, and the trumpet player Charles Moore helped to kick off the Detroit Artists' Workshop, which soon resulted in formation of the Artists' Workshop Cooperative Housing Project. After police harassment, Sinclair and Leni Arndt, whom he had married, joined with the artist Gary Grimshaw to establish Trans-Love Energies Unlimited, a "total cooperative tribal living and working commune."[20] Rock bands, includ-

ing the MC-5, along with artists, the staff members of underground newspapers, and operators of headshops became part of what was variously
called the Hill Street, the MC-5, or the White Panther commune. The
1967 Steering Committee, which included Sinclair and Grimshaw, appeared in January of that year, declaring they had been readying all their
lives for the New Year. The committee members aspired, they declared,
to "live and work to make the world a human place for us all—a place we
can LIVE in, as a man lives in his home, or in his skin—IS his skin. We
feel equal with the universe and with this city, at one with them, and
would have this unity spread throughout our lives, to move toward a
human universe." The steering committee saw itself "as an agent of the
Sun—to bring people light and colour. . . . To illuminate them, and bring
them together." The intention was to hold an early event, "a benefit for
GUERRILLA," then to support the Zen temple community from San
Francisco, and to hold a regional conference focusing on consciousness
expansion. During the summer, the committee envisioned a continental
congress allowing for the creation of "a new nation firmly based on
human need and spirit," which would help to bring about "a new civilization."[21]

In the summer of 1965, Robert Anton Wilson published an article,
"The Religion of Kerista and Its 69 Positions," the religion founded a
decade earlier by John Presmont, which had caught on in Greenwich
Village. Now known as Jud the Prophet by thousands of followers "in
such odd places as London, Berlin, Tangier, New York City, San Francisco, and Passaic, New Jersey," Presmont no longer referred to his religion
as "our thing," a phrase readily employed by the mafia. Having received
another vision three years earlier, in which he spotted Buddhas dwelling
on an island called Kerista, containing a mammoth mountain, Presmont
now spoke of the religion of Kerista. This was "a religion of freedom and
joy, a religion without dogma or restriction, and a religion of ecstasy,"
and Keristans proved determined to act accordingly. As Wilson began
interviewing a batch of Keristans dwelling in Greenwich Village, he
asked to see their leader, but received the following response, "No, no,
man, you don't get it. Kerista has no *leader*. Jud is the *prophet*. Kerista
doesn't need leaders, or teachings, or theories, or stipulations, or restrictions, Kerista is *freedom*." One large man, sporting a full black beard and
a mass of hair, added that "Kerista is freedom *and* love." Having heard
that Keristans practiced bisexuality, free love, and heavy doping, Wilson

gingerly inquired about this. Another young man responded, "Well, first of all, we're not trying to enforce anything on anybody. That goes against freedom, and freedom is our first law. People can keep any hang-up they've got, as long as they want to keep it. Of course, if they want to get over their hang-ups, we'll help them. But we don't pressure anybody to try anything that they're still square about." As the conversation proceeded, one Keristan revealed that they obtained new names—such as Tre, Dau, E. Z., Good, Marquel—from an Ouija board. They had all tossed aside middle-class status, rejecting the so-called Affluent Society, voluntarily choosing instead to reside in East Village slums, which they saw as emancipated "from a living death." Most fundamental to Kerista, they offered, was "Buddho, the art of no-defense," which at its more advanced stage also involved overcoming "greed, sexual jealousy, and other 'hang-ups.'" As the black-bearded giant said, "We're trying to live according to the pure self, not full of bullshit." When asked how that distinguished them from other East Villagers with similar determinations, the same young man stated, "No difference. Except we have purpose, directions, goals, and love." They pooled their economic resources, with only four having jobs, a like number on welfare, and eighteen "living hand-to-mouth." But they rotated and helped out one another when it came to babysitting, shopping, or cleaning clothes. [22]

A couple of days later, Wilson met the patriarchal-looking Jud Presmont, a large, friendly, white-haired man, who talked about the Keristan philosophy regarding sexual freedom. "We believe in love. People shouldn't be like balloons, ready to explode if they're touched. We believe in total sharing, and that means sharing love and affection as well as property." Keristans required only mutual consent, with one of its members homosexual, and most, bisexual. "People either dig that this is the natural, decent, loving way to behave, or they don't," Presmont said. Asserting that his work was completed, he also pointed to fifty-year-old Desmond Slattery as the man to help Kerista construct "an island colony." Slattery immediately expressed disdain for all religions, and referred to Kerista as a social movement. Not concerned if people considered Kerista "a religion or a social movement," Presmont offered, "The important thing is that they act naturally and decently." At that point, Slattery explained that the island colony would revolve around ecology, his religion, and become "the hip San Juan." Presmont explained another facet of his philosophy. He had no desire to toil for a living, and envisioned his colony as a place where no one would work. Then he stated, "When you're doing what you want to do, it isn't *work*; it's *play*. One cat is raising rabbits, another is raising chickens, somebody's growing vegetables, they're all having a ball, is that *work*? Work is when you're taking orders from somebody you hate."[23]

John Gruen's *The New Bohemia*, published in the mid-1960s, contained a chapter on Kerista, which the author called "a spreading paradisiacal cult" with the calling card, "Love Conquers All," although he detected distrust of outsiders. The group put out a newspaper, *Kerista Speeler*, which proclaimed that "a new concept of man" was being shaped by dedicated individuals who only sought "the betterment and advancement of the human race." The newspaper envisioned "a series of neopolynesian, with our own flavored architecture, villages and ranches," and propounded the gospel of love and sex. "Balling through life is the Kerista way."[24]

Patterned after B. F. Skinner's utopian novel, Walden House opened in Washington, D.C., in 1965, founded by thirty-four-year-old Kathleen "Kat" Kinkade and other devotees of *Walden Two*. In the *Walden House Newsletter*, Kinkade asserted that "the holding of property in common" was not a dogmatic issue suggested by Jesus or Karl Marx, but rather simply saved money and helped to lessen envy. The larger American culture, she warned, emphasized selfishness, the exploitation of one's fellow human beings, and the receipt of the largest honors by those who benefited most from accomplishing "nothing at all." Those at Walden House, by contrast, sought to devise "a miniature society in which every member considers his neighbor's needs equally with his own, where exploitation is unthinkable, and where it is assumed that every member is doing his share of the necessary work." They were not aspiring to literal equality, but rather "a general feeling of fairness, a logical first step in the pursuit of happiness."[25]

Soon determining that Walden House was "a dismal failure in every way," Kinkade nevertheless quickly moved on to help establish Twin Oaks Community, a rural commune located on a 123-acre tobacco farm, purchased for approximately $36,000 and situated thirty-five miles southeast of Charlottesville, Virginia. The community emphasized "cooperation, sharing, nonviolence, equality, and ecology." Its members strove for economic self-sufficiency, engaging in income-sharing while having each member devote forty-two hours a week to the community's basic needs.

Along with managers, Twin Oaks had a "Generalized Bastard," whose assignment was "to be officially nasty" in goading others to attend to necessary tasks. In spite of such efforts, Twin Oaks' members were often compelled to work in Charlottesville to maintain the community's economic viability. Kinkade "led through persuasion," while believing devotedly in communal life. In *A Walden Two Experiment*, she acknowledged that its inhabitants still aspired to "the big dream—a better world . . . for as many people as we can . . . support." They hoped to create "a new kind of human to live in that world: happy, productive, open-minded people who understand that in the long run, human good is a cooperative and not a competitive sort of thing."[26]

An artists' community, Drop City, was formed in southern Colorado near Trinidad in 1965, providing an iconic example of rural communal living during the period. Distinctive with its geodesic domes, drawn from the ideas of Buckminster Fuller, Drop City, rooted on six acres of land, strove to foster experimental artistic endeavors; other influences included the composer John Cage and the artist Robert Rauschenberg. Writing in *Inner Space*, its founders discussed what artists Jo Ann Bernofsky, Richard Kallweit, and Clark Richert, and filmmaker Gene Bernofsky sought to shape in Drop City. "We have attempted to create a total living environment outside the structure of society, where the artist can remain in touch with himself, the universe and other creative living beings." All Droppers considered themselves free, able to do what they wanted, without rules, duties, and obligations. They lauded anarchy and "the pleasure principle," proclaiming that their largest concern was "being alive." They lacked jobs and steady incomes, but not necessary materials. To the affluent, wasteful society that was the United States, they appeared as "scrounges, bums, garbage pickers." They considered themselves sensualists, all fourteen Droppers, and came in various "sizes, shapes and colors: painters, writers, architects, panhandlers, filmmakers, magicians, gluttons, musicians, wizards, unclassifiables." Uniting them was a belief that their art and lives could not be separated. They were not a psychedelic community, in that they deemed drugs unnecessary, but "etymologically, perhaps" they were, serving as "one spark of a great chain reaction." Of particular note was "The Ultimate Painting," a large multicolored globe that Drop Artists crafted by 1966.[27] The following year, *Time* magazine's feature, "Youth: The Hippies," contained a description and color illustration of Drop City.[28]

By that point, other communes had achieved notoriety, including the Hog Farm Collective, founded by Hugh Romney, earlier a promoter and standup comic once managed by Lenny Bruce, on land situated north of Los Angeles in the San Fernando Valley. A friend of the Merry Pranksters, Romney and friends accepted an offer to tend to a pig farm, but soon formed "an expanded family, a mobile hallucination, a sociological experiment, an army of clowns" that became famous within the ranks of the counterculture.[29] The Hog Farm provided light shows at Los Angeles' Shrine Exposition Hall for leading rock bands, but became best known when Romney later served as the unofficial master of ceremonies at the Woodstock Music Festival. The Hog Farm helped to provide easygoing security, medical assistance, refreshments, and other food supplies. It had earlier made another wise decision: to compel the visiting Charles Manson and his flock of young women, with their "bad vibes," to leave the Hog Farm.[30]

In 1966, folk musician Mel Lyman, a banjo and harmonica player in Jim Kweskin's jug band, founded the Lyman Family, also called the Fort Hill Community, in the dilapidated Roxbury district in South Boston. Having relocated from the West Coast, Lyman hooked into the burgeoning LSD scene in Cambridge that revolved around Timothy Leary, Richard Alpert, and Ralph Metzner. After the folk audience listened in dismay to Bob Dylan and Robbie Robertson play rock 'n' roll music at the 1965 Newport Folk Festival, Lyman entertained the crowd with a mouth harp rendition of "Rock of Ages." Drawing on psychedelic experiences and a millennial sensibility, the Lyman Family seemingly subscribed to the founder's belief that he was Jesus Christ, "the twentieth-century Savior." Devotees purportedly included Mark Frechette and Daria Halprin of *Zabriskie Point* fame, *Crawdaddy* rock journalist Paul Williams, and Kweskin. Taking control of the Boston *Avatar*, the underground newspaper, Lyman immediately introduced himself in curious fashion. "To those of you are unfamiliar with me let me introduce myself by saying that I am not a man, not a personality, not a tormented struggling individual. I am all those things but much more. I am the truth and I speak the truth. . . . In all humility I tell you that I am the greatest man in the world and it doesn't trouble me in the least. . . . I am going to attack everything you believe in, everything you cling to, I am going to shed light on your dark truths, I'm going to show you things as they REALLY ARE and not how you would like them to be." Soon, the family put out a new publication,

American Avatar, in which Lyman proclaimed himself to be Jesus Christ, who was "about to turn this foolish world upside down."[31]

Lou Gottlieb, an ex-communist, former member of the folk music group, the Limeliters, and possessor of a doctorate in musicology, settled on nearly thirty-two acres of land that previously constituted a chicken farm and apple orchard, at Morningstar in Sonoma County, also in 1966. The closest neighbor was the famed cartoonist of the *Peanuts'* comic strip, Charles Schultz. The grizzly bearded Gottlieb played his grand piano, calling himself the "resident piano player," and stayed at a modest cabin on the Morningstar ranch.[32] His friend and fellow musician Ramon Sender actually spent more time at the ranch, at least initially, because Gottlieb resided in San Francisco, where he served as the *San Francisco Chronicle*'s music critic. Subscribing to the philosophy of open land and believing in "voluntary primitivism," Gottlieb welcomed anyone to live at Morningstar for free.[33] Gottlieb referred to LATWIDNO, the notion of Land Access to Which Is Denied No One. He later explained to Timothy Miller why Morningstar became a historically significant "beacon." In addition to the principle of LATWIDNO, the commune involved an attempt to address the fundamental conundrum communards encountered: "who stays and who's gotta go, by letting the land choose its inhabitants thereby forming a tribe."[34] Sender also subscribed to the idea of voluntary primitivism, which entailed reuniting "man with his greater self—God's nature"; that required harmoniously existing "with the four elements—earth, air, fire, and water." It involved constructing biodegradable housing; avoiding electricity, natural gas, running water, and telephone service; and relying on manpower to plant and harvest crops.[35]

Seeking spirituality, Sender and other friends read out loud from the nineteenth century communitarian John Humphrey Noyes, the Russian philosopher P. D. Ouspensky, and Lama Anagarika Govinda, the German-born follower of Tibetan Buddhism. Gottlieb invited hippies to dwell at Morningstar, and by November 1966, seven had arrived from the Haight-Ashbury district. Tree houses appeared, people cavorted in the nude, and the commune soon participated in the free food programs the Diggers conducted in San Francisco. Several Diggers came to the ranch and informed Gottlieb in early 1967, "We're expecting two million freaked out teenagers and these people gotta have something to eat."[36] The Diggers asked if they could harvest apples from the orchard, and Gottlieb readily agreed. Soon, the Digger store in San Francisco posted a sign, "Visit the Digger Farm," referring to Morningstar. Gottlieb also willingly accepted homeless migrants sent to the ranch. Consequently, Morningstar, after barely a year of existence, had, to the chagrin of the local police, attracted approximately two hundred residents, along with *Time* magazine. Many came to view Morningstar as the Diggers' commune, following as it did Digger principles, including open earth, air, fire, and water. Gottlieb's own philosophy was perhaps best exemplified in the quote he delivered from the communard and writer Elia Katz: "The idea of communes 'working,' flourishing, succeeding is always brought up, but this is beside the point in the case of the communes now existing in America. What is essential is to expose ourselves to a life of voluntary poverty, or life for minimal cost, and a life of sharing . . . because this is what it is, alone, that makes the commune endeavor an important thing in America."[37]

Bill Wheeler, another friend of Gottlieb and a believer in open land, soon established another commune nearby, the heavily wooded Wheeler's Ranch, also considered Digger territory. Wheeler, who had attended Yale University and was a high-level executive in his family's sewing machine company by the age of twenty, immediately fell in love with the 315-acre plot of land, one untamed ridge removed from the ocean. He became enamored with the ridge, wanting to reside there permanently, viewing it "as the perfect woman, spacious and lyrical, closed and secure, yet having great vistas."[38] After four years, he came to another determination, appreciating that he possessed more land than he needed and deciding he should share it, particularly choosing to assist the Morningstar family, which was constantly harassed and required a home. A tent became his new place of residence, while he employed a studio to paint and hold community meetings.

Wheeler also recalled that the communards at his ranch wanted to express themselves through art, music, and creativity. Wheeler's Ranch soon boasted over two hundred residents, who dwelled in shacks, and relied on a community garden while raising chickens. A communal orientation prevailed, as exemplified by a regular Sunday dinner, sweat baths, nudity, and psychedelics. Called the "benevolent king of the land," Wheeler prohibited open fires at various points, dogs, and feces scattered about the ranch.[39]

The Diggers established some of the first of the many urban communes that appeared in San Francisco, beginning in 1966 and 1967. The

Sutter Street commune was among the most significant, following the Digger belief in Free Everything and participating in a food-buying cooperative. Sutter Street eventually offered a weekly intercommunal newspaper, *Kaliflower*, containing "practical, philosophical and household tips."[40] Adapted from the Hindu name, Kaliyuga, pointing to humankind's final, most cataclysmic epoch, represented the notion of a "flower coming out of this current age of destruction." Thursdays became Kaliflower Day, during which members would carry both *Kaliflower* and groceries to other communes on a "routing list."[41]

One of the early mentors for the counterculture, Paul Goodman, delivered a utopian prediction of "The Diggers in 1984," published in the September 1967 issue of *Ramparts*. Looking ahead to the beginning of the following decade, he foresaw two large efforts pertaining to "rural reconstruction." The first involved the decision to end the harassment of radical youth, and the resulting determination to support "their reservations," in the manner the government now treated Native Americans. Greater difficulty arose concerning urban communes in places like the Haight-Ashbury district or New York City's East Village, but "an inventive tribe, the Diggers," offered "a solution: settlement in the countryside." The other wave involved the large number "of hermits and monks," concerned about people's souls. While tagged as lawless, the Diggers, Goodman wrote, subscribed to "Live and Left Live, and . . . the Golden Rule." These were "peaceable people," favoring fresh food, music and all kinds of automobiles, while disdaining "moral legislation" and taxes. They were good citizens, little utilizing public services and believing in the need to address ecological problems.[42]

Crash pads, in the fashion of Digger hangouts, cropped up in urban centers around the country. The Switchboard in San Francisco helped people, including runaways and dropouts, find places to stay, sometimes for the briefest amount of time, while others were connected to specific political or countercultural designs. Allen Cohen later described them as "not quite communes," which nevertheless helped to foster the notion of communal living, necessary intimacy, and sharing. Crash pads ranged from the well-organized to dysfunctional endeavors where "infectious diseases . . . chaotic childrearing and resultant high pediatric disease rates" ensued, Timothy Miller reports. Thousands easily moved about from urban crash pads to rural communes, and back again, at least for a time while the economy remained strong and rents low.[43]

From the summer of 1967 through the end of the year, more communes appeared, perhaps fueled by the idea of the Summer of Love and the disappointment that ensued. In June, as events in San Francisco's Haight-Ashbury district wound on, three young men from Pittsburgh parlayed a grant of land of 105 acres with water rights from a friend, Rick Klein, who purchased it for $55,000, into the New Buffalo Commune in northern New Mexico, north of Taos, with the idea of participating in a peyote church. Klein later recalled, "I was going to be a literature professor and then I took LSD, and saw that there's more to it than just this. . . . The first thing we did was have a peyote meeting." Klein and his friends, assisted by the Taos Pueblo, constructed a large, five-thousand-square-foot adobe structure, and a pair of smaller buildings. Young people flocked to the site, spurred by reports in the underground press, but typical of most communes, rapid turnover ensued. Striving for self-sufficiency, communards raised chickens, while growing corn, squash, and beans.[44]

In New Mexico alone, more than two dozen communes emerged, including several that became well known in countercultural circles like New Buffalo, the relocated Morningstar East, Lama Foundation, Hog Farm, also relocated, and the Reality Construction Company. The Lama Foundation was also started in 1967, located on 110 beautiful acres of land next to a federal forest, at an altitude of almost nine thousand feet twenty miles north of Taos, which itself would be referred to as Haight-Ashbury East. Founders Barbara and Stephen Durkee set up a center for Spiritual Realization and Interfaith Studies on their commune. They were particularly close to Richard Alpert, Barbara having introduced her husband to him at Millbrook. Alpert and Stephen, along with another friend of the Durkees, traveled to India, with the hope, as Barbara remembered, that her husband would become enlightened and they could create "a place where people in this country could come, do retreats, and study great spiritual teachings."[45] Eclectic religious idea came into play, drawn from Hinduism, Buddhism, Zen, Sufi, Christian, and Native American tenets.

Some of the newer communes involved hippies escaping from earlier ones, or from the greater pressures many members of the counterculture experienced as more attention and notoriety occurred. As scores of young people descended on Morningstar Ranch, neighbors of Lou Gottlieb complained to local authorities in Sonoma County about noise, nudity, and a dearth of sanitation. Reputed health violations led to a $500 fine, while several of the guests of the ranch, along with Gottlieb himself, suffered arrests and incarceration. Accusing of orchestrating an organized camp, while failing to heed sanitation regulations, Gottlieb responded, "If they find any evidence of organization here, I wish they would show it to me."[46] Other communards, including those at Tolstoy Farm, suffered harassment and major busts, often revolving around sanitation, building inspections, underage guests, or drugs. They also experienced sometimes troubled individuals, including runaways, speed freaks, and teenyboppers seeking something, however transient.

By the fall of 1967, the Diggers were proclaiming the Death of Hippie in the Haight-Ashbury district, while the East Village and other counter-cultural enclaves were also experiencing a sense of loss regarding once held millennial sensibilities. At the same time, utopian notions hardly dissipated altogether, given the relocating of communes and the appearance of many new ones during the next few years. And this was true not only in areas like Southern California, Northern California, and New York City, long receptive to bohemian experiments, but throughout the American heartland. Among the most celebrated were the Olompali Ranch, situated near Novato, California, led by the well-heeled Don McCoy and featuring the Chosen Family; Black Bear Ranch, originally featuring "revolutionary activists," dwelling in Northern California's Siskiyou County[47], Table Mountain Ranch in Mendocino County; the Reality Construction Company and Morningstar East in the Taos area; and Packer Corner, also known as Total Loss Farm, in southern Vermont.

Many even viewed the Jesus movement as a spinoff from the counter-culture. Emerging out of the West Coast by 1967, it spread across the country and into Europe, with its adherents often referred to, initially somewhat derisively, as "Jesus freaks." It began with early evangelical attempts to attract young people, in such seemingly unlikely venues as the Haight-Ashbury district, the University of California at Berkeley campus, and Los Angeles' Sunset Strip. Among those attracted to the movement, its hundreds of communal houses, and publications like the *Hollywood Free Paper* and *Right On!*, were former hippies seeking lifestyle changes, having endured difficulties with drugs or sexually transmitted diseases.[48]

As historians Maurice Isserman and Michael Kazin note, thousands of young Americans eventually resided in communes of all sorts. "Individual bands of communards lived in teepees, geodesic domes, ramshackle and sometimes hand-made farmhouses, buses, and in crowded urban apartments." They got by through a variety of means, including subsistence farming, selling pot, running health-food stores or restaurants, establishing bookshops, publishing newspapers, even operating day-care centers. Diverse strands of thought guided them as well, including Christianity, Buddhism, Native American spiritual beliefs, sexual liberation, anarchism, pacifism, gender equality, and a belief in imminent revolution of a decidedly secular cast.[49]

14

FROM HIPPIE TO YIPPIE ON THE
WAY TO REVOLUTION

The Diggers, like Allen Ginsberg, the staff of *The Rag* in Austin, Texas, and Liberation News Service, among many other individuals and organizations, including some communards, refuted the stereotypical notion that participants in the counterculture were necessarily apolitical. At a bare minimum, most hippies opposed the war, even if many failed to participate in protest gatherings. Others did, however, and the line between the movement and the counterculture remained murky, at a minimum. In fact, additional seminal events in 1967 and 1968 demonstrated that if anything the ability to differentiate between those two great flowerings became more difficult still. At the SDS Conference, held in Denton, Michigan, in June 1967, Peter Berg of the Diggers told the political activists, "Property is the enemy—burn it, destroy it, give it away. Don't let them make a machine out of you, get out of the system, do your thing. Don't organize students, teachers, Negroes, organize your head. Find out where you are, what you want to do and go out and do it. Johnson's a commie. The Kremlin is more fucked up than Alabama. Get out! Don't organize the schools, burn them. Leave them, they will rot." Emmett Grogan attacked those in attendance as "Faggots! Fags! Take off your ties, they are chains around your necks," then exclaimed, "You haven't got the balls to go mad. You're going to make a revolution?—you'll piss in your pants when the violence erupts." One of the senior SDS leaders, Bob Ross, responded to Grogan, "If the CIA wanted to disrupt this meeting they couldn't have done it any better than by sending you."[1] By contrast, Abbie Hoffman was elated, stating, "Holy shit. Excitement, Drama, Revolution."[2]

Appearing at a press conference in late August, Hoffman, political activist Jerry Rubin, the socially engaged comedian Dick Gregory, and SNCC chairman H. Rap Brown discussed plans for a gathering at the Pentagon to conduct an "exorcism to cast out the evil spirits," as the Diggers had suggested months earlier.[3] The thirty-one-year-old Hoffman, a native of Worcester, Massachusetts, was a graduate of both Brandeis University and the University of California at Berkeley, who became involved in first the civil rights movement, and then the antiwar campaign. After SNCC largely purged whites from its ranks, Hoffman concentrated more on the youth scene on the Lower East Side, while drawing ideas and tactics from the San Francisco Diggers, eventually turning to a kind of street theater to garner public attention and reshape youth consciousness. During the spring of 1967, in response to a "Support Our Boys in Vietnam" march led by the Veterans of Foreign Wars, Hoffman oversaw a "Flower Brigade," whose members were attacked as he had anticipated before contacting the media. Reports followed of "warmongers" beating up hippies, while Hoffman delivered his own account in *WIN*, sponsored by the War Resisters League. He breezily admitted, "We were poorly equipped with flowers from uptown florists. Already there is talk of growing our own. . . . The cry of 'Flower Power' echoes through the land. We shall not wilt."[4]

Coming from a less affluent Jewish family in Cincinnati, Jerry Rubin graduated from the University of Cincinnati, lived in Israel for a year-and-a-half, and eventually briefly enrolled in the PhD program in sociology at UC Berkeley. After participating in the Free Speech Movement, Rubin went to Cuba on a trip sponsored by the Progressive Labor Party, and then helped to organize the large Vietnam teach-in in Berkeley. A leader of the antiwar movement in the Bay Area, Rubin received a subpoena from the House Un-American Activities Committee in mid-1966. Following the advice of the San Francisco Mime Troupe's Ronnie Davis, he appeared attired in the garb of an American revolutionary soldier. Not allowed to testify, Rubin was removed from the congressional hearing by federal marshals, and faced a disorderly conduct charge. He subsequently happily noted, "Socrates is turning in his grave."[5] The following year, Rubin ran for mayor of Berkeley, capturing 22 percent of the vote.

Hoffman later pointed to Gary Snyder and Ed Sanders, a poet and member of the Fugs, as the inspirations for massive protest, recalling a stoned Sanders declaring, "A pentagon is a five-sided symbol of evil. . . . Lordy, Lord. . . . Make it rise, you motherfuckers. If you're so goddamn good, make it rise in the air."[6] At the first press conference held by the National Mobilization Committee to End the War in Vietnam, Hoffman pledged that the "flower power contingent" would ring the Pentagon, deliver spells, and compel it to "rise in the air" three hundred feet. To ward off Mace, which the federal government promised to use against protestors at the Pentagon, Hoffman indicated that the Diggers possessed Lace, "a high potency sex juice." Calling himself George Metesky, Hoffman gleefully delivered an extended pledge in the *East Village Other*:

> We will dye the Potomac red, burn the cherry trees, panhandle embassies, attack with water pistols, marbles, bubble gum wrappers, bazookas, girls will run naked and piss on the Pentagon walls, sorcerers, swamis, witches, voodoo, warlocks, medicine men, and speed freaks will hurl their magic at the faded brown walls. . . . We will dance and sing and chant the mighty OM. We will fuck on the grass and beat ourselves against the doors. Everyone will scream "VOTE FOR ME.". . . Schoolchildren will rip out their desks and throw ink at stunned instructors, office secretaries will disrobe and run into the streets, newsboys will rip up their newspapers and sit on the curbstones masturbating, storekeepers will throw open their doors making everything free, accountants will all collapse in one mighty heart attack, soldiers will throw down their guns.[7]

Meanwhile David Dellinger, who headed the MOBE, selected Rubin as project director for an impending march on Washington in mid-October.

"A Call to Resist Illegitimate Authority" appeared in the October 12, 1967, issue of the *New York Review of Books*, and in other venues as well, condemning the Vietnam War as "unconstitutional and illegal" and urging young men, including those in the military, to refuse to support the conflagration. An array of well-known figures signed the document, including several associated with the counterculture in different manners, such as Lawrence Ferlinghetti, Allen Ginsberg, Paul Goodman, Herbert Marcuse, and Dr. Benjamin Spock. The manifesto was designed to support the Resistance, the antidraft organization whose members refused to accept the legitimacy of the Selective Service System, some opting for jail instead. [8]

Marshall Bloom and Raymond Mungo envisioned the upcoming protests at the Pentagon as a means for representatives of the underground press to get together. The meeting occurred at the Institute for Policy Studies, which Mungo later called "the sugar daddy of New Left operations in the area," and resulted in the founding of Liberation News Service (LNS). Bloom explained that LNS was intended to connect antiestablishment publications and to provide "hard information to the Movement," while Walter Bowart and various staff members of the *East Village Other* sang the praises of the UPS. In turn, two *Washington Free Press* staff members accused the UPS and the *East Village Other* of embezzlement. As a rhetorical battle raged, it was clear that campus editors, pacifists, and hippies remained concerned about their own particular areas of interest, and then fist fights actually occurred. At a minimum, Mungo seemed to recognize that LNS would "be an uneasy coalition," at best. [9]

Seventy thousand demonstrators congregated in Washington, D.C., on October 21, 1967, to "Confront the War Makers." The National Mobilization Committee to End the War in Vietnam orchestrated the rally, conducted at the Lincoln Monument on the Capital Mall. Featured speakers included the radical pacifist David Dellinger, who had spoken of the need "to disrupt and block the war machine," and Dr. Benjamin Spock, the famed pediatrician and author of the internationally renowned book, *Baby and Child Care*, originally published in 1946, which urged loving parental treatment of infants. Following the address, an estimated fifty thousand people headed for the Pentagon, the architectural symbol of the mammoth American military establishment. Hoffman, Sanders, and various leading figures from the Lower East Side "passed out noisemakers, wild costumes, and witches' hats." According to historian David Farber, this involved "comic theater and a genuine hunger for the liberating force of the irrational lined up against the fierce and deadly reason of the Military Machine." [10] At one point, Sanders delivered his own incantation: "In the name of the generative power of Priapus, in the name of totality, we call upon the demons of the Pentagon to rid themselves of the cancerous tumors of the war generals." [11] Allen Ginsberg later considered that the Pentagon's authority was "demystified," thus "in that sense we *did* levitate it." This appeared to be "a triumph of the human imagination

over heavy metal materialism." As demonstrators headed for the Pentagon, Hoffman reflected that it "looked a lot like the storming of the
Bastille in the French Revolution."[12] Hoffman, who thought "the peace
movement has gone crazy and it's about time," felt empowered, believing
he was able to manipulate the media.[13] After Hoffman was arrested, he
yelled at the police, "I'm in here with Jews and Commies. Let me out!"[14]

Writing in *The Rag* on October 30, Thorne Dreyer discussed the recently concluded march on the Pentagon. Referring to "the gala Pentagon
confrontation," which he deemed indicative of the New Left's shift "from
'protest to resistance,'" Dreyer declared it "a dramatic and intense political event" that augured something new. The actions in Washington, in
Oakland during Anti-Draft week, in Madison, and in Brooklyn, enabled
black Americans to view the white left with greater respect. The "Confrontation" at the Pentagon fostered "a dynamic spirit of community,"
with "the actual storming of the Pentagon" little anticipated, Dreyer insisted. New too was the unwillingness to allow oneself to be dragged off
to jail, in civil disobedient fashion, which Dreyer dismissed as "the same
old liberal bullshit." Instead, young kids, many less than twenty years old,
behaved more militantly, while refusing to "lose their heads." Diggers
served food and passed around joints, helping to cultivate "a real festival
atmosphere." A number of people conversed with the soldiers, stating,
"We're on the same side," unlike the generals who were "fucking with
their lives." Protestors told the soldiers, "We've got food. Grass—we'd
love to turn you on." A chant rang out, "JOIN US! JOIN US!" Several
campfires began, with a number of young men burning draft cards. Dreyer felt thrilled "by the romantic vision of this beautiful revolutionary
army, occupying the lawn of the Pentagon." Purportedly, a soldier "de-
fected," leading to cheers and cries, "We Love You," as well as "We Are
All Brothers." Later, the communication between the protestors and the
soldiers waned, and police became "really brutal," freely employing billy
clubs. Still, "beautiful little hippie chicks" with "tears streaming down
their faces" refused to leave. Dreyer acknowledged that it "wasn't all love
and flowers from our side," as some "baited the soldiers, threw objects at
them." Nevertheless, Dreyer believed that he had witnessed "such a moving thing" that demonstrated the genuine changes the movement was
undergoing. There was a growing appreciation, he wrote, that the movement had to "speak for America," had to battle against "those fuckers in
the Pentagon, and those social institutions that enslave us." Moreover,

movement participants needed to view soldiers like "brothers who are being victimized." This did not call for getting beaten and responding in kind with declarations of love. Possibly the movement was not ready for "these kinds of confrontations yet," and perhaps its adherents had to "move into the communities and start talking to people as people." And yet maybe they had "the makings of a second American revolution," but one far removed from "this moral witness crap."[15]

The folksinger Phil Ochs, Abbie Hoffman, Jerry Rubin, and Paul Krassner orchestrated a rally involving three thousand demonstrators, who gathered in Washington Square on November 25, ran from Grand Central Station up Fifth Avenue to Times Square, returned to Washington Square, and then took off for Tompkins Square, shouting "The war is over." Ochs deemed the Vietnam War "only a figment of our propagandized imagination, a psychodrama out of *1984*."[16] He considered it necessary to conduct "an attack of mental disobedience on an obediently insane society," and to "step outside the guidelines of the official umpires and make your own rules and your own reality."[17]

On December 5, 1967, Allen Ginsberg joined with Dr. Benjamin Spock and nearly three thousand protestors in staging a demonstration, which was part of "Stop the Draft Week," at the induction center located at 39 Whitehall Street in Manhattan's South End. Police arrested the poet, the noted pediatrician, and 262 others on charges of disorderly conduct. Two individuals—one of them, the Fugs' Tuli Kupferberg—also faced charges of resisting arrest.

The Beatles released *Magical Mystery Tour* on December 8. Appearing the next month was *Steppenwolf*, the first album by the Canadian-American rock group based in Los Angeles.[18] The album included Mars Bonfire's "Born to Be Wild" and Hoyt Axton's "The Pusher," both later commercial hits popular among hip young people. With an energetic thrust, Steppenwolf sang "Born to Be Wild," talking about heading for the highway to seek adventure, whatever it might be, while acting to "take the world in a love embrace" by firing "all of yours guns at once / And explode into space." The band indicated that "like a true nature's child / We were born, born to be wild" and able to "climb so high."[19] One of the greatest and most disturbing songs of the era, "The Pusher" had the protagonist smoking a good deal of marijuana and popping a large number of pills, but refusing to touch anything "That my spirit couldn't kill." He damned the pusher, who cared nothing at all if his clients lived or died, in contrast to the dealer, who only doled out grass, enabling one to achieve "lots of sweet dreams." The pusher, for his part, would destroy individuals physically and mentally. The protagonist envisioned "total war" being declared against the pusher, including the meting out of death "with my bible (sic), and my razor and my gun."[20]

In mid-December, Rubin, Ed Sanders, and Keith Lampe talked about holding a free music festival during the Democratic National Convention, scheduled for Chicago in late August. Norman Mailer exclaimed "Wow!" on hearing of the impending summer plans.[21] As Rubin informed him about "a festival of life" amid the Democratic convention, Mailer was "overcome by the audacity of the idea." He told Rubin, "It's a beautiful and frightening idea. . . . You're a brave man." Rubin also explained that he hoped to induce one hundred thousand individuals or scores of rock groups to go to Chicago, to "so intimidate and terrify the establishment that Lyndon Johnson would have to be nominated under armed guard." Mailer recalled Rubin's statement that the protestors wouldn't have to do anything to induce that. Rubin continued, "The establishment is so full of guilt they'll do it all themselves. They won't be able to take it."[22]

The Hoffmans, Krassner, and Ellen Sander soon gathered in the Florida Keys, where Abbie and Ed, high on acid, "rapped about revolution. . . . guns and warfare."[23] Writing to an old friend, Father Bernard Gilgun, Hoffman spoke of inducing a quarter of a million people to come to Chicago, with "about 100,000 . . . committed to disruption or sabotage." He deemed each approach "worthwhile."[24] On New Year's Eve, Hoffman, his wife Anita, Rubin, Rubin's girlfriend, Nancy Kurshan, and Krassner, gathered at the Hoffmans' apartment on St. Marks Place in the East Village, close to Tompkins Square and the Fillmore East; they all got stoned. At one point, Krassner began crying out, "Yippie! Yippie!" That was what "the festival of life" would amount to, he exclaimed. Anita insisted on the necessity of a more formal name for the establishment media: the Youth International Party. Discussion was also had about nominating a pig for the presidency, and setting up a newspaper. As historian David Farber indicates, Yippie thus "began as a dope joke, as a half-cocked combination of hippie ethos and New Left activism, only the real joke was that the inventors meant it."[25]

A few days later, Rubin appeared at the Labor Forum in New York City to debate Old Leftist and antiwar activist Fred Halstead. To his debate partner's dismay, Rubin declared, "I support everything which puts people into motion, which creates disruption and controversy, which creates chaos and rebirth . . . people who burn draft cards . . . burn dollar bills . . . say FUCK on television . . . freaky, crazy, irrational, sexy, angry, irreligious, childish, mad people." Regarding the possibility of repression in Chicago, Rubin sermonized, "Repression turns demonstration protests into wars. Actors into heroes. Masses of people into a community. Repression eliminates the bystander, the neutral observer, the theorist. It forces everyone to pick a side." Rubin went on to contend, "A movement cannot grow without repression. The left needs an attack from the right and the center. Life is theater and we are the guerrillas attacking the shrines of authority, from the priests and the holy dollar to the two party system. Zapping people's minds and putting them through changes in action in which everyone is emotionally involved. The street is the stage. You are the star of the show." Young people would take the lead in "a revolution against privilege and a revolution against the boredom of steel-concrete plastic." Moreover, he stated, "Chicago is LBJ's stage and we are going to steal it."[26]

Additional meetings about the Democratic Party national convention followed, including one at the Hoffmans' on January 11 that added Ed Sanders, Keith Lampe, and Bob Fass, a pioneer of listener-based, non-commercial radio in New York City, to the planning group. An even larger gathering occurred shortly afterward at the posh apartment of Peggy Hitchcock. Liberation News Service editor Marshall Bloom was present, along with the *East Village Other*'s Allen Katzman, Timothy Leary, and Allen Ginsberg, who pledged to publicize the Yippie Festival of Life. On January 16, Sanders, Krassner, Rubin, and Hoffman issued "An Announcement: Youth International Party (or Yip!) Is Born." The proclamation called for "an international festival of youth music and theater" in Chicago in August, urging, "Rise up and abandon the creeping meatball! Come all you rebels, youth spirits, rock minstrels, truth seekers, peacock freaks, poets, barricade jumpers, dancers, lovers and artists." The manifesto warned that "the NATIONAL DEATH PARTY" was gathering to anoint President Lyndon Baines Johnson. By contrast, "There are 500,000 of us dancing in the streets, throbbing with amplifiers and harmony. We are making love in the parks. We are reading, singing, laughing, printing newspapers, groping and making a mock convention and celebrating the birth of FREE AMERICA in our own time." The announcement declared that "new tribes will gather in Chicago. We will be completely open, everything will be free. Bring blankets, tents, draft cards, eager skin and happiness." Notwithstanding warnings from President Johnson, Chicago Mayor Richard Daley, and the FBI's "J Edgar Freako. . . . We are coming! We are coming from all over the world!" Charging that the American spirit was being shredded "by the forces of violence, decay, and the napalm, cancer fiend," the Yippie leaders insisted on "the politics of ecstasy." They pledged, "We will create our own reality, we are Free America." Among those signing the document were Arlo Guthrie, Country Joe McDonald, Phil Ochs, the Fugs, Timothy Leary, and Allen Ginsberg.[27]

In late January 1968, the Tet Offensive, a systematic assault by North Vietnamese Army soldiers and Viet Cong guerrillas against South Vietnamese cities and provincial capitals, began. Notwithstanding earlier intelligence warnings, American policymakers, both civilian and military, appeared taken aback by the ferocity and enormity of the attacks, which involved approximately eighty thousand enemy forces. American families proved at least equally startled by televised images of Tet, including an incursion onto the U.S. embassy grounds in Saigon. Public opinion regarding the war began to shift, although the prevailing animosity toward the antiwar movement hardly subsided. Nevertheless, the antiwar candidacy of Minnesota Senator Eugene McCarthy, soon followed by that of the far more charismatic New York Senator Robert F. Kennedy, gathered momentum as the presidential primaries occurred. Movement activists such as Tom Hayden exhibited a tortured attitude toward the antiwar candidates, especially Kennedy, but countercultural figures generally proved more skeptical still. Kennedy delivered his own warning, "We seem to fulfill the vision of Yeats: 'Things fall apart, the center cannot hold; / mere anarchy is loosed upon the world.'"[28]

In February 1968, Rubin informed the *San Francisco Oracle*'s Allen Cohen about a massive counter demonstration to the Democratic Party presidential convention, which would be held in Chicago that summer.

> Our idea is to create a cultural, living alternative to the Convention. It could be the largest gathering of young people ever: in the middle of the country at the end of the summer. . . . We want all the rock bands, all the underground papers, all the free spirits, all the theater groups— all the energies that have contributed to the new youth culture—all the tribes—to come to Chicago and for six days we will live together in the park, sharing, learning, free food, free music, a regeneration of

spirit and energy. In a sense, it is like creating a SF-Berkeley spirit for
a brief period in the Midwest . . . thereby breaking people out of their
isolation and spreading the revolution.[29]

In *The Village Voice*, Rubin declared, "We say the hell with middle-class
'security' and phony status games, we are going to screw up this society.
And we can do it." He foresaw "a massive white revolutionary youth
movement" linked with black eruptions that "could seriously disrupt this
country, and thus be an internal catalyst for a breakdown of the American
ability and will to fight guerrillas overseas."[30] In an interview with John
Wilcox, the British journalist who had cofounded *The Village Voice* and
more recently had established *Other Scenes*, an underground newspaper
in New York City, Hoffman warned, "Revolution's a lot like a river, you
know, it sort of seeks its own level." He predicted that if American
television displayed "kids running through the streets yelling and screaming . . . there'd be blood, violence, boom."[31]

Also in February, Jefferson Airplane began recording *Crown of Creation*, which featured "Lather," David Crosby's "Triad," and "The House
at Pooneil Corners."[32] Written by Grace Slick in homage to drummer
Spencer Dryden's turning thirty, "Lather" began with its protagonist hit-
ting that age mark, and, consequently, having all of his toys taken away.
On top of that, his mother mailed newspaper clippings about "old friends
who'd stopped being boys," including a banker and a tank commander.
By contrast, Lather still enjoyed lounging "about nude in the sand" and
playing his drums. While children referred to him as famous, old men
considered Lather insane.[33] "Triad" referred to a ménage-à-trois, with
Heinlein-like "Sister lovers water brothers."[34] Notwithstanding its title,
"The House at Pooneil Corners" offered a not so whimsical look at the
world around despite the attempt "to get far and high," with "Somebodys
dealing, somebodys stealing," the war continuing, and images of castles
disappearing.[35] Late in the month, the Beatles headed to India to spend
several weeks with Maharishi Mahesh Yogi, who had introduced
Transcendental Meditation to India in the mid-1950s; that provided a spur
for more Western youth to travel to the East. Ringo Starr left first, then
Paul McCartney, while John Lennon and George Harrison stayed somewhat longer. Lennon, in particular, was trying to kick a growing addiction
to hard drugs, but talk that the Maharishi had made a pass at the
American actress Mia Farrow provided an excuse to depart. While in

India the Beatles wrote many of the songs that later appeared on either *The White Album* or *Abbey Road*.

The March 11 issue of *Newsweek* suggested that "the hippie movement . . . is at a crossroads." Some were following the lead of the Maharishi, opting for meditation rather than social engagement. Others were joining in "a partly political, partly put-on group called the Youth International Party—yippies." The Yippies appeared to be "a non-group," but included in their ranks Rubin, Hoffman, Ginsberg, Leary, and *The Realist*'s Paul Krassner. As Rubin explained, "It's the politics of ecstasy. The Youth International party begins with the premise that politics should be a party. It's dancing, it's guerrilla theater."[36] The Yippies intended to conduct a "freak out" during the Democratic National Convention, while Hugh Romney of the Hog Farm envisioned nominating a pig for President during a mock convention. In the radical pacifist publication *WIN* on March 15, Hoffman dismissed the Democratic national convention as "a political circus," then stated, "Ours will be the real thing complete with sawdust and laughing bears." Rather than "meaningless resolutions," the protestors would listen to Country Joe and the Fish and Allen Ginsberg. When the president arrived at the podium, "We will run naked through the streets."[37]

In a letter dated March 16 that appeared in the *Berkeley Barb*, Michael Rossman, long involved with political and countercultural activities in the Bay Area, presciently warned his friend Jerry Rubin "about this Yippie thing." Rossman feared that blood would be forthcoming with even black radicals in Chicago telling their white organizer buddies, "Stay off the street, we won't be able to protect you." He saw the Yippies operating in "deeply and dangerously irresponsible" fashion, a charge Rossman also tossed at New Left activists Rennie Davis and Tom Hayden for suggesting the possibility of "peaceful . . . multicentered independent demonstrations" taking place near the Convention site. Rossman saw Rubin "surrounded by Death," and about to be known "as a politico who dropped acid."[38]

The Village Voice of March 21 included an article by Sally Kempton, "Yippies Anti-Organize a Groovy Revolution," with Hoffman quoted as saying, "We're not leaders, we're cheerleaders."[39] The Yippies planned a demonstration, the Yip-in, to be conducted at New York's Grand Central Station in the early hours of March 22. The advance publicity playfully indicated, "It's a spring mating service celebrating the equinox, a back-scratching party, a roller skating rink, a theater . . . with you as performer and audience." Participants were advised to bring "Flowers, Beads, Music, Radios, Pillows, Eats, Love and Peace.[40] As the Yip-in started at 1 a.m., chants soon rang out, ranging from "Yippie" to "Burn, Baby, Burn." The Motherfuckers attempted to provoke the police, who began clubbing individuals indiscriminately, even smacking commuters awaiting train service. Don McNeill of *The Village Voice* decried the Yip-in as "a pointless confrontation in a box canyon" that presaged upcoming events in Chicago.[41] Agreeing with the latter analysis, Hoffman was thrilled that "the Grand Central Station Massacre knocked out the hippie image of Chicago and let the whole world know there would be blood on the streets in Chicago."[42] The *New York Times* reported, "Political Activism New Hippie 'Thing.'"[43]

In late March, the African American author Julius Lester applauded the Yippies in his column for the *Guardian*.

> In a country where the picket sign march and demonstration have become respectable, other means of communicating a political point of view must be found. Regis Debray talks of armed propaganda. . . . The Yippies have begun to explore the techniques of disarming propaganda. They have their roots not in Mao or Che but in the Provos, rock and Lenny Bruce. They ignore what a man thinks and grab him by the balls to communicate their message. They seek to involve people in an experience, not argue with them. They are like Zen monks who never answered a question directly, never set forth a list of Dos and Don'ts, Rights and Wrongs but answered students with a hard slap. The Yippies are a hard slap, a kick in the crotch, a bunch of snipers pinning the enemy down and making him afraid to move.[44]

But as Jerry Rubin admitted in *The Village Voice* on March 21, "I am more confident of our ability to survive concentration camps than I am of our ability to survive Bobby" Kennedy, whose campaign style appeared to duplicate the charisma of his slain brother, but from a more impassioned vantage point.[45] President Johnson's stunning announcement on March 31 that he would not seek renomination for another possible presidential term only appeared to enhance RFK's chance to ascend to the White House. Abbie Hoffman responded to LBJ's declaration by acknowledging, "Lyndon is out-flanking us on our hippie side."[46]

Professor Theodore Roszak from California State University, Hayward, wrote about "Capsules of Salvation" in the April 8 issue of *The Nation*. Roszak, in the midst of drafting his classic work, *The Making of a Counterculture*, began by asserting, "At the bohemian fringe of the disaffected youth culture, all roads lead to dope." During the past ten years, "the drug experience" had served as "the common denominator," but, Roszak warned, "the frantic search for a narcotic nirvana can destroy many of the young, as well as all that is most valuable in their rebellion." By contrast, "controlled samplings and restrained observations" characterized earlier endeavors by William James, Havelock Ellis, Aldous Huxley, and Alan Watts. Roszak offered, "I doubt that anyone could have predicted what a wretched aftermath these pioneering experiments were to have." Some individuals who took psychedelics, Roszak continued, were simply too young, with minds too undeveloped "for such psychic adventures." The inability "to recognize this fact is the beginning of disaster," he stated. Simply put, "there is nothing whatever in common between a man of Huxley's experience and intellectual discipline sampling mescaline, and a 15-year-old tripper whiffing airplane glue until his brain turns to oatmeal." Moreover, drug usage did indeed become "a hangup which too many of the young can't shake." Part of this was "typically American," with passage from "a gimmick" to the selling of "a new way of life." "Decadence," with the fixation on the drug experience, characterized hippie culture. Roszak named Leary, "the promoter, apologist and high priest of dope," the leading proponent of the "lamentable campaign" contending that drugs could lead to "a total and autonomous culture." The professor also pointed to Kesey, but indicated that at least his sessions "were mainly fun and games." Ominously, Roszak referred to Herbert Marcuse's 1964 book, *One-Dimensional Man*, with its Marxist and Freudian influences, as emphasizing how the most sophisticated brands of totalitarianism involved "repressive sublimation," rather than brutal repression. Roszak concluded with the observation that "it only took Timothy Leary and his ilk to formulate the proposition that personal salvation and the social revolution can be packed in a capsule."[47]

In April, Raymond Mungo, one of the founders of Liberation News Service (LNS), continued his travels around the country, visiting Austin. There, as in Boston, Chicago, Ann Arbor, and Berkeley, a feeling existed that this was "all there is." As Mungo saw it, "if you live in the heart of Texas, you would know that there is no place else." On or around the

University of Texas campus could be found "head shops, libraries, an underground newspaper, a local Narc, and 90 percent of America's mescaline." He mentioned the *Rag*, the local underground paper, calling it one the nation's first but warned, it was "growing old." Mungo referred to "bureaucratic hassles," similar to those experienced by LNS, that had "become utterly and hopelessly unmanageable." At the same time, the *Rag* had avoided the "personality war" some papers suffered, which Mungo attributed to the "gentle and decent" stewardship of Thorne Dreyer.[48]

Writing in *Rolling Stone* magazine, Ralph Gleason discussed the anger and ire directed against the counterculture in his essay, "The Final Paroxysm of Fear." New rock music, he admitted, had hardly changed the world. And yet he believed that it had created a type "of *Stranger in a Strange Land* head community." Gleason saw what he referred to as "the counter-revolution," serving as "the last dying gasp of the Logical Generation," terrified by the unknown. Young people appeared to repulse the dominant "Elders," the police, and many other adults, who devolved "into a snarling mob of hysterical, crazed bigots" regarding long hair, rock music, drugs, and sex.[49]

A series of unsettling events transpired in the spring of 1968. On April 4, an assassin, later discovered to be James Earl Ray, fired a bullet that took the life of civil rights leader Martin Luther King Jr. Over one hundred American cities, including the nation's capital, experienced race riots in the wake of the killing of America's apostle of nonviolence. Responding to a priest who suggested a protest march in Memphis, Abbie Hoffman responded, "I ain't marching anymore."[50] Later that month, students at Columbia University went on strike and occupied campus buildings, led by black militants and the campus chapter of SDS, headed by Mark Rudd. "Liberation classes" were held, and concerts delivered, with the Grateful Dead and Phil Ochs performing. Among those showing up to display support for the students, protesting the university's complicity with the Pentagon and its encroachment on black-held property in Harlem, were Allen Ginsberg, Tom Hayden, H. Rap Brown, and Stokely Carmichael, the coauthor of *Black Power: The Politics of Liberation* and a relatively new addition to the leadership of the Black Panther Party. SDS envisioned "two, three, many Columbias," with the campus unrest at Morningside Heights ushering in a new wave of militant tactics.[51] By early May, a strike involving students from the University of Paris and

Sorbonne University and workers threatened to topple the conservative French government of Charles DeGaulle.

On May 7, 1968, Ginsberg sat for an interview with William F. Buckley, the right-wing editor of *The National Review*, to be aired later in the year on Buckley's PBS program, *Firing Line*. When asked about hippies and "the new order," Ginsberg quizzically responded, "New order?" before stating, "I'm hoping it will be orderly and gentle, yes." At one point, Ginsberg said, "I think the LSD clarified my mind and left it open to get that sense of giant, vast consciousness." Referring back to Buckley's initial query, Ginsberg said "the primary hippie, and beatnik originally, that '56 perception was a recognition of that unity of being and a recognition of that great consciousness which we all were identical with, see?" Ginsberg suggested that the notions of "flower power" or "make love, not war" were "grounded in an understanding of the nature of the universe in that you can't fight *us*, we can't fight *us*." The need existed to appreciate "our unity, particularly black and white, particularly square and hippie, particularly police and student, particularly Birchite and faggot individualist." As Buckley expressed concerns that the hippie attitude regarding love failed to take into consideration humanity's essence, Ginsberg denied that love was what most shone in the Haight-Ashbury; instead, it was "a widening of awareness from the feeling that we were separate, alienated, isolated individuals to be regimented and made into advertising workers or soldiers going off with short Prussian haircuts to napalm in Vietnam." To Ginsberg, the beats and hippies said nothing new, other than emphasizing "the old gnostic (sic) tradition which had been somewhat suppressed by the Whore of Babylon . . . the organized, rigidified, militarily crusading Church."[52]

Michael Rossman again expressed displeasure about the Yippies' plans for Chicago, warning,

> This style of organizing is dangerously irresponsible. For the formless publicity building the magical beckoning symbol of Music projects an image that is recklessly and inescapably slanted. It promises grooving and warmth, and does not warn that joy there must be won from within—not absorbed from others—in a landscape of total hostility whose ground conditions may well be the terror and death of one's brothers.

Rossman continued, "And once triggered, the energies there may not soon subside."[53]

Janis Joplin and Big Brother and the Holding Company began recording *Cheap Thrills* during the spring of 1968, with her powerful voice dominating "Piece of My Heart" and the Big Mama Thornton classic, "Ball and Chain."[54] As she admitted, "My music isn't supposed to make you riot. It's supposed to make you fuck."[55] Almost as noteworthy was the collage-like album cover produced by Robert Crumb, with cartoonish images of band members, an indication that live recordings had taken place at Bill Graham's Fillmore Auditorium, and the insignia of the Frisco chapter of the Hell's Angels. Quicksilver Messenger Service recorded its debut album, which included "Dino's Song" by Dino Valenti, who had helped to found the band but was presently incarcerated because of a dope bust.[56] John Lennon and his new lover Yoko Ono delivered an album, *Two Virgins*, in which they stood naked on the front and back covers.[57]

The Beatles attained notoriety in another arena that spring, on beginning the operations of Apple, their own record company. Conducting a radio interview to announce that launching, Lennon referred to the Vietnam War as "insane," and talked about the need to change the Establishment "completely." Paul McCartney informed Ray Connolly, writing for the London *Evening Standard*, "We've got all the money we need. I've got the house and the cars and all the things that money can buy. So instead of trying to amass money for the sake of it, we're setting up a business with a social and cultural environment where everyone gets a decent share of the profits. I suppose it'll be like a sort of Western communism."[58]

Hopes for peaceful transformation of American society further dissipated for many, including political activists like Tom Hayden, with the shooting of Senator Robert F. Kennedy in the early morning of June 5. The death of a second Kennedy brother, who appeared to have a good shot at garnering the Democratic Party presidential nomination, followed closely the assassination of Martin Luther King Jr. and weakened the already tenuous belief in the system held by a growing number of young people, both in the movement and the counterculture. At SDS's national convention, held at Michigan State University in East Lansing, Bernadine Dohrn, a graduate of the University of Chicago Law School, elected Inter-organizational Secretary, had proclaimed, "I consider myself a revolutionary communist."[59] SDS leaders began envisioning harsher confrontations in Chicago, with some, like Jeff Jones, welcoming that prospect.

In mid-June, a jury in Boston convicted Dr. Benjamin Spock, Yale University chaplain William Sloane Coffin Jr., author Mitchell Goodman, and Harvard graduate student Michael Ferber of conspiring to counsel young men to violate the Selective Service Act. Spock responded by asserting that the Vietnam War "violates the United Nations Charter, the Geneva accords and the United States' promise to obey the laws of international conduct. It is totally, abominably illegal."[60]

On a far more whimsical note, the Beatles' cartoon-etched movie, *Yellow Submarine*, appeared in mid-July, complete with the band members looking as they had during *Sgt. Pepper's*, the fantasy Pepperland, and nasty Blue Meanies, hardly enamored with songs like the title tune, "Baby, You're a Rich Man," and several from *Sgt. Pepper's*.[61]

Based in Detroit, still the automobile capital of the world, the proto-punk band MC-5, managed by John Sinclair, began acquiring something of a following. Greatly influenced by Sinclair, the MC-5 strongly identified with the white working class, and adopted a political posture that drew from both Marxism and Maoism. Sinclair was the founder of the White Panther Party, which believed in "a total assault on the culture by any means necessary."[62] While attending Albion College, Sinclair, a native of Flint, Michigan, became enamored with beat writers and avant-garde jazz. Later, Sinclair reflected on his reading of Norman Mailer's *The White Negro*: "I was a White Negro in a purer sense. By the time that came out, I was on the streets. I was hangin' in the barbershops, in the pool rooms. . . . [I was] doing it."[63] He participated in Detroit's Artist Workshop, with its avant-garde emphasis; another participant was John Kay, later the lead singer for Steppenwolf. The collective put out some of the region's first underground publications, such as *Guerrilla* with its masthead reading, "A Newspaper of Cultural Revolution."

Another commune, Om, soon to become legendary in countercultural lore, thrived for a brief spell in mid-1968. Originally from Southern California, but escaping from that region's sprawling cities, pollution, and commercial bent, members of Om had lived for about a-year-and-a-half in several cabins close to Santa Cruz, although the high cost of rent compelled them to consider relocating. They soon accepted a friend's offer of free use of the land near the village of Harmonsburg, outside of Meadville, Pennsylvania, he had recently inherited, along with its ramshackle three-story farmhouse, which lacked, as Robert Houriet later reported, "windows, a working stove, indoor plumbing, electricity." Thirty-five people, including fourteen women and a little girl, made up the Om family, with half the women regularly paired with a lone male partner. Most were in their early thirties, while the purported leader, thirty-year-old George Hurd, viewed the commune as a "working anarchy," absent officers, work regimens, and only a few "tribal councils." Financial resources proved limited, however, and even those who worked on nearby farms received only crops in return. At the same time, communal "happenings," including regular readings from the work of Dr. Seuss, A. A. Milne, and Frank Baum, heightened "the family's almost mystical feeling of oneness." They were part of an attempt to attain "inner peace and exaltation by natural means," rather than through drugs. Those were hardly absent altogether, and ranged from morphine to methadrine. Sexual practices seemed somewhat less free-flowing than on many communes, and birth control was considered "unnatural." Some farmers willingly helped out the Om family, providing surplus food stuffs and instructions on cultivating crops. However, the appearance of new arrivals, including teenyboppers and drunken motorcyclists, the latter of whom fired a rifle near the farmhouse, hardly helped the family's image. A number of unfortunate incidents occurred, including the shooting of one of the family's dogs, the repeated rape of a family member, and the admission to the local hospital of a communard with infectious hepatitis. Tensions rose, and arrests of four family members, charged with vagrancy, followed. A raid of the farm occurred, with an ensuing charge of "maintaining a disorderly house." An injunction was posted on the farmhouse, denying its use for "fornication, assignation and lewdness." Merchants, including the operator of the nearby grocery store, refused to deal with the family. Its members soon scattered, and arson resulted in the gutting of the farm's main house. [64]

In July, the British group the Moody Blues put out "Legend of a Mind," recorded six months earlier, and serving as a tribute to Timothy Leary. The song denied that Leary was dead, declaring that instead he was "outside looking in," flying "his astral plane," taking individuals on trips that took one up and down. [65] Leary spent considerable time with the Brotherhood of Eternal Love, while his son Jack stayed at the group's ranch in Garner Valley, close to Idyllwild, California, for a good while longer. The Brotherhood revered Timothy, and deemed *The Psychedelic Experience* virtually sacrosanct.

Margaret Sankot, the head nurse at the Haight-Ashbury Medical Center, and Dr. David E. Smith, the medical director of the Haight-Ashbury Clinic, delivered a report on "Drug Problems in the Haight-Ashbury," which appeared in the August 1968 issue of the *American Journal of Nursing*. The original hippie subculture in the district, they began, revolved around a small group of individuals determined "to share creative, emotional, and transcendental experiences." Adopting a communal lifestyle, they propounded a gospel "of love and brotherhood," while employing pot and LSD to foster their quest for self-enlightenment. Initially, they were able to devise their own subculture, complete with rules they concocted. However, by the previous summer, many others rushed into the area, lacking any appreciation "of the 'new community' philosophy." The results were catastrophic, with a paucity of housing, food, and health care. Drug usage of the street variety escalated, with predictable results. Consequently, "the original subculture was shattered by thousands of upset, unhappy young people looking for immediate answers to life's problems." The Haight-Ashbury Clinic had opened in June 1967, with its staff determined "not to judge, but to inform and to care," quickly offering treatment for many on bad acid trips or on methamphetamine. The latter became the most frequently abused drug in the district. The *San Francisco Express Times*, an underground newspaper, also reported that "for at least a year now . . . the community as a common commitment of its parts, has deteriorated steadily. Most of the old crowd is gone. Some say they haven't actually left but are staying away from the street because of bad vibrations." A sense of despair had taken hold, while even the Diggers had stopped handing out free food in Golden Gate Park. As one explained, "Well, man, it took a lot of organization to get that done. We had to scuffle to get the food. Then the chicks or somebody had to prepare it. Then we got to serve it. A lot of people got to do a lot of things at the right time or it doesn't come off. Well, it got so that people weren't doing it." Plus, "you hate to get into a power bag and start telling people what to do but without that, man, well."[66]

Also in August 1968, Tom Wolfe's book, *The Electric Kool-Aid Acid Test*, began garnering reviews widely. Writing in the *New York Times*, Eliot Fremont-Smith referred to "the great freak-out of the nineteen-sixties," the adventures of Ken Kesey and the Merry Pranksters. Fremont-

Smith called *The Electric Kool-Aid Acid Test* "not simply the best book on the hippies," but "the essential book" on the Kesey band of acidheads, who underwent cross-country trips, complete with outlandish outfits and drug-laden orgies, "doing whatever it was mystically, communally, evangelically felt, an urge needed doing, only always further out, nearer the edge."[67] The writer C. D. B. Bryan, also reviewing Wolfe's book for the *New York Times*, deemed it "astonishing," and a work that captured the hippie movement as Norman Mailer's *The Armies of the Night* had antiwar protest. Bryan discussed the evolution of Kesey from an esteemed author "to an LSD enthusiast, to the messianic leader of a mystical band of Merry Pranksters, to a fugitive from the F.B.I., California police and Mexican Federales." Wolfe's book itself, Bryan offered, was "a celebration of psychedelia, of all its sounds and costumes, colors and fantasies." Bryan effectively characterized the Pranksters as a cult led by one man, all of whom proved unable to actually move beyond acid in the manner that Kesey urged. What Bryan considered most significant about *The Electric Kool-Aid Acid Test* was how it captured the transformation young people were undergoing, as they appeared more concerned about aesthetic than social values, rejecting the Protestant Ethic for "the Pleasure Now principle."[68] The novelist Joel Lieber, writing in *The Nation*, also praised Wolfe's book as conveying as accurately as possible "the entire mental atmosphere of a scene in which one's understanding is based on feeling rather than verbalization." Looking back at the Pranksters, Lieber indicated that "what started out as being a fun trip became a mission and the mission became a religion, a religion totally dedicated to *Now*, the ecstasy of living in the present," with Kesey serving as "an exemplary prophet."[69]

15

FIGHTING IN THE STREETS AND THE
LATEST BATTLE OF THE BANDS

In August 1968, LNS splintered into two irreconcilable factions, with Marshall Bloom and Raymond Mungo heading the one that set up shop at a farm in Montague, Massachusetts. The coming apart of LNS presaged impending divisions within the counterculture and the movement. Mungo spun the story of LNS's fracture into the Virtuous Caucus—his—and the Vulgar Marxists, in the autobiographically laden *Famous Long Ago: My Life and Hard Times with Liberation News Service*, complete with embellishments. "Their story was communal socialism, ours was something like anarchism, and while we could cheerfully keep a few socialists around, they couldn't function as they planned with even one anarchist in the house, one Marshall Bloom. . . . Their method of running the news service was the Meeting and the Vote, ours was Magic. We lived on Magic, and still do, and I have to say it beats anything *systematic*." Members of the Virtuous Caucus referred to their lifestyle as "Kool Space," believing that "one united family" beckoned on the planet Earth. Those communards sought to construct "a fair and just society . . . of equals," rooted in "kindness and compassion." They possessed a cow, a pig, a horse, twenty-four chickens, and plenty of dogs and cats. Mungo recalled, "Plants, flowers, and trees framed our universe," while magic was "on our side." He would never depart, Mungo knew, if, as he later wrote, "I could just avoid growing up."[1]

Responding to news of LNS's "hard times," FBI director J. Edgar Hoover fired off a memo to the agency's New York office. "Recent issues of the underground press have carried articles relating to the split within the Liberation News Service (LNS). It would seem this is an excellent opportunity to take advantage of the split to further disrupt the underground press and to attack the New Left." Agents at the New York office proceeded to devise a letter, purportedly signed by a former staffer and titled "And Who Got the Cookie Jar?" that ridiculed LNS staffers, deemed the breakup "a real kindergarten performance by all concerned," labeled an LNS founder "a bit of a nut," and bemoaned the devolution of the organization "from an efficient news service into a complete mess." The FBI followed up by seeking an audit of LNS by the Internal Revenue Service, which proved obliging. Additional efforts to discredit LNS included the sending of a letter to the antiwar Student Mobilization Committee posing the question, "How has the Liberation News Service survived these many years?" and answering, "Federal bread constitutes its main support." The letter also ominously warned, "LNS is in an ideal position to infiltrate the Movement at every level," and "LNS representatives all carry police press cards too."[2]

The Democrats' long-awaited presidential convention, held in Chicago in late August, proved calamitous for their retaining the White House. Cries that "the whole world is watching" rang out, as violent clashes occurred between demonstrators and the police in Grant Park. Police went on a rampage, smashing into protestors and innocent bystanders alike, with violence even seeping into the hotel headquarters of antiwar Senator Eugene McCarthy and onto the convention hall itself. This was precisely the scenario that the Yippies, led by Abbie Hoffman and Jerry Rubin, had envisioned months earlier, although the intervening months had resulted in far fewer than the one hundred thousand young people once predicted as coming to the Windy City. The authoritarian image cast by Mayor Richard Daley and the Chicago police department convinced many not to make the trek, an image hardened by recent events. Riots that followed the killing of Martin Luther King Jr. on April 4 led to Daley's adoption of a hardline law-and-order policy, and his pronouncement that Chicago police in the future should "shoot to kill arsonists" and "shoot to maim looters."[3] An antiwar gathering weeks later saw police seemingly target protestors with nightsticks.

Consequently, many who initially intended to participate in the Yippies' Festival of Life chose not to do so. *The Seed*, the Chicago underground paper edited by Abe Peck, warned, "Don't come to Chicago if you expect a five-day Festival of Life, music and love," and advised, "If you're going to Chicago, be sure to wear some armor in your hair." The *Seed* foresaw the possibility of a "Festival of Blood," inferring that the police would riot.[4] The *Berkeley Barb* also delivered an admonition: "Yippies will need to be a tough breed . . . Flower children may be quickly 'radicalized' by having their heads busted by a cop's billy club."[5] As Peter Coyote later explained, the Diggers too were little enamored with both the Yippies and politicos like Tom Hayden, who seemed to be proclaiming themselves "the new leaders of the radical left." The Diggers worried that Abbie Hoffman, Jerry Rubin, and Hayden were enticing kids to come to Chicago as part "of Police Theater," with no permits available and no rock bands. Coyote charged, "It was as capricious and as manipulative a trick as anything Lyndon Johnson or Kennedy ever did, to get these kids out there to create this huge event, called radicalizing America."[6]

Hoffman delivered the last Yippie manifesto before the convention, including the slogan from the Paris uprisings in the spring, "Be realistic-demand the impossible," and signing it "A. Hippie." "This is my personal statement. There are no spokesmen for the Yippies. . . . We are all our own leaders. . . . We demand a society based on humanitarian cooperation and equality, a society which allows and promotes the creativity of all people, especially youth." Hoffman wrote, "Political pigs, your days are numbered. We are the second American Revolution. We shall win. Yippie." The Steering Committee of the Mobe urged supporters to come to Chicago, warning that the city "is fast becoming the Prague of the middle west," but insisting on the need to "not lose our democratic rights by default."[7]

Allen Ginsberg expressed displeasure at the Yippies and their "bloody visions of apocalypse" at the convention, but appeared at the park, quickly becoming enmeshed in the protest gatherings, trying to dampen tensions by chanting "Om, ommm."[8] Others who arrived included National Mobe leaders Tom Hayden, Rennie Davis, and David Dellinger, and the Yippie contingent headed by Hoffman and Rubin. Hoffman urged young people to adopt a militant stance. "Fuck nuns: laugh at professors: disobey your parents: burn your money: . . . break down the family, church, nation, city, economy: turn your life into an art form, a theatre of the soul and a theatre of the future." Rumors floated that the Yippies intended to spike Chicago's reservoirs with LSD, and also hoped "to paint cars like independent taxi-cabs and forcibly take delegates to Wisconsin; . . . to engage Yippie girls as 'hookers' to attract delegates and dose their drinks with LSD; to bombard the Amphitheater with mortars from several miles away; to jam communication lines." They planned "to assemble 100,000 people to burn draft cards; . . . to dress Yippies like Viet Cong and walk the streets shaking hands and passing out rice; . . . to have ten thousand nude bodies floating on Lake Michigan."[9] But only a few thousand protestors gathered in Chicago, along with six thousand soldiers from the U.S. Army, five thousand National Guardsmen, twelve thousand policemen, and possibly one thousand operatives from the FBI, the CIA, and military intelligence. As the city refused to issue permits for demonstrators to camp out in Grant Park, Rubin and Hoffman called for the kids to prevent police from shutting it down. When Hoffman threatened looting and pillaging by roaming bands, an enraged Ed Sanders responded, "I'm sick and tired of hearing people talk like that. . . . You're urging people to go out and get killed for nothing. Man, that's like murdering people."[10] Ginsberg agreed. "The park isn't worth dying for."[11] Finally, Rubin, Hoffman, Sanders, Ginsberg, and Paul Krassner issued notes calling for the park to be abandoned if the curfew were enforced; SDS leaders agreed that the alternative was too dangerous, potentially.

On August 27, in Lincoln Park, Hoffman delivered his "Yippie Workshop Speech," which began with a blast at both the mainstream media and the police. Quickly, Hoffman exclaimed,

> So if you are good at guerrilla theater, you can look a pig right in the eye and say that to him, you know, and he'll do it. You know, that's the thing, to get him to do it. You just let 'em know that you're stronger psychically than they are. And you are, because you came here for nothin' and they're holdin' on to their fuckin' pig jobs 'cause of that little fuckin' paycheck and workin' themselves up, you know. Up to what? To a fuckin' ulcer. Sergeant. We got them by the balls. The whole thing about guerrilla theater is gettin' them to believe it. Right.[12]

The Yippies went ahead with their Festival of Life, which including a performance by the MC-5.

In reality, the scene in Chicago was ugly and about to get uglier still, as many, including Hoffman earlier, had predicted and as was occurring elsewhere. As the Democratic Party convention approached, television viewers had watched scenes of tanks rolling into Czechoslovakia's capital city, where during the past several months, the reform government of Alexander Dubcek had attempted to bring about "socialism with a human face" as part of the so-called Prague Spring. The events in Chicago seemed eerily similar, with police shouting "Kill!" and "Commie!" as they smashed into the bodies and heads of protestors, who delivered cries of their own like "Motherfucker!," "Pigs!," "Shithead!," and "Zieg Heil!" At one point, Connecticut Senator Abraham Ribicoff denounced "Gestapo tactics in the streets of Chicago," as a visibly enraged Mayor Daley could be seen mouthing, "Fuck you, you Jew son of a bitch, you lousy motherfucker, go home."[13] Another almost surreal moment occurred during a televised debate on August 28 between writers William F. Buckley and Gore Vidal, when Vidal demanded that Buckley "shut up a minute" and called him a "pro-crypto-Nazi." An enraged Buckley responded, "Now listen, you queer. Stop calling me a crypto-Nazi or I'll sock you in the goddamn face and you'll stay plastered."[14] On another occasion, CBS anchorman Walter Cronkite proved visibly upset and frustrated on learning that reporter Dan Rather had been roughed up on the convention floor. Democratic Party presidential nominee Hubert Humphrey hardly ingratiated himself with the movement, in seemingly siding with the Chicago police.

> I know what caused these demonstrations. They were planned, premeditated by certain people in this country that feel that all they have to do is riot and they'll get their way. They don't want to work through the peaceful process. I have no time for them. The obscenity, the profanity, the filth that was uttered night after night in front of the hotels was an insult to every woman, every mother, every daughter, indeed, every human being, the kind of language that no one would tolerate at all. . . . Is it any wonder police had to take action?[15]

Yippie Keith Lampe insisted, "We have ripped the smiling mask from the face of the man," while Stew Albert referred to the clashes in Chicago as amounting to "a revolutionary wet dream come true."[16] Jerry Rubin appeared delighted by what Chicago had wrought. "We wanted exactly what happened. We wanted the tear gas to get so heavy that the reality was tear gas. We wanted to create a situation in which the Chicago police and the Daley administration and the federal government and the United States would self-destruct. We wanted to show that America wasn't a democracy, that the convention wasn't politics. The message of the week was of America ruled by force. This was a big victory." Rubin admitted, "We were guilty as hell."[17]

But the radical journalist I. F. Stone worried that the finest young people "were being lost—some among the hippies to drugs, some among the radicals to an almost hysterical frenzy of alienation."[18] In a subsequent *Playboy* interview, Ginsberg stated, "I think everybody who watched television during the convention experienced a widening of consciousness because . . . outright police brutality was shown so clearly that even TV and radio commentators were saying, 'This is a police state!'"[19]

The *East Village Other*'s Allen Katzman penned an essay, "Bandages and Stitches Tell the Story," starting with the opening quote from Charles Dickens's *A Tale of Two Cities*: "It was the best of times. It was the worst of the times." To Katzman, "thus began the battle of Chicago, a tale of two cities within a city, an armed camp where stupidity, ideology, and power politics have set the stage for the fall of the Holy American Empire." Hardly employing the language of the love generation, Katzman lambasted "the technology of the Pig, Chicago's blue brute force otherwise known as Mayor Daley's Dervishes." Piqued by their disdain for the mayor, the media had ushered in "the most viable revolution in this country since the Boston Tea Party," while Daley enabled young revolutionaries to become schooled in guerrilla warfare antics. Meanwhile, the residents of Chicago supposedly had never been more cognizant "of the police state they live in." Katzman concluded, "The battle for Chicago will be remembered in the heavy years to come as the beginning of a Revolution." As beatings had continued, Chicago featured the "Death Headquarters" of Democratic Party presidential nominee Hubert Humphrey, and looked like Vietnam and Prague.[20] SDS National Secretary Mike Klonsky soon suggested, "Chicago has shown us that young people in this country are not necessarily caught up in the bullshit that is the American electoral process."

Recorded from late May through the first three weeks in June, "Revolution" came out on August 26, and was John Lennon's response to mounting cries within the antiwar movement for moving into the streets. To those who professed a desire for revolution, Lennon declared, "We all want to change the world." But he drew the line, at least in the most commercially successful version of the song, in conveying his opposition to "destruction" and to supporting "people with minds that hate." And regarding calls to alter the Constitution or institutions in general, Lennon warned, "You better free your mind instead" and that sporting photographs of Chinese communist leader Mao Zedong would hardly prove appealing.[21] Also recorded during the spring of 1968, the Rolling Stones' "Street Fighting Man" appeared to offer that rock band's take on the youthful eruptions of the period. While Lennon admonished would-be revolutionaries to carefully reflect, Mick Jagger and Keith Richards seemingly stood shoulder-to-shoulder with those who favored action in the streets. Their song opened with the cacophony "of marching, charging feet," as summer had arrived and the timing was propitious "for fighting in the street." Declaring that "the time was right for a palace revolution" and that his name was "disturbance," the protagonist promised to bellow out, "I'll kill the king." Jagger and Richards only somewhat softened the edges of "Street Fighting Man" by admitting that "a poor boy" could only "sing for a rock 'n' roll band . . . in sleepy London town."[22] Talking to the London *Sunday Mirror*, Jagger, who had studied at the elite London School of Economics, suggested, "War stems from power-mad politicians and patriots," "Anarchy is the only slight glimmer of hope," and "There should be no such thing as private property."[23]

The Beatles' rendition of "Revolution" resulted in criticism of John Lennon's song from the New Left and the underground press, with *Ramparts* labeling it a "betrayal" and asserting, "You *know* it's *not* gonna be all right," while the *New Left Review* dismissed it as "a lamentable petty bourgeois cry of fear." The *Berkeley Barb* assailed the tune even more harshly: "'Revolution' sounds like the hawk plank adopted in the Chicago convention of the Democratic Party." By contrast, rock critic Greil Marcus insisted there was "a message in the music which is ultimately more powerful than anyone's words. There is freedom and movement in the music, even as there is sterility and repression in the lyrics. The music doesn't say 'cool it' or 'don't fight the cops.'"[24] *Time* magazine also pointed to the Beatles' refrain, "We all want to change the world," as well as their admonition regarding destruction and "minds that hate."[25] Historian Jon Weiner points to another consideration, the fact that the supposed "B" side of "Revolution," proved to be far more appealing to Beatles' fans: "Hey Jude." Writing for LNS, Jon Landau praised the Beatles' top British rivals instead, declaring that "The Stones strike for realism in contrast to the Beatles' fantasies. They want to transcend the escapist and the self-congratulatory."[26]

Perhaps the headline that the *New York Times* offered in late August was unsurprising, given the unsettling nature of major events that continued to take place, "Hippies Fading from City Scene." Many hippies, John Kifner noted, had headed "to the country in search of a life of rustic simplicity that has become the new dropout ideal." Hippies had gathered in communal farms back East in Vermont and Massachusetts, and in Colorado ghost towns out West. As the *East Village Other*'s editor, Peter Leggieri, observed, "Everybody's left the city. There was a belief that the city was not fit to live in, that it was going to explode." Driving hippies away were police harassment and slum violence. Another change involved those who were abandoning "indolence for radical politics."[27] Jeff Shero, who had founded *The Rat*, an underground newspaper in New York City, with other former staff members from *The Rag*, such as Gary Thiher and Alice Embree, reported, "The heroes aren't Leary and Ginsberg anymore; they're Che Guevera and Eldridge Cleaver of the Black Panthers."[28] Even radical pacifists were adopting more militant tactics, as exemplified by the actions of the "Ultra Resistance," Catholic activists, led by Father Daniel Berrigan and his brother, Father Philip Berrigan, who destroyed draft records. As Philip Berrigan saw it, there existed "no other human course except to say by one's life and one's acts, 'This is me against genocide in Vietnam, against thermonuclear paranoia, against Third World rape, against Black containment, against environmental ruin—against a society which defines itself as a technological tribe!'" All the while, more reports floated that "the kids on the street are talking revolution."[29]

New York Times reporter John Leo saw one possibility as he examined the turn of the underground press toward championing greater political activism. Previously, he noted, the underground press reflected and helped to mold "the withdrawn life style of hippies and dropouts." More recently, it had experienced a decided shift in the direction of radical politics. Earlier, the top underground papers focused on drugs, sex, rock 'n' roll, Eastern religions, and psychedelic art, but now those same publications highlighted student protest, the antiwar campaign, guerrilla activities, resistance to the draft, and wholesale assaults on the Establishment. Leo pointed to some 150 underground papers around the country, the vast majority founded within the past three years and most on shaky financial footing. The writing contained in the underground press was frequently "freewheeling, lurid, superficial," but also "imaginative and impassioned" with attention drawn to issues given short shrift by the mainstream press. The turn to "radical politics" could be seen in papers like the Los Angeles *Free Press* and the *Avatar*, as well as in the shutting down of the San Francisco *Oracle*. Jeff Shero of *The Rat*—"New York's muckraking subterranean newspaper"—stated forthrightly, "The drug culture is dead." He continued, "It's now impossible to believe in any kind of salvation from drugs," not with young people being drafted or smacked by cops on drug busts, real or concocted. The *Berkeley Barb*'s Max Scherr pointed to police harassment as politicizing those who read the underground papers. People were forced to become involved, discovering "they can't hide from society as they thought they could." For others, hippie existence had amounted to "danger, poverty, overcrowding, police raids and a slow brutalizing of the spirit." The *East Village Other*'s Peter Leggieri analyzed this situation: "The concept of flower people in America today is absurd." Paul Krassner of *The Realist* asserted, "The repressive aspects of society are just being seen more and more clearly." Many of the newest underground papers were explicitly radical, following SDS's line. Earlier heroes of the counterculture like Timothy Leary and Alan Watts garnered less attention, as even comic strips were more politicized. As for objectivity, LNS's Thorne Dreyer deemed that "a farce. We made our biases clear. That frees our writers to talk about their guts." Still, Leggieri issued a warning, despite acknowledging that as times were changing, the underground press had to also. "We don't believe politics can lead to anything beneficial to mankind. This is a political year, but when it's over the political papers will be gone and we'll still be here." With regard to the media establishment, LNS cofounder Raymond Mungo admitted, "The media is the enemy. I'd much rather put *The Times* out of business than the New York City police. It does much more damage."[30]

A turn to the streets and possibly revolution also occurred in other countries during this period, including America's immediate neighbor to the south. That occurred as the 1968 Olympics Games approached in Mexico City, where the Tlatelolco massacre took place on October 2. Mexican soldiers and police killed hundreds of protestors gathered at Mexico City's Plaza de las Tres Culturas, as young demonstrators shouted "No queremos olimpiadas, queremos revolucion!"[31] The infuriated Mexican government, with the Olympic Games slated to begin in the national capital days later, rained bullets on thousands of high school and university students. Protest cropped up during the actual games, as when American sprinters Tommie Smith and John Carlos held aloft single, black-fisted gloves in solidarity with the black power movement in the United States.

Again subpoenaed by the House Committee on Un-American Activities, a bearded Jerry Rubin had shown up at a congressional hearing on October 1, wearing, as historian William L. O'Neill relates, "a Black Panther beret, Viet Cong pajama bottoms, a Mexican bandolier with live ammunition, bells, bracelets, and earrings. His feet, face, and naked chest were painted with psychedelic designs and peace symbols. He carried a toy M-16 rifle."[32] Guards removed his ammo. Abbie Hoffman came affecting an Indian-image, with "sporting feathers in his hair, a hunting knife and a bullwhip." In addition, members of the Women's International Terrorist Conspiracy from Hell, a group known as WITCH, held brooms and encircled Rubin, while burning incense, dancing, and chanting. At one point, Rubin interrupted the proceedings to yell out, "Last night, the Nazis tear-gassed my room." On October 3, police arrested Hoffman, who was sporting a red, white, and blue shirt with stripes that could be likened to an American flag, when he tried to enter the building where the committee was convening. Charged with desecrating the American flag, Hoffman was also charged with resisting arrest. His wife Anita faced a charge of carrying out a felonious assault against a police officer. Meanwhile, Rubin sat quietly with a Vietcong flag drawn around his neck.[33]

That month, *Traffic* appeared, having been recorded in London and New York City during the first months of the year.[34] This masterwork contained "You Can All Join," "Pearly Queen," "Feelin' Alright," and "40,000 Headsmen," among other songs. Written by Steve Winwood, "You Can All Join In" talked about setting someone else free, while just being "what you want to be."[35] Winwood and Jim Capaldi's "Pearly Queen" had "some gypsies blood" and flowers blooming around her feet, "made of silk and sequins."[36] The brilliant "Feelin' Alright" spoke of the need for a change of scenery due to "the strangest dreams" nightly.[37] Also written by Winwood and Capaldi, "40,000 Headsmen" pointed to sea travels, hidden treasures, and thousands of shotguns firing.[38]

In early October 1968, Governor Ronald Reagan, in a speech in Sacramento explained, "We have some hippies in California. For those of you who don't know what a hippie is, he's a fellow who has hair like Tarzan, who walks like Jane, and who smells like Cheetah."[39] Meanwhile, SDS recruiters like Terry Robbins and Bill Ayers asserted, "Youth is the revolution . . . politics is about life, struggle, survival."[40] As many as one hundred thousand young people claimed to be members of the New Left organization, which boasted over three hundred chapters nationwide. New Left activism sharpened, with greater numbers of violent incidents, including the bombing of ROTC facilities and campus buildings. Underground newspapers such as *The Rat* in New York City delivered diagrams explaining how to construct explosives. Mike Klonsky emphasized the need to veer "toward a revolutionary youth movement."[41]

On November 1, John Sinclair issued the White Panther Party Statement, opening with a call for "Cultural Revolution through a total assault on the culture." That required, Sinclair stated, members of his group to use every means to expose the American people to it. "Our culture, our art, the music, newspapers, books, posters, our clothing, our homes, the way we walk and talk, the way our hair grows, the way we smoke dope and fuck and eat and sleep—it is all one message, and the message is FREEDOM!" The White Panthers represented the only lifestyle fitting for America's "kids," and "THESE KIDS ARE READY!" Defiantly, Sinclair wrote, "We are a bunch of arrogant motherfuckers," who would not tolerate the police or any pseudo-authorities who desired "to put us down." Indeed, for the initial time in the nation's history, there existed "a generation of visionary maniac white motherfucker country dope fiend rock and roll freaks" prepared "to get down and kick out the jams—ALL THE JAMS" and unleash everyone "from their real and imaginary prisons." Simply put, Sinclair asserted, "We demand total freedom for everybody! And we will not be stopped until we get it. We are bad." The White Panthers were also "THE SOLUTION," working for everybody, dismissing money, leaders, school, and "the white honkie culture." As Sinclair put it, "We breathe revolution. We are LSD driven total maniacs of the universe. We will do anything we can to drive people crazy out of their heads and into their bodies." Leading the charge were rock 'n' roll and "organic high-energy guerrilla bands" already "destroying millions of minds." Admittedly, the White Panthers did not possess guns yet, at least not all of them did, but they boasted a powerful weapon: "direct access to teenagers." And yet, "we will use guns if we have to—we will do anything—if we have to. We have no illusions."[42] SDS's *New Left Notes* editorialized, "THE ELECTIONS DON'T MEAN SHIT. VOTE WHERE THE POWER IS. OUR POWER IS IN THE STREET."[43]

Operating from a different vantage point, Stewart Brand, an old compatriot of Ken Kesey and the Merry Pranksters, and the producer of the Trips Festival, began publishing *The Whole Earth Catalog*, a sixty-four page compendium that sold for five dollars and discussed "whole systems," shelter and land use, industry and crafts, communications, community, nomadics, and learning.[44] Brand was also influenced by the time he spent at Drop City, the six-acre artists' community in southern Colorado, initially inspired by architectural pathfinders Buckminster Fuller and Steve Baer. All the while, the counterculture and the movement both experienced a devastating setback, which some radicals foolishly welcomed, with the election of Richard Nixon as president of the United States.

The Beatles' three-record collection, referred to as the *White Album*, recorded during the previous several months, appeared on November 22, 1968.[45] The British artist Richard Hamilton, best known for his 1956 collage, "Just what is it that makes today's homes so different, so appealing?" that had helped to kick off Pop Art, designed the starkly white cover, containing only the band's name and a production number. While the Lennon-McCartney songwriting team continued to receive credits, John and Paul all but crafted many of their own offerings individually, as did George and Ringo. The best of the thirty songs included McCartney's hard-rocking "Back in the U.S.S.R.," "Birthday," and "Helter Skelter"; Harrison's mystical sounding "While My Guitar Gently Weeps," the tongue-in-cheek "Piggies," and "Savoy Truffle"; and several of Lennon's. John's top contributions included "Dear Prudence," "Glass Onion," "Happiness Is a Warm Gun," "I'm So Tired," "Julia," "Everybody's Got Something to Hide Except Me and My Monkey," "Sexy Sadie," "Revolution 1," and "Cry Baby Cry," songs that skirted from the deeply personal to those reflecting about drug experiences ranging from LSD to heroin. In "Glass Onion," Lennon began by referring to Strawberry Fields, "where nothing is real," then pointed to another place "where everything flows." He talked about "the walrus," indicated that it was McCartney, and also spoke of "the fool on the hill" and "fixing a hole in the ocean."[46] The tormented "Happiness Is a Warm Gun" repeated that refrain, along with "Bang bang, shoot shoot," and intoned, "And I can feel my finger on your trigger / I know nobody can do me no harm."[47]

The Rolling Stones, still featuring Mick Jagger, Keith Richards, Brian Jones, Bill Wyman, and Charlie Watts, released *Beggars Banquet* on December 6, recorded from mid-March through the end of July.[48] The album included the eerie "Sympathy for the Devil," the rambunctious "Street Fighting Man," and "Salt of the Earth," a paean to "hard working people." "Sympathy for the Devil," recorded by the Rolling Stones in June 1968, presented an encyclopedic sweep of some of history's darkest moments, including the torture of Jesus Christ, the murder of Nicholas II and his family by the Bolsheviks, the German blitzkrieg, and the assassinations of the Kennedy brothers. Among the song's most famous passages were the lines declaring "Just as every cop is a criminal / And all the sinners saints."[49] On a more leavened note, the Stones' production of "Salt of the Earth" called for a "drink to the hard working people," to those of "lowly" birth, and "a prayer for the common foot soldier" and his family.[50] The political left, as exemplified by *Ramparts*, lauded the Stones, while tossing another dig at the Beatles. "The Beatles were always nice kids, a little weird maybe," *Ramparts* asserted. "The Stones are still freaks and outlaws."[51]

Jack Newfield of *The Village Voice* reviewed Abbie Hoffman's book *Revolution for the Hell of It* in the December 29, 1968, edition of the *New York Times*. Newfield referred to Hoffman as "a charming combination of Ernie Kovacs, Artaud, and Prince Kropotkin . . . a put-on artist, an acid head . . . a mass-media guerrilla." The author, Newfield noted, was "a pure Marxist-Lennonist—Harpo Marx and John Lennon," who "prefers theater to politics." At the same time, Newfield believed that Hoffman considered *Revolution for the Hell of It* to be "a serious manifesto for the growing counterculture." As Newfield read Hoffman, the Yippie leader wanted to employ street theater and the media to reach out to youth, extolled a "politics of ecstasy," and disdained the "property fetish." Newfield worried that Hoffman's anarchistic thrust would play into the hands of the Chicago police, Southern highway patrolmen, and the demagogic, race-baiting George Wallace. "The Absurd," Newfield warned, would not bring about redistribution of power in the United States, while drugs and satire would not quell Richard Daley or Spiro Agnew, a formerly moderate Republican who had undergone a sharp turn rightward, recently elected vice president of the United States. Those desirous of rekindling the American Dream, Newfield offered, would be better served by read-ing radical elder statesmen such as I. F. Stone, Norman Mailer, and Ho-ward Zinn. [52]

16

COINTELPRO AND THE MILLENNIUM

The ushering in of the administration of Richard M. Nixon coincided with a temporary revival of the movement, along with a simultaneous determination by some to disrupt the American political system altogether and by others to withdraw to the communitarian enclaves the nation had long, but intermittently, experienced. Too little appreciated was the fact that American radical political and cultural currents generally thrived amid a liberal or progressive atmosphere at the national level. Racial unrest, the Vietnam War, and the growing alienation of larger numbers of America's youth resulted in disdain for the liberal administrations, particularly that of Lyndon Baines Johnson, that governed the United States during much of the 1960s. Under LBJ, the American welfare state mushroomed in the fashion it had not since the New Deal era of Franklin Delano Roosevelt, but notwithstanding strong presidential support for civil rights legislation, race riots marked the era, along with mounting protest on college and university campuses regarding U.S. involvement in Vietnam. As a consequence, the largest antiwar movement in American history emerged, alongside increasingly militant civil rights forces, and a seemingly still burgeoning counterculture. New protest groups had also appeared or were soon about to, including movements professing to speak for women, Native Americans, Puerto Ricans, gays, and the elderly. But these movements within the movement experienced splinters of their own, divided as they often were between activists willing to accept incremental change and those demanding that alterations involving longstanding practices, lifestyles, and even the American system itself occur all but instantaneously. While some seemed to hope or believe that the far more conservative administration of Richard Nixon would further alienate the American public, thereby fostering the continued growth of the movement, some recognized that reform and radical campaigns could hardly have been less timely.

On January 20, 1969, Richard Milhous Nixon, the inveterate Cold Warrior and red-baiter, became the thirty-seventh president of the United States. Nixon and his running mate, Spiro Agnew, had run on a law-and-order campaign and an at least implicit promise of a plan to end the war in Vietnam. Counter-inaugural protest activities occurred in Washington, D.C., from January 18–20, with the Mobe leading a march of ten thousand protesting the war in Vietnam, and smoke bombs and rocks hurled at the limousine carrying Nixon. Rennie Davis acknowledged that lacking the ability to control "guerrilla street activity," the Mobe should no longer hold mass demonstrations as they had become too "dangerous."[1] Others disagreed, determined to intensify protest tactics, while bandying about talk of revolution.

The federal government responded by again targeting countercultural and movement endeavors. The same day Nixon took the oath of office as president, J. Edgar Hoover, the aged but still seemingly all-powerful head of the FBI, fired off a memo to branch offices across the country. Agents had expressed great concern regarding the underground press' "vast growth."[2] Hoover instructed all FBI agents to undertake an extensive examination of New Left–oriented publications, and demanded information about staffs, printers, and advertisers. This was in keeping with the FBI's Counter Intelligence Program (COINTELPRO), initiated in the mid-1950s against the American Communist Party, but quickly expanded to a host of civil rights, antiwar, and New Left groups and individuals. Over the next several months, a campaign against the underground press unfolded, which included the setting up of phony publications, the use of obscenity and drug laws, reliance on agents provocateurs, and physical assaults of various kinds. Operatives included agents from the FBI, the CIA, the Federal Drug Administration, and the U.S. military, as well as local police, some associated with so-called red squads. In 1967, President Lyndon B. Johnson had authorized establishment of Operation CHAOS within the CIA, designed to ferret out foreign influences affecting the antiwar movement. Among the targets was *Ramparts* magazine.

Documents later released under the Freedom of Information Act demonstrated that subsequent COINTELPRO operations included attempts to pique hostilities between leaders, shape an impression some were government agents, and publish articles in student papers and the underground press emphasizing "the depravity of New Left leaders and members," including the resort to drugs "and free sex."[3] The FBI actually created a number of supposed underground newspapers or operations, including the *Armageddon News* in Bloomington, the *Longhorn Tale* in Austin, the New York Press Service, and the Pacific International News Service in San Francisco. Agents were urged to abet drug busts, to spread misinformation within the ranks of the New Left, and to devise damaging anonymous letters about New Leftists and underground newspapers that could be sent to family members, neighbors, the employers of parents, university officials, state legislators, members of Boards of Regents, and the media. Obscenity laws were resorted to in an effort to drive underground publications like *NOLA Express* in New Orleans and *Open City* in Los Angeles out of business, due to expenses incurred in staving off convictions. In similar fashion, the busting of all staff members of the *Argus* in Ann Arbor, Michigan, resulted in the closure of that newspaper. In addition, "landlords, printers, distributors or advertisers were intimidated, harassed, boycotted, otherwise" compelled to stop dealing with underground papers, while street vendors were hassled, detained, or arrested. Columbia Records, which had put out a short-lived "The Man Can't Bust Our Music" campaign, cut off a vital financial subsidy.[4]

There were also cases of actual violence, sometimes initiated by vigilantes, directed against the underground press, such as the ransacking of the office of the *Washington Free Press*, physical assaults against the staff of the *Philadelphia Free Press*, and the firebombing of several other publications, including *Helix* (Seattle), *Space City* (Houston), *Orpheus* (Phoenix), *The Great Speckled Bird* (Atlanta), and the *Los Angeles Free Press*. As investigative journalist Chip Berlet indicates, the UPS itself experienced "mail openings, physical office stakeouts, staff surveillance, and the obtaining and copying of bank records, credit card records, postage meter records, car rental records, telephone call records, traffic ticket records, income tax records, and more."[5]

In a lengthy article distributed by the LNS, Thorne Dreyer and Victoria Smith discussed "The Movement and the New Media," beginning with the wholesale manner in which the underground press was being legally and physically assaulted. This occurred, they offered, because the radical press had shifted course, discarding its early "sweetness and light" for a more recent "culturally outrageous and politically revolutionary" stance. They also affirmed that underground publications needed to shift along with the movement, as in the case of *The Rag* in Austin, Texas, which no longer served as a unifying force for political activists in that community.[6]

Paul A. Robinson, a newly minted PhD in history from Harvard, teaching at Stanford University, completed an intriguing book in February that undoubtedly remained little known to both the New Left and the counterculture but nevertheless touched on aspects pertinent to each. *The Freudian Left: William Reich Geza Roheim Herbert Marcuse* explored the work of the Jewish intellectuals who left Hitler-dominated Europe during the 1930s. All three emphasized the singular importance of sex, and considered sexuality and politics inextricably intertwined. Sexual repression, they emphasized, provided "one of the principal mechanisms of political domination." They underscored the significance of "stylistic radicalism" too, deeming "psychoanalysis as a revolutionary or critical doctrine."[7]

In the February 16, 1969, edition of the *New York Times*, Robert Houriet discussed the "Life and Death of a Commune Called Oz." Working on his sweeping examination of the commune movement, *Getting Back Together*, Houriet sympathetically but unflinchingly explored the utopian hopes and stark realities that had confronted the Oz family, originally based in California but relocated to western Pennsylvania. Pressured by the "straight" society its members sought to escape from, as well as problems engendered by young drifters and almost stereotypically antisocial motorcyclists, the Oz family came apart, scattering across the nation.[8]

Singling out supposed leaders of the movement in a conspiracy trial, the Justice Department initiated official proceedings against the so-called Chicago Eight, accused of having headed across state borders "to incite a riot" during the 1968 Democratic Party presidential convention. On March 20, a grand jury indicted Yippies Abbie Hoffman and Jerry Rubin, the radical pacifist David Dellinger, Black Panther leader Bobby Seale, New Leftists Davis and Tom Hayden, and academicians John Froines and Lee Weiner. Among the unindicted co-conspirators were Stewart E. Albert, Sidney M. Peck, Kathy Boudin, and Thomas W. Neumann.

In a special issue of *Rolling Stone* published on April 5, Ralph Glea-son posed the question, "Is There a Death Wish in the U.S.?" Politics, Gleason asserted, had failed, while the counterculture offered "no Pro-gram for Improvement of the Society." At the same time, the hippies and pop musicians did suggest "a program for improvement of the young people of the world." Transforming society, Gleason indicated, required the attainment of "a state of grace." Conducting a revolution, he contin-ued, would have to occur differently than in the past: "without killing people or it won't work."[9] Offering a different approach in that same issue, Michael Rossman, a former leader of the Free Speech Movement at Berkeley, delivered "American Revolution 1969." He wrote about the likelihood of a quarter of a million marijuana-related arrests during the year, pointing to police having "planted dope on friends of" his, including organizers for SDS, Yippies, editors of high school underground publica-tions, and self-styled educational reformers like Rossman himself, who traveled the campus circuit championing free universities, new curricula, and student empowerment. Conspiracy theories abounded about "a small, hard-core minority of freak maniac anti-Christs" helping to pique discon-tent.[10]

That spring semester college and university campuses witnessed even more protests, and more violent ones, as SDS's chronicler, Kirkpatrick Sale, indicates. Black students at Cornell wielded guns, a lengthy boycott of classes crippled San Francisco State University, bombing incidents disrupted university life, and street fighting broke out in Washington, D.C.; Madison, Wisconsin; and Berkeley. *New Left Notes* called for "Power to the People!" and "DEATH TO THE PIG!" The Nixon admin-istration promised to rein in "radical, revolutionary, anarchistic kids" and to smack down both "draft-dodgers" and student radicals. Attorney Gen-eral John Mitchell insisted that "Campus militants, directing their efforts at destruction and intimidation, are nothing but tyrants."[11] Government operatives, university administrators, and local officials targeted New Left organizations, particularly SDS, and leaders. Clashes involving the so-called People's Park, constructed on University of California property a few blocks from the main campus, culminated in days of street fighting, the shooting of several individuals, and Governor Ronald Reagan's dec-laration on May 15, "If it's to be a blood bath, then let it be now."[12] Berkeley poet John Oliver Simon considered the park "at the very center of our struggle" pertaining to "the total liberation of the ecology." Simon

quoted from Gary Snyder, who claimed, "The most revolutionary consciousness is to be found among the most oppressed classes—animals,
trees, grass, air, water, earth." To Simon, the battle over the park introduced "the concept of the Whole Earth, the Mother Earth, into the vocabulary of revolutionary politics."[13] Another poet, Denise Levertov,
deemed the park "a little island of Peace and hope in a world made filthy
and hopeless by war and injustice."[14]

In May, the British group Thunderclap Newman, set up by The Who's
Peter Townshend, released "Something in the Air," which spoke of "in-
stigators" and the presence of revolution here and now. "Something in the
Air" talked about the need "to get it together," to pass out guns and
ammunition, and "to blast our way through here."[15]

The U.S. Supreme Court issued a unanimous ruling on May 19, tossing aside the marijuana conviction of Timothy Leary, on the grounds that
federal legislation pertaining to the drug violated the self-incrimination
clause of the Fifth Amendment. Issuing the ruling for the High Court,
Justice John Marshall Harlan proclaimed that Leary and other defendants
could not be prosecuted for refusing to pay a large marijuana transfer tax.
State marijuana laws remained in place, as did a federal measure providing for lengthy sentences for sellers of the drug. That summer, the Fifth
Circuit Court of Appeals overturned the convictions of Benjamin Spock
and Michael Ferber for conspiring to abet draft resistance, and remanded
the cases against William Sloane Coffin and Mitchell Goodman; the
charges involving a fifth defendant, Marcus Raskin of the Institute for
Policy Studies, had earlier been dropped. By contrast, John Sinclair of the
White Panther Party received a prison sentence of 9½ to 10 years, following a conviction for the possession of a pair of marijuana joints. Tom
Forcade reported that friends of Sinclair "openly wept when they heard
the news."[16]

During the spring, John Lennon, now married to Yoko Ono, with
whom he had conducted a bed-in for peace, released "The Ballad of John
and Yoko," as a Beatles' song, with lyrics about "We're only trying to get
us some peace" and expressions of concern, "Christ you know it ain't
easy. . . . They're gonna crucify me."[17] Initially not allowed to return to
the United States because of an earlier drug bust in England, John publicized another bed-in with Yoko, this one held in Montreal, where a recording of his new song, "Give Peace a Chance," took place. Among
those present during the session were Timothy Leary, Allen Ginsberg,

Dick Gregory, British pop star Petula Clark, New York City disc jockey Murray the K, and comedian Tommy Smothers, costar of the television program, *The Smothers Brothers*. Several of those individuals were mentioned in the song, as were isms of all kinds, along with revolution and evolution. Lennon repeatedly sang "All we are saying is give peace a chance."[18] Robert Christgau of *The Village Voice* proved unimpressed with Lennon's pacifistic stance, writing, "All revolutions are unpleasant, but the ones you lose are really for shit. But if it happens, it happens, and everybody chooses sides. All of John Lennon's rationalizations are correct. Violence does lead to more violence." However, "Lennon would never have achieved enlightenment if thousands of his forebears hadn't suffered drudgery far worse than protest marches and cared enough about certain ideals—and realities—to risk death for them."[19]

In mid-June, during the SDS National Convention, held at the Chicago Coliseum, two thousand members witnessed or participated in the destruction of that leading New Left organization. Egged on by Black Panthers, SDS tore itself apart, thanks to its Maoist Progressive Labor and the counterculture-inflected Revolutionary Youth Movement factions. Emerging out of RYM itself was Weatherman, which included the new national officers of the badly shrunken remnant of SDS: Mark Rudd, Bill Ayers, and Jeff Jones. Bernadine Dohrn led a walkout of several hundred from the convention, after she shouted, "Long live the victory of people's war," a slogan borrowed from the Chinese communist military leader Lin Biao. With fists raised, they bellowed, "Power to the people! Power to the people!," "Ho! Ho! Ho Chi Minh!"[20] From a membership approaching one hundred thousand, the ranks of SDS rapidly plummeted to the three-hundred-person contingent that made up Weatherman, along with affiliated splinter groups. Weatherman drew its name, ironically, from Bob Dylan's 1965 song, "Subterranean Homesick Blues," which insisted, "You don't need a weatherman / To know which way the wind blows."[21] Happily watching SDS implode, Abbie Hoffman said, "We have come to praise SDS, not to bury it." A New York City police detective soon warned the Senate Permanent Subcommittee on Investigations that SDS posed a "grave threat to society generally," possessing an "unbending aim of destroying every vestige of an ordered society under a capitalistic system."[22]

The law, or at least New York City policemen, and portions of the counterculture butted heads in another manner in late June, when the

Stonewall riots occurred after a raid on a bar located in the West Village at 51 and 53 Christopher Street, just down the street where Yoko Ono once lived. Operated by the Genovese crime syndicate, the Stonewall Inn had turned into a gay bar and experienced frequent police raids. During an attempted bust in the early morning hours of June 28, patrons and community residents began to fight back, while shouting "Gay power!" Some drag queens sang, "We are the Stonewall girls / We wear our hair in curls / We wear no underwear / We show our pubic hair."[23] As protestor Michael Fader later explained, "We all had a collective feeling like we'd had enough of this kind of shit. . . . Everyone in the crowd felt that we were never going to go back. It was like the last straw. It was time to reclaim something that had always been taken from us . . . mostly it was total outrage, anger, sorrow. . . . It took different forms, but the bottom line was, we weren't going to go away. And we didn't."[24]

One of the mainstays of the counterculture on the West Coast, the *Berkeley Barb* splintered in early July, due to complaints by staff members who considered themselves underpaid. The *Barb on Strike* contained an article by Steve Haines charging, "Capitalist pig Max Scherr has locked us . . . out of our office and fired us for trying to turn *The Barb* into a model of the people's revolution."[25] *Berkeley Barb* editor Scherr countered, "It may be that one man cannot resist a gang determined to destroy him," signing his editorial, "Max the Pig."[26] The staff members who had put out the special issue, *Barb on Strike*, began publishing the *Berkeley Tribe*.

In mid-July, Columbia Pictures released a low-budget film—shot during the first half of 1968 and produced for just over $300,000—that captured something of the spirit of the times. Directed by Dennis Hopper, who costarred with Peter Fonda and Jack Nicholson, veterans of such B-movies as *Wild Angels* and *The Trip*, *Easy Rider* proved a remarkable commercial hit, tapping into the zeitgeist involving the counterculture. Fonda played the part of Wyatt, with his motorcycle jacket sporting an American flag on the back, and tight leather pants, and Hopper was Billy, with his long hair and bushy mustache. On their quest to see America, they picked up a hippie hitchhiker, whom they took to his commune. Declining to stay there, Wyatt, called Captain America by his buddy, and Billy got arrested in a small town, meeting up with an alcoholic lawyer in jail, George Hanson, who joined them outside for a brief spell. George, played by Jack Nicholson, offered sage advice as they sat around a campfire: "You know, this used to be a hell of a good country. I can't understand what's gone wrong with it." He explained that many Americans were fearful of hippies like Wyatt and Billy, because they represented freedom. George warned, "Don't ever tell anyone they're not free cause they're going to get real busy killing and maiming to prove to you that they are." In the dead of night, townsmen murdered George. Later, following an LSD-shadowed venture in New Orleans, Wyatt and Billy suffered a similar fate, when shotgun-toting rednecks blew them off their motorcycles. The musical score added greatly to the film's ambiance, with such cult songs as Hoyt Axton's "The Pusher," Steppenwolf's "Born to Be Wild," the Band's "The Weight," the Fraternity of Man's rendition of "Don't Bogart Me," Bob Dylan's "It Alright, Ma (I'm Only Bleeding)," performed by Roger McGuinn, and McGuinn's "Ballad of Easy Rider."[27]

The commune movement that *Easy Rider*'s Wyatt and Billy drifted through received greater attention, not all of it positive, in the mainstream press during the last several months of 1969. The *New York Times'* Steven V. Roberts, soon to write about a very different group of communards, delivered an article titled "Some Enter Communal Seclusion to Escape Turmoil, Others to Find Religion," in the paper's August 2, 1969, edition. He referred to Big Tree and his wife Little Tree, who had moved from Hollywood to a pristine valley in southern Oregon, where they now had a three-month-old daughter Lotus Tree, a horse, some chickens, several acres of rocky land, a yet-to-be finished stone house, no electricity or running water, and "a deep contentment." As the long-haired Big Tree, formerly a well-paid chemist who had driven a Jaguar, expressed it, "We had to get everything off our backs. Then we had to decide what we wanted to put back—what was valid." Hundreds of other young people had also escaped from California cities to reside in the "Magic Valley" across the state border.[28]

As Roberts noted, young people had established dozens of their own communities, in the warm climes of California, Arizona, and New Mexico, but also in Colorado, the Midwest, Pennsylvania, and New England. Many existed in rural areas, others in urban centers, such as Mel Lyman's Fort Hill Community in Boston's Roxbury district. Oracle, Arizona, featured a ranch run by approximately thirty adults, many who taught at the University of Arizona. These communities, Roberts wrote, exemplified a general rejection of the lifestyles of most Americans, riddled as those were with impersonality, stress, chaos, pollution, and police crackdowns. Their inhabitants desired "a reduction of life to its essentials, to the simple things they can understand and hold onto in a time of turmoil." As one California transplant now residing in Oregon put it, "We lost the connection with the land in the cities. We were not part of anything, we had no roots." Not everyone was delighted with this turn of events, with local authorities and vigilantes hassling communards. Shootings, rapes, and narcotic charges mounted, while townsfolk often proved divided about the merits of the new community residents. Nevertheless, the movement continued as Big Tree explained, while pointing to Lotus Tree. "We're waiting for these kids to talk so we can find out the next step. We're waiting for instructions."[29]

In August, both a still darker and a fresher side to the counterculture appeared. On August 9, the beautiful film actress Sharon Tate, eight-and-a-half months pregnant and married to film director Roman Polanski, and three friends were found stabbed to death at the Tate-Polanski home in Benedict Canyon in the Santa Monica Mountains. A young man was discovered shot to death in the driveway. The *New York Times* reported that "the word 'pig' was scrawled in blood on the door of the main house." Polanski, returned from devising a film script in London, soon issued denials that "a wild drug party" had taken place at the hillside home on the evening when the murders occurred. Moreover, he declared, "Sharon did not use drugs. She did not touch alcohol, and she did not smoke cigarettes."[30] On August 10, Leon and Rosemary LaBianca, wealthy grocery-store owners, were found murdered in their home situated in Los Angeles' Silverlake neighborhood, a dozen miles from the Tate-Polanski estate.

As rumors floated about actors fleeing the Hollywood scene, an event took place on the other side of the country that soon overshadowed the Tate murders, at least for a time. From August 15 through August 18, the Woodstock Music and Art Fair played out in the Catskills Mountains, northwest of New York City. The site was a six-hundred-acre dairy farm owned by forty-nine-year-old Max B. Yasgur, located forty-three miles southwest of the village community of Woodstock. Orchestrated by Michael Lang, John Roberts, Joel Rosenman, and Artie Kornfield, the Woodstock Festival proved to be a defining moment for the counterculture. Twenty-nine months earlier, Roberts and Rosenman had posted an ad in the "Capital Available" sections of both the *Wall Street Journal* and the *New York Times*, "Young Men with Unlimited Capital looking for interesting, legitimate investment opportunities and business propositions," before setting up Media Sound Studios in mid-Manhattan. In February 1969, music promoter Lang broached the idea of a festival in the Woodstock area, where Dylan, folk singer Tim Hardin, the Band, and the Loving Spoonful resided. A bit earlier, Lang had met Kornfield, who had become director of East Coast Contemporary Product for Capitol Records. Kornfield had established a reputation as a songwriter, delivering or helping to craft tunes like "Dead Man's Curve" for Jan and Dean, and "Rain, the Park, and Other Things," for the Cowsills, with its profession of love for "the flower girl." Lang spoke to Kornfield about a music retreat, "a rock festival, sorta."[31]

Nearly two hundred thousand advance tickets were sold for $18 apiece, but at least one hundred thousand additional individuals arrived for the festival, resulting in the declaration of a state of emergency by Sullivan County, where Woodstock is situated. Barnard L. Collier reported in the *New York Times* on August 15 that no violence had taken place, as a state police lieutenant acknowledged. "There hasn't been anybody yelling pig at the cops and when they asked directions they are polite and none of them has really given us any trouble yet." Louis Ratner, sheriff of Sullivan County, noted that about fifty arrests had occurred, most for drug possession. By contrast, a state police sergeant admitted, "As far as I know the narcotic guys are not arresting anybody for grass. If we did there isn't enough space in Sullivan or the next three counties to put them in." Something of a cultural war appeared to be taking place in Bethel, New York, the home of Max Yasgur's farm. An early sign read, "Stop Max's Hippie Music Festival. No 150,000 hippies here. Buy no milk." A more recent sign, posted near the music site, declared, "Don't bother Max's cows. Let them moo in peace."[32]

During the festival, top rock, folk, and pop performers appeared, including Richie Havens, the Grateful Dead, Janis Joplin, Sly and the Family Stone, The Who, Jefferson Airplane, Creedence Clearwater Revival, Joe Cocker, the Band, Country Joe and the Fish, Jimi Hendrix, and Crosby, Stills, Nash and Young. Among the most riveting moments were the renditions of "With a Little Help from My Friends" by Cocker, "Piece of My Heart" by Joplin, and "The Star Spangled Banner" by Hendrix. Jefferson Airplane presented "Volunteers," yet to be released as a single, but in keeping with the theme of revolution that had taken hold in both the counterculture and the movement during the past several months. The band sang about what was occurring "in the streets," and repeatedly exclaimed, "Got a revolution Got to revolution," while pointing to a generational divide that led some to become "volunteers of America."[33]

After battling with the festival promoters, Abbie Hoffman was allowed to include an article, "The Hard Rain's Already Fallin'," in the official program. He predicted that very soon posters at the post office would feature photographs of top rock groups, alongside the declaration, "WANTED FOR CONSPIRACY TO INCITE RIOT." He pointed out that both blacks and radicals faced arrest, underground newspapers endured harassment, dissident GIs experienced "harsh sentences," and the police had moved from clubs and tear gas to shotguns and buckshot. Hoffman underscored the fact that numerous rock and folk performers had recently been busted, including "Jimi Hendrix, MC-5, The Who, Phil Ochs, Tim Buckley, Jefferson Airplane, Grateful Dead, Jim Morrison, Creedence Clearwater, The Turtles, Moby Grape, Ray Charles, The Fugs, Dave Van Ronk, Joan Baez." They had been "busted because the authorities want to destroy our cultural revolution in the same way they want to destroy our political revolution." Referring to the trial of the Chicago Eight, Hoffman admitted, "We are guilty of being members of a vast conspiracy," one opposing the Vietnam War and the Nixon administration, and battling "the oppression of black communities . . . the harassment of our cultural revolution . . . an educational system that seeks only to channel us into a society we see as corrupt and impersonal . . . the growing police state . . . dehumanizing work roles that a capitalist economic system demands." Bluntly, Hoffman admitted, "What we are for quite simply is a total revolution. We are for a society in which the people directly control the decisions that affect their lives." In recent years, this movement has mushroomed "from hundreds to millions of young people," while growing more militant. Yes, "flower children have lost their innocence and grown their thorns. We have recognized that our culture in order to survive must be defended. Furthermore we have realized that the revolution is more than digging rock or turning on. The revolution is about coming together in a struggle for change." It required the destruction of a boss-led, competitive system, and the construction "of a new community based on people and cooperation." The "old system" was withering all about, as "we joyously come out in the streets to dance on its grave. With our free stores, liberated buildings, communes, people's parks, dope, free bodies and our music we'll build our society in the vacant lots of the old and we'll do it by any means necessary."[34]

In the midst of The Who's set on August 16, Hoffman bolted onto the stage and grabbed ahold of the microphone, initiating a rap about John Sinclair, the jailed leader of the White Panther Party. He blurted out, "I think this is a pile of shit while John Sinclair rots in prison!" before The Who's lead guitarist Peter Townshend hollered, "Fuck off my stage!" leading Hoffman to retort, "Fascist pig."[35]

That same day, John Roberts admitted that the massive turnout at the Woodstock Festival had proven "a little nightmarish for us, actually," and confessed to not understanding "why this had picked up so much steam." He revealed that the program had been "designed, conceived and operated by young people, all 26 years old and under." As Roberts explained, "I had felt for a long time that the polarization of the generations is a very serious threat to our society, and we felt that a cultural exposition created by youth could be of inestimable value in bridging that gap." He noted, "Ours was going to be in the country. It was going to be away from the urban and suburban areas in a very rustic setting with a lot of room, grass, trees, lakes. It was going to be a youth cultural exposition and that is where the culture of this generation expresses itself more naturally." The promoters had poured in less than $200,000 on advertising, while garnering "a tremendous amount of excitement and speculation on the radio stations where disk jockeys talked it up in the last couple of months." But he predicted there would not likely be another such undertaking, because "we've had a very adverse situation up here." The fair's theme was "three days of peace and music," but the undertaking had become a bit "scary," Roberts stated. He went on to say, "If we had any inkling that there was going to be this kind of attendance, we certainly would not have gone ahead." Staff had proven "terribly short-handed," and "the money and ticket collection" quickly gave way. "Financially speaking, of course, the festival is a disaster," Roberts admitted.[36]

In a front-page article that same day, "300,000 at Folk-Rock Fair Camp Out in a Sea of Mud," Barnard L. Collier referred to the crowd as "well-behaved." Max Lang was quoted as stating, "It's about the quietest, most well-behaved 300,000 people in one place that can be imagined. There have been no fights or incidents of violence of any kind." Agreeing with Lang's assessment, a state police officer confessed, "I can hardly believe that there haven't been even small incidents of misbehavior by the young people." There had been bad trips, with a warning delivered at the podium that the acid was "not poison. It's just badly manufactured acid. You are not going to die." Scores of volunteer physicians and nurses provided medical assistance. In another piece in the *Times*, "Back in the City," some young people, already returned to New York City, were said to look "like infantrymen back from a battle zone." One twenty-year-old from Brooklyn was quoted as saying, "We're vestiges of our former selves."[37]

By August 17, Lang, Roberts, Rosenman, and Kornfeld extolled the appearance of a new "youth culture" in the United States, which "came out of the alleys and the streets." As Lang put it, "This generation was brought together and showed it was beautiful." He continued, "The peace they were screaming about is what they really want—they're living it. They value each other more than material things." But the profit-making venture the promoters envisioned had not panned out, saddling them with a $2 million financial loss.[38] On a more positive note, the concerns earlier expressed about the wave of young people flooding into the Catskills had clearly abated. The man who led Monticello's constabulary praised them highly, in his own fashion. "Notwithstanding their personality, their dress and their ideas, they were and they are the most courteous, considerate and well-behaved groups of kids I have ever been in contact with in my 24 years of police work," Lou Yank offered.[39] No longer receiving threatening calls, farmer Max Yasgur was now being praised and asked if he needed help. Admitting that he too never anticipated the festival mushrooming to the size it had, Yasgur declared, "But if the generation gap is to be closed, we older people have to do more than we have done." An acquaintance expressed doubts whether Yasgur had "made a good business deal," but suggested that "he was motivated at least as much by his principles as by the thought of making money." Another local businessman stated, "Max is not just a successful farmer. He is an individualist."[40]

But the *New York Times* also offered a blistering editorial on August 18, "Nightmare in the Catskills." The *Times* editorial staff declared that the drug-inflected dreams and rock 'n' roll that drove hundreds of thousands to the Woodstock festival "had little more sanity than the impulse that drive the lemmings to march to their deaths in the sea." The festival concluded with "a nightmare of mud and stagnation" that crippled the surrounding community for the entire weekend, the *Times* intoned. While dismissing the "maddened youth," the editorial nevertheless acknowledged "that the great bulk of the freakish-looking intruders behaved astonishingly well" and clearly possessed great potential "if it can just be aroused to some better purpose than the pursuit of LSD."[41]

Almost immediately, however, the *Times* began delivering a different, more favorable spin about Woodstock. The following day, another editorial referred to the festival as "a social phenomenon, comparable to the Tulipmania or the Children's Crusade." But more significantly, the *Times* now deemed the mass gathering "essentially a phenomenon of innocence." It praised the patience and good humor displayed by hundreds of thousands of young people, notwithstanding the "mud, rain, hunger and thirst" they endured. Also in the *Times*, Patrick Lydon soon wrote about a half million young people coming to the farm "high and . . . only got higher." Awed local members of the community offered exclamations of "peace," free water, and smiles. Miracles recurred, including kind acts by the police, the delivery of food courtesy of an Army helicopter, and the raining of flowers from the air. Lydon offered, "Yet faith makes miracles and it was the astonishing peace and joy of the youthful masses that brought happy results." After noting the free food presented by the Hog Farm and the assistance provided by the Red Cross Station for those who became sick, Lydon underscored "the joy of confirmation, the delight in accenting what others could give." He declared, "Hippies had never been quite so successful before, never before had they so impressed the world that watched."[42]

Time magazine presented its own analysis of what it called "history's largest happening." More important than "the good vibrations" emanating from top rock groups, Bethel suggested, *Time* indicated, "the potential power of a generation that in countless disturbing ways has rejected the traditional values and goals of the U.S." Spawned at Woodstock was "the spontaneous community of youth . . . the stuff of which legends are made," the extended editorial asserted. Many adults were deeply troubled by the festival, seeing it as "a squalid freakout, a monstrous Dionysian revel, where a mob of crazies gathered to drop acid and groove to hours of amplified cacophony." To *Time*'s editorial staff, however, other lessons could be learned from Woodstock. It demonstrated "the pervasiveness of a national subculture of drugs," but also "the unique sense of community that seems to exist among the young, their mystical feeling for themselves as a special group" characterized by "friendship, camaraderie and . . . love." After referring to Jefferson Airplane's singing of

"Volunteers," *Time* insightfully declared, "In its energy, its lyrics, its advocacy of frustrated joys, rock is one long symphony of protest." Moreover, notwithstanding the discomfiture of adults, "the revolution it preaches, implicitly or explicitly, is basically moral; it is the proclamation of a new set of values as much as it is the rejection of an old system." *Time* insisted that the same type of young people who reveled at the festival protested at both Harvard and Columbia, and had battled in the streets of Chicago the previous summer.[43]

Again, thoughtfully, *Time* referred to both Theodore Roszak and Herbert Marcuse, who considered the counterculture to include children of the middle class engaged in "the absolute refusal" to accept the ravages of modern technology and society. Those children favored "the pleasure principle . . . over the Puritan ethic of work." While many young people had been drawn, however briefly, to the recent political campaigns of Eugene McCarthy and Bobby Kennedy, they appeared to lack a leader. Singer Janis Joplin agreed, saying that was not necessary. "We have each other. All we need is to keep our heads straight and in ten years this country may be a decent place to live in." For *Time*, a rock festival such as Woodstock served "as the equivalent of a political forum for the young." And as Jimi Hendrix offered, "This was only the beginning," then declared, "The kids are not going to be in the mud all the time. From here they will start to build and change things. The whole world needs a big wash, a big scrub-down." *Time* ended its generally favorable account of the counterculture by warning that "a revolution based on unreason may just as easily bring a New Barbarism rather than the New Jerusalem." It quoted from W. B. Yeats, "And what rough beast, its hour come round at last, / Slouches toward Bethlehem to be born?"[44]

Writing in *Hard Times*, Andrew Kopkind quoted Donovan's line, "beatniks out to make it rich," in referring to hip entrepreneurs Michael Lang and John Roberts, who, he suggested, initially designed the Woodstock Festival "to consolidate the culture revolution and extract the money of its troops." The festival managers, Kopkind contended, had to confront its inherent "contradiction . . . how to stimulate the energies of the new culture and profit thereby, and at the same time control them." They sought to apply the "co-optation theory," spending freely through SDS and the underground press to promote the festival and acquire "hip legitimacy," barring "real cops," and offering "free food, water, camping festival." Particularly important were the Hog Farmers, who helped to "spread

the love/groove ethic," while also serving as the camp's "only good organizers," providing everything from the delivery of free food to the dispensing of advice for those undergoing bad acid trips. The Hog Farmers
were "hip beyond any doubt," emitting cool, low-key hippie talk about
making love not war, the mystical integrity of earth, and the importance
of doing your own thing, preferably alone."[45]

Kopkind also wrote about the different makeup of the crowd itself,
with half of the "weekend-hip" variety and the other half "composed of
tribes dedicated to whatever gods now seem effective and whatever
myths produce the energy needed to survive," ranging from Mother Earth
to street-fighting man, from Janis Joplin and Jimi Hendrix to Che. He
believed the American nation, at least in the twentieth century, had never
witnessed "a 'society' so free of repression," with nude swimming, easy
sex, and smiling cops. "For people who had never glimpsed the intense
communitarian closeness of a militant struggle—People's Park or Paris in
the month of May or Cuba—Woodstock must always be their model of
how good we will all feel after the revolution." To Kopkind, what was
"not illusionary" was "the reality of a new culture of opposition," which
contested "all the inane and destructive values of privatism, competition,
commercialism, profitability and elitism." Predicting that "something will
survive," Kopkind warned that "when the dope freaks and nude swim-
mers and loveniks and ecological cultists and music groovers find out that
they have to fight for love, all fucking hell will break loose."[46]

The counterculture received another public relations' boost with the
release of Arthur Penn's *Alice's Restaurant*, based on the song by Arlo
Guthrie and starring the singer as himself.[47] In late August, the *New York
Times*' film critic Vincent Canby coupled a review of *Alice's Restaurant*
with one of Haskell Wexler's *Medium Cool*, about the 1968 Democratic
Party presidential convention in Chicago. Canby saw these as contrasting
political perspectives emanating from American youth, whom he divided
into "the already liberated and the would-be liberators." Near the close of
Medium Cool, Wexler displayed young demonstrators, who had just endured billy clubs and tear gas, optimistically singing Woody Guthrie's
anthem, "This Land Is Your Land." Woody's former on-again, off-again
musical partner, Pete Seeger, appeared in *Alice's Restaurant*, singing
"Pastures of Plenty," a patriotic ode also crafted by the elder Guthrie.
That movie revolved around Arlo's arrest for littering, and subsequent
conviction, which supposedly precluded him from entering the U.S. mili-

tary. Optimism, Canby offered, drove Woody Guthrie's movement, while ridicule propelled his son's. Woody, so close to the CPUSA, wanted "to modify the system" that Arlo eventually ignored altogether, albeit "with such wild good humor, even joy" to allow one to "see the continuity between father and son." Wexler's "brilliant" film, by contrast, was filled with anger, and presented "a montage of sheer violence, a warning that our house is on fire and that the roof has already caved in." While *Medium Cool* was politically engaged, *Alice's Restaurant* was "committed to life," in the manner of "the colonizing hippies of today," Canby wrote. In an earlier review, the film critic referred to Joni Mitchell's singing of her hauntingly beautiful and sadly prophetic "Songs to Aging Children."[48]

Clearly building on their experience at Woodstock and the nation's political atmosphere, the members of Jefferson Airplane issued "We Can Be Together" in September, declaring themselves to be "outlaws in the eyes of America." In the fashion of the Yippies and influenced by the Black Panthers, Paul Krassner admitted that young people stole, cheated, lied, hid, and dealt. "We are obscene lawless hideous dangerous dirty violent and young," targeting private property, supporting "chaos and anarchy," and ordering their antagonists, "Up against the wall fred (motherfucker)," as well as a tearing down of walls.[49] By contrast, singer-songwriter Joni Mitchell, Graham Nash's lover, crafted "Woodstock," which began with "a child of God" heading to Yasgur's farm to join a rock 'n' roll band, to camp out, and "get my soul free." Declaring that members of the counterculture were "stardust . . . golden," Mitchell wrote, "We've got to get ourselves back to the garden."[50] Crosby, Stills, Nash and Young would also put out their own version of "Woodstock," which appeared on the *Déjà Vu* album then being recorded.[51] Other seminal songs on *Déjà Vu*, released the following spring, included Nash's "Teach Your Children" and "Our House," and David Crosby's "Almost Cut My Hair," paeans to the counterculture.[52]

Two important chroniclers of the counterculture, including one who arguably helped to plant seeds for its emergence, offered similar but contrasting analyses of American youth. In *The Making of a Counterculture*, Professor Theodore Roszak warned that "a technocratic totalitarianism" would appear, more efficient than George Orwell and Aldous Huxley predicted, should the youth revolt and its version of "the Great Refusal" fail. Roszak particularly focused on important intellectual threads, including C. Wright Mills's radical sociology, "the dialectics of liberation" offered by Herbert Marcuse and Norman Brown, the "journey to the east" undertaken by Allen Ginsberg and Alan Watts, the aspiring to "the counterfeit infinity" linked to "Timothy Leary's impenetrably occult narcissism" and the more fun-filled games of Ken Kesey, and the examination of utopia by Paul Goodman.[53] In his review of Roszak's book, Columbia University philosopher professor Robert Paul Wolff stated upfront that many of the nation's smartest and most gifted youth had recently "been turning against reason," resorting instead to drugs, mysticism, Zen Buddhism, and other Eastern religions. Wolff admonished Roszak for supposedly encouraging this flight from reason, which he feared could "play into the hands of reaction."[54]

Paul Goodman, whose warning that young people were "growing up absurd" had served as a harbinger for the youthful explosions of the 1960s, wrote about "The New Reformation," in the September 14, 1969, edition of the *New York Times*. In advanced industrialized nations, he contended, science and technology had "become the system of mass faith," no matter the dominant political ideology in place. However, such a "basic faith" now appeared imperiled, as young dissidents termed science "antilife . . . a Calvinist obsession" employed by white Europeans to control people of color, while scientific technology had proven "diabolical." Also apparently discredited were the professions and academic instruction. Goodman suggested that a new religious crisis was taking place, akin to the Reformation. Bringing this about, he wrote, were the alienation young people experienced and their determination "to be taken seriously." Goodman credited them with operating in a creative manner religiously, employing music, drugs, and even sexuality as sacraments while striving to prevent competition. Rock festivals such as Woodstock and another recent gathering on the Isle of Wight, in which Dylan participated, appeared to Goodman as "pilgrimages." He considered this religiosity genuine and likely to endure, although he could not predict "into what."[55]

17

THE CONSPIRACY, STREET FIGHTING MAN, AND THE APOCALYPSE

Another facet of what many referred to as Woodstock Nation played out with the well-publicized Trial of the Chicago Eight, which began on September 24, 1969, soon devolving into something of a circus-like atmosphere. Judge Julius Hoffman proved incapable of reigning in the defendants or their counsel, known collectively as the Conspiracy, whose members soon became celebrity figures on college and university campuses across the United States. Abbie Hoffman and Jerry Rubin, in particular, played the part of spoiled children, bantering with the judge in Yiddish, as Hoffman did, and making a mockery of the court proceedings. The trial went on for months, during which time Judge Hoffman, enraged by Bobby Seale's characterizations of him as a "fascist dog" and a "racist," ordered the Black Panther leader bound and gagged, thereby only accentuating the presupposition that radicals could not obtain justice in American courtrooms.[1] While testifying, Hoffman proclaimed himself "a child of the 60s . . . a cultural revolutionary," who "tries to shape and participate in the values, and the mores, the customs and the style of living of new people who eventually become inhabitants of a new nation and a new society through art and poetry, theater, and music." Continuously verbally jousting with the judge, Hoffman at one point admonished him as a "disgrace to the Jews."[2] Also appearing as defense witnesses were various luminaries drawn from the American left and the counterculture, including Pete Seeger, Timothy Leary, Country Joe McDonald, Phil Ochs, Judy Collins, and Arlo Guthrie.

On September 26, as if on cue, the Beatles issued *Abbey Road*, which included George Harrison's masterpieces "Something" and "Here Comes the Sun," and John Lennon's pulsating "Come Together."[3] The latter song offered Alice in Wonderland–inflected lyrics, and the repeated refrain, "Come together right now over me."[4] Meanwhile, the band was effectively breaking up, after Lennon told George, Paul McCartney, and Ringo Starr that he was leaving the group. This followed the recent release of *Great White Wonder*, a lengthy bootleg album of Bob Dylan's recordings, containing renditions of songs ranging from Woody Guthrie's "I Ain't Got No Home" to Dylan's own "Mighty Quinn" and "I Shall Be Released." In October, Plastic Ono Band issued "Cold Turkey," attributed only to John Lennon, not his longtime writing partner Paul McCartney, and was a pained admission of heroin withdrawal, with its declaration, "I wish I was a baby / I wish I was dead."[5]

On October 4, *Rolling Stone* presented a timely special report by John Burks, "The Underground Press." It opened with a look at the three-year-old Detroit *Fifth Estate*, among the nation's two hundred or so underground papers, and the one most tied to John Sinclair, the MC-5, and the White Panther Party. A local commune, Trans-Love Energies, had centered on Sinclair, but the now commercially successful MC-5 had split off, doling only 10 percent of the band's earnings to the commune until Sinclair was released from jail. Reflecting on the deadly riot that swept through Detroit during the summer of 1967, editor Peter Werbe, a year shy of thirty, recalled, "It was *beautiful*. So beautiful. You've never seen anything like it." Eighteen-year-old Ken Kelley, editor of the Ann Arbor *Argus*, thought little of SDS and believed his paper should have a role "beyond the Movement." LNS's George Cavaletto acknowledged that the underground press was experiencing "a cultural crisis." Three years before, Cavaletto contended, drugs involved "the first revolutionary step a lot of people took," but that passed, and the turn toward confrontation "as a way of life" also was proving unsatisfying. And yet a staffer at the *Washington Free Press* insisted "the greatest thing that could happen would be for rock and roll really to take an active role in the revolution." The *Great Speckled Bird*'s Miller Francis Jr. remained "equally committed to the Movement and to rock and roll," but dismissed the MC-5 as "an emasculated version" of the early Who. At Philadelphia's *Distant Drummer*, it had appeared at one time that Don DeMaio would push the paper "toward the netherland of SDS and White Panthers and Motherfuckers."

Now, he was considering selling the paper, whose audience drove Volkswagens and smoked marijuana, but refrained from taking LSD. Burks visited Tom Forcade in Phoenix, where he coordinated the UPS and also edited the underground magazine *Orpheus*. A fire-bombing several months earlier led Forcade to insist that the front door remain barred. On hearing that John Sinclair had referred to the underground press as "a great bunch of motherfuckers," Forcade said that the White Panther leader "has genius. A deeply poetic vision of the revolution." Forcade expressed belief in nonviolence, and indicated that the movement was at "the point of diminishing returns with the techniques of shock and separatism."[6]

Pointing to the nitty-gritty of underground newspapers, Burks mentioned the low wages staffers received and the need for advertisements, which included sex pitches of various kinds. Some staff members, as at the *Berkeley Tribe*, deemed such ads exploitative. Editor and publisher Art Kunkin stated that the *Los Angeles Free Press* turned down illegal advertisements, and sought to temper "crude appeals to sex," but had no problems with "homosexual personals." Kunkin considered his paper a "conscience for the Movement," ready to criticize the Black Panthers when necessary. Another early underground paper, the *East Village Other* was suffering from an abundance of democracy or anarchy at its helm, Burks wrote. Attempts to foster "democratic participation" continued at the *Washington Free Press*, the San Francisco *Good Times*, the Chicago *Seed*, and Atlanta's *Great Speckled Bird*, but the *Berkeley Tribe* had opted, for efficiency's sake, to place "certain dictatorial powers" in its editor's hands. A number of important underground editors criticized LNS for its top-down approach and lack of accountability, while LNS's Allen Young insisted its operation was "very democratic" as it provided news coverage supportive of the movement. The *New York Times* acknowledged, "Liberation News Service is one of the few functional alternatives, or counter-institutions, that the Movement has produced."[7]

Finances beset *The Rat*, which Burks deemed "politically the most revolutionary of New York's underground papers." In two recent issues, a letter went out to subscribers, addressed as "Brothers and Sisters," discussing the troubled economic state of affairs. "Trying to get through to you. Amerika hassles in between us. We've been evicted from our old offices, turned down by printers, subjected to intricate bureaucratic runarounds by the U.S. post office. CBS subsidiary, Columbia Records, has

cancelled all advertisements in the underground press. The great Amerikan Pig is trying to sit on us. It's been hard to run the paper, fight hassles
and get out your subscription." The letter closed with the sign off, "Hold
on, it's a'comin. Armed love, *The Rat*." Jeff Shero, formerly of the *Rag*
and a one-time SDS national officer, served as editor, dealing when necessary with the Motherfuckers, who traipsed in and out of the office.[8]

By this period, the idea of revolution filtered through the underground
press. However, John Kois of the Milwaukee *Kaleidoscope* stated, "We
don't see ourselves as an instrument of the revolution, because we don't
see any revolution." In fact, Kois foresaw a greater likelihood of a right-
wing revolutionary situation than one emanating from the left. He admitted to hating politics, offering, "This will all be bullshit anyway." The
Ann Arbor Argus' Ken Kelley dismissed SDS altogether. "Fuck 'em.
They're getting more and more absurd, SDS. They missed their chance
because they never listen to what people want, what people are into, and
now SDS is just into rhetoric." The *San Francisco Good Times'* Marvin
Garson recalled conversing with "an SDS chick from Detroit" who employed "a fake hillbilly accent," and warned him that come the revolution, he was "gonna be *offed*." The *Chicago Seed*'s Marshall Rosenthal
believed that each individual had to "make his own revolution on his own
terms," and offered support for Abbie Hoffman's call for "revolution for
the hell of it." The *Seattle Helix*'s Roger Downey considered revolution a
type "of Constitutional duty."[9]

Members of Weatherman, many wearing helmets, wielding clubs, and
holding aloft the National Liberation Front flag, tore out of Chicago's
Lincoln Park, crying out, "Long live the victory of the people's war," at
the start of the "Days of Rage," October 8–11, leading to the calling in of
2,500 National Guardsmen and the eventual arrest of three hundred protestors. The dates were selected to commemorate the death of Che Guevara, killed two years earlier. Running down Clark Street, members of
Weatherman hurled rocks through plate-glass windows, then averting a
line of police, dashed over to State Street. The action, designed, as John
Jacobs had urged, to "bring the war home," was supposed to be "very
heavy" and to induce "street kids" to participate but to little avail.[10] *New
Left Notes* nevertheless soon extolled the Weatherman street action.

> We came to Chicago to join the other side . . . to do material damage to pig Amerika and all that it's about . . . to do it in the road—in the open—so that white America could dig on the opening of a new front . . . to attack . . . to vamp on those privileges and destroy the motherfucker from the inside. . . . FROM HERE ON IN IT'S ONE BATTLE AFTER ANOTHER—WITH WHITE YOUTH JOINING IN THE FIGHT AND TAKING THE NECESSARY RISKS. PIG AMERIKA—BEWARE: THERE'S AN ARMY GROWING RIGHT IN YOUR GUTS, AND IT'S GOING TO HELP BRING YOU DOWN.[11]

Many Weatherman leaders were arrested, and nearly a quarter of million dollars bail had to be posted. Writing in the *New York Times*, John Kifner tellingly declared members of Weatherman "almost religiously obsessed with turning themselves into true revolutionaries and in escaping their own middle-class backgrounds, which they scornfully term 'white skin privilege.'"[12]

The militants who had joined Weatherman viewed with disdain the Moratorium to End the War in Vietnam, orchestrated by Sam Brown and David Hawk, which involved a one-day calling to a halt of business-as-usual. Carried out around the United States on October 15, the Moratorium featured a protest rally by one hundred thousand on the Boston Common and a gathering of a quarter-million people at Bryant Park in Midtown Manhattan, while another one hundred thousand showed up in Chicago.

On October 21, forty-seven-year-old Jack Kerouac, having been reduced to heavy drinking and loneliness, notwithstanding a third marriage (to Stella Sampas), and disapproving of the radical politics associated with the New Left, died of massive abdominal hemorrhaging. In an interview the previous year with William F. Buckley on the PBS program, *Firing Line*, Kerouac had acknowledged that the beats and the hippies were part of one "Dionysian movement," and that "the hippies are good kids, they're better than the Beats."[13] Now writing in the *New York Times*, Joseph Lelyveld deemed Kerouac's *On the Road* "a basic text for youth who found their country claustrophobic and oppressive," but also "a spontaneous and passionate celebration of the country itself." While noting that *On the Road* had plenty of caustic critics, Lelyveld also praised its passages containing finely drawn social commentary, including when the protagonist Sal Paradise acknowledged wanting to be "a

Negro, feeling that the best the white world had offered was not enough ecstasy for me, not enough life, joy, kicks, darkness, music, not enough life." As Lelyveld revealed, Black Panther leader Eldridge Cleaver declared that passage in *On the Road* "a cultural turning point for white America."[14] Allen Ginsberg praised his deceased friend as "the first one to make a new crack in the consciousness."[15] It was Kerouac who "broke open the fantastic solidity in America, as solid as the Empire State Building, that turned out not to be solid at all. His vision was what the universe as we will experience it is—golden ash, blissful emptiness, a product of our own grasping speed."[16] *Time* magazine also acknowledged that when Kerouac wrote about easy sex or pot, they remained "exotic and forbidden fruit."[17]

In mid-November, the New Mobilization Committee to End the War in Vietnam triggered rallies around the country, including one in Washington, D.C., involving as many as a half million demonstrators. The vast majority were peaceful, although a Yippie-led contingent tossed rocks and bottles, and also burned American flags. Among those speaking on the National Mall were Eugene McCarthy, South Dakota Senator George McGovern, Coretta Scott King, and Dick Gregory, while Arlo Guthrie, Pete Seeger, and the touring cast of *Hair* helped to provide entertainment, albeit with a political twist. Warnings frequently made about war criminality appeared to gather momentum following the announcement on November 30 of charges against Lieutenant William Calley for having participated in and then covered up the slaughter of hundreds of Vietnamese civilians that had taken place in the village of My Lai some twenty months earlier. Young Americans proved riveted to other news that at least potentially involved the war in Vietnam, particularly the televised introduction on December 1 of a draft lottery, which effectively allowed young men with high draft numbers to avoid military service altogether. Other than for those with safe lottery numbers, December 1969 hardly proved hopeful for those involved with either the movement or the counterculture. On December 4, Chicago police fired scores of bullets into an apartment where Black Panthers Fred Hampton and Mark Clark dwelled, killing both as they lay in their beds. The radical San Francisco attorney Charles Garry reported these "were the 27th and 28th Black Panthers killed in clashes with the police since January of 1968."[18]

The next day, the Rolling Stones released their latest album, *Let It Bleed*, while thousands of rock fans gathered at the Altamont Speedway in Tracy, California, to hear the Grateful Dead, Jefferson Airplane, Crosby, Stills, Nash and Young, the Stones, and other bands at a free rock concert.[19] Along with Oakland policemen and security guards, the Rolling Stones purportedly hired the Hell's Angels for a promised $500 worth of beer to help maintain order at the Altamont Festival. Some three hundred thousand fans attended, but the outbreak of violence, much of it associated with the Hell's Angels, convinced the Grateful Dead, who had helped to bring about the festival, to decline to perform. Both Jefferson Airplane's manager Bill Thompson and the Family Dog's Chet Helms considered Altamont "a permanent holding ground for tense vibrations." The Rolling Stones' set included "Jumpin' Jack Flash," "Sympathy for the Devil," "Midnight Rambler," "Street Fighting Man," and "Gimme Shelter," from *Let It Bleed*. The atmosphere was fraught with tension, with singer Marty Balin of Jefferson Airplane knocked unconscious when he attempted to prevent a member of the Hell's Angels from attacking a concertgoer. In one particularly terrible moment, the Hell's Angels' Alan Passaro repeatedly stabbed a young black student, Meredith Hunter, who was also stomped on by other members of the motorcycle group, as the Stones played "Sympathy for the Devil"; the band halted as the violence took hold. Hunter had attempted to go onstage during the Rolling Stones' performance, and appeared to have a gun. A stunned Jagger declared that evening, "I know San Francisco by reputation. It was supposed to be lovely here—not uptight. What happened? What's gone wrong? If Jesus had been there, He would have been crucified." An autopsy revealed that Hunter had been on speed, and an ensuing murder trial resulted in Passaro's acquittal, following the showing of film footage demonstrating that Hunter had pointed a gun in the air.[20]

Writing for *Liberation*, former SDS president Todd Gitlin termed Altamont "The End of the Age of Aquarius."[21] *Rolling Stone* magazine later featured a cover story of the festival titled "Let It Bleed," an obvious takeoff on both the band's recent album and the Altamont fiasco.[22] Rock critic Michael Lydon noted the all-too-familiar signs there: "the dancing beaded girls, the Christ-like young men, and smiling babies . . . but the weirdos too, whose perverse and penetrating intensity no camera ever captures. Speed freaks with hollow eyes and missing teeth, dead-faced acid heads turned out by countless flashes, old beatniks clutching gallons of red wine, Hare Krishna chanters with shaved heads and acned cheeks." Still, there was something strangely unfamiliar too, with countless numbers immersed in "the first swirling, buzzing, euphoric-demonic hours of acid," causing Lydon to wonder, "is this Bosch or Cecil B. DeMille, biblical, medieval, or millennial? Are we lost or found?" This was clearly not "Woodstock West," and despite the early feeling that things were "friendly enough and loose," there appeared "too much of something." And then violence broke out, as a Hell's Angel rammed a pool cue into someone, but the crowd proved largely "passive and afraid," intimidated by the motorcycle gang members. The sense of community dissipated, while afterward the festival became known as "the disaster at Alta-mont."[23]

Rolling Stone magazine would refer to it as the Altamont Death Festi-val, and the *San Francisco Chronicle*'s Ralph Gleason suggested "it wasn't just the Stones and it wasn't just the Angels, it was all of us." Gleason deemed Altamont "the most significant act ever . . . associated with rock music." The concert "abruptly" terminated "the San Francisco rock mythology" that included the Hell's Angels, Allen Ginsberg, and Ken Kesey. The high ticket prices and "extraordinary profits" from the Rolling Stones' recent tour also called into question their posture "as musical revolutionary spokesmen," who had supplanted both Bob Dylan and the Beatles. As Gleason saw it, "The name of the game is money, power, and ego, and money is first as it brings power. The Stones didn't do it for free, they did it for money, only the tab was paid in a different way. Whoever goes to the movie paid for the Altamont religious assem-bly."[24]Freelance writer Robert Draper contends, "San Francisco had been rushing kamikaze-style toward the disaster that became Altamont."[25]

In mid-December 1969, billboards in several cities around the world displayed a more hopeful message, "WAR IS OVER! If you want it. Happy Christmas from John and Yoko." An angry John Sinclair re-sponded, "You are going to sound awfully fucking stupid trying to tell the heroic Vietnamese people that 'the war is over if you want it' while they are being burned and bombed and blown out of their pitiful little huts and fields."[26]

Notwithstanding John and Yoko's message, a shroud covered the counterculture throughout the month, which proved enduring. That re-sulted from the discovery of the killers of Sharon Tate, her friends, and Leno and Rosemary LaBianca, slain in Southern California in August. Arrests were made in early December of members of the so-called Man-son family, headed by thirty-five-year-old, pathologically dysfunctional

Charles Manson, who had spent much of his life in institutions for unwanted or troubled boys, or incarcerated for a variety of offenses, including burglaries, auto theft, sodomy of another boy, forgery, and violation
of the Mann Act (transporting girls or women across state borders for
illicit purposes). Released from jail on March 21, 1967, despite a request
to remain behind bars, the slightly built, five-foot-seven-inch-tall Manson, ever the con man, moved to Berkeley, becoming something of a guru
in Haight-Ashbury during the Summer of Love. As one of his followers
later recounted, "He was magnetic. His motions were like magic," while
others considered him a "beautiful man" who "loved us all totally."[27]
Joined by a pack of women and a smaller number of men, Manson established the "Family" that soon became so notorious. Beginning in the
spring of 1968, Manson and various Family members resided for several
months at the Pacific Palisades residence of Dennis Wilson of the Beach
Boys, who later recorded a song Manson wrote. With Wilson footing the
bill, Manson recorded several songs, but in August, Wilson's manager
ordered the Family to leave the drummer's home. Manson then relocated
his followers to the five-hundred-acre Spahn Ranch near the Topanga
Canyon, once owned by silent film star William S. Hart, and where a
number of western films and television programs had been shot. At one
point, Terry Melcher, the record producer of the Byrds and the Beach
Boys and the son of actress Doris Day, made a couple of visits to Spahn
Ranch, to hear Manson and some of the women members of the Family
sing. Manson, in turn, showed up uninvited at the residence where Melcher had previously resided but that had recently been rented by Sharon
Tate and Roman Polanski.[28]

Following the release of the Beatles' *White Album*, Manson had become obsessed with "Helter Skelter," which he insisted was the famous
group's warning about impending race war. Manson convinced his followers that they were the chosen ones, certain to prevail after a bloody
racial conflagration. Desirous of speeding "Helter Skelter" along but even
more determined to deflect investigation of the Manson-spawned murder
of a former family member, the cult leader instructed his followers to
commit mayhem at Terry Melcher's former home, where they proceeded
to murder Tate and several of her friends on the morning of August 9.
The following evening, the Family killed the LaBiancas, scrawling
"Rise," "DEATH TO PIGS," and "HEALTER [sic] SKELTER" in the
house. By early December, investigators from the Los Angeles Police

Department had arrested Family members, including its ringleader. A sensational trial would begin the following summer. Meanwhile, news accounts referred to the Svengali-like hold Manson had over the young women and men who followed him; the women viewed themselves as his "slaves" and called him "God," "Jesus," and "Satan."[29]

News of the Manson slayings proved devastating in many countercultural circles, including the famed Laurel Canyon, just outside of Los Angeles, as Michael Walker explains in his spirited book, *Laurel Canyon: The Inside Story of Rock-and-Roll's Legendary Neighborhood*. Rock musician Graham Nash acknowledged, "That's when it really started to turn weird. Because up until then everybody's door was open, nobody gave a shit—y'know, come on in, what the fuck—and then all of a sudden it was like: I gotta lock my car. I gotta lock my door. It was the beginning of the end, I think." Nash was also struck by the fact that Manson was a musician who had auditioned for Neil Young. He considered the Manson murders "the entire antithesis of what the peace-and-love movement was about," but transformative as "everybody knew that something had happened that had changed the vibe of the area dramatically forever." Paul Body, a musician who also worked as a doorman for the Troubadour, recalled, "Once people found out that hippies were killing people, it was a whole different thing." Los Angeles record executive Sally Stevens remembered, "It was really scary suddenly. People used to just hitchhike merrily everywhere and that really slowed down." Another resident of Los Angeles, David Strick, who soon became a renowned photographer, reflected back to that period, pointing to "a huge number of whacked losers who were part of the hippies scene—I mean, they were absolutely demented." A photo groupie, Pamela Des Barres declared, "The Manson murders changed the idea that hippies were safe, that hippies were harmless, that hippies could inflict no harm on anybody. That the only guy with long hair and the beard could turn out to be the devil was really a nightmare." A&R executive Michael James Jackson stated, "We were in this peaceful mentality about sharing, that it was a community, that there was no judgment." That changed because of Manson and the Family, whose actions had proven "purely frightening." The British singer and actor Michael Des Barres concluded, "In truth, the devil had always been there. The '60s created the devil, and Manson came out of that."[30]

The *New York Times* offered an explanatory piece on December 14, "Many Religious Communes of Young People Are under the Sway of Compelling Leaders." Possibly written by Stephen V. Roberts, who had been tracking communes and was closely following the Manson story, the article discussed charismatic figures inside the commune movement. It opened by discussing nineteen-year-old Michael Metelica, who had once desired to become a member of the Hell's Angels but was now linked to forty followers awaiting both the Second Coming and the Aquarian Age, during which all men would view others as their brothers. Metelica headed the group known as the Brotherhood of the Spirit, situated in a rented summer camp located in Heath, Massachusetts, in the state's northwestern sector. He devised rules precluding the use of drugs or alcohol, as well as "sex without love."[31]

The article referred to Metelica's commune as one of dozens established by young people aspiring to "mystical and religious experience, refuge from the material world." The inspiration for those communes frequently derived from a compelling figure who possessed some of the charisma that Manson exuded. One member of Mel Lyman's Fort Hill Community offered that Manson was "full of spirit, but in a primitive form and without heart." The religions driving communards appeared to involve belief "in man's potential for producing a transcendent 'creative energy' once he is freed from cultural inhibitions, or 'hang-ups.'" There existed profound distrust of the purely rational, and a corresponding belief in the mystical, in the fashion of the counterculture. Steve Diamond, who had worked for LNS and now resided on the Montague Farm, one of two communes (one in Massachusetts and one in Vermont) resulting from LNS's split, asserted, "What we have isn't farming or dropping out or revolution. It's just people relating to people." He referred to New York City, where he had attended Columbia University, as "a prison," with people knowing "they are locked up, but they just don't know how to get free."[32]

The *New York Times'* Roberts wrote about "The Hippie Mystique," which appeared in the newspaper in mid-December. After noting that Manson denied being a "hippie," Roberts quoted from a psychiatrist, who stated, "Manson was really a mirror image of the hippie. The hippie stresses the beatific side of his character almost to the exclusion of everything else. Manson embodied the demonic characteristics that are in all of us but seldom come out." Referring to the hippie community in Topanga,

Roberts spoke of whimsical notions, but also "loneliness and despair, bad drug 'trips' and fear of a future cast adrift from the moorings of the past." Additionally, violence could appear, involving the emotionally troubled or defenseless individuals preyed on by others. In early January, Roberts wrote about "Charlie Manson: One Man's Family." While the guilt of Manson and his compatriots had yet to be proven, Roberts wrote, what was obvious was the "strange family of wandering young people" who followed Manson. "Living on the fringes of a hostile society, they posed just by their presence a basic challenge to the values and institutions of their parents," labeled by Roberts as "middle- or upper-middle-class." He asked, "Where did they come from? What were they like? What road did they travel to that crowded courtroom?" Roberts viewed Manson as the byproduct of both "parental neglect" and a failed "public correctional system." Moreover, as Dr. David Smith of the Haight-Ashbury Free Clinic analyzed matters, "If the delusional system turns hostile, and you're committed to whatever your spiritual leader says is right, and he says, 'Kill,' you can kill."[33] Meanwhile, the *Los Angeles Free Press*, one of the first of the underground publications, highlighted stories about Manson for three straight weeks.

Ed Sanders, one of the founders of the Fugs and an originator of the idea to levitate the Pentagon, would write *The Family: The Story of Charles Manson's Dune Buggy Attack Battalion* (1971), an attempted definitive examination of the deadly cult that many saw as besmirching the counterculture.[34] In his review in the *New York Times*, Robert Christgau considered Sanders's exploration into Manson natural as both were "into sex, dope, the occult and the downfall of straight society." Unfortunately, however, as Christgau put it, "in the age of the new togetherness, it isn't just the good guys who get together." Sanders recognized this, warning, "The flower movement was like a valley of thousands of plump white rabbits surrounded by wounded coyotes. Sure, the 'leaders' were tough, some of them geniuses and great poets. But the acid-dropping middle-class children from Des Moines were rabbits." In contrast to Sanders, a devotee of nonviolence, "a distressing minority," as exemplified by Bernadine Dohrn of Weatherman, who initially sang Manson's praises, and those who worried that a frame-up was taking place, refused "to believe that a long-haired minstrel could also be a racist and a male supremacist who used dope and orgasm and even some variety of love to perpetuate his own murderous sadism."[35] Jerry Rubin, after speaking with

Manson, declared, "I fell in love with Charlie Manson the first time I saw his cherub face and sparkling eyes on national TV." Rubin continued, "His words and courage inspired us."[36]

Only weeks after Manson and the Family became household names, SDS, now largely reduced to the increasingly cult-like Weatherman, headed by Dohrn and a small group of her compatriots, gathered in ghetto-riddled Flint, Michigan, for the organization's final convention. During the past few weeks, the Weatherman collectives had undergone intensive self-criticism sessions, with the deliberate tearing apart of longtime relationships, amid group drug and sexual experiences. One Weatherman flyer indicated, "We're moving, dancing, fucking, doing dope, knowing our bodies as part of our lives, becoming animals again after centuries of repression and uptightness." Referred to as the National War Council, the proceedings in Flint went on from December 27–31, 1969, in a "Giant Ballroom," sporting mammoth posters of revolutionary figures like Fidel Castro, Che Guevara, Ho Chi Minh, Vladimir Lenin, Mao Zedong, Malcolm X, and Eldridge Cleaver. One wall displayed photographs of Fred Hampton, the Black Panther recently killed by police in Chicago, while a banner sported bullets coupled with images of former president Lyndon B. Johnson, defeated Democratic Party presidential nominee Hubert Humphrey, President Richard M. Nixon, Vice President Spiro T. Agnew, Governor Ronald Reagan, Mayor Richard Daley, and Sharon Tate. Posters featured scoped rifles tagged "PIECE NOW," and a massive cardboard machine gun hung from the ceiling. As would later be reported, "the war council was frenzy . . . in anticipation of the armed struggle they were calling for." After sleeping for an hour or so, most Weather people spent the rest of the time involved in "heavy, heavy rapping, heavy listening, heavy exercising, heavy fucking, heavy laughing." Frenzied mass meetings, called "wargasms," took place at night. Dohrn said, "That's what we're about, being crazy motherfuckers and scaring the shit out of honky America," while Mark Rudd exclaimed, "It's a wonderful feeling to hit a pig. It must be a really wonderful feeling to kill a pig or blow up a building." John Jacobs declared, "We're against everything that's 'good and decent,' in honky America. We will burn and loot and destroy. We are the incubation of your mother's nightmare." At one point, Dohrn applauded the Manson Family murder. "Dig it: first they killed those pigs, then they ate dinner in the same room with them, then they even shoved a fork into the victim's stomach." Weatherman would herald

"MANSON POWER—THE YEAR OF THE FORK!" Increasingly, talk was heard of moving to "higher levels of struggle," which referred to armed struggle, the breaking into small cells or affinity groups, and heading underground. [37]

18

THE NOT SO SLOW FADE

In January 1970, the first women's issue of *The Rat*, the underground New York newspaper, appeared, offering the seminal essay, "Goodbye to All That." Written by Robin Morgan, a former antiwar activist and Yippie turned founder of WITCH (the Women's International Terrorist Conspiracy from Hell), the piece slammed "the counterfeit male-dominated Left." It castigated easy references to "pussy power" and "clit militancy" heard around the New Left and underground newspaper staffs, as well as "the little jokes, the personal ads, the smile, the snarl." White males, Morgan stated, were "most responsible for the destruction of human life and environment on the planet today." But it was also white males who led "the supposed revolution to change all that." A genuine revolution, she wrote, had to be "led by, *made* by those who have been most oppressed: black, brown, and white *women*," with men serving as auxiliaries. She urged women to be "bitchy, catty, dykey, frustrated, crazy, Solanisesque, nutty, frigid, ridiculous, bitter, embarrassing, man-hating, libelous, pure, unfair, envious, intuitive, low-down, stupid, petty, liberating." Indeed, "WE ARE THE WOMEN THAT WOMEN HAVE WARNED US ABOUT." Morgan dismissed the notion that men were oppressed, and contended that both sexism and racism antedated capitalism and thrived under socialism as well. Women were determined to "kick out all the jams, and the boys" would have to struggle to keep up or fall by the wayside. Declaring "goodbye, goodbye forever, counterfeit Left, counterleft, male-dominated cracked-glass mirror reflection of the Amerikan Nightmare," Morgan asserted that "women are the real left," with their "unclean bodies . . . inferior brains . . . wild eyes . . . wild voices."[1] Later that year, Morgan edited *Sisterhood Is Powerful*, an early anthology of radical feminist writings.[2]

About the same time as Morgan's blistering denunciation of misogyny, the radical feminist periodicals, *It Ain't Me Babe* and *off our backs*, appeared in Berkeley and Washington, D.C., respectively. Dismayed New Leftists, the women staffers of *It Ain't Me Babe* sought to meld fervent feminism with support for global revolution. The collective putting out of *off our backs* included other veterans of the New Left such as Marilyn Webb, Marlene Wicks, and Colette Reid. Their founding statement read, "We seek through the liberation of women, the liberation of all peoples."[3]

At their posh, thirteen-room penthouse located on Manhattan's Park Avenue, famed conductor Leonard Bernstein and his wife, the actress Felicia Montealegre, hosted, on January 14, the first of a series of parties, the attendees later derisively referred to by Tom Wolfe as engaged in "radical chic."[4] Almost ninety guests were present, as Bernstein discussed the Black Panther Party with Donald Cox, a leading member of the radical organization, at the gathering, designed to raise money for the legal defense fund of the so-called New York Panther 21, whose trial was impending on charges of conspiring to murder policemen and blow up department stores, police stations, railroad facilities, and the famed New York Botanical Gardens.[5] An editorial in the *New York Times* on January 16 assailed the development of the Panthers as "romanticized darlings of the politico-cultural jet set." The *Times* referred to the Panthers as possessing a strange mixture "of Mao-Marxist ideology and Fascist paramilitarism." The paper dismissed the "group therapy plus fund-raising soirée" put on by Bernstein and Montealegre, characterizing it as "the sort of elegant slumming that degrades patrons and patronized alike."[6] Montealegre in turn charged that the *Times* had treated the "deeply serious" event frivolously, which necessarily offended anyone devoted "to humanitarian principles of justice."[7]

City College political scientist Marshall Berman reviewed two works by the Scottish psychiatrist R. D. Laing, considered a guru for the counterculture, in the *New York Times* in February 1970. Earlier best known for *The Politics of Experience and the Bird of Paradise*, Laing had more recently written *The Divided Self* and *Self and Others*, which only added to his already controversial reputation. In *The Politics of Experi-*

ence, Laing exclaimed, "If I could turn you on, if I could only drive you out of your wretched mind, if I could tell you I would let you know."[8] Berman opened his systematic analysis by pointing to the 1960s as a period when "two of the deepest streams of consciousness—self-consciousness and social consciousness—converged." As those strands merged, the Freudian Left, associated with "Wilhelm Reich, Erich Fromm, Herbert Marcuse, Paul Goodman, Norman O. Brown," acquired greater acclaim, while influencing American thought. Those intellectuals particularly impacted American radicalism, offering the New Left both "a new direction and a new vocabulary" while pointing to society's propensity to foster alienation within oneself. Laing went further still, seemingly suggesting that madness could provide "existential truth."[9]

Vincent Canby and Richard Goldstein reviewed Michelangelo Antonioni's film, *Zabriskie Point*, featuring a gorgeous young couple, played by Mark Frechette and Daria Halprin, real-live members of the Lyman Family.[10] Appropriately performing the roles of Mark and Daria, respectively, they wrestled a bit over conflicting beliefs—his inclination to revolutionary engagement, and hers to countercultural activities. Both critics deemed the film vacuous, although Goldstein credited Antonioni with ultimately presenting the United States "as a bouquet of shapes and colors, eagerly grotesque, plosive or sedately unreal."[11] Subsequent films dealing with the movement and the counterculture, such as *Getting Straight* and *The Strawberry Statement*, each focusing on the campus revolution, garnered mixed reviews at best.[12] Refusing to simply dismiss them as "bad," Canby more importantly saw these films as "opportunistic, unworthy," in which ideas and characters were treated less than seriously.[13] Dotson Rader, author of *I Ain't Marching Anymore! An Honest Look of Life among the Disaffected Young—Their Violence, Politics, and Sex*, took particular umbrage at the film version of *The Strawberry Statement*, which, in contrast to the memoir by James Simon Kunen, relocated scenes from Columbia University during the spring of 1968 to San Francisco. Rader deemed it "a cheap attempt at the commercial cooption and exploitation of the anguish of a generation." Not stopping there, he damned it as "as slander" directed at those determined to end injustice at home or abroad, and as "a palpably counterrevolutionary film."[14]

The number of bombings or attempted bombings on college and university campuses continued to mount during the winter and spring, along with trashing incidents, but government and corporate buildings were also targeted. As Kirkpatrick Sale reports, self-professed revolutionaries included Weatherman, "the New Year's Gang, the Quartermoon tribe (Seattle), the Proud Eagle Tribe (Boston), the Smiling Fox Tribe (New York City), one unnamed group around Columbia University, the John Brown Revolutionary League (Houston), the Motherfuckers (now living in New Mexico), and various (generally unofficial) branches of the White Panthers and the Black Panthers."[15] A representative for the U.S. Treasury Department, whose Alcohol, Tobacco and Firearms Division tracked the stockpiling of illegal guns by militant groups, reported that some SDS factions, particularly "the Mad Dogs and the Crazies, were arming themselves." But he also noted that no large gun caches had been seized from SDS factions. [16]

In his summation to the jury on February 13, 1970, U.S. Attorney Thomas A. Foran referred to the defendants in the Chicago Seven trial as "evil men" who wished to "stand on the rubble of our destroyed system of government." He termed them "profligate extremists, more concerned with their own needs than the common good." The defendants, Foran emphasized, were "sophisticated . . . smart and . . . well-educated and . . . as evil as they can be." He accused them of deliberately exploiting alienated young people, and of waging an "assault on the law." Earlier, defense counsel William Kunstler had quoted from both Allen Ginsberg and Judy Collins, while insisting it was the responsibility of the jury to ensure the right of individuals "to speak boldly unafraid, to be masters of their souls, to live free and to die free." Jurors subsequently acquitted the defendants of conspiracy charges, but found Abbie Hoffman, Jerry Rubin, David Dellinger, Rennie Davis, and Tom Hayden guilty of possessing the intent to pique a riot after crossing state boundaries. Prior to being sentenced, Hoffman urged Judge Julius Hoffman to take LSD, while Rubin informed him, "Julius, you radicalized more people than we ever could. You're the country's top Yippie." The judge ordered fines of $5,000 and sentenced the convicted defendants to five years' imprisonment. In addition, he doled out lengthy prison terms to the defendants and their attorneys, William Kunstler and Leonard Weinglass, for criminal contempt. Judge Hoffman had already handed out a four-year jail sentence to Bobby Seale, for contempt of court. [17]

Street battles ensued between young people and the police in the Isla Vista community, situated next to the idyllic University of California at Santa Barbara campus. Rioting occurred from the evening of February 25 until the early morning, with the local Bank of America building burned to the ground. Governor Ronald Reagan issued a declaration of an "extreme emergency," with members from the California Highway Patrol joining with local police, while the National Guard prepared for possible action.[18]

On March 6, 1970, the affluent townhouse located at 18 West 11th Street, in the heart of Greenwich Village, exploded, as a result of a failed attempt to build bombs in the basement of the four-story building owned by the family of Cathy Wilkerson of Weatherman. Members of Weatherman offered contrasting accounts of what was being attempted, but general agreement existed that nail bombs were being put together in an effort "to bring the war home" when a blast killed three members of the organization: Teddy Gold, Diana Oughton, and Terry Robbins. One account indicated that Columbia University's main library was being targeted, but others pointed to Fort Dix, New Jersey, where a dance involving noncommissioned officers was scheduled that evening. Among those escaping from the explosion were Wilkerson and Kathy Boudin.

In an essay published in the *New York Times* on March 15, Thomas R. Brooks underscored "a new mood among frustrated radicals," in the wake of trials involving the Black Panthers and the Chicago Seven. Brooks noted that a number of militant black and white groups employed "a rhetoric of violence and a Marxist-Leninist jargon," talking "of the need to arm in self-defense if not for outright guerrilla warfare." He pointed out that most members of Weatherman "are the educated children of middle-class, if not outright wealthy parents." After grappling with the question of what led such individuals to become revolutionaries, Brooks determined, "It is difficult to escape the feeling that these youngsters are demented. How else explain the admiration for Sirhan Sirhan, the murderer of Senator Robert F. Kennedy, or for Charles Manson." Brooks referred to "open jokes about assassinations, and a salivating over violence."[19]

Jerry Rubin's book, *Do It!: Scenarios of the Revolution*, with an introduction by Eldridge Cleaver, appeared in the spring, resulting in a thoughtful book review by Christopher Lehmann-Haupt in the *New York Times*.[20] The journalist, writing only weeks after the Greenwich Village townhouse explosion, indicated that Rubin's book lightly referred to blowing up toll booths and Howard Johnson motels. Damningly, Lehmann-Haupt suggested that the thinking of Rubin, who condemned "Amerika" as racist, sexist, and warmongering, appeared logically to lead to "annihilation, symbolized far better by the rubble on 11th Street, with its excavated corpses and its charred library, than by a book." Rubin, of course, did not appear to take himself seriously, preferring rather to produce theater and mythology.[21]

Freelance writer Bennett Kremen later questioned whether "anything about this headline-hungry media-hustler" should be taken seriously. Kremen bluntly stated that Rubin's insistence on taking more LSD and a curbing of discipline would lead "any self-respecting revolutionary general in command to shoot him dead." Nor could the reviewer imagine Rubin, with his dreams of a "fantacized (sic), carefree Xanadu" setting the path for greater liberty and an improved, albeit "more self-indulgent world," making it through "the brutality of a true revolutionary struggle." Also looking back to Abbie Hoffman's *Revolution for the Hell of It*, Kremen dismissed the author's "grandiose, mind-blown world."[22]

Richard Todd, an editor at *The Atlantic* magazine, examined another type of utopia, B. F. Skinner's *Walden Two* and the commune movement. The book's sales had now surpassed six hundred thousand copies, which Todd explained as resulting from the desire for "community," exemplified by both new towns and rural communes. His book, Skinner believed, provided no handbook for hippies and had fostered no revolution, but it had propounded ideas now very much in vogue. A student had written him, declaring that Thoreau's notion of "living a life of quiet desperation" possessed no appeal to him. But having read and discussed *Walden Two*, he considered the book "a ray of sanity and hope in the midst of an otherwise insane confusion," with its depiction of a self-sustaining community. Skinner informed Todd, "I don't claim to have invented the hippie movement, but the idea of communities seems to have come around again. People are looking for alternative ways of life. What hippies share with the book is a belief that people can get along together." He went on to warn, "Much of what we see, however, is a quest for *instant* community," as in the case of Woodstock, which he considered to have no future. Young people were interested in his novel, Skinner determined, for it provided "a chance to plan a lasting community." However, as Todd remarked, many hippie communes hardly operated in the fashion of *Walden Two*. Still, Skinner retained hope in the young, despite worrying that they didn't choose to reason. After all, some did "want to do better, to go beyond smoking pot." He attributed the high failure rate for communes to the "desire for immediate ecstasy, a mistaken belief in egalitarianism, and sheer lack of capital." The Twin Oaks community in Virginia, Todd suggested, could probably best be compared with *Walden Two*. One recent teenage arrival acknowledged having read the book, but admitted, "It was *Easy Rider* that turned me on to communes." The community's psychology instructor expressed reverence for Skinner, declaring, "He is to psychology what Einstein was to physics." His reading of *Walden Two* led him to search for such a community. As for Skinner, he believed "an experimental attitude toward life" to be essential.[23]

The March 29, 1970, edition of the *New York Times* contained Steven V. Roberts's report on Ecology Action, the radical environmental group, only a few weeks before the initial Earth Day celebration that helped to publicize the modern environmental movement. Roberts discussed the commune-like house at 3029 Benvenue in Berkeley, where former anti-war activist and Ecology Action founder Cliff Humphrey resided with his wife Mary and some ten volunteers, many completing the alternative service required of conscientious objectors by the Selective Service System. The Humphreys revered Native Americans for having lived in harmony with the land, with Cliff pointing to the fact "that the biosphere, the life-support system for the earth, is finite and fragile." Like many ecologists, Humphrey believed society had to experience "a cultural transformation" involving movement away from "growth, consumption and progress." Humphrey became one of the key figures in sparking a recycling campaign involving paper products, glass, steel, aluminum, clothes, and machinery. His group members desired to grow pesticide-free vegetables, baked their own bread, and attempted to restrict water usage.[24]

Gregory Voelm, a young man and recent graduate of Antioch College, who had become a conscientious objector, explained that his was "the first protest graduating class." Various friends headed for Canada, Mexico, or rural communes, afflicted with a large sense of meaninglessness. Voelm saw ecology as "the answer to alienation," explaining, "We're alienated from nature and alienated from our ability to relate to each other, to love. But to break down that alienation between the individual and his environment is really a radical thing. When you destroy part of the environment, you have to realize you're destroying part of yourself." Turned on by Allen Ginsberg and Gary Snyder, former Yippie Keith Lampe had also become involved with the environmental campaign, publishing *Earth Read-Out*, an ecology newsletter given to the underground press, but planned to do more. He intended to head to Colorado to acquire some land. "I have to get out of the typewriter things and into reality. We take this population-food squeeze very seriously, and we're going to go out and grow more food than we can consume." Once again, reporter Stephen V. Roberts analyzed the back-to-the-land movement, deeming it "a search for simplicity, for privacy, for meaningful work, for basic pleasures, for harmony with nature, for roots, for wholeness." Existing in a badly splintered world of machines and oppressive technology, its participants sought "personal communion . . . magic," self-empowerment, time, peace, and joy. Simply put, "in a world of fragments, they want to be put back together." This explained the furor over People's Park, the appeal of *The Whole Earth Catalog*, and the whole ecology movement, with its seeking of "the spiritual values buried by the advent of rationality and technology." Peggy Datz, a former teacher now working at the Ecology Center in Berkeley, declared, "It really is a new religion. I went camping in the Sierras last summer and we were three days from the nearest road. It did fantastic things for my head. I had a really mystical feeling about being part of a total living community."[25]

In April, leading members of the Ultra-Resistance, brothers Daniel and Philip Berrigan, facing lengthy prison sentences, headed underground, with Philip captured within weeks; Daniel remained on the run for several months. In the April 5 edition, *New York Times* reporter Agie Salpukas discussed the thriving yet tenuous nature of the underground press caused by heightened harassment. As the number of such papers continued to grow so did the targeting by law enforcement officials at all levels. The *East Village Other*'s Allen Katzman indicated that his paper had always mirrored shifts involving "the radical youth movement," initially focusing on the birthing of an alternative culture, but the Vietnam War, events in Chicago surrounding the 1968 Democratic Party national convention, and the Chicago Conspiracy trial altered that, leading to the need "to expose the present culture with facts and fists." LNS's Alan Young again reported that both investigative reporting and larger engagement in radical politics resulted in intensified police harassment. "We're trying to build a radical movement. Now they're out to get us," Young asserted.[26]

On April 12, the *New York Times* presented an extended treatment, "Political Terrorism: Hysteria on the Left," by the writer Irving Howe, a man who had been a radical since his college days in the latter stages of the 1930s and was the editor of *Dissent*, the democratic socialist journal. The vast bulk of American youth, politically engaged or not, Howe wrote, continued to support democratic, nonviolent paths, no matter how inarticulately. Now, however, New Left offshoots were "inflamed with the rhetoric of violence. Some flirt with sabotage and terror; others inflict minor physical brutalities on intra-left opponents." Possibly some had been involved in bombings. Howe acknowledged that there existed very good reasons for individuals to feel terribly alienated from American society, but denied that such frustration should lead to revolutionary violence. The despair experienced by New Left extremists, he warned, had received "an explosive or . . . hysterical quality" through linkage to foreign ideologies like Maoism and Castroism that only "cut them off from both American realities and democratic norms." Of little help was the splintering of SDS into Maoist and anarcho-authoritarian mindsets. Howe too was struck with how many New Leftists were "upper-class youth," members of "the upper *bourgeoisie*." He was also troubled by the fact that "Jewish boys and girls, children of the generation that saw Auschwitz" despised democratic Israel, while championing Gamal Abdel Nasser's "revolutionary" Egyptian dictatorship. Disturbing too were the actions of various intellectuals, including the "erudite" Herbert Marcuse, "who taught the young that tolerance is bourgeois deception and liberal values are a mask for repression"; Andrew Kopkind, who said that "morality comes out of the barrel of a gun"; and the *New York Review of Books*, which had effectively published a primer on "how to make a Molotov cocktail." Such intellectuals, in Howe's eyes, provided "an aura of intellectual respectability" for the New Left's turn to "elitism . . . authoritarianism . . . contempt for democracy . . . worship of charismatic dictators . . . the mystique of violence." Additionally, Howe warned that any identification with terrorism would prove disastrous for the American left, while terrorism itself would prove catastrophic for civil liberties. Ultimately, Howe argued, opposing terrorism was simply the right thing to do. "To throw bombs is wrong. It is wrong because it is inhumane, because it creates an atmosphere in which brute force settles all disputes." Howe worried about the moral consequences of terrorism, and reminded readers that Stalin's secret police also undoubtedly justified their actions by their "revolutionary commitment," "fight against injustice," "sacrifice and ideology."[27]

That spring, American colleges and universities experienced their greatest paroxysm of violence following the Nixon administration's decision to extend the war by undertaking an extensive ground operation into Cambodia. In the midst of escalating protests, President Nixon was heard muttering, "You see these bums, you know, blowing up the campuses. Listen, the boys that are on the college campuses today are the luckiest people in the world, going to the greatest universities, and here they are burning up the books, storming around this issue."[28] Several ROTC buildings were burned or bombed, including one at the Midwestern campus of Kent State University. On May 4, National Guardsmen called to Kent State fired into a mass of students—some protesters and others simply attempting to move from class to class—killing four and wounding nine others. Ten days later, police gunned down two students at the largely black campus of Jackson State in Mississippi. The Kent State killings resulted in massive student protest, but the shootings at Jackson State engendered little response. The Kent State tragedies also induced Neil Young to write "Ohio," soon released by Crosby, Stills, Nash and Young. The song referred to "Four dead in Ohio," "soldiers . . . cutting us down," "Tin soldiers and Nixon coming."[29] The Beatles completed their final album, *Let It Be*, produced by Phil Spector, and released on May 8.[30] Weeks before, Paul McCartney had announced his departure from the Beatles, just prior to release of his first solo album.[31]

On May 13, Thomas King Forcade spoke in Washington, D.C., before the congressional Commission on Obscenity and Pornography, which he derisively called the "Keystone Kommittee" that was purportedly conducting "a blatant McCarthyesque witch hunt" with "inquisitional 'hearings'" throughout the nation. It stood, Forcade charged, as "the vanguard of the Brain Police, Mind Monitors, Thought Thugs, Honky Heaven Whores" striving to convert millions into "thought criminals." He declared, "You ARE 1984, with all that implies." He dismissed the supposed design of the committee, declaring instead that it would lead to "total state control of every man, woman, child, hunchback and midget." By contrast, Forcade testified, the underground press sought "liberation— total freedom," and insisted that its participants were "the solution to America's problems. We are revolution. . . . We are tomorrow, not you. We are the working model of tomorrow's paleocybernetic culture, soul, life, manifesting love, force, anarchy, euphoria, positive, sensual, communal, abandoned, united, brotherhood, universal, orgasmic, harmonious, flowing new consciousness media on paper, coming from our lives in the streets. So fuck off, and fuck censorship!"[32]

Weatherman completed its first underground communique on May 21 (although it would not be published immediately), with Bernadine Dohrn offering "A DECLARATION OF A STATE OF WAR." Dohrn spoke of blacks "fighting almost alone for years"; the manifesto affirmed, "We've known that our job is to lead white kids to armed revolution." She asserted, "Kids know that the lines are drawn; revolution is touching all of our lives. Tens of thousands have learned that protest and marches don't do it. Revolutionary violence is the only way." Weatherman was now following "the classic guerrilla strategy" employed by the Vietcong, as well as "the urban guerrilla strategy of the Tupamaros," and Che's pronouncement that "revolutionaries move like fish in the sea." Dohrn continued, "The alienation and contempt that young people have for this country has created the ocean for this revolution." Members of Weatherman planned to "fight in many ways," Dohrn warned. "Dope is one of our weapons. The laws against marijuana mean that millions of us are outlaws long before we actually split. Guns and grass are united in the youth underground. Freaks are revolutionaries and revolutionaries are freaks. If you want to find us, this is where we are. In every tribe, commune, dormitory, farmhouse, barracks and townhouse where kids are making love, smoking dope and loading guns—fugitives from Amerikan justice are free to go."[33]

The May 25, 1970, edition of *New Times* presented a cover with a handcuffed Charles Manson and the heading, "The Media Assassination of Charlie Manson: Last Interview from Jail."[34] The June 25 cover of *Rolling Stone* magazine featured Manson, along with promotion for its "Special Report: Charles Manson," with the subheading, "The incredible story of the most dangerous man alive."[35] The August 11 issue of the *East Village Other* also displayed Manson, with the headline, "Manson Declares Nixon Guilty."[36] Later in the year, *Harper's* displayed a cartoon-sketch of an upside-down Manson, and a story by Frank Conroy, "Manson Wins: A Fantasy."[37] *Tuesday's Child*, a Los Angeles–based countercultural newspaper, founded by disgruntled members of the *Los Angeles Free Press*, tagged Manson "Man of the Year."[38]

Earlier that summer, Jack Newfield, who had written a prescient book on SDS and SNCC, *A Prophetic Minority*, reviewed LNS cofounder Raymond Mungo's autobiographical offering, *Famous Long Ago: My Life and Hard Times with Liberation News Service*. Newfield noted that the New Left had not produced many memorable books of its own until recently, but was beginning to do so, as indicated by "this honest, literate and loving memoir of the Movement." *Famous Long Ago*, Newfield continued, was one young man's journey through war, assassinations, the counterculture, and political schisms, resulting in Mungo's becoming "a post-Beatles Thoreau, digging nature and privacy on a farm in Vermont." Written from within "the stormy center of the Movement," Mungo's account discussed its evolution "from flowers and yellow submarines, peace and brotherhood, to sober revolutionary committees, Che-inspired berets, even guns." As for Mungo, he had opted for "nature, the country, private virtue, community, writing and his friends." At his book's close, Mungo confessed, "I am an indigent dropout. I no longer have any program to save the world, let alone nineteenth-century Marxism, except perhaps to pay attention to trees. . . . Let us now then cease with our complaining about the state the world is in, and make it *better*. We're not trying to convince the world. . . . We're only trying to change ourselves."[39]

The journalist Sara Davidson wrote a lengthy essay that appeared in the June 1970 issue of *Harper's* magazine, under the heading, "Open Land: Getting Back to the Communal Garden." She began by recounting her visit to Wheeler's Ranch, where she was greeted with a sign that read, "Welcome, God, love." She discovered that all the inhabitants were vegetarians, with Wheeler offering that diet was "very very central to the revolution." Wheeler called the ranch "the land," which had been "opened" during the winter of 1967, to assist individuals at Morningstar whom officials were forcing off that commune. Lou Gottlieb had introduced Wheeler to the concept of open or free land, which was catching on in other parts of the Far West. Davidson found it surprising that individuals on Wheeler's Ranch called themselves "hippies," but as she discovered, "being a hippie, to them, means dropping out completely and finding another way to live, to support oneself physically and spiritually." It required rejecting competition, the work ethic, technology, and political operations. Gottlieb, an ex-communist, stated, "The entire Left is a dead end." Hippies, for their part, chose "to turn inward and reach backward for roots, simplicity, and the tribal experience." Having found slums cold, unfriendly, and dangerous, they began moving back to the land, engaging in voluntary primitivism, as Ramon Sender noted. Aspiring to "retribalization," the inhabitants of the ranch called on a childbirth ritual and weekly feasts. At the same time, in the manner of many other communes, Wheeler's Ranch preferred "a loose community of individuals," not communal living. Problems existed, with a sexual double standard favoring straying males, poor sanitation resulting in dysentery, and "periodic waves of hepatitis, clap, crab, scabies, and streptococcic throat infections."[40]

For her article, Davidson also interviewed Stewart Brand of *The Whole Earth Catalog* fame, who talked about the impulse to go back to the land to set up "intentional communities." He revealed, "What we want are alternative economies and alternative political systems. Many alternative ecologies." New social programs, he admitted, were "always parasitic," having to "feed off the parent culture until they're strong enough to be self-sustaining." Eventually, he believed, the New Mexico communes could shape their own economy through the swapping of goods and services. Davidson also visited Huw Williams of the former Tolstoy Farm, one of the oldest open land communes, now called Freedom Farm. When asked how the community had endured for so long, Williams replied, "The secret is not to try. We've got a lot of rugged individualists here, and everyone is into a different thing." Like many other communes, Freedom Farm experienced difficulties when some "speed freaks, transients, addicts, and crazies" began arriving about four years earlier. Not all the "permanents" agreed with Williams's anarchist philosophy, desiring more in the way of authority and discipline. Williams stated, "The thing about anarchy is that I'm willing to do a job myself, if I have to, rather than start imposing rules on others."[41]

On August 3, 1970, Steven V. Roberts offered yet another look at communes in a *New York Times'* article featuring the Taos scene. He referred to a young woman, in exile from Lansing, Michigan, who headed for the mountains in New Mexico, after seeing *Easy Rider*. Hippie migration to the area around Taos had been occurring now for three or four years, Roberts noted, with thousands arriving but few managing to endure financial problems, brutal winters, scorching summers, water scarcity, poor soil, and violence, including beatings, rapes, and shootings. Another problem resulted from the seeming waves of troubled young people, lacking much in the way of resources, who appeared to be wanting "the great commune in the sky," declared a clerk who worked at the General Store, which catered to local hippies. Thus the warning went out, "Don't come to Taos." Even members of the Hog Farm bemoaned the fact that "any more people will kill us." A few, however, appeared to be carving out alternative institutions and lifestyles. One of the founders of the Lama Foundation, Jonathan Altman, explained, "When you see something doesn't work, you don't just stand there and scream at it. You find something else." The Family, a commune made up of about fifty people, including ten babies, resided in a large old house close to central Taos. The adults practiced a version of group marriage, and took on new names, several culled from the story of King Arthur and his Round Table. Viewing itself as a "service commune," the Family desired to help others, operating the General Store and an information center, located next door. Steve Durkee, another one of the founders of the Lama Foundation, considered his community as attempting to nurture the "three bodies" human beings possess: physical, mental, and emotional. "What we're working for is the development of the human personality through the harmonicus growth of all three bodies."[42]

Also during the summer of 1970, Doubleday and Company, Inc. issued an autobiographically drawn novel, William J. Craddock's *Be Not Content*. The finest single encapsulation of the LSD experience and a brilliant portraiture of acidheads in mid-1960s' California, this work presented the story of Abel Egregore, a well-read college student and member of the Night Riders motorcycle gang, which hung out with the Hell's Angels. Following his first LSD trip, Abel opted to become a different kind of outlaw, engaged in an elusive search for enlightenment. His days as "a street fighter" ended immediately, as he explained. "I saw my world shrink to a micro-speck floating in the eternity of the cosmos, and I smelled enlightenment, and was promised answers to the questions I didn't even know how to ask, and I relearned that hostility and working it out on other beings was utterly wrong, and I refelt the feelings. I had learned it was sophisticated and cool to ignore and I said, 'God forgive me.'" LSD, Abel appreciated, "cut right through the Zen games and intellectual disillusionment of the once worshipped Beat generation." Moreover, "Acid's first and most powerful message was love." A second acid trip enabled him to appreciate "the unfathomable *beauty* and joy that was *right there*, all around, everywhere, just waiting to be seen and appreciated." Abel became immersed in the counterculture, joining in efforts to establish "independent tribes in the forests," only to be reviled "by property owners, cops, the board of health, forest rangers, and Smokey the

Bear." Forced to return to the cities, they discovered tensions mounting but believed that something big was going to occur. Along with his compatriots, Abel participated in a series of antiwar demonstrations, while one friend after another got busted. [43]

Owsley's White Lightning led Abel to experience that "in the beginning there was nothing. Nothing. So much all-cool nothing that it was everything. Nothing. Perfect Nothing. . . . And from the Eternal Nothing came an illusion of a separate something faced with a task. A quest, the beginning and end of which are exactly the same." And yet Abel existed, as did "the world—the illusion. . . . The universe and all its intricate beauty." He reasoned that "it's too complex to be nothing. It exists!" as did the Void. Moreover, "the nothing of the Void embraces and cancels all other existences." Unable to let go, Abel was informed, "Then you'll have to go back." [44]

Later in the story, a friend, Baxtor, stated, "Acid was a sad mistake. First it promised us things that we'll never obtain—states of existence that we'll never attain and hold. Then it showed us a glimpse of the end. Now that's a dirty trick. Once you've seen the end, the race *to* the end becomes an all-out drag. We're going to grow old and die. That's all. That's all there is. The enlightenment-game is just *that* . . . another game." With Abel unable to counter his contention, Baxtor continued, "We're a cosmic experiment that failed. Freaks. Acid freaks." [45] Although everyone around Abel was tired of hearing about love, and attempted so futilely to experience it, he underwent another acid trip when, at least momentarily, he again felt that "everything is perfect—OM-endlessly—OM—infinity is ours—peace, my friends. I love you. I am you. We are simply IT. There's nothing else to know." [46]

On August 24, a powerful bomb tore apart Sterling Hall at the University of Wisconsin-Madison, resulting in the killing of a married postdoctoral researcher in physics, Robert Fassnacht, and injuries suffered by three other individuals. The bomb was designed to destroy the Army Mathematics Research Center, housed at Sterling Hall, but Fassnacht and his department had no involvement with the center. The self-named "New Year's Gang," which included two brothers, Karleton and Dwight Armstrong, along with David Fine and Leo Burt, carried out the bombing and presented a communiqué, "Vanguard of the Revolution." [47] FBI director J. Edgar Hoover's office sent a memo on September 1 declaring, "In view of seriousness of this case, and possibility this bombing could trigger similar tragic consequences elsewhere, it is imperative that early solution be made in this case." The memo went on to state, "New Left extremists have previously announced their targets include Federal buildings, FBI offices, and other law enforcement facilities." It called for "aggressive prosecutive steps."[48]

Timothy Leary, facing a twenty-year prison sentence for drug convictions, escaped on September 13 from the minimum security prison, California Men's Colony West, in San Luis Obispo, where he was held.[49] Assisting the breakout were members of the Brotherhood of Eternal Love, which footed the bill, and Weatherman. As one leader of the Brotherhood, Eddie Padilla, related, "The Weathermen didn't care about Timothy Leary; they cared about their cause. We were revolutionaries, too, but they were violent revolutionaries. They wanted to overthrow the government through violent means. We were into overthrowing it through love."' The Brotherhood believed they could "turn on the world" through LSD.[50] Through Weatherman, Leary sent out a manifesto declaring,

> There is a time for peace and a time for war. There is the day of laughing Krishna and the day of Grim Shiva. . . . Brothers and sisters, this is a war for survival. Ask Huey and Angela. They dig it. Ask the wild free animals. They know it. . . . There are no non-combatants at Buchenwald, My Lai or Soledad. . . . Remember the Sioux and the German Jews and the black slaves. . . . If you fail to see that we are the victims—defendants of genocidal war, you will not understand the rage of the blacks, the fierceness of the browns, the holy fanaticism of the Palestinians, the righteous mania of the Weathermen, and the pervasive resentment of the young. Listen, Americans. Your government is an instrument of total lethal evil. Remember the buffalo and the Iroquois! Remember Kennedy, King, Malcolm, Lenny!

Then Leary exclaimed, "To shoot a genocidal robot policeman in the defense of life is a sacred act. . . . Listen, comrades. The liberation war has just begun. Resist, endure, do not collaborate. Strike. You will be free. . . . Listen, the hour is late. Total war is upon us. Fight to live or you'll die. Freedom is life. Freedom will live." Wrapping up his diatribe, Leary declared, "WARNING: I am armed and should be considered dangerous to anyone who threatens my life or my freedom."[51]

Members of Weatherman helped to spirit Leary and his wife Rosemary out of the country and into Algeria, where they joined Black Panther Party leader Eldridge Cleaver, on the run from an attempted murder charge. Leary was soon reported attempting, albeit unsuccessfully, to link up with Palestinian guerrillas in Lebanon and Egypt. Shortly joining the Learys and Cleaver in Algeria was Bernadine Dohrn, who had abetted Leary's prison break. Dohrn had recently been added to the FBI's expanded list of ten most wanted fugitives, which included radicals Angela Davis, Dwight Allen Armstrong, Karleton Lewis Armstrong, David Sylvan Fine, Leo Frederick Burt, Katherine Ann Power, and Susan Edith Saxe. From Algeria, Leary wrote to Allen Ginsberg, whom he addressed as "Beloved Brother." Deeming his escape "a miracle," Leary declared "weathermen are the most beautiful brave, wise people. Young gods and goddesses." Expressing pride in being connected to Weatherman, Leary proceeded to acclaim the Black Panthers "the hope of the world" and Cleaver a "genial genius," and to praise Algeria as "perfect." He affirmed complete support for "the Panthers and the third world—Algeria, N. Vietnam, N. Korea, China."[52]

One of the first countercultural figures to respond to Leary was Ken Kesey, who penned an open letter widely reproduced in underground papers in the United States. "Dear Good Doctor Timothy. Congratulations! The only positive memories I have from all my legal experiences was getting away. A good escape almost makes up for the fucking bust." However, Kesey proceeded to admonish Leary. "In this battle, Timothy, we need every mind and every soul, but oh my doctor we don't need one more nut with a gun. I know what jails makes you feel but don't let them get you into their cowboys-and-Indians script. . . . What we need, doctor, is inspiration, enlightenment, creation, not more headlines. Put down that gun, clear that understandable ire from your Irish heart and pray for the vision wherein lies our only true hope." Kesey continued, "I do not mean to scold someone so much my senior in so many ways; I just don't want to lose you. What I really mean is stay cool and alive and high and out of cages. . . . And keep in mind what somebody, some Harvard holy man I think it was, used to tell us years ago: 'The revolution is over and we have won.'"[53]

Countering Kesey's charges, Leary agreed to an interview in Algeria with a *Rolling Stone* reporter, during which he suggested that the FBI had crafted the letter attributed to the Merry Prankster. Responding to a question about resorting to guns, Leary agreed "it's inevitable. Their system is based on guns. The Weathermen and I have rapped this through on acid and agree totally. Arms is one of their weapons . . . and one of ours." Leary insisted, "Anyone who's been through the LSD experience with us is an acid revolutionary now. Dynamite is just the white light, the external manifestation of the inner white light of the Buddha."[54]

In "An Open Letter to Allen Ginsberg on the Seventh Liberation," Leary declared that he now subscribed to the refrain, "Shoot to live / Aim for Life." Ginsberg wrote back to Leary, expressing pleasure that he was out of jail, but admitting to an "odd effect of your Weatherman letter." Ginsberg acknowledged, "I don't know what good 'armed and considered dangerous' mantra will do," but also admitted that he was unaware what an "'unarmed and not considered dangerous' mantra" would accomplish either. Ginsberg felt compelled to point out to his friend that Algeria, in the fashion of Arab, socialist, and western states, was "very puritanical about grass."[55] As matters turned out, Algeria proved unsafe for the Learys in another manner, when armed Black Panthers held them captive with Cleaver demanding a ransom, in effect. Eventually, the Learys were allowed to leave Algeria, arriving in Zurich, but were temporarily detained in a Swiss prison.

Leary's strange turn was hardly the only setback those in the counterculture experienced as word was transmitted of his glorification of violent revolution. The rock world suffered another kind of loss, that of three of its brightest lights, all twenty-seven-years-old, in a matter of months, beginning on September 18, 1970, when Jimi Hendrix died in the Kensington district of West London after a heavy dosage of barbiturates. Just over two weeks later, on October 4, Janis Joplin experienced a heroin overdose in Los Angeles; she had recently slammed hippies, declaring "They're frauds, the whole goddamn culture. They bitch about brainwashing from their parents, and they do the same damn thing."[56] The following summer, a bloated Jim Morrison also apparently died from an overdose of heroin in Paris.

Ironically, in the very period when Hendrix, Joplin, and Leary fell from grace, a series of books poured forth celebrating the ideals associated with the counterculture. In early September, Kenneth Keniston, the director of Yale Medical School's Behavioral Sciences Study Center and the author of two seminal books related to the counterculture and the movement, *The Uncommitted: Alienated Youth in American Society* and *Young Radicals: Notes on Committed Youth*, explored recent works that provided a radical examination of contemporary America, including Philip E. Slater's *The Pursuit of Loneliness: American Culture at the Breaking Point*. Someone revisiting the United States after being away, Slater, a professor of sociology at Brandeis University, contended, "is struck first of all by the grim monotony of American facial expressions—hard, surly, and bitter—and by the aura of deprivation that informs them. One goes abroad forewarned against exploitation by grasping foreigners, but nothing is done to prepare the returning traveler for the fanatical acquisitiveness of his compatriots." Slater appeared particularly dismayed by the hostility directed at "blacks, hippies, and student radicals," at the same time little concern was expressed about the chance of an epochal nuclear or ecological disaster. He bemoaned the lack of community and engagement, and the stultifying competiveness and individualism of American society. In Marcusean fashion, Slater also decried Madison Avenue's propensity "to maximize sexual stimulation and minimize sexual availability."[57]

In his review of *The Pursuit of Loneliness*, Paul Goodman's *New Reformation*, and Richard Sennett's *The Uses of Disorder: Personal Identity and City Life*, Keniston discussed crises befalling both the New Left and the counterculture, which he saw as intertwined. The early New Left, Keniston wrote, fractured, to a considerable extent, owing to its lack of a firm intellectual foundation, having opted for a "shallow and eclectic" melding of "populism, liberal reform and ever-larger doses of C. Wright Mills and Marcuse." Eventually, various New Leftists sought inspiration in Marxism, albeit it "leavened with Mao Tse-tung, Che Guevara, and Frantz Fanon." While linking American radicals and the Third World, it stoked the fantasy of American workers becoming the new revolutionary vanguard. Keniston referred to the counterculture as "another faction of the New Left" that sought cultural revolution through "light shows, macrobiotics, Timothy Leary, acid, Zen, Norman O. Brown, astrology, encounter groups and meditation." To Keniston, "cultural revolutionists" most desired "'unalienated consciousness,' spontaneous human relationships and a rediscovery of the subjective world." At the same time, it proved strikingly susceptible to cooptation by mass circulation publications and Madison Avenue, even threatening to devolve into "a harmless caricature of American culture," instead of a genuine alternative.[58]

In his review in the *New York Times*, Keniston labeled Slater's work "a brilliant, sweeping and 'relevant' critique of modern America," and one that refused to applaud either "apocalyptic radicalism or its apotheosis of the world of pure consciousness." To Keniston, *The Uses of Disorder* by Sennett, another Brandeis sociologist, presented the finest present-day "defense of anarchism," contending that affluent America could move beyond earlier "'adolescent' conformisms" and sustain small anarchic communities, absent both police and rules. Goodman's *New Reformation*, an expansion of his earlier essay with the same title, again examined youth revolt as largely religiously determined. All three authors, Keniston suggested, were "post-Marxist and post-Freudian," both critical and appreciative of young radicals. In the fashion of anarchists, Goodman condemned "the Leninist cast of some modern radicals," and continued to believe that the discarding "of old authority relations" would result in "a more spontaneous and better society." At the same time, Goodman urged American youth to better appreciate history, learning, the humanities, reason, and science. For his part, Keniston appreciated that Slater and Sennett recognized technological advances made "possible the most radical vision of a possible future" in which man could shape "the social process he has created."[59]

The September 26, 1970, issue of *The New Yorker* contained an essay by Yale Law School Professor Charles A. Reich on "The Greening of America," also the title of a new book he was publishing. Reich began by declaring a unique revolution was taking place. "It has originated with the individual and with culture." If successful, it would ultimately reshape political structures too. It would be nonviolent, and could not be based on violence. It was presently spreading in rapid-fire fashion, having already influenced "laws, institutions, and social structure." It could well result in "a higher reason, a more human community, and a new and liberated individual." This was, Reich wrote, "the revolution of the new generation," which invariably promised to transform American society, to end disorder, war, poverty, environmental spoilation, "the artificiality of work and culture," the lack of community, and the loss of self resulting from suppression, repression, and alienation. In his book, which proved a mammoth bestseller, Reich talked about Consciousness I, Consciousness II, and Consciousness III. The first combined belief in American possibilities and rapacity, the second the thinking of the corporate state, and the third that of youth, "the energy of enthusiasm, of hope . . . of openness."[60]

In his review of *The Greening of America* in the *New York Times*, Peter Marin warned that "the flower children" he had encountered had "been driven to exile or heroin, or else now arm themselves with guns instead of flowers." After the first exhilarant surge subsided, the young "moved on to something lonelier and far more real, a kind of mythic struggle in a darkness more profound than any Reich recognizes or has chosen to enter." Marin then pointed to, among others, John Sinclair, Timothy Leary, slain Kent State students, and murdered Black Panthers.[61] Longtime U.S. diplomat and renowned historian George F. Kennan also denied that "Con III" was "the answer," dismissing Reich's analysis as "seductive and contagious" and accusing him of exaggerating actual "evils" as did "fanatical political movements, including the totalitarian ones."[62] Philosopher Herbert Marcuse, considered one of the mentors to the New Left, criticized Reich's failure to acknowledge the role played by elites in determining "life and death, war and peace." In his estimation, *The Greening of America* falsely transmuted "social and political radicalism into moral rearmament."[63] New Left leader Tom Hayden, dwelling in a Berkeley commune called the Red Family, agreed with the need "for a new foundation to guarantee life, liberty and the pursuit of happiness," but questioned Reich's belief that a revolutionary alteration of consciousness would accomplish that. Such a mindset, Hayden wrote, was "utopian," for actual "institutions of protest and resistance" were required to foster a newer brand of self-government. Also necessary were "a socialist economic system," proportional representation for underrepresented groups, the dismantling of "the American Empire," and "an internationalist movement."[64]

In the late fall, George Harrison and John Lennon offered solo albums, underscoring the fact that the counterculture's former greatest rock band was no more. At the end of November, Harrison put out the appropriately titled *All Things Must Pass*, a three-album compendium with the smash hit "My Sweet Lord" and its declarations of "Hallelujah," "Hare Krishna," "Gurur Brahma," "Gurur Vishnu," "Gurur Devo," and "Gurur Sakshaat."[65] John Lennon issued his own solo album, far more critically acclaimed than Paul McCartney's, in early December.[66] It reflected the deeply introspective turn Lennon and Yoko Ono had engaged in, which included primal therapy sessions with Arthur Janov in Los Angeles. The highly personal offerings included "Mother," "Love," and "God," while Lennon also displayed his growing determination to recast himself as a "Working Class Hero." Lennon referred to God as a concept that enabled one to measure pain, and then emphatically stated what he did not believe in, including many of the iconic forces associated with both the counter-culture and the movement: magic, I-Ching, the Bible, tarot, Jesus, Kennedy, Buddha, mantra, Gita, yoga, Elvis, Dylan, and the Beatles. He emphasized instead his belief both in himself and the couple he was part of, while declaring, "The dream is over" and that he had been the "dream-weaver . . . the walrus," but now he was John.[67] The embittered "Working Class Hero" underscored how difficult it was both at home and school, the Marcusean determination to anesthetize individuals with religion, sex, and television, and society's insistence on young men becoming soldiers. In the end, people remained "fucking peasants," but they should aspire to the status of "a working class hero."[68]

As the first year of the new decade neared a close, Weatherman delivered its own reassessment of revolutionary possibilities and youth subculture. The "New Morning" communiqué, posted on December 6, bragged about "a growing illegal organization of young women and men" who could "live and fight and love inside Babylon," outside the FBI's reach. At the same time, the Weathermen acknowledged the townhouse explosion had "forever destroyed our belief that armed struggle is the only real revolutionary struggle." They understood the difficulty of standing as "a group of outlaws" outside of youth communities. This was, the communiqué continued, "a question of revolutionary culture." They declared that "people become revolutionaries in the schools, in the army, in prisons, in communes and on the streets. Not in an underground cell." Over the past few months, they stated, "freaks and hippies and a lot of people in the Movement have begun to dig in for a long winter." People were involved in experimenting with their lives, learning "how to survive together in the poisoned cities and how to live on the road and the land. They've moved to the country and found new ways to bring up free wild children. People have purified themselves with organic food, fought for sexual liberation, grown long hair. People have reached out to each other and learned that grass and organic consciousness-expanding drugs are weapons of the revolution," albeit not for everyone. "The enemy" recognized how potent this youth culture was, and thus it called on "killer-drugs" like "smack and speed" to cripple young people. Still, people went on creating new families, while collectives appeared across the American landscape, made up of those willing "to trust each other both to live together and to organize and fight together." The revolution, Weathermen affirmed, was about "our whole lives; we aren't part-time soldiers or secret revolutionaries." Women in particular were adopting more assertive stances, taking leading roles in the struggle to bring about "a New Nation."[69]

19

IT'S ALL OVER NOW

Meanwhile, the increasingly politicized John Lennon participated in a revelatory interview with *Rolling Stone* and produced songs like "Power to the People," "Imagine," "Woman Is the Nigger of the World," "John Sinclair," and "Happy Xmas (War Is Over)." During the interview, conducted in New York City on December 8, 1970, Lennon affirmed, "The dream is over. I'm not just talking about the Beatles, I'm talking about the generation thing. It's over, and we gotta—I have to personally—get down to so-called reality." He admitted to having taken LSD one thousand times, saying "I used to just eat it all the time." He also praised "Give Peace a Chance" as "beautiful," and labeled "Working Class Hero . . . a revolutionary song." Discussing "Revolution" and the idea behind it, Lennon acknowledged, "I don't know; I've got no more conception than you. I can't see . . . eventually it'll happen, like it will happen—it has to happen; what else can happen? It might happen now, or it might happen in a hundred years, but—." Lennon soon sang the refrain, "Power to the people," over and over again, and indicated that those who wanted a revolution better head to the streets. By contrast, the lyrical "Imagine" called for reflecting on the absence of heaven and heaven, "living for today," the dissolving of countries, recognizing there was literally "nothing to kill or die for," the dissipating of religion, and humankind's "living in peace" as human brotherhood took hold "and the world will live as one." Lennon's feminist "Woman Is the Nigger of the World" termed her "the slave of the slaves," while "Happy Xmas" asserted, "War is over, if you want it."[1]

Another facet of the counterculture, the commune movement, hardly disappeared as the new decade continued. In fact, Bill Kovach of the *New York Times* noted in mid-December 1970 that "Communes Spread as the Young Reject Old Values." Kovach began his impressionistic delivery by stating, "In remote valleys and canyons or cluttered city apartment houses, thousands of young adults, seeking economic advantages, social revolution, love, pot, God, or themselves, are creating a new life style in America." These arrangements, referred to as communes, colonies, cooperatives, affinity groups, or families, promised to become a major social force in the years ahead. Most participants did not consider themselves to be engaging in an experiment, but rather traversing "a path from things as they are to things as they should be." In the Bay Area, Marin County alone featured "several dozen hippie-style communes." An ex-Marine, former writing instructor at San Francisco State College, and Haight-Ashbury veteran, Stephen Gaskin, joining in a caravan across the country, helped to found The Farm in Summertown, Tennessee, which propounded the gospel of nonviolence and reverence for Mother Earth.[2]

UCLA Psychology Professor Louis West considered the communes part of a green rebellion opposing the "sterile family and community life style of the suburbs, which produced most of these young people." Presently residing in a Cambridge commune, a Harvard graduate student stated, "We're trying to share our lives and ideas in a way never possible in a dormitory or in separate apartments. It's an attempt to be truly human beings in the way we've always been taught to believe human beings were supposed to live with one another—with love and understanding." In addition to college-rooted communes, revolution-directed ones existed, focusing on women's liberation, draft counseling, and other issues. Work-oriented communes similarly had emerged, including those connected to many underground newspapers, as had religiously based ones. Albert Solnit, an urban planner for Marin County, saw the latest communards as carving out "a kind of new social frontier for the disaffected of the last third of the twentieth century," devising different kinds of human relationships.[3]

A series of thoughtful book-length treatments of the commune movement soon appeared, including Robert Houriet's *Getting Back Together*, Stephen Diamond's *What the Trees Said: Life on a New Age Farm*, Richard Fairfield's *Communes USA: A Personal Tour*, and Keith Melville's *Communes in the Counterculture: Origins, Theories, Styles of Life*.

None, however, really offered predictions on the future of "a new green order," which was continuously threatened by hostile neighbors, technological encroachments, and the large number of disaffected young people lacking much in the way of skills or direction.

Steven V. Roberts's "Halfway between Dropping Out and Dropping In," published in the September 12, 1971, edition of the *New York Times*, highlighted the Red Fox legal cooperative in Berkeley, where new patterns of domesticity, child-rearing, and work were in operation.[4] Two months later, sociology professor Bennett M. Berger of the University of California at Davis, through a collective book review, also in the *New York Times*, examined the commune movement and the seeking of solutions—through eroticism, drugs, mysticism, community, "anything that promises transcendence of the lonely and insatiable self." Berger was struck by how little communards seemed to appreciate "the socially structured character of their convictions and the self-congratulatory nature of them." He contended that the entire counterculture was based, at least in part, "in large scale impersonal processes which juvenilize the young as a way of keeping them out of mainstream adult society, which has few if any important roles for them to play."[5]

At different points, Berger likened countercultural participants to Peter Pan and Huck Finn, calling Raymond Mungo "a brilliant celebrant" who "writes with enormous joy and magic and eagerness for the future, like a boy who has had a lot of love." But Berger indicated that Steve Diamond perhaps pinpointed one of the grave sources of difficulty for communards, who "had to suffer the fickleness of random energy. . . . It takes time, time to work out painfully all the personal hassles and complications that result from a structureless society." They seemingly were unaware that society required structure, and that personal difficulties were never fully "worked out." Gently but damningly, Berger suggested that neither writer piqued hope that anarchistic communes could survive. They remained financially dependent on welfare and the beneficence of parents, among others, had to contend with the tenuousness of personal relationships, and were afflicted by a "distrust of democratic process" likely to culminate in either authoritarianism or political paralysis. Berger praised Houriet's encyclopedic look at communes, stating "It is all there: the talk of vibes and karma and meditation and energy flow and getting it together; the farmhouses and domes, the tipis and the pueblos, the organic gardens, the peyote rituals, the Oming; the problems of money, authority, size, self-sufficiency, mobility, and so on."

But all the books he examined, Berger determined, lacked analytical perspective regarding the commune movement, including an understanding that alternative lifestyles hardly involved "a very deviant choice" presently due to high levels of unemployment, a diminishing of educational opportunities, and worsening familial pathologies. This was the case, notwithstanding the movement's association with "The Family and The Land" that resulted in at least portions "of an almost ready made 'noble' ideology." In addition, it remained shocking to Berger that American society failed to sanctify its institutions, goals, and role models. Meanwhile, the commune movement attracted some of the nation's "best but some of the worse as well," and its future remained in flux.[6]

Nevertheless, even in the opening stages of the new decade a changed perspective appeared to be taking hold. John Sinclair, the founder of the White Panther Party, acknowledged as much in reflecting back to the period when discussion of hippies first became something of a national obsession.

> It's hard to describe the feeling we had. Everybody was taking acid and dancing and screaming in the music and uniting on every level with everybody else around him. . . . We had a whole new vision of the world, and we knew that everything would be all right once the masses got the message we were sending out through our music, our frenzied dancing, our outrageous clothes and manners and speech, our mind-blowing, consciousness-expanding, earthshaking dope.[7]

In exploring the latest literary favorites, Peter Marin, in an essay in the *New York Times* in late February 1971, also worried about what young people were experiencing. He ticked off the usual suspects: Kurt Vonnegut's *Cat's Cradle*, Robert Heinlein's *Stranger in a Strange Land*, Hermann Hesse's *Steppenwolf*, Frank Herbert's *Dune*, J. R. R. Tolkien's *Lord of the Rings* trilogy, Jerry Rubin's *Do It!*, Abbie Hoffman's *Revolution for the Hell of It*, Eldridge Cleaver's *Soul on Ice*, *The Autobiography of Malcolm X*, and *Quotations From Chairman Mao Tsetung*. He also pointed to works by Theodore Roszak, Kenneth Keniston, and Edgar Z. Friedenberg that attempted to examine American youth. But he feared that "we are in for a tangled and difficult time of it," with "exhaustion and implosion, psychic pain and delight, darkness and light and nightmare and paradise" impending. The end result might "be a new consciousness or a real counter culture," Marin asserted,[8] but even heading in that direction would prove "far more difficult than we have imagined."

The less-than-stellar economic times the nation began to experience as the new decade opened proved troublesome for both the counterculture and the movement. Affluent times had undergirded the youth movement. By contrast, the unprecedented phenomenon of stagflation—of simultaneous rising unemployment and high inflation—made it more difficult to get by cheaply as many had during the first several years of the postwar era. A near quarter century of strong economic growth, albeit with some temporary dips along the way, had allowed for a tremendous increase in the ranks of the middle class, an explosion in enrollments at colleges and universities, and enough prosperity to enable a bohemian fringe to get by at relatively minimal cost. Rents and food prices remained low, even in places like Greenwich Village, North Beach, Haight-Ashbury, and Venice, as well as within youth-based enclaves situated around institutions of higher learning. That began to change markedly as the job market tightened, the costs of basic goods increased, and those cheap rents began to disappear. The initially gentle aging of the baby boomers and their slightly elder siblings also came into play, as many began to take on the responsibilities of adulthood, including those involving personal relationships and the workplace. Some opted for what Andrew Kopkind referred to as "sea-level" organizations, located, as Paul Starr explained, at a midpoint "between underground and the aboveboard."[9] The shift to the draft lottery and the winding down of the Vietnam War removed threads that had bound many young people to radical possibilities and to each other. So did the collapse of de jure segregation, the empowerment of African Americans at the ballot box and the resulting election of many black officials, and the appearance of a larger black bourgeoisie, all the while an ever-more depressed underclass existed. Helpful too was the shattering of glass ceilings as male-only institutions began to give way to female aspirants, affirmative action practices, and legal rulings, including the 1973 U.S. Supreme Court ruling of *Roe v. Wade* that enabled many women to avoid backstreet abortionists.

In a sense, both the counterculture and the movement went mainstream, being incorporated into the larger American society, albeit in highly diluted fashion. The seeking of nirvana and the millennium associated with many of rock's greatest performers during the 1960s clearly dissipated, but a good number of those same musicians and younger ones as well retained a commitment to social activism as exemplified by festivals from the No Nukes Concert in 1979 to Live Aid six years later to the annual Farm Aid concerts associated with outlaw country singer Willie Nelson. The underground press waxed and waned, but alternative newspapers, however gentrified in their own manner, can still be found in many urban communities today. Communes are still sprinkled across the American landscape, notwithstanding the horror stories associated with Jim Jones and the Peoples Temple that relocated so tragically to Jonestown, Guyana. Dedicated attorneys and physicians remain committed to collective solutions, offering legal and medical assistance to the indigent, battling against supposed budget hawks determined to eviscerate social programs, and supporting such solutions as single-payer medical coverage. Health food stores, many with an upscale flavor but many retaining a countercultural twist too, can be found even in smaller cities and towns, as well as in every major urban community. Concerns about the environment propelled a large number of former movement activists to remain politically engaged, and to adopt simpler lifestyles seemingly less taxing to a planet containing an ever-increasing number of inhabitants, many lacking material comforts Americans had come to take for granted. Some, like social critic Thomas Frank, prove troubled by the apparent too easy melding of Establishment and countercultural ways as he explains in *The Conquest of Cool: Business Culture, Counterculture, and the Rise of Hip Consumption* (1997).[10]

By the end of the 1960s and the beginning of the ensuing decade, many young people chose to engage in the long march through the institutions, whether or not they were aware of Italian Marxist Antonio Gramsci's admonition several decades earlier to do precisely that. This resulted in a series of admitted paradoxes, with some concerned about loss of an original, true commitment to utopian possibilities, and others dismissive of the latest version of radical chic. Hence, charges arose of sellout and the seeming appearance, in higher education, for instance, of an Academic Left determined to keep the ideals of the 1960s alive in a different guise, albeit as "tenured radicals." Ironically, a batch of young men and women drawn to the counterculture helped to bring about as many changes in American lifestyles and work habits as any: those who operated in pristine pockets like the Bay Area before expanding into Seattle, Austin, and other areas around the country that featured large numbers of well-educated, industrious professionals. In an essay for *Time* magazine in 1995, "We Owe It All to the Hippies," Stewart Brand asserted that "the counterculture's scorn for centralized authority provided the philosophical foundations of not only the leaderless Internet but also the entire personal-computer revolution."[11] The journalist John Markoff examines the fuller story in *What the Dormouse Said: How the Sixties Counterculture Shaped the Personal Computer Industry* (2005), as does Fred Turner in *From Counterculture to Cyberculture: Stewart Brand, the Whole Earth Network, and the Rise of Digital Utopianism* (2006).[12]

The sexual liberation of the 1960s occurred for some and passed others by, but it certainly helped to reshape American social mores for decades to come. The upside included the dissipating of hypocritical notions, double standards, and repressive gender-based restrictions, along with the ushering in, at times at least, of genuine liberation. More negatively, sexual emancipation itself led to the easy tearing apart of relationships, exploitation, an explosion in pornography, and license, which caused some to worry about a culture of narcissism and others to reflect on the very real costs engendered by the tossing aside of sexual restraints in the age of acquired immune deficiency syndrome or acquired immunodeficiency syndrome, also referred to as AIDS. Not all Americans were pleased to leave behind Victorian-styled sexual constraints, with new efforts cropping up to restrict sexual practices and declare that life begins at conception. Tolerance, including regarding various modes of cohabiting and parenting, appeared far greater than earlier, but there remained millions of Americans, longing for halcyon days that undoubtedly never occurred, who were disturbed by attitudinal and behavioral transformations.

Historians continue to aptly convey the possibilities inherent in the counterculture of the 1960s, its strengths, and its weaknesses. John Diggins astutely offers, "Countercultural radicalism moved far beyond New Left radicalism, for it sought a new consciousness not so much to realize as to obliterate the Western industrial idea of consciousness."[13] Despite acknowledging the "ephemeral" quality of "the hippies movement," Allen J. Matusow contends it was "profoundly significant," foreshadowing "the erosion of the liberal values that had sustained bourgeois society, the character type that had been its foundation, and the ethic that had undergirded efforts to accomplish its reform."[14] Terry H. Anderson writes that the counterculture particularly impacted the baby boomers, altering their ethics, fostering greater skepticism regarding "experts, leaders, politicians, and about institutions," both religious and secular. In his estimation, the boomers have proven "more flexible, introspective, and tolerant" of race, sex, and personal relationships. In the process, they have helped to produce "a much more open society" than the one existing right after World War II, with citizen engagement expected on all sides of the political spectrum.[15] Irwin and Debi Unger credit the counterculture for helping to bring about both the ecological and the gay liberation movements.[16] Alice Echols argues, by contrast, that the counterculture failed to contest prevailing stereotypes regarding both women and homosexuals.[17] Martin A. Lee and Bruce Shlain refer to "the tremendous outburst of energy in the sixties" opening up "avenues of choice," including the use of psychedelic drugs, whose "experience carries the impress of a constellation of social forces that are always shifting and up for grabs."[18] David Chalmers applauds the counterculture for bringing about "freer expressive behavior," but he points out that it did not lead to "a broad new culture of opposition or the new world it had once seemed to promise."[19] Notwithstanding its "hopes and dreams," James J. Farrell reveals, the counterculture "couldn't escape human nature or American socialization." Farrell quotes one communard who admitted, "We still carried with us the repressions of the old environment, in our bodies and our minds."[20]

Still, Morris Dickstein, one of the first chroniclers to reexamine the counterculture from a distance, as brief as it then was, recognizes something telling in his 1977 treatment, *Gates of Eden: American Culture in the 1960s*. He emphasizes the fact that "the sixties survive as more than a memory. . . . They survive in us, survive in those who experienced them most intensely." At the very close of his book, he also tellingly points to the counterculture's millennialism. "Utopian hopes may be disappointed but can rarely be forgotten. The gates of Eden, which beckoned to a whole generation in many guises, still glimmer in the distance like Kafka's castle, unapproachable but unavoidable." Dickstein quotes from the British poet and cultural critic Matthew Arnold, who, while talking about literature, cast a wider cultural swath, at least potentially, in speaking of "the promised land." Arnold offered, "To have desired to enter it, to have saluted it from afar, is already, perhaps, the best distinction among contemporaries."[21]

Even more pertinent to the American counterculture of the 1960s is the opening statement delivered by a famed English author just a century before that decade began. Charles Dickens's reflection on the period during and shortly following the French Revolution seems equally apropos for that later time, and for those who aspired to a new millennium only to encounter something far different than what they once envisioned.

> It was the best of times, it was the worst of times, it was the age of wisdom, it was the age of foolishness, it was the epoch of belief, it was the epoch of incredulity, it was the season of Light, it was the season of Darkness, it was the spring of hope, it was the winter of despair, we had everything before us, we had nothing before us, we were all going direct to heaven, we were all going direct the other way—in short, the period was so far like the present period, that some of its noisiest authorities insisted on its being received, for good or for evil, in the superlative degree of comparison only. [22]

As for the four men who helped to usher in the American counterculture of the 1960s, they headed down different paths in their own final days. Kerouac died first, in 1969, and was the youngest to do so, at the age of forty-seven, physically bloated and lacking the movie star–like appearance that once distinguished him. Kerouac's literary career had long stalled and he had undertaken a political shift rightward, but the man who had been the beats' brightest star, however briefly, refused to disavow either them, whom he considered "pure," or the hippies.

Timothy Leary died in 1996, having undertaken a strange migration of his own, during which he was deemed by the president of the United States "the most dangerous man in America," imprisoned, went into exile, and passed on information about Weatherman to the FBI. He later lectured widely, became enamored with the possibility of space colonization, and looked to personal computers as "the LSD of the 1990s." [23] Following his death, the *New York Times* called Leary the "Pied Piper of Psychedelic 60's." [24] The British newspaper, *The Independent*, referred to him as a "Sixties messiah" and noted that the Internet contained his last messages, "Why Not" and "Yeah," along with the declaration, "Our friend, teacher, guide and inspiration will continue to live within us." [25] As the media highlighted Leary's involvement with the FBI during the mid-1970s, Ken Kesey, Paul Krassner, Tom Robbins, and Robert Anton Wilson were among the well-known writers and artists who defended him. "An Open Letter from the Friends of Timothy Leary" insisted that "nobody was seriously injured by [his] interaction with the FBI." Summarizing matters, Kesey affirmed, "Tim knew he had to make the same sort of rollover when he was in the belly of the beast. He also knew he wasn't telling the Feds anything they didn't already know. And he figured it the same way I did: our true allies and comrades would understand." Kesey concluded, "Tim was a great warrior, funny and wise and clever and, above all, courageous. I judge myself blessed to have battled alongside a revolutionary like this blue-eyed brother. Those who want to gnaw on his bones never knew his heart."[26]

Ginsberg was the next to go, in 1997, having moved full circle from being a pariah to a celebrated figure in the American intelligentsia, serving as Distinguished Professor of English at Brooklyn College and winning the National Book Award. Never backing off from his celebration of pansexuality or drug experimentation, he remained a political activist, championing civil liberties from Czechoslovakia before the Velvet Revolution to his own country. William Burroughs proclaimed that "Allen was a great person with worldwide influence. He was a pioneer of openness and a lifelong model of candor. He stood for freedom of expression and for coming out of all the closets long before others did." The *New York Times* acclaimed Ginsberg the "Master Poet of Beat Generation."[27]

The youngest of the countercultural godfathers, Ken Kesey, appropriately, was the last to depart, dying in 2001, also never having disavowed his belief in or usage of psychedelic substances. Following a jail stint, he spent a great deal of time at his family farm in Pleasant Hill, Oregon, writing prolifically at times but never coming close to recapturing the literary magic of *One Flew over the Cuckoo's Nest*. No matter, he was enormously proud of the fact that his *Little Tricker the Squirrel Meets Big Double the Bear* was included on a list of suggested children's books offered by the Library of Congress. His friend and fellow Merry Prankster Ken Babbs reflected on Kesey, calling him "a great good friend and great husband and father and grand dad, he will be sorely missed but if there is one thing he would want us to do it would be to carry on his life's work. Namely to treat others with kindness and if anyone does you dirt forgive that person right away. This goes beyond the art, the writing, the performance, even the bus. Right down to the bone."[28] The *New York Times* delivered its own editorial about "The Prankster's Death": "Jack Kerouac went on the road, but that was a private trip. Mr. Kesey mapped the road out for the rest of us, whether we took it or not, whether we found him merry or not, whether we like his kind of pranks or not. The

Kesey road began in La Honda, where for years afterward you could still feel the echo of the acid tests, and it eventually led everywhere."[29]

NOTES

I. THE PRECURSORS: FROM UTOPIA TO HUXLEY

1. Lois Boe Hyslop, *Charles Baudelaire Revisited* (Twayne Publishers, 1992), 45; CityRoom Staff, "Charles Baudelaire: The Dark Genius of the City of Light," September 19, 2013, http://cityroom.com/charles-baudelaire-the-dark-genius-of-the-city-of-light/.

2. Walt Whitman, *Leaves of Grass* (Dover, 2007), 21.

3. Joanna Levin, *Bohemia in America, 1858–1920* (Stanford University Press, 2009), 107.

4. John Boyle O'Reilly, *In Bohemia* (University of California Libraries, 1886), 14.

5. William Dean Howells, *The Coast of Bohemia* (BiblioBazaar, 2009), 197.

6. Daniel Aaron, *Writers on the Left* (Columbia University Press, 1992), 25.

7. Langston Hughes, *The Collected Poems of Langston Hughes* (Vintage, 1995), 50.

8. Anatole Broyard, "A Portrait of the Hipster," *Partisan Review* 15 (June 1948): 721–27.

9. Albert Hoffman, *LSD: My Problem Child* (Oxford University Press, 2013), 18–23.

10. Martin A. Lee and Bruce Shlain, *Acid Dreams: The Complete History of LSD: The CIA, the Sixties, and Beyond* (Grove Press, 1994), 3–43.

11. Lucy Freeman, "2 Drugs Expected to Aid Mind Study," *New York Times*, May 11, 1951.

12. "Button, Button . . .," *Time* (June 18, 1951): 82–83.

13. "Mescal Madness," *Newsweek* (February 23, 1953): 92–94.

14. "Mescaline and the Mad Hatter," *Time* (June 13, 1953): 62.

15. Aldous Huxley, "A Treatise on Drugs," *Complete Essays: Volume 3, 1930–1935*. Eds. Robert S. Baker and James Sexton (Ivan R. Dee Publisher, 2000), 303–5.

16. Aldous Huxley, *Brave New World* (Harper Perennial Modern Classics, 2006), 36. For a careful examination of Huxley's psychedelic experiences, see David King Dunaway, *Huxley in Hollywood* (Harper & Row Publishers, 1989), 285–304, 322–32, 369–72.

17. Jay Stevens, *Storming Heaven: LSD and the American Dream* (Grove Press, 1987), 7.

18. Aldous Huxley, *The Devils of Loudun* (Harper Perennial Modern Classics, 2009), 324.

19. William Blake, *The Marriage of Heaven and Hell* (Dover Publications, 1994), 36.

20. Aldous Huxley, *The Doors of Perception* and *Heaven and Hell* (Fontal Lobe Publishing, 2011).

21. David King Dunaway, "Huxley, Aldous Leonard (1894–1963)," *Oxford Dictionary of National Biography* (Oxford University Press, 2004; online edition, January 2011).

22. William Sargant, "Chemical Mysticism," *British Medical Journal* 1 (May 1, 1954): 1024.

23. Berton Roueche, "Shimmering Hours: The Doors of Perception," *New York Times*, February 7, 1954.

24. Thomas Mann, *Letters of Thomas Mann, 1889–1955* (University of California Press, 1975), 463–64.

25. Lee and Shlain, *Acid Dreams*, 73, 48.

26. Huxley, *The Doors of Perception*, 69.

27. Stevens, *Storming Heaven*, 57.

28. "Artificial Psychoses," *Time* (December 19, 1955): 60, 63.

29. John Dollard, "In the Eden of the Mind," *New York Times* (April 8, 1956).

30. D. V. Hubble, *British Medical Journal* 2 (July 14, 1956): 86.

31. Paul Zucker, review of *Heaven and Hell*, *The Journal of Aesthetics and Art Criticism* 15 (March 1957): 363.

32. "Mushroom Madness," *Time* (June 16, 1958): 44, 47.

33. Lee and Shlain, *Acid Dreams*, 35–43.

34. Stevens, *Storming Heaven*, 64–65. Anais Nin's ancestry was Spanish, Cuban, Danish, and Cuban.

35. "The Psyche in 3-D," *Time* (March 28, 1960): 83, 85.

2. TROUBADOURS FOR A NEW AMERICAN BOHEMIA: ALLEN GINSBERG, JACK KEROUAC, AND THE BEATS

1. Jonah Raskin, *American Scream: Allen Ginsberg's Howl and the Making of the Beat Generation* (University of California Press, 2004), 33, 47.

2. Andrew Jamison and Ron Eyerman, *Seeds of the Sixties* (University of California Press, 1995), 150.

3. Kevin J. Hayes, *Conversations with Jack Kerouac* (University Press of Mississippi, 2005), 14.

4. Alison Behnke, *Jack Kerouac* (Twenty-First Century Books, 2007), 29; Raskin, *American Scream*, 51.

5. Jamison and Eyerman, *Seeds of the Sixties*, 152.

6. Martin Torgoff, *Can't Find My Way Home: America in the Great Stoned Age, 1945–2000* (Simon & Schuster, 2004), 33.

7. Torgott, *Can't Find My Way Home*, 30–31.

8. Jack Kerouac and Allen Ginsberg, *Jack Kerouac and Allen Ginsberg: The Letters* (Penguin Books, 2011), 5.

9. Allen Ginsberg, *The Letters of Allen Ginsberg* (Da Capo Press, 2008), 394.

10. Hilary Hollady, *American Hipster: A Life of Herbert Huncke, the Times Square Hustler Who Inspired the Beat Movement* (Magnus Books, 2013), 10.

11. Jack Kerouac, *On the Road* (Penguin Books, 1999), 5.

12. Thomas Clark, "Allen Ginsberg: An Interview," *Paris Review* 10 (Spring 1966): 23.

13. Raskin, *American Scream*, 78, 14.

14. *The Beat Book: Writings from the Beat Generation*, ed. Anne Waldman (Shambhala, 2007), xxii.

15. Jack Kerouac, "Aftermath: The Philosophy of the Beat Generation," *Esquire* (March 1958): 24–26.

16. Ann Charters and Samuel Charters, *Brother-Souls: John Clellon Holmes, Jack Kerouac, and the Beat Generation* (University Press of Mississippi, 2010), 99, 150.

17. Raskin, *American Scream*, 97–98.

18. Grant David McCracken, *Transformations: Identity Construction in Contemporary Culture* (Indiana University Press, 2008), 92–93.

19. Raskin, *American Scream*, 103.

20. Bill Morgan, *I Celebrate Myself: The Somewhat Private Life of Allen Ginsberg* (Viking Adult, 2006), 125.

21. David Creighton, *Ecstasy of the Beats: On the Road to Understanding* (Dundurn, 2007), 185.

22. Charles Poore, "Books of the Times," *New York Times*, March 2, 1950.

23. John Brooks, "Of Growth and Decay," *New York Times*, March 5, 1950.

24. Poore, "Books of the Times," *New York Times*, July 10, 1950.

25. John Lardas, *The Bop Apocalypse: The Religious Visions of Kerouac, Ginsberg, and Burroughs* (University of Illinois Press, 2000), 256; Rich Kelley, "The Library of America Interviews Douglas Brinkley about Jack Kerouac," Library of America e-Newsletter (September 2007).

26. John Leland, *Why Kerouac Matters: The Lessons of On the Road (They're Not What You Think)* (Viking Adult, 2007), 149.

27. Steven Watson, *The Birth of the Beat Generation: Visionaries, Rebels, and Hipsters, 1944–1960* (Pantheon, 1995), 125–26.

28. Morgan, *I Celebrate Myself*, 142.

29. Allen Ginsberg, *Journal: Early Fifties, Early Sixties* (Grove Press, 1994), 6.

30. Ellis Amburn, *Subterranean Kerouac: The Hidden Life of Jack Kerouac* (St. Martin's Griffin, 1999), 183.

31. Clellon Holmes, "This Is the Beat Generation," *New York Times*, November 16, 1952.

32. Holmes, "This Is the Beat Generation."

33. Ginsberg, *Journals: Early Fifties, Early Sixties*, 8.

34. William S. Burroughs, *The Letters of William Burroughs: Volume I: 1945–1959* (Viking Adult, 1993), 119–20.

35. Allen Ginsberg, "Junkie: An Appreciation," in William S. Burroughs, *Junky: The Definitive Text of "Junk"* (Grove Press, 2012), 146–49. *Junky* was first titled *Junk*, then *Junkie*, before later being issued as *Junky*.

36. Ginsberg, *Journals: Early Fifties, Early Sixties*, xxii.

37. Kenneth Rexroth, *The Selected Poems of Kenneth Rexroth* (New Directions, 1984), 94–101.

38. James Campbell, *This Is the Beat Generation: New York-San Francisco-Paris* (University of California Press, 2001), 164–65; Paul Maher, *Kerouac: The Definitive Biography* (Taylor Trade Publishing, 2004), 280.

39. Barry Gifford, *Jack's Book: An Oral Biography of Jack Kerouac* (Penguin Books, 2012), 185–86.

40. *On the Poetry of Allen Ginsberg*, ed. Lewis Hyde (University of Michigan Press, 1985), 404–6.

41. James J. Farrell, *The Spirit of the Sixties: The Making of Postwar Radicalism* (Routledge, 1997), 58.

42. John Whiting, "The Lengthening Shadow: Lewis Hill and the Origins of Listener-Sponsored Broadcasting in America," in "Cracking the Ike Age: Aspects of Fifties America," *The Dolphin*, No. 23 (Autumn 1992) (Aarhus University Press, 1992).

43. Raskin, *American Scream*, 6–13.

44. Jack Kerouac, *The Dharma Bums* (Penguin USA, 1991), 13.

45. Heidi R. Moore, *The Aesthetics of Place and the Comedy of Discomfort: Six Humorist*s (UMI Microform, 2008), 129.

46. Allen Ginsberg, *Howl: Original Draft Facsimile, Transcript, and Variant Versions, Fully Annotated with Contemporaneous Correspondence* (Harper Perennial Modern Classics, 2006); Raskin, *American Scream*, xiii; Bill Morgan, *The Typewriter Is Holy: The Complete, Uncensored History of the Beat Generation* (Free Press, 2010), 101–10.

47. Allen Ginsberg, *Howl and Other Poems* (City Lights Publishers, 2001).

48. Ginsberg, *Howl and Other Poems*.

49. Ginsberg first read from "Howl" at the San Francisco Arts Festival. *Howl on Trial: The Battle for Free Expression*. Ed. Bill Morgan (City Lights Publishers, 2006), 35; *Queer Beats: How the Beats Turned America on to Sex*, ed. Regina Marler (Cleis Press, 2004), xxix.

50. Raskin, *American Scream*, 7; Charters and Charters, *Brother-Souls*, 248.

51. *Howl on Trial*, 47–48, 37–38.

52. Allen Ginsberg, "America," *Howl and Other Poems*, 20–22.

53. William Carlos Williams, "Introduction," *Howl and Other Poems* (City Lights Books, 2006).

54. Allen Ginsberg, *The Letters of Allen Ginsberg* (Da Capo Press, 2008), 130.

55. Michael Kimmage, *The Conservative Turn: Lionel Trilling, Whittaker Chambers, and the Lessons of Anti-Communism* (Harvard Historical Studies, 2009), 404–5.

56. Ginsberg to Richard Eberhart, May 18, 1956, in *The Letters of Allen Ginsberg*, 130–39.

57. Denise Levertov to William Carlos Williams, February 7, 1957, in *The Letters of Denise Levertov and William Carlos Williams* (New Directions, 1998), 62.

58. Richard Eberhart, "West Coast Rhythms," *New York Times*, September 2, 1956.

59. Thomas F. Merrill, *Allen Ginsberg* (Twayne Publishers, 1988), 87.

60. Paul Iorioi, "Birth of the Beat Generation: 45th Anniversary of 'Howl' Read at Six Gallery," *San Francisco Chronicle*, October 28, 2000.

61. Paul J. Mariani, *William Carlos Williams: A New World Naked* (W.W. Norton, 1990), 731.

62. *Howl on Trial*; Hyde, *On the Poetry of Allen Ginsberg*, 48.

63. Judge Clayton W. Horn, "The Decision," in *Howl on Trial*, 197–99.

64. David Perlman, "How Captain Hanrahan Made *Howl* a Best-Seller," in *Howl on Trial*, 201–7.

65. Carolyn Bird, "Born 1930: The Unlost Generation," *Harper's Bazaar* (February 1957): 104+.

66. John Hollander, "Poetry Chronicle," *Partisan Review* 24 (Spring 1957): 296–98.

67. James Dickey, "From Babel to Byzantium," *Sewanee Review* 65 (Summer 1957): 508–11.

68. Allen Ginsberg to John Hollander, September 7, 1958, in *Howl on Trial*, 88.

69. Charles I. Glicksberg, "The Lost Generation of College Youth," *Journal of Higher Education* 28 (May 1957): 257–64, 294.

70. Norman Mailer, "The White Negro: Superficial Reflections of the Hipster," *Dissent* 4 (Summer 1957): 276–93.

71. Mailer, "The White Negro."

72. Marc D. Schleifer, "Here to Save Us," *The Village Voice*, October 15, 1958.

73. Peter Manso, *Mailer: His Life and Times* (Washington Square Press, 2008), 260.

3. THE CONTINUED RECEPTION
OF THE BEATS

1. Kenneth Rexroth, *Rexroth Reader* (Jonathan Cape, 1972), 259.

2. Gilbert Millstein, "Books of the Times," *New York Times*, September 5, 1957.

3. Millstein, "Books of the Times."

4. Allen Ginsberg to Jack Kerouac, *Kerouac: Selected Letters: Volume 2: 1957–1969* (Penguin Books, 2000), 73.

5. Bruce Cook, *The Beat Generation and the Tumultuous '50s Movement and Its Impact on Today* (Charles Scribner's Sons, 1971), 7.

6. Arthur Oesterreicher, "'On the Road,'" *The Village Voice*, September 18, 1957.

7. Ralph Gleason, "Kerouac's Beat Generation," *Saturday Review of Literature* (January 11, 1958): 75.

8. David Boroff, "The Roughnecks," *New York Post*, September 8, 1957.

9. Thomas F. Curley, "Everything Moves but Nothing Is Alive," *Commonweal* (September 13, 1957): 595–96.

10. Ray B. Browne, "Vocal, The Frantic Fringe," *Washington Post*, September 8, 1957.

11. "What Capote Said about Kerouac," *New York Times*, October 25, 1992.

12. Carlos Baker, "Itching Fell," *Saturday Review* (September 7, 1957): 32–33.

13. David Dempsey, "In Pursuit of Kicks," *New York Times*, September 8, 1957.

14. Ben Ray Redman, "Living It Up with Jack Kerouac," *Chicago Tribune*, October 6, 1957.

15. "Books: The Ganser Syndrome," *Time* (September 16, 1957): 120.

16. "Flings of the Frantic," *Newsweek* (September 9, 1957): 115.

17. Kenneth Rexroth, "On the Road," *San Francisco Chronicle*, September 1, 1957.

18. Ekbert Faas, *Robert Creely: A Biography* (UPNE, 2001), 217.

19. Robert Briggs, *Ruined Time: The 1950s and the Beats* (RBA Publishing, 2006), 398.

20. Thomas Lask, "An Angry Poet's Call to Arms," *New York Times*, September 29, 1957.

21. Herbert Gold, "Hip, Cool, Beat—and Frantic," *The Nation* (November 16, 1957): 349–55.

22. Gold, "Hip, Cool, Beat—and Frantic."

23. Gold, "Hip, Cool, Beat—and Frantic."

24. Morgan, *The Typewriter Is Holy*, 133–47.

25. Watson, *The Birth of the Beat Generation*, 253–56.

26. Jerry Talmer, "Back to the Village—But Still on the Road," *The Village Voice*, September 18, 1957.

27. Howard Smith, "Jack Kerouac: Off the Road, Into the Vanguard, and Out," *The Village Voice*, December 25, 1957.

28. Allen Ginsberg to Paul Carroll, December 9, 1957; Ginsberg to Carroll, "Wait!" n.d., *Chicago Review* 12 (Autumn 1958): 46–49.

29. Barry Miles, *The Beat Hotel: Ginsberg, Burroughs and Corso in Paris, 1957–1963* (Grove Press, 2001), 72.

30. John Clellon Holmes, "The Philosophy of the Beat Generation, *Esquire* (February 1958): 35–38.

31. Jack Kerouac, "Aftermath: The Philosophy of the Beat Generation," *Esquire* (March 1958): 24–25.

32. David Boroff, "Beatville, U.S.A.," *New York Post*, February 23, 1958.

33. Kenneth Rexroth, review of *The Subterraneans*, *San Francisco Chronicle*, February 16, 1958.

34. Esta Seaton, "The Beat Generation," *The Phylon Quarterly* 19 (1958): 342–43.

35. Norman Podhoretz, "The Know-Nothing Bohemians," *Partisan Review* 25 (Spring 1958): 305–11, 313–16, 318.

36. Herb Caen, "Herb Caen," *San Francisco Chronicle*, April 2, 1958; Jesse Hamlin, "How Herb Caen Named a Generation," *San Francisco Gate*, November 26, 1955.

37. J. Donald Adams, "Speaking of Books," *New York Times*, May 18, 1958.

38. Ernest van den Haag, "Kerouac Was Here," *Social Problems* 6 (Summer 1958): 21–28.

39. "The Disorganization Man," *Time* (June 9, 1958): 98, 100–101.

40. Lawrence Lipton, "'Beat' Writers See Barbarians at the Gates, Seek Succor in Pad, Pod and Self-Abasement," *Los Angeles Times*.

41. Alan W. Watts, "Beat Zen, Square Zen, and Zen," *Chicago Review* 12 (Summer 1958): 3–11.

42. Robert Brustein, "The Cult of Unthink," *Horizon* (September 15, 1958): 38–45, 134–35.

43. "Priest Belittles 'Beat Generation,'" *New York Times*, September 8, 1958.

44. Michael Grieg, "The Old Beat Gang in San Francisco," *San Francisco Examiner*, September 28, 1958.

45. Allen Ginsberg, *Spontaneous Mind: Selected Interviews, 1958–1996* (Harper Perennial, 2002), 4–5.

46. Kerouac, *The Dharma Bums*, 97.

47. Paul Maher Jr., *Empty Phantoms: Interviews and Encounters with Jack Kerouac* (Thunder's Mouth Press, 2005), 278.

48. Charles Poore, "Books of the Times," *New York Times*, October 2, 1958.

49. Nancy Wilson Ross, "Beat—and Buddhist," *New York Times*, October 5, 1958.

50. Samuel I. Bellman, "On the Mountain," *Chicago Review* 13 (Winter–Spring 1959): 68–72.

51. Allen Ginsberg, "The Dharma Bums," *The Village Voice*, November 12, 1958.

52. Marc Schleifer, "The Beat Debated—Is It or Is It Not?" *The Village Voice*, November 19, 1958.

53. Seymour Krim, "King of the Beats," *Commonweal* (January 2, 1959): 359–60.

54. Stephen D. Edington, *The Beat Face of God: The Beat Generation as Spirit Guides* (Trafford Publishing, 2006), 49.

55. "Laughing Gas" and "Lysergic Acid" in Allen Ginsberg, *Kaddish and Other Poems: 1958–1960* (City Lights Books, 1961): 66–82, 86–91.

56. Allen Ginsberg to Louis Ginsberg, May 20, 1959, in *The Letters of Allen Ginsberg*, 223–24.

57. Gilbert Millstein, "Man, It's Like Satire," *New York Times*, May 3, 1959.

58. Gerald Nachman, *Seriously Funny: The Rebel Comedians of the 1950s and 1960s* (Pantheon, 2009), 410.

59. Harry T. Moore, "Cool Cats Don't Dig the Squares," *New York Times*, May 24, 1959.

60. Lawrence Lipton, *The Holy Barbarians* (Julian Messner, 1959).

61. Eugene Burdick, "The Politics of the Beat Generation," *Western Political Quarterly* 12 (June 1959): 553–55.

62. "Nightclubs: The Sickniks," *Time* (July 13, 1959): 42.

63. "Bang Bong Bing," *Time* (September 7, 1959): 80.

64. *The Many Loves of Dobie Gillis*, CBS (1959–1963).

65. Allen Ginsberg, "On a Throne Made of Vanishing Ink," November 4, 1959.

66. Thalia Selz, "The Beat Generation," *Film Quarterly* 13 (Autumn 1959): 54–56.

67. Paine Knickerbocker, "Imports Dominate San Francisco Film Fete," *San Francisco Chronicle*, November 29, 1959.

68. Kenneth Rexroth, "Discordant and Cool," *New York Times*, November 29, 1959.

69. Paul O'Neil, "The Only Rebellion Around," *Life* (November 30, 1959): 47, 113–14, 119, 131.

70. Lawrence E. Davies, "'Beats' in Center of Coast Unrest," *New York Times*, January 31, 1960.

71. Bennett M. Berger, "How Long Is a Generation?" *British Journal of Sociology* 11 (March 1960): 10–23.

72. Gilbert Millstein, "Rent a Beatnik and Swing," *New York Times*, April 17, 1960.

73. Richard Schickel, "A Gone Group," *New York Times*, May 15, 1960.

74. Schickel, "A Gone Group."

75. "Beatnik: The Magazine for Hipsters," *Mad* (September 1960).

76. Norman Mailer, "Ode to Allen Ginsberg," in *Mailer: His Life and Times*, 261–62.

77. Ginsberg, *Journals: Early Fifties, Early Sixties*, 200.

78. Alice Echols, *Shaky Ground* (Columbia University Press, 2002), 18.

4. FROM HARVARD TO MILLBROOK: TIMOTHY LEARY

1. Robert Greenfield, *Timothy Leary: A Biography* (Harcourt, 2006), 342.

2. Jeanne Watson, "Interpersonal Diagnosis of Personality: A Functional Theory and Methodology for Personality," *American Journal of Sociology* 63 (September 1957): 244–45.

3. H. J. Eysenck, "Interpersonal Diagnosis of Personality: A Functional Theory and Methodology for Personality," *British Medical Journal* 2 (December 21, 1957): 1478.

4. Bert Kaplan, "Interpersonal Diagnosis of Personality: A Functional Theory and Methodology for Personality," *American Anthropologist* 60 (February 1958): 210.

5. Toshio Yatsushiro, "Interpersonal Diagnosis of Personality: A Functional Theory and Methodology for Personality," *Administrative Science Quarterly* 3 (June 1958): 123–27.

6. Robert Gordon Wasson, "Seeking the Magic Mushroom," *Life* (June 10, 1957): 100–120.

7. Timothy Leary, *Flashbacks: An Autobiography* (Tarcher, 1989), 16.

8. Mikal Gilmore, *Stories Done: Writings on the 1960s and Its Discontents* (Free Press, 2009), 34.

9. Robert Greenfield, *Timothy Leary: A Biography* (Harcourt, 2006), 104.

10. Don Lattin, *The Harvard Psychedelic Club: How Timothy Leary, Ram Dass, Huston Smith, and Andrew Weil Killed the Fifties and Ushered in a New Age for America* (HarperOne, 2011), 20.

11. Greenfield, *Timothy Leary*, 113.

12. Timothy Leary, *The Politics of Ecstasy* (Ronin Publishing, 1998), 13.

13. Daniel Pinchbeck, *Breaking Open the Head: A Psychedelic Journey into the Heart of Contemporary Shamanism* (Broadway Books, 2003), 181–82.

14. Aldous Huxley, *Island* (Harper Perennial Modern Classics, 2009).

15. Jill Jonnes, *Hep-Cats, Narcs, and Pipe Dreams: A History of America's Romance with Illegal Drugs* (Scribner, 1996), 219.

16. W. J. Rorabaugh, *Kennedy and the Promise of the Sixties* (Cambridge University Press, 2004), 208.

17. Marion S. Goldman, *The American Soul Rush: Esalen and the Rise of Spiritual Privilege* (New York University Press, 2012), 75.

18. Leary, *Flashbacks*, 44.

19. Lattin, *The Harvard Psychedelic Club*, 52.

20. Leary, *The Politics of Ecstasy*, 101.

21. Torgoff, *Can't Find My Way Home*, 72.

22. Peter Conners, *White Hand Society: The Psychedelic Partnership of Timothy Leary and Allen Ginsberg* (City Lights Publishers, 2010), 80–86.

23. Stevens, *Storming Heaven*, 146.

24. Conners, *White Hand Society*, 91–92.

25. Morgan, *I Celebrate Myself*, 321.

26. Leary, *Flashbacks*, 55.

27. Morgan, *I Celebrate Myself*, 324.

28. "Dear Coach," Jack Kerouac to Timothy Leary, January 20, 1961.

29. Greenfield, *Timothy Leary*, 138–39.

30. Greenfield, *Timothy Leary*, 127.

31. Ram Dass, "Turning On" in *Be Here Now* (Lama Foundation, 1971).

32. Leary, *Flashbacks*, 78.

33. Conners, *White Hand Society*, 50.

34. Peter O. Whitmer, *Aquarius Revisited: Seven Who Created the Sixties Counterculture That Changed America* (Citadel, 2007), 29.

35. Whitmer, *Aquarius Revisited*, 29–32.

36. Greenfield, *Timothy Leary*, 159.

37. Stevens, *Storming Heaven*, 160–61.

38. Ted Morgan, *Literary Outlaw: The Life and Times of William S. Burroughs* (W.W. Norton, 2012), 391.

39. Leary, *Flashbacks*, 96.

40. Morgan, *Literary Outlaw*, 406.

41. Whitmer, *Aquarius Revisited*, 126.

42. Jane Dunlap, *Exploring Inner Space: Personal Experiences under LSD-25* (Harcourt, Brace and World, 1961).

43. Gilmore, *Stories Done*, 38.

44. Greenfield, *Timothy Leary*, 167.

45. John Higgs, *I Have America Surrounded: A Biography of Timothy Leary* (Barricade Books, 2006), 41.

46. Andrew T. Weil, "The Strange Case of the Harvard Drug Scandal," *Look* (November 5, 1963): 38, 43–44, 46, 48.

47. Higgs, *I Have America Surrounded*, 49.

48. Gilmore, *Stories Done*, 37.

49. Robert E. Smith, "Psychologists Disagree on Psilocybin Research," *The Harvard Crimson*, March 15, 1962; "Hallucination Drug Fought at Harvard—350 Students Take Pills," *Boston Herald*, March 16, 1962.

50. Joseph Lee Auspitz, "Leary Analyzes Work on Psilocybin Effects, Praises Mystical View," *The Harvard Crimson*, April 23, 1962.

51. Stevens, *Storming Heaven*, 171.

52. Lee and Shlain, *Acid Dreams*, 88.

53. Torgoff, *Can't Find My Way Home*, 85.

54. Don Lattin, *Distilled Spirits: Getting High, Then Sober, with a Famous Writer, a Forgotten Philosopher, and a Hopeless Drunk* (University of California Press, 2012), 191–92.

55. Leary, *Flashbacks*, 134, 138.

56. Donald Janson, "Doctors Report a Black Market in Drug That Causes Delusions," *New York Times*, July 14, 1962.

57. Jonnes, *Hep-Cats, Narcs, and Pipe Dreams*, 229.

58. Stevens, *Storming Heaven*, 189.

59. "Harvard Men Told of Mind-Drug Peril," *New York Times*, November 29, 1962.

60. Fred M. Hechinger, "Harvard Debates Mind-Drug 'Peril,'" *New York Times*, December 14, 1962; Richard Alpert and Timothy Leary, "To the Editors of the Crimson," *Crimson Review*, December 13, 1962.

61. Greenfield, *Timothy Leary*, 192–93.

62. Joseph M. Russin and Andrew T. Weil, "An Editorial," *Harvard Crimson*, May 28, 1963.

63. "No Illusions," *Newsweek* (June 10, 1963): 92–93.

64. Josiah Lee Auspitz, untitled article, *The Harvard Review* 1 (Summer 1963).

65. Timothy Leary and Richard Alpert, "The Politics of Consciousness Expansion," *Harvard Crimson* 1 (Summer 1963).

66. Emma Harrison, "Psychiatrist Warns of Health Peril in Mind Drug," *New York Times*, June 4, 1963.

67. "Statement of Purpose," *Psychedelic Review* 1 (June 1963): 6.

68. Stevens, *Storming Heaven*, 197.

69. "Mexico Ousts 20 in Drug Research," *New York Times*, June 15, 1963.

70. Timothy Leary, "The Religious Experience: Its Production and Interpretation," *Psychedelic Review* (Number 3, 1964): 324–46.

71. Dana L. Farnsworth, "Hallucinogenic Agents," *Journal of the American Medical Association* 185 (September 14, 1963): 878–80.

72. "Editorial," *Psychedelic Review* 1 (Fall 1963): 119.

73. "Instant Mysticism," *Time* (October 25, 1963): 86–87.

74. Weil, "The Strange Case of the Harvard Drug Scandal," 38, 43–44, 46, 48.

75. Bob Gaines, "LSD: Hollywood's Status-Symbol Drug," *Cosmopolitan* (November 1963): 78–81.

76. Alan Harrington, "Hallucinogens: A Novelist's Personal Experience," *Playboy* (November 1963): 84+; Aldous Huxley, "Hallucinogens: A Philosopher's Visionary Prediction," *Playboy* (November 1963): 84+.

77. Greenfield, *Timothy Leary*, 209.

78. "Psychic-Drug Testers Living in Retreat," *New York Times*, December 15, 1963.

79. Kay Parley, "Supporting the Patient on LSD Day," *American Journal of Nursing* 64 (February 1964): 80–82.

80. "Consciousness Expanders: Therapeutic Aids or Mind Distorters?" *American Journal of Nursing* 64 (February 1964): 82–83.

81. Joseph Havens, "A Working Paper: Memo on the Religious Implications of the Consciousness-Changing Drugs (LSD, Mescaline, Psilocybin)," *Journal for the Scientific Study of Religion* 3 (Spring 1964): 216–26.

82. Timothy Leary, Ralph Metzner, and Richard Alpert, *The Psychedelic Experience: A Manual Based on the Tibetan Book of the Dead* (University Books, 1964).

83. Timothy Leary, "Introduction," in *LSD: The Consciousness-Expanding Drug*, ed. David Solomon (G. Putnam's Sons, 1964), 11–28.

84. Robert Anton Wilson, "Timothy Leary and His Psychological H-Bomb," *The Realist* (August 1964): 1, 17–20.

5. THE MERRY PRANKSTER: KEN KESEY

1. Rick Dodgson, *It's All a Kind of Magic: The Young Ken Kesey* (University of Wisconsin Press, 2013), 22.

2. Richard Rayner, "Aging Gracefully: Ken Kesey's 'Cuckoo' and 'Notion,'" *Los Angeles Times*, December 9, 2007; Malcolm Cowley, *The Portable Malcolm Cowley* (Viking Penguin, 1990), 508.

3. Philip L. Fradkin, *Wallace Stegner and the American West* (Knopf, 2008), 134, 131.

4. Mark Christensen, *Acid Christ: Ken Kesey, LSD and the Politics of Ecstasy* (Schaffner Press, 2010), 58–59.

5. Lee and Shlain, *Acid Dreams*, 119.

6. Stevens, *Storming Heaven*, 126.

7. Torgoff, *Can't Find My Way Home*, 90–91.

8. Whitmer, *Aquarius Revisited*, 202.

9. Tom Wolfe, *The Electric Kool-Aid Acid Test* (Bantam, 1969), 34.

10. Stevens, *Storming Heaven*, 228.

11. Christensen, *Acid Christ*, 123.

12. Ed McClanahan, *I Just Hitched in from the Coast: The Ed McClanahan Reader* (Counterpoint, 2011), 41–42.

13. Blair Tindall, "Psychedelic Palo Alto," *Palo Alto Weekly* (May 8, 2000).

14. Torgoff, *Can't Find My Way Home*, 88–89.

15. Whitmer, *Aquarius Revisited*, 198.

16. McClanahan, *I Just Hitched in from the Coast*, 41.

17. Stevens, *Storming Heaven*, 229.

18. McClanahan, *I Just Hitched in from the Coast*, 40; Robert Stone, *Prime Green: Remembering the Sixties* (Ecco, 2007), 87.

19. Maher, *Kerouac*, 422; Ann Charters, *Beat Down to Your Soul: What Was the Beat Generation?* (Penguin Books, 2001), 605.

20. "Life in a Loony Bin," *Time* (February 16, 1962): 90.

21. Martin Levin, "A Reader's Report," *New York Times*, February 4, 1962; Ken Kesey to Drama Mailbag, January 7, 1964.

22. Sam Zolotow, "Role in Play Set for Kirk Douglas," *New York Times*, February 6, 1962.

23. Christensen, *Acid Christ*, 371.

24. Robert Stone, "The Prince of Possibility," *New Yorker* (June 14, 2004): 70–72, 74, 77–78, 81–82, 85–86, 89.

25. Gus Blaisdell, "Shazam and the Neon Renaissance," *Author and Journalist* (June 1963): 7.

26. Hunter S. Thompson, *Songs of the Doomed* (Simon and Schuster, 2002), 118.

27. Torgoff, *Can't Find My Way Home*, 97.

28. Lee and Shlain, *Acid Dreams*, 121.

29. Wolfe, *The Electric Kool-Aid Acid Test*, 194.

30. Mark Hamilton Lytle, *The Uncivil Wars: The Sixties Era from Elvis to the Fall of Richard Nixon* (Oxford University Press, 2006), 202.

31. Christensen, *Acid Christ*, 97.

32. Torgoff, *Can't Find My Way Home*, 95–96.

33. Blair Jackson, *Garcia: An American Life* (Penguin Books, 2000), 79

34. Christiansen, *Acid Christ*, 112, 104.

35. Watson, *The Birth of the Beat Generation*, 289–90.

36. Christiansen, *Acid Christ*, 112; Stone, *Prime Green*, 119–23.

37. Kenn Thomas, *Cyberculture Counterconspiracy: A Steamshovel Web Reader*, Volume One (Book Tree, 1999).

38. Torgoff, *Can't Find My Way Home*, 115.

39. Stone, "The Prince of Possibility."

40. Richard Kostelanetz, "Ginsberg Makes the World Scene," *New York Times*, July 11, 1965.

41. Allen Ginsberg, *The Visions of the Great Rememberer* (Haystack Book, 1974), 42.

42. Wolfe, *The Electric Kool-Aid Acid Test*, 102.

43. Ginsberg, *The Visions of the Great Rememberer*, 42.

44. Orville Prescott, "A Tiresome Literary Disaster," *New York Times*, July 27, 1964.

45. Conrad Knickerbocker, "Any Dream May Come True," *New York Times*, August 2, 1964.

46. Reviews of *Birth of a Psychedelic Culture* and *Acid Christ*, *The Bloomsbury Review* (Fall 2010): 5+.

47. Christensen, *Acid Christ*, vii.

48. William McKeen, *Outlaw Journalist: The Life and Times of Hunter S. Thompson* (W.W. Norton, 2008), 107–8.

49. Hunter S. Thompson, *Hell's Angels: The Strange and Terrible Saga of the Outlaw Motorcycle Gangs* (Random House, 1966), 234.

50. Allen Ginsberg, "First Party at Ken Kesey's with Hell's Angels."

51. Wolfe, *The Electric Kool-Aid Acid Test*, 222.

52. Barry Miles, *Hippie* (Sterling, 2005), 50.

53. Allen Ginsberg, "Demonstration or Spectacle as Example, as Communication or How to Make a March/Spectacle," *Berkeley Barb*, November 19, 1965.

54. Charles Perry, *The Haight-Ashbury: A History* (Random House, 1988), 34.

55. Bill Graham, *Bill Graham Presents: My Life Inside Rock and Out* (Da Capo Press, 2004), 199.

56. Torgoff, *I Can't Find My Way Home*, 119.

57. Lee and Shlain, *Acid Dreams*, 147.

58. Torgoff, *Can't Find My Way Home*, 121.

59. Nicholas Schou, *Orange Sunshine: The Brotherhood of Eternal Love and Its Quest to Spread Peace, Love, and Acid to the World* (St. Martin's Griffin, 2011), 8.

60. Perry, *The Haight-Ashbury*, 45.

6. THE MAGIC ELIXIR OF SEX AND
A TOUCH OF ANARCHISM

1. "Manners and Morals—How to Stop Gin Rummy," *Time* (March 8, 1948): 16.

2. Howard A. Rusk, "Concerning Man's Basic Drive," *New York Times*, January 4, 1948.

3. "Speakers Assail Kinsey on Report," *New York Times*, March 31, 1948.

4. "Scientific Parley Finds the Kinsey Report 'Incomplete,' 'Full of Facts' Aid to Law," *New York Times*, December 31, 1949.

5. William Barrett, "News Designs in Our Bohemia, *New York Times*, August 20, 1950.

6. Clyde Kluckhohn, "The Complex Kinsey Study and What It Attempts to Do," *New York Times*, September 13, 1953.

7. *Roth v. United States*, 354 US. 476, 492 (1957); *Alberts v. California*, 354 U.S. 476 (1957).

8. Howard Whitman, *The Sex Age* (Doubleday, 1962), 64.

9. David Allyn, *Make Love, Not War: The Sexual Revolution* (Routledge, 2001), 65.

10. *Grove Press, Inc. v. Gerstein*, 378 U.S. 577 (1964).

11. *Attorney General v. A Book Named Naked Lunch*, Supreme Judicial Court of Massachusetts, 218 N.E. 2d 571 (1966).

12. Irwin Unger and Debi Unger, *America in the 1960s* (Brandywine Press, 1988), 267.

13. Allyn, *Make Love, Not War*, 9.

14. Irwin Unger and Debi Unger, *America in the 1960s*, 277.

15. William Reich, *The Function of the Orgasm: Sex-Economic Problems of Biology Energy: Volume 1 of The Discovery of the Orgone* (Farrar, Straus and Giroux, 1973), 21.

16. William Reich, *The Mass Psychology of Fascism* (Farrar, Straus and Giroux, 1933).

17. Mildred Edie Brady, "The New Cult of Sex and Anarchy," *Harper's Magazine* (April 1947): 312–21.

18. Brady, "The New Cult of Sex and Anarchy."

19. Brady, "The New Cult of Sex and Anarchy."

20. Brady, "The New Cult of Sex and Anarchy."

21. Mildred Edie Brady, "The Strange Case of William Reich," *The New Republic* (May 26, 1947): 20–23.

22. A. S. Neil to William Reich, October 22, 1956, in *Record of a Friendship: The Correspondence between William Reich and A. S. Neil*, ed. Beverley R. Placzek (Farrar Straus Giroux, 1981), 418–19.

23. Myron Sharaf, *Fury on Earth: A Biography of William Reich* (Da Capo Press, 1004), 474.

24. Gerald Grow, "William Reich: Imperfect Master," Original Web Publication, 2007.

25. Barbàra Celarent, "Eros and Civilization by Herbert Marcuse," *American Journal of Sociology* 115 (May 2010): 1964–72.

26. Herbert Marcuse, *Eros and Civilization: A Philosophical Inquiry into Freud* (Vintage Books, 1955).

27. Marcuse, *Eros and Civilization*.

28. Clyde Kluckhohn, "A Critique on Freud," *New York Times*, November 27, 1955.

29. Kurt H Wolff, review of *Eros and Civilization*, *American Journal of Sociology* 62 (November 1956): 342–43.

30. Herbert Fingarette, "Eros and Utopia," *The Review of Metaphysics* 10 (June 1957): 660–65.

31. Herbert Marcuse, *One-Dimensional Man* (Beacon Press, 1964).

32. Herbert Marcuse, *A Critique of Pure Tolerance* (Beacon Press, 1965).

33. Herbert Marcuse, *One-Dimensional Man* (Beacon Press, 1966); Herbert Marcuse, *The New Left and the 1960s: The Collected Papers of Herbert Marcus: Volume 3* (Routledge, 2004), 11.

34. Marcuse, *The New Left and the 1960s: The Collected Papers of Herbert Marcus: Volume 3*, 106.

35. "Marcuse Defines His New Left Line," *New York Times*, October 27, 1968.

36. Norman O. Brown, *Life against Death: The Psychoanalytical Meaning of History* (Vintage, 1959).

37. Norman O. Brown, *Love's Body* (University of California Press, 1966).

38. Nicholas Murray, *Aldous Huxley: A Biography* (Thomas Dunne Books, 2003), 444.

7 THE MAGIC IN THE MUSIC

1. Robert Shelton, "20-Year-Old Singer Is Bright New Face at Gerde's Club," *New York Times*, September 29, 1961.

2. Bob Dylan, "Mr. Tambourine Man" (1965).

3. Bob Dylan, *Another Side of Bob Dylan* (1964).

4. Bob Dylan, "My Back Pages" (1964).

5. Bob Dylan, "Chimes of Freedom" (1964).

6. Bob Dylan, "The Gates of Eden" (1964).

7. Bob Dylan, "It's Alright Ma, I'm Only Bleeding" (1964).

8. Bob Dylan, *Bringing It All Back Home* (1965); Bob Dylan, *Highway 61 Revisited* (1965).

9. Bob Dylan, "Subterranean Homesick Blues" (1965).

10. Bob Dylan, "It's All Over Now, Baby Blue" (1965).

11. Bob Dylan, "Ballad of a Thin Man" (1965).

12. Bob Dylan, "Desolation Row" (1965).

13. Bob Dylan, "Like a Rolling Stone" (1965).

14. The Byrds, *Mr. Tambourine Man* (1965).

15. The Byrds, "Turn! Turn! Turn!" (1965).

16. The Byrds, "Eight Miles High" (1965).

17. Dino Valenti, "Let's Get Together" (1964).

18. Country Joe McDonald and the Fish, "I Feel Like I'm Fixin' To Die Rag" (1965).

19. Farrell, *The Spirit of the Sixties*, 203.

20. The Warlocks, "Can't Come Down" (1965).

21. Perry, *The Haight-Ashbury*, 29–30.

22. Lee and Shlain, *Acid Dreams*, 142–43.

23. David Crosby, "Stranger in a Strange Land" (1965).

24. Bob Dylan, "Rainy Day Women No. 12 and 35" (1965).

25. Bob Dylan, *Blonde on Blonde* (1966); Bob Dylan, "Absolutely Sweet Marie" (1966).

26. The Beatles, *The Beatles Anthology* (Chronicle Books, 2000), 158; Jacqueline Edmondson, *John Lennon: A Biography* (Greenwood, 2010), 82; Philip Norman, *John Lennon: The Life*, 375 (Ecco, 2009).

27. The Beatles, *A Hard Day's Night* (1964); The Beatles, "I Want to Hold Your Hand" (1963); The Beatles, "I Should Have Known Better" (1964).

28. The Beatles, "Help" (1965); The Beatles, *Help* (1965).

29. The Beatles, "Ticket to Ride" (1965).

30. The Beatles, *Rubber Soul* (1965).

31. The Beatles, "Norwegian Wood" (1965).

32. The Beatles, "Nowhere Man" (1965).

33. The Beatles, "The Word" (1965).

34. The Beatles, *Yesterday and Today* (1965).

35. The Beatles, "Day Tripper" (1966).

36. The Beatles, "Doctor Robert" (1966).

37. Maureen Cleave, "How Does a Beatle Live?" *London Evening Standard*, March 4, 1966.

38. The Beatles, *Revolver* (1966).

39. The Beatles, *The Beatles Anthology*, 177.

40. Joshua M. Greene, *Here Comes the Sun: The Spiritual and Musical Journey of George Harrison* (Wiley, 2006), 54.

41. David Sheff, Interview with John Lennon and Yoko Ono, *Playboy* (January 1981):75+.

42. The Beatles, "She Said She Said" (1966).

43. Sheff, Interview with John Lennon and Yoko Ono; Interview with Peter Fonda, *Playboy* (September 1970): 85+.

44. The Beatles, "Tomorrow Never Knows" (1966).

45. The Beatles, "Rain" (1966).

46. Jann S. Wenner, Interview with John Lennon, *Rolling Stone* (January 21, 1971).

47. Donovan Leitch, "Sunshine Superman" (1966).

48. Donovan Leitch, "Sunshine Superman" (1966).

49. Donovan Leitch, "Season of the Witch" (1966).

50. Donovan Leitch, "The Trip" (1966).

51. Donovan Leitch, *Mellow Yellow* (1966).

52. Country Joe and the Fish, "Section 43" (1966).

53. The Great Society, "Somebody to Love" (1966).

54. Jefferson Airplane, "White Rabbit" (1966).

55. The 13th Floor Elevators, *The Psychedelic Sounds of the 13th Floor Elevators* (1966).

56. Cream, *Fresh Cream* (1966).

57. The Beatles, *The Beatles Anthology*, 229.

58. The Doors, *The Doors* (1967); The Doors, "Break on Through (to the Other Side)" (1967).

59. The Doors, "The Crystal Ship" (1967); The Doors, "Light My Fire" (1967).

60. The Doors, "The End" (1967).

61. The Electric Prunes, "I Had Too Much to Dream (Last Night)" (1966).

62. Jefferson Airplane, *Surrealistic Pillow* (1967); Jefferson Airplane, "Somebody to Love" (1967).

63. The Jimi Hendrix Experience, *Are You Experienced* (1967).

64. The Jimi Hendrix Experience, "Purple Haze" (1967); The Jimi Hendrix Experience, "Fire" (1967); The Jimi Hendrix Experience, "Foxey Lady" (1967); The Jimi Hendrix Experience, "Are You Experienced" (1967).

65. The Jimi Hendrix Experience, *Axis: Bold as Love* (1967); The Jimi Hendrix Experience, "Up from the Skies" (1967); The Jimi Hendrix Experience, "Spanish Castle Magic" (1967); The Jimi Hendrix Experience, "If 6 Was 9" (1967).

66. The Beatles, "Strawberry Fields Forever" (1966).

67. The Beatles, *Sgt. Pepper's Lonely Hearts Club Band* (1967).

68. The Beatles, "Sgt. Pepper's Lonely Hearts Club Band" (1967); The Beatles, "With a Little Help from My Friends" (1967).

69. The Beatles, "Lucy in the Sky with Diamonds" (1967).

70. The Beatles, "Within You Without You" (1967).

71. The Beatles, "Sgt. Pepper's Heart Club Band" reprise (1967, The Beatles, "A Day in the Life" (1967).

72. The Beatles, *Magical Mystery Tour* (1967).

73. The Beatles, "All You Need Is Love" (1967).

74. The Beatles, "I Am the Walrus" (1967).

75. The Beatles, "Strawberry Fields Forever" (1967); The Beatles, "The Fool on the Hill" (1967).

76. Traffic, *Mr. Fantasy* (1967).

77. Traffic, "Dear Mr. Fantasy" (1967); Traffic, "Heaven Is in Your Mind" (1967); Traffic, "Dealer" (1967); Traffic, "Hole in My Shoe" (1968); Traffic, "Paper Sun" (1968); Traffic, "Coloured Rain" (1968).

78. Traffic, "Dear My Fantasy"; Traffic, "Heaven Is in Your Mind."

8. CALIFORNIA DREAMING AND HAIGHT-ASHBURY

1. The Mamas and the Papas, "California Dreamin'" (1965).

2. Christensen, *Acid Christ*, 152.

3. Perry, *The Haight-Ashbury*, 44–45.

4. David W. Bernstein, "Emerging Art Forms and the American Countercul-ture, 1961–1966," in *The San Francisco Tape Music Center: 1960s Countercul-ture and the Avant-Garde* (University of California Press, 2008), 7.

5. "Can You Pass the Acid Test?" *Grateful Dead Sources*, February 12, 2013.

6. Lee and Shlain, *Acid Dreams*, 143.

7. Wolfe, *The Electric Kool-Aid Acid Test*, 263.

8. Allen Cohen, "Notes on the San Francisco *Oracle*," Rockument.com.

9. Lee and Shlain, *Acid Dreams*, 146.

10. Jay Stevens, "The Counterculture" in *The Sixties*, ed. Peter Stine (Wayne State University Press, 1996), 132.

11. Lisa Montanareli and Ann Harrison, *Strange But True: San Francisco: Tales of the City by the Bay* (Globe Pequot, 2005), 206.

12. Mark Hamilton Lytle, *America's Uncivil Wars: The Sixties Era from Elvis to the Fall of Richard Nixon* (Oxford University Press, 2006), 211–16.

13. Cohen, "Notes on the San Francisco *Oracle*."

14. Perry, *The Haight-Ashbury*, 58–59; Wolfe, *The Electric Kool-Aid Acid Test*, 265.

15. Perry, *The Haight-Ashbury*, 290–91.

16. Gene Anthony, *The Summer of Love: Haight-Ashbury at Its Highest* (Last Gasp, 1995), 6.

17. "The Silver Snuffbox," *Time* (March 18, 1966): 85.

18. "Specious Marijuana Defense," *New York Times*, March 18, 1966.

19. John Corry, "Drugs a Growing Campus Problem," *New York Times*, March 21, 1966.

20. "The Exploding Threat of the Mind Drug That Got Out of Control," *Life* (March 25, 1966).

21. "Editor's Note," *Life* (March 25, 1966): 3.

22. Gerald Moore, "A Remarkable Mind Drug Suddenly Spells Danger LSD," *Life* (March 25, 1966): 28.

23. Albert Rosenfeld, "The Vital Facts about the Drug and Its Effects," *Life* (March 25, 1966): 30–31.

24. "Scientists, Theologians, Mystics Swept Up in a Psychic Revolution," *Life* (March 25, 1966): 30D.

25. "U.S. Plot to 'Set Up' Ginsberg for Arrest Is Described to Jury," *New York Times*, April 14, 1966.

26. William Borders, "Prof. Leary Calls LSD Raid 'Intolerable Violation' of Rights," *New York Times*, April 19, 1966.

27. "New York: Time to Mutate," *Time* (April 29, 1966): 34.

28. Aubrey Lewis, "L.S.D.," *The British Medical Journal* 1 (June 18, 1966): 1529.

29. Allen Ginsberg's testimony, U.S. Senate Special Subcommittee of the Committee on the Judiciary, June 14, 1966 (United States Senate 488).

30. Jonathan Randal, "Poet and U.S. Aide Back Drug Study," *New York Times*, August 25, 1966.

31. Bernard Gravzer, Interview with Timothy Leary, *Playboy* (September 1966): 93+.

32. Perry, *The Haight-Ashbury*, 85–86.

33. John Brownson, "Anarchy 66 Provo: Provos Si, Yankee No," San Francisco *Oracle*, September 20, 1966.

34. Lee and Shlain, *Acid Dreams*, 170. For a fascinating look at the Diggers, see Peter Coyote, *Sleeping Where I Fall: A Chronicle* (Counterpoint, 1999) and "The Free-Fall Chronicles," The Digger Archives.

35. "A-Political Or, Criminal Or Victim Or Or Or . . .," *The Diggers Papers*, September 30, 1966.

36. Lytle, *America's Uncivil Wars*, 213.

37. Allen Cohen, "A Prophecy of a Declaration of Independence," San Francisco *Oracle*, September 20, 1966.

38. Montanarelli and Harrison, *Strange But True*, 207.

39. Anthony, *The Summer of Love*, 119, 122.

40. George Metevsky, "Delving the Diggers," *Berkeley Barb*, October 21, 1966, 3.

41. Sandy Troy, *Captain Trips: A Biography of Jerry Garcia* (Thunder's Mouth Press, 1995), 99–100.

42. Tom Wolfe, *The Electric Kool-Aid Acid Test*, 395–97.

43. Bill Graham, *Bill Graham Presents*, 170.

44. Bernard Hoskyns, *Beneath the Diamond Sky: Haight-Ashbury 1965–1970* (Simon and Schuster, 1997), 121, 123, 125.

45. George Metevsky, "The Ideology of Failure," *Berkeley Barb*, November 18, 1966, 6.

46. "In Search of a Frame," *Berkeley Barb*, November 25, 1966, 6.

47. Ralph Gleason, "Like a Rolling Stone," *American Scholar* 36 (Autumn 1967): 555–63.

48. Etan Ben-Ami, Interview with Peter Coyote, January 12, 1989.

49. Ben-Ami, Interview.

50. "Trip without a Ticket," *The Digger Papers* (Winter 1966–1967).

9. SPREADING THE WORD:
ALTERNATIVE MEDIA

1. Robert Stein, *Media Power: Who Is Shaping Your Picture of the World?* (Authors Choice Press, 2005), 182.

2. "An Angry Young Magazine . . .," *The Realist* (June–July 1958): 2.

3. Lionel O'Lay, "500 See Psychedelic Art at Free American Gallery," *Los Angeles Free Press* 2 (September 24, 1965), 1–2.

4. Roger Streitmatter, *Voices of Revolution: The Dissident Press in America* (Columbia University Press, 2001), 202.

5. Tom Weller, "Max Scherr," *The Berkeley Barb* (2011), California Digital Library.

6. Harvey Ovshinsky, "Editorial," *The Fifth Estate* 1 (November 19–December 2, 1965).

7. Allen Katzman, "Poor Paranoid's Almanac," *East Village Other* (August 1, 1966).

8. Doug Rossinow, *The Politics of Authenticity: Liberalism, Christianity, and the New Left in America* (Columbia University Press, 1998), 261.

9. Laurence Leamer, *The Paper Revolutionaries: The Rise of the Underground Press* (Simon and Schuster, 1972), 62.

10. Rossinow, *The Politics of Authenticity*, 260; *Abe Peck, Uncovering the Sixties: The Life and Times of the Underground Press* (Pantheon, 1985), 58.

11. Thorne Dreyer, letter to underground newspaper editors, October 3, 1966.

12. John McMillian, *Smoking Typewriters: The Sixties Underground Press and the Rise of Alternative Media in America* (Oxford University Press, 2011), 53–59.

13. Carol Neiman, "The Truth—Beep—Is On Page . . . ," *The Rag* 1 (October 10, 1966), 1.

14. Jeff Shero, "Playboy's Tinsel Seductress," *The Rag* (October 10, 1966): 4, 7–8.

15. "I AM THE LIGHT" sketch, *The Rag* 1 (October 10, 1966): 5.

16. Gary Chason, "Sexual Freedom League: The Naked Truth," *The Rag* 1 (October 17, 1966), 1, 4–8, 17.

17. McMillian, *Smoking Typewriters*, 59.

18. "Super-Scoop," *The Rag* 1 (October 17, 1966), 20.

19. Allen Pasternak, "God Dead from Heroin Overdose; Underground Seeks Replacement, *The Rag* 1 (October 24, 1966), 9, 12–13.

20. "THIS THURSDAY IS GENTLE THURSDAY," *The Rag* 1 (October 31, 1966), 4.

21. Glenn W. Jones, "Gentle Thursday: An SDS Circus in Austin, Texas, 1966–1970," in *Sights on the Sixties*, ed. Barbara L. Tishcler (Rutgers University Press, 1992), 75–85.

22. Photo montage of Gentle Thursday, *The Rag* 1 (November 7, 1966), 10–11.

23. McMillian, *Smoking Typewriters*, 61.

24. Larry Freudiger, "Ken Kesey Crew Pays SF Mayor High Tribute OR Thar's Gold in Them Thar Hills," *The Rag* 1 (October 31, 1966), 17–20.

25. "A Soldier Says 'Humbug,'" *The Rag* 1 (October 24, 1966), 1, 15.

26. Thorne Dreyer, "All-Woman Sit-In at S.S. Office," *The Rag* 1 (October 31, 1966), 1, 3, 10–11.

27. Sandra F. Wilson, Mrs. Robert Pardun, Mrs. Larry Freudiger, et al. to Col. Morris S. Schwartz, n.d., *The Rag* 1 (October 31, 1966), 13.

28. Paul Deglau, "Disagreements with the New Left," *The Rag* 1 (October 24, 1966), 8–9, 12–13.

29. Larry Freudiger, "SNCC and Black Power Defended," *The Rag* 1 (November 7, 1966), 1, 6–8.

30. Gary Thiher, "Malcolm X; Wretched of the Earth Black Men Speak Out," *The Rag* 1 (November 7, 1966), 4–5, 9, 12–13.

31. "SDS Supports Black Power," *The Rag* 1 (November 14, 1966), 8.

32. "The Art of the Possible, or Who Controls the Court House: One Man—One Vote," *The Rag* 1 (November 14, 1966), 12–13; Larry Freudiger, "Panther Sharpens Claws on White Rooster," *The Rag* 1 (November 14, 1966), 13–15.

33. Larry Freudiger, "The Supreme Court: Two Decisions Strike at Social Deviants," *The Rag* 1 (November 21, 1966), 12–14.

34. Bruce Schmiechen, "Finding Fault with the Family Doctor," *The Rag* 1 (November 7, 1966), 14–16.

35. Tuli Kupferberg, "The Uses and Fuses of Education," *The Rag* 1 (November 28, 1966), 9–11.

36. Larry Freudiger, "The Great Headline Fiasco or Who Are the Brain Police?" *The Rag* 1 (December 5, 1966), 5–7.

37. Alan Locklear, "Merry Christmas: Buy a War Toy," *The Rag* 1 (December 12, 1966), 1, 12–13.

38. Rachel Maines, "Schools Squelch Smut," *The Rag* 1 (January 2, 1967), 1, 4; "Desolation Row," *The Rag* 1 (January 2, 1967), 16; "Clergymen Protest Hanoi Bombing," *The Rag* 1 (January 2, 1967), 17–18.

39. Chet Briggs, "The Artful Dodger," *The Rag* 1 (January 2, 1967), 7–9.

40. Anthony Homf, "I Would Suggest That the Situation of Texas Hippies Vis-à-Vis Their Physical Well-Being Could Rightly Be Termed Very Dangerous or Paranoia," *The Rag* 1 (January 2, 1967), 11, 15–16.

41. "Meanwhile, a Dozen Issues Later . . . ," *The Rag* 1 (January 9, 1967), 18.

42. "Fair Warning," *All New Zap Comix No. 1* (Apex Novelties, 1967); David Armstrong, *A Trumpet to Arms: Alternative Media in America* (J. Tarcher, 1981), 84–85.

10. PEOPLE OF THE BOOK

1. Helen Perry, *The Human Be-In* (Basic Books, 1970), 19–20.

2. D. T. Suzuk, *An Introduction to Zen Buddhism* (Grove, 1964).

3. Hermann Hesse to Gerhard Friedrich, June 20, 1940.

4. Alfred Werner, "Nobel Prize Winner," *New York Times*, December 8, 1946.

5. "For Service to Mankind," *New York Times*, November 16, 1946.

6. "Nobel Prize Winner," *New York Times*, November 20, 1946.

7. Alfred Werner, "Nobel Prize Winner," *New York Times*, December 8, 1946.

8. Claude Hill, "Herr Hesse and the Modern Neurosis," *New York Times*, March 16, 1947.

9. "Prizewinner," *Time* (March 17, 1947): 104.

10. Alice S. Morris, "The Will to Perish," *New York Times*, February 1, 1948.

11. Richard Plant, "Seven Titles of Interest . . .," *New York Times*, October 30, 1949.

12. Christopher Lazare, "A Measure of Wisdom," *New York Times*, December 2, 1951.

13. Dwight Macdonald, *New Yorker* (January 23, 1954): 99.

14. Seymour L. Flaxman, "Der Steppenwolf: Hesse's Portrait of the Intellectual, *Modern Language Quarterly* 15 (December 1954): 349–358.

15. Colin Wilson, *The Outsider: The Seminal Book on the Alienation of Modern Man* (Delta, 1956), 51–68.

16. Richard Plant, "Mystical Pilgrims," *New York Times*, July 21, 1957.

17. Claude Hill, "Hermann Hesse at Eighty," *Books Abroad* 31 (Summer 1957): 248–49.

18. Gisela Stein, "Hermann Hesse at 85," *New York Times*, July 1, 1962.

19. "Hermann Hesse, Novelist, Dead; Winner of Nobel Prize in 1946," *New York Times*, August 10, 1962.

20. Timothy Leary and Ralph Metzner, "Hermann Hesse: Poet of the Interior Journey," *The Psychedelic Review* 1 (Fall 1963): 167–82.

21. "A God Within," *Time* (July 30, 1965): 68–69.

22. Robin White, "The Search," *New York Times*, February 27, 1966.

23. Hermann Hesse, *Siddhartha* (New Directions, 1951).

24. Hesse, *Siddhartha*.

25. Hesse, *Siddhartha*.

26. John Simon, "Unique and Necessary," *New York Times*, May 19, 1968.

27. Hermann Hesse, *Narcissus and Goldmund* (Farrar, Straus and Giroux, 1968).

28. Hesse, *Narcissus and Goldmund*.

29. Hesse, *Narcissus and Goldmund*.

30. Eliot Fremont-Smith, "The Relevancy of Hermann Hesse," *New York Times*, November 1, 1968.

31. Hermann Hesse, *The Journey to the East* (Farrar, Straus and Giroux, 1968).

32. Hesse, *The Journey to the East*.

33. Hermann Hesse, *Demian* (Harper and Row, 1965).

34. Hesse, *Demian*.

35. Hesse, *Demian*.

36. Hermann Hesse, *Steppenwolf* (Holt, Rinehart and Winston, 1962).

37. Hesse, *Steppenwolf*.

38. Hesse, *Steppenwolf*.

39. Hesse, *Steppenwolf*.

40. Theodore Ziolkowski, "Saint Hesse among the Hippies," *American-German Review* 35 (1969): 19–23.

41. Ralph Freedman, "The Glass Bead Game," *New York Times*, January 4, 1970.

42. John Leonard, "Somewhere between Swinburne and Salinger," *New York Times*, February 17, 1970.

43. Egon Schwartz, "Hermann Hesse, the American Youth Movement, and Problems of Literary Evaluation, *PMLA* 85 (October 1970): 977–87.

44. Lewis Carroll, *Alice's Adventures in Wonderland and Through the Looking-Glass* (Grosset and Dunlap Publishers, 1946).

45. Jefferson Airplane, "White Rabbit"; Jefferson Airplane, "The House at Pooneil Corners" (1968).

46. Henry Resnik, "The Hobbit-Forming World of J. R. R. Tolkien," *Saturday Evening Post* (July 2, 1966): 90–92, 94.

47. Robert Sklar, "Tolkien and Hesse: Top of the Pops," *The Nation* (May 8, 1967): 598–601.

48. Orville Prescott, "Books of the Times," *New York Times*, August 4, 1961.

49. Robert A. Heinlein, *Stranger in a Strange Land* (G. Putnam's Sons, 1961).

50. Arthur C. Clarke, *Childhood's End* (Ballantine Books, 1953).

51. Basil Davenport, "The End, and The Beginning, of Man," *New York Times*, August 23, 1953.

52. Arthur C. Clarke, *2001: A Space Odyssey* (New American Library, 1968).

53. Kahlil Gibran, *The Prophet* (Alfred A. Knopf, 1923).

54. Carlos Castaneda, *The Teachings of Don Juan: A Yaqui Way of Knowledge* (Washington Square, 1968); Charles Simmons, "The Sorcerer's Apprentice," *New York Times*, August 14, 1968.

55. Dudley Young, "The Magic of Peyote," *New York Times*, September 29, 1968.

56. Peter Marin, "Tripping the Heavy Fantastic," *New York Times*, February 21, 1971.

I I. FROM THE HUMAN BE-IN TO
THE SUMMER OF LOVE

1. "Man of the Year: The Inheritor," *Time* (January 6, 1967): 18.

2. Walter Medeiros, "Mapping San Francisco 1965–1967: Roots and Florescence of the San Francisco Counterculture," *Summer of Love: Psychedelic Art, Social Crisis, and Counterculture in the 1960s* (Liverpool University Press, 2006), 341.

3. Allen Cohen, "A Gathering of the Tribes."

4. Conners, *White Hand Society*, 200.

5. Allen Cohen to Art Kunkin, January 1, 1967.

6. Stevens, *Storming Heaven*, 261.

7. The Communication Company, "Our Policy," January 1967.

8. The Communication Company, press release, January 24, 1967.

9. Richard M. Harnett, "All Kinds of 'Kooks' Gather for 'Happening,'" *Cleveland Plain Dealer*, January 16, 1967.

10. Steve Levine, "A Gathering of the Tribes—A Baptism Notes from the San Andreas Fault," San Francisco *Oracle*, January 1967.

11. Miles, *Hippie*, 191.

12. Perry, *The Human Be-In*, 16.

13. The Communication Company, "To the people," February 6, 1967.

14. The Communication Company, "Invitation/to/…/a/Be-In," February 16, 1967.

15. "The Houseboat Summit: February, 1967, Sausalito, Calif.," the *Oracle*, vol. 1, no. 7; Allen Ginsberg, Timothy Leary, Gary Snyder, Alan Watts, "Changes," in *Notes from the New Underground*, ed. Jesse Kornbluth (An Ace Book, 1968), 139–204.

16. "The Houseboat Summit: February, 1967, Sausalito, Calif."; Ginsberg, Leary, Snyder, Watts, "Changes."

17. "Dropouts with a Mission," *Newsweek* (February 6, 1967): 92, 95.

18. Hendrik Hertzberg, "Dropouts with a Mission."

19. Hertzberg, "Dropouts with a Mission."

20. Hertzberg, "Dropouts with a Mission."

21. Gladwin Hill, "'Turn On, Tune In and Drop Out': LSD Users Describe Their Experiences During a Psychedelic Trip," *New York Times*, February 23, 1967.

22. Warren Hinckle, "The Social History of the Hippies," *Ramparts* (March 1967): 5–12, 17–20, 24–26.

23. Hinckle, "The Social History of the Hippies," 9–12.

24. Hinckle, "The Social History of the Hippies," 17–18.

25. Hinckle, "The Social History of the Hippies," 19, 24.

26. Hinckle, "The Social History of the Hippies," 25–26.

27. Hinckle, "The Social History of the Hippies," 26.

28. Peter Richardson, *A Bomb in Every Issue: How the Short, Unruly Life of Ramparts Magazine Changed Magazine* (The New Press, 2009), 83, 107–8.

29. The Communication Company, "More Words on Other Side," n.d.

30. David Farber, *Chicago '68* (University of Chicago Press, 1994), 26–27.

31. Chester Anderson, "Uncle Tim's Children," The Communication Company, April 16, 1967.

32. Anderson, "Uncle Tim's Children."

33. The Communication Center, "street news for the tenth of may," May 10, 1967.

34. Claude Hayward and Chester Anderson, "To The Erstwhile Underground Press, Greeting," The Communication Company.

35. Charles E. Alverson, "Offbeat 'Diggers' Aid Drifters in Bohemian Area of San Francisco," *Wall Street Journal*, April 27, 1967.

36. David Talbot, *Season of the Witch: Enchantment, Terror, and Deliverance in the City of Love* (Free Press, 2013), 92.

37. Susan J. Douglas, *Listening In: Radio and the American Imagination* (University of Minnesota Press, 2004), 270; Tom Donahue, "A Rotting Corpse, Stinking up the Airways . . .," *Rolling Stone* (November 1967): 14–15.

38. Susan Krieger, *Hip Capitalism* (Sage, 1979).

39. Hunter S. Thompson, "The 'Hashbury' Is the Capital of the Hippies," *New York Times*, May 14, 1967.

40. Thompson, "The 'Hashbury' Is the Capital of the Hippies."

41. Martin Arnold, "Organized Hippies Emerge on Coast," *New York Times*, May 5, 1967.

42. Strawberry Alarm Clock, "Incense and Peppermints" (1967).

43. Buffalo Springfield, "For What It's Worth" (1967).

44. Robert Christgau, "Anatomy of a Love Festival," *Esquire* (January 1968): 60–67.

45. John Phillips, "San Francisco (Be Sure to Wear Flowers in Your Hair)" (1967).

46. The Communication Company, "When You Come to San Francisco."

47. Philip Charles Lucas, *The Odyssey of a New Religion: The Holy Order of MANS from New Age to Orthodoxy* (Indiana University Press, 1995), 27.

48. Perry, *The Haight-Ashbury*, 192.

49. Hunter S. Thompson, "The Hippies," http://distrito47.wordpress.com/2014/02/03/the-hippies-by-hunter-s-thompson/. From *Collier's Encyclopedia 1968 Yearbook*.

50. Miles, *Hippie*, 195.

51. Sylvan Fox, "9 Hurt, 38 Arrested as Hippies Clash with Police," *New York Times*, May 31, 1967.

52. Stephen A. O. Golden, "At a Commune for Diggers Rules Are Few and Simple," *New York Times*, June 1, 1967.

53. Paul Hofman, "Hippies Heighten East Side Tensions," *New York Times*, June 3, 1967.

54. *Summer of Love*, Gail Doglin and Vicente Franco, directors (American Experience, 2007).

55. Jack Newfield, "One Cheer for the Hippies," *The Nation* (June 26, 1967): 809–10.

56. "The Hippies: Philosophy of a Subculture," *Time* (July 7, 1967): 18–22.

57. Ibid; "Drugs: LSD and the Unborn," *Time* (August 11, 1967): 60.

12. THE DEATH OF HIPPIE AND EARLY POSTMORTEMS

1. "End of the Dance," *Time* (August 18, 1967): 22–23.

2. Allen Cohen, "In Memoriam for Superspade and John Carter," *San Francisco Oracle* 1 (August 22, 1967).

3. "The Hippie Temptation," CBS News, August 23, 1963; Jack Gould, "TV: Program Examines Hippies' Life," *New York Times*, August 23, 1967.

4. John Kifner, "Hippies Shower $1 Bills on Stock Exchange Floor," *New York Times*, August 25, 1967.

5. The Grateful Dead, *Anthem of the Sun* (1968).

6. Ralph J. Gleason, "The Power of Non-Politics or the Death of the Square Left," *Evergreen Review* (September 1967): 41–45, 95–96.

7. "Our Mysterious Children," *Saturday Evening Post* (September 23, 1967): 102.

8. Joan Didion, "Hippies Generation," *Saturday Evening Post* (September 23, 1967): 25–94.

9. Nicholas von Hoffman, *We Are the People Our Parents Warned Us Against* (Quadrangle, 1968), 6, 17–20.

10. Von Hoffman, *We Are the People Our Parents Warned Us Against*, 30–31, 55, 71.

11. Von Hoffman, *We Are the People Our Parents Warned Us Against*, 116–19.

12. Von Hoffman, *We Are the People Our Parents Warned Us Against*, 119–20.

13. Von Hoffman, *We Are the People Our Parents Warned Us Against*, 124–25.

14. Mark Harris, "The Flowering of the Hippies," *Atlantic Monthly* (September 1967): 63–72.

15. Lawrence Swaim, "Hippies: The Love Thing," *North American Review* 252 (September 1967): 16–18.

16. Richard Blum, untitled review of "The Varieties of Religious Experience," *Journal of Criminal Law* 58 (September 1967): 385–86.

17. Miles, *Hippie*, 210–11.

18. Free City Collective, "October Sixth Nineteen Hundred and Sixty Seven," *Free City News Sheets*, October 6, 1967.

19. George McKay, "The Social and (Counter-) Cultural 1960s in the U.S.A. Transatlantically," in *Summer of Love*, 43.

20. Perry, *The Haight-Ashbury*, 243.

21. Miles, *Hippie*, 211.

22. Von Hoffman, *We Are the People Our Parents Warned Us Against*, 238–40.

23. "Hippies: Where Have All the Flowers Gone?" *Time* (October 13, 1967): 30–31.

24. Martin Arnold, "The East Village Today: Hippies Far From Happy as Slum Problems Grow," *New York Times*, October 15, 1967; Golden, "At a Commune for Diggers Rules Are Few and Simple."

25. Richard Goldstein, "Love: A Groovy Idea While He Lasted," *The Village Voice*, October 19, 1967, reprinted in Richard Goldstein, *Reporting the Counterculture* (Unwin Hyman, 1989), 119–22.

26. Earl Shorris, "Love Is Dead," *New York Times*, October 29, 1967.

27. "David Crosby," reprinted from *The Oracle of Southern California, Ann Arbor Sun*, April 1968, in *The Hippie Papers: Notes from the Underground Press* (Signet Books, 1968), 219–21.

28. Clive Barnes, "'Hair'—It's Fresh and Frank," *New York Times*, April 30, 1968.

29. Eric Burdon and the Animals, "Monterey" (1967).

30. Cream, *Disraeli Gears* (1967).

31. Cream, "Strange Brew" (1967); Cream, "Tales of Brave Ulysses" (1967).

32. Cream, "Sunshine of Your Love" (1967).

33. Jann Wenner, *Rolling Stone* (November 9, 1967).

34. "The High Cost of Music and Love: Where's the Money from Monterey?" *Rolling Stone* (November 9, 1967): 1.

35. Nicholas Schou, *Orange Sunshine*, 70–71.

36. The Jimi Hendrix Experience, *Axis: Bold as Love* (1967).

37. Hans Toch, "Last Word on the Hippies," *Nation* 205 (December 4, 1967): 582–88.

38. Barry Miles, *Paul McCartney: Many Years From Now* (Holt Paperbacks, 1998), 444.

39. The Rolling Stones, *Their Satanic Majesties Request* (1967).

40. The Rolling Stones, "She's a Rainbow" (1967).

13. ALTERNATIVE LIVING

1. Timothy Miller, *The 60s Communes: Hippies and Beyond* (Syracuse University Press, 2000).

2. Robert Houriet, *Getting Back Together* (Coward, McCann and Geoghegan, 1971), xii–xiii.

3. Houriet, *Getting Back Together*, xiii–xiv.

4. Canned Heat, "Going Up the Country" (1968).

5. Robert S. Fogart, *All Things New: American Communes and Utopian Movement, 1860–1914* (University of Chicago Press, 1990).

6. Percival Goodman and Paul Goodman, *Communitas: Means of Livelihood and Ways of Life* (University of Chicago, 1947).

7. Charles K. Agle, "The Science of Community Planning," *New York Times*, June 1, 1947.

8. David Riesman, "Some Observations on Community Plans and Utopia," *Yale Law Journal* 57 (December 1947): 173–200.

9. B. F. Skinner, *Walden Two* (MacMillan, 1948).

10. Orville Prescott, "Books of the Times," *New York Times*, June 11, 1948.

11. Charles Poore, "Tour of an Almost Perfect Utopia," *New York Times*, June 13, 1948.

12. Donald C. Williams, "The Social Scientist as Philosopher and King," *Philosophical Review* 58 (July 1949): 345–59.

13. Helen and Scott Nearing, *Living the Good Life: Being a Plain Practical Account of a Twenty Year Project in a Self-Subsistent Homestead in Vermont, Together with Remarks on How to Live Sanely and Simply in a Troubled World* (Social Science Institute, 1954).

14. Scott Nearing, *The Making of a Radical: A Political Autobiography* (Chelsea Green Publishing Company, 2000).

15. Miller, *The 60s Communes*.

16. Tom Wolfe, *The Electric Kool-Aid Acid Test*, 51–52.

17. Charles Poore, "Books of the Times," *New York Times*, March 29, 1962.

18. Chad Walsh, "Can Man Save Himself?" *New York Times*, April 1, 1962.

19. Miller, *The 60s Communes*, 20–26.

20. "John Sinclair and the Sixties Counterculture in Michigan" webpage, University of Michigan-Flint.

21. Emil Bacilla, Gary Grimshaw, Jim Semark, John Sinclair, Robin Tyner, and Alan van Newkirk, "1967 Steering Committee."

22. Robert Anton Wilson, "The Religion of Kerista and Its 69 Positions," *Fact* 2:4 (July–August 1964): 23–29.

23. Wilson, "The Religion of Kerista and Its 69 Positions," 23–29.

24. John Gruen, *The New Bohemia* (A Cappella Books, 1966), 52–60.

25. Kathleen Kinkade, "Journal of a Walden Two Commune," *Walden House Newsletter* (August 1966): 8, 14.

26. Kathleen Kinkade, *Walden Two Experiment* (Morrow, 1973).

27. Mark Matthews, *Droppers: America's First Hippie Commune, Drop City* (University of Oklahoma Press, 2010); John Curl, *Memories of Drop City: The First Hippie Commune and the Summer of Love (iUniverse, Inc., 2006)*; Peter Rabbit, *Drop City* (The Olympia Press, 1971).

28. "The Hippies," *Time* (July 7, 1967): 18–22.

29. Miles, *Hippie*, 270.

30. Gary Keyes and Mike Lawler, *Wicked Crescenta Valley* (History Press, 2014), 70.

31. Mel Lyman, *Mirror at the End of the Road* (American Avatar Publication, 1971); David Felton, Robin Green, and David Dalton, *Mindfuckers: A Source Book on the Rise of Acid Fascism in America* (Straight Arrow Books, 1972).

32. "In Memoriam: Lou Gottlieb," The Digger Archives.

33. Farrell, *The Spirit of the Sixties*, 225.

34. Miller, *The 60s Communes*, 51–52.

35. Fairfield, Richard, "Morningstar Ranch," in *The Modern Utopian: Alternative Communities of the '60s and '70s* (Process, 2010), 69.

36. Miller, *The 60s Communes*, 47.

37. Elia Katz, *Armed Love: Communal Living—Good or Bad?* (Blond and Briggs, 1972), 136.

38. "Early Days on the Ridge and the Naked Cop," in *Home Free Home: A History of Two Open-Door California Communes*, The Digger Archives.

39. "Wheeler's Ranch," in *Modern American Communes: A Dictionary*, ed. Robert Sutton (Greenwood, 2005), 175.

40. Joshua Gamson, *The Fabulous Sylvester: The Legend, the Music, the Seventies in San Francisco* (Picador, 2006), 50.

41. "A Publication of the Free Print Shop," *Kaliflower: The Intercommunal [Free] Newspaper*, The Digger Archives.

42. Paul Goodman, "The Diggers in 1984," *Ramparts* (September 1967): 28–30.

43. Miller, *The 60s Communes*, 45.

44. Jack Loeffler, "Land of Clear Light," *El Palacio* (Spring 113), 40–51.

45. Ahad Cobb, "Early Lama Foundation."

46. Miller, *The 60s Communes*, 51.

47. Timothy Miller, "The Historical Communal Roots of Ultraconservative Groups," in *The Cultic Milieu: Oppositional Subcultures in an Age of Globalization*. Ed. Jeffrey Kaplan and Helene Loow (AltaMira Press, 2002), 100.

48. Larry Eskridge, *God's Forever Family: The Jesus People Movement in America* (Oxford University Press, 2013).

49. Maurice Isserman and Michael Kazin, *America Divided: The Civil War of the 1960s* (Oxford University Press, 2008), 170.

14. FROM HIPPIE TO YIPPIE ON THE WAY TO REVOLUTION

1. Todd Gitlin, *The Sixties: Years of Hope, Days of Rage* (Bantam, 1987), 220.

2. Abbie Hoffman, *Revolution for the Hell of It: The Book That Earned Abbie Hoffman a Five-year Prison Term at the Chicago Conspiracy Trial* (Da Capo Press, 2005), 35.

3. T. V. Reed, *Fifteen Jugglers, Five Believers: Literary Politics and the Poetics of American Social Movements* (University of California Press, 1992), 107.

4. Marty Jezer, *Abbie Hoffman: American Rebel* (Rutgers University Press, 1993), 105.

5. Jerry Rubin, "A Yippie Manifesto."

6. Abbie Hoffman, *The Autobiography of Abbie Hoffman* (Da Capo Press, 2000), 129.

7. Raskin, *For the Hell of It*, 119–20.

8. "A Call to Resist Illegitimate Authority," *New York Review of Books*, October 12, 1967.

9. Raymond Mungo, *Famous Long Ago: My Life and Hard Times with Liberation News Service* (Beacon Press, 1970), 5–45.

10. Farber, *Chicago '68*, 60, 13.

11. Ed Sanders, *Fug You: An Informal History of the Peace Eye Bookstore, the Fuck You Press, the Fugs, and Counterculture in the Lower East Side* (Da Capo Press, 2011).

12. Raskin, *For the Hell of It*, 124, 122.

13. Hoffman, *Revolution for the Hell of It*, 43.

14. Raskin, *For the Hell of It*, 123.

15. Thorne Dreyer, "People Call for Revolution: Pentagon Up-Tight," *The Rag* 2 (October 30, 1967).

16. Raskin, *For the Hell of It*, 125.

17. Charles DeBenedetti, *An American Ordeal: The Antiwar Movement of the Vietnam Era* (Syracuse University Press, 1990), 223.

18. Steppenwolf, *Steppenwolf* (1967).

19. Steppenwolf, "Born to Be Wild" (1968).

20. Steppenwolf, "The Pusher" (1968).

21. Paul Berman, "Mailer's Great American Meltdown," *New York Times*, August 22, 1968.

22. Testimony of Norman Mailer, *Conspiracy in the Streets: The Extraordinary Trial of the Chicago Eight* (New Press, 2006), 188–91.

23. Raskin, *For the Hell of It*, 126.

24. Jezer, *Abbie Hoffman*, 121.

25. Farber, *Chicago '68*, 3; Abbie Hoffman, *Soon to Be a Major Motion Picture* (Perigee Books, 1980), 137.

26. Jerry Rubin, *Do It!: Scenarios of the Revolution* (Simon and Schuster, 1970), 247–50, 123.

27. Farber, *Chicago '68*, 17.

28. Thurston Clarke, *The Last Campaign: Robert F. Kennedy and 82 Days That Inspired America* (Henry Holt, 2008), 35.

29. Michael William Doyle, "Staging the Revolution: Guerrilla Theater as a Countercultural Practice," in *Imagine Nation: The American Counterculture of the 1960s and '70s*, eds. Peter Braunstein and Michael William Doyle (Routledge, 2002), 90.

30. Jezer, *Abbie Hoffman*, 125.

31. Raskin, *For the Hell of It*, 132.

32. Jefferson Airplane, *Crown of Creation* (1968).

33. Jefferson Airplane, "Lather" (1968).

34. Jefferson Airplane, "Triad" (1968).

35. Jefferson Airplane, "The House at Pooneil Corners" (1968).

36. "Here Comes the Yippies," *Newsweek* (March 11, 1968): 68.

37. Jezer, *Abbie Hoffman*, 126.

38. Michael Rossman to Jerry Rubin, March 16, 1968, *Berkeley Barb*.

39. Sally Kempton, "Yippies Anti-Organize a Groovy Revolution," *The Village Voice*, March 2, 1968.

40. Vincent Cannato, *The Ungovernable City* (Basic Books, 2002), 222.

41. Gitlin, *The Sixties*, 229.

42. Hoffman, *Revolution for the Hell of It*, 91.

43. "Political Activism New Hippie 'Thing,'" *New York Times*, March 24, 1968.

44. Farber, *Chicago '68*, 33–34.

45. Jerry Rubin, "The Election-High Is a Bad Trip," *The Village Voice*, March 21, 1968.

46. Hoffman, *Revolution for the Hell of It*, 104.

47. Theodore Roszak, "Capsules of Salvation," *Nation* (April 8, 1968): 466–71.

48. Raymond Mungo, *Famous Long Ago*, 125–26.

49. Ralph Gleason, "The Final Paroxysm of Fear," *Rolling Stone* 1 (April 6, 1968).

50. Raskin, *For the Hell of It*, 138.

51. Sale, *SDS*, 449.

52. William F. Buckley interview with Allen Ginsberg, taped on May 7, 1968, for *Firing Line* segment, "The Avant Garde."

53. Armstrong, *A Trumpet to Arms*, 123.

54. Big Brother and the Holding Company, *Cheap Thrills* (1968).

55. Isserman and Kazin, *America Divided*, 161.

56. Quicksilver Messenger Service, *Quicksilver Messenger Service* (1968); Dino Valenti, "Dino's Song" (1968).

57. John Lennon and Yoko Ono, *Two Virgins* (1968).

58. Ray Connolly, "Apple-The Short, Strange Blossoming of The Beatles' Dream," *The Independent*, October 22, 2010.

59. Kirkpatrick Sale, SDS (Vintage, 1974), 451.

60. Bart Barnes, "Pediatrician Benjamin Spock Dies," *Washington Post*, March 17, 1998.

61. The Beatles, Yellow Submarine (1968); The Beatles, "Yellow Submarine" (1968"; The Beatles, "Baby, You're a Rich Man" (1967).

62. John Sinclair, "White Panther Party Statement," November 1, 1968.

63. Jeff A. Hale, "The White Panthers' 'Total Assault on the Culture,'" in *Imagine Nation*, 127.

64. Robert Houriet, "Life and Death of a Commune Called Om," *New York Times*, February 16, 1969; Houriet, *Getting Back Together*.

65. The Moody Blues, "Legend of a Mind" (1968).

66. Margaret Sankot and David E. Smith, "Drug Problems in the Haight-Ashbury," *American Journal of Nursing* 68 (August 1968): 1686–89.

67. Eliot Fremont-Smith, "Freak-Out in the Day-Glo," *New York Times*, August 12, 1968.

68. C. D. B. Bryan, "The SAME Day: heeeeeewack!!!" *New York Times*, August 18, 1968.

69. Joel Lieber, Day-Glo and Light Nights," *Nation* (September 23, 1968): 282–83.

15. FIGHTING IN THE STREETS AND THE LATEST BATTLE OF THE BANDS

1. Mungo, *Famous Long Ago*, 163–202; Raymond Mungo, *Beyond the Revolution: My Life and Times since Famous Long Ago* (Contemporary Books, 1990).

2. Chip Berlet, "The FBI, COINTELPRO, and the Alternative Press," Political Research Associates.

3. Frank Kusch, *Battleground Chicago: The Police and the 1968 Democratic National Convention* (University of Chicago Press, 2008), 35.

4. Kusch, *Battleground Chicago*, 54.

5. Farber, *Chicago '68*, 53.

6. Etan Ben-Ami interview with Peter Coyote.

7. Farber, *Chicago '68*, 55, 168.

8. Farber, *Chicago '68*, 56.

9. Raskin, *For the Hell of It*, 152.

10. Sanders, *Fug You*, 325.

11. Toni Apicelli, *A Sixties Story* (Dog Ear Publishing, 2011), 80.

12. Abbie Hoffman, "Yippie Workshop Speech," August 27, 1968.

13. Abe Ribicoff, Democratic Party National Convention, August 28, 1968; Richard Daley, Democratic Party National Convention, August 28, 1968; Norman Mailer, *Miami and the Siege of Chicago* (Primus, 1968).

14. Debate between Gore Vidal and William F. Buckley, August 28, 1968, ABC News.

15. Mark Kurlansky, *1968: The Year That Rocked the World* (Random House Trade Paperbacks, 2005), 285.

16. Raskin, *For the Hell of It*, 166; David Farber, *The Age of Great Dreams: America in the 1960s* (Hill and Wang, 1994), 224.

17. Kusch, *Battleground Chicago*, 134.

18. I. F. Stone, "When a Two-Party System Becomes a One-Party Rubber Stamp," *I. F. Stone's Weekly* (September 9, 1968): 2.

19. Paul Carroll Interview with Allen Ginsberg, *Playboy* (April 1969): 81–92, 236–44.

20. Allen Katzman, "Bandages and Stitches Tell the Story," *East Village Other* (August 30, 1968).

21. The Beatles, "Revolution" (1968).

22. The Rolling Stones, "Street Fighting Man" (1968).

23. Alex Constantine, *The Covert War Against Rock* (Feral House, 2000), 45; Telegraph Reporters, "Why the Queen 'Refused to Hand Mick Jagger a Knighthood,'" *The Telegraph*, July 11, 2012; Dorian Lynskey, "Mick: The Wild Life and Mad Genius of Jagger by Christopher Andersen—Review," August 17, 2012.

24. Jon Wiener, *Come Together: John Lennon in His Time* (Random House, 1984), 60–63; "100 Greatest Beatles Songs: 'Revolution,'" *Rolling Stone* (September 19, 2011).

25. "Recordings: Apples for the Beatles," *Time* (September 7, 1968): 59–60.

26. Wiener, *Come Together*, 63, 66.

27. John Kifner, "Hippies Fading From City Scene," *New York Times*, August 26, 1968.

28. Nat Hentoff Interview with Eldridge Cleaver, "Eldridge Cleaver: A Candid Conversation with the Black Panther Leader," *Playboy* (December 1968): 89+.

29. DeBenedetti, *An American Ordeal*, 231–32.

30. John Leo, "Politics Now the Focus of Underground Press," *New York Times*, September 4, 1968.

31. Armando Tinoco, "What Happened in Mexico City Today? Twitter Remembers October 2, 1968 Student Massacre by Police in Tlatelolco Square," *Latin Times*, October 2, 2013.

32. William O'Neill, *The New Left: A History* (Harlan Davidson, 2001), 56.

33. David E. Rosenbaum, "Yippie Leader Arrested on Flag-Desecration Charge Outside House Hearing," *New York Times*, October 4, 1968.

34. Traffic, *Traffic* (1968).

35. Traffic, "You Can All Join In" (1968).

36. Traffic, "Pearly Queen" (1968).

37. Traffic, "Feelin' Alright" (1968).

38. Traffic, "40,000 Headsmen" (1968).

39. Lou Cannon, *Governor Reagan: His Rise to Power* (Public Affairs, 2005), 285.

40. David Barber, *A Hard Rain Fell: SDS and Why It Failed* (University Press of Mississippi, 2010), 149.

41. Mike Klonsky, "Toward a Revolutionary Youth Movement," *New Left Notes* (December 23, 1968).

42. Sinclair, "White Panther Party Statement."

43. Cathy Wilkerson, *Flying Close to the Sun: My Life and Times as a Weatherman* (Seven Stories Press, 2011), 228–29.

44. *Whole Earth Catalog: Access to Tools* (Portola Institute, 1969).

45. The Beatles, *White Album* (1968).

46. The Beatles, "Glass Onion" (1968).

47. The Beatles, "Happiness Is a Warm Gun" (1968).

48. The Rolling Stones, *Beggars Banquet* (1968).

49. The Rolling Stones, "Sympathy for the Devil" (1968).

50. The Rolling Stones, "Salt of the Earth" (1968).

51. Wiener, *Come Together*, 65.

52. Jack Newfield, "Put-Ons and Fraternal Hotfoots for the New Left; Revolution for the Hell of It," *New York Times*, December 29, 1968.

16. COINTELPRO AND THE MILLENNIUM

1. DeBenedetti, *An American Ordeal*, 244.

2. McMillian, *Smoking Typewriters*, 115.

3. Amy Stevens, *Daniel Shays' Legacy: Marshall Bloom, Radical Insurgency and the Pioneer Valley* (Collective Copies, 2005), 65.

4. McMillian, *Smoking Typewriters*, 124, 122.

5. Berlet, "The FBI, COINTELPRO, and the Alternative Press."

6. Thorne Dreyer and Victoria Smith, "The Movement and the New Media," *Liberation News Service* packet 144, March 1, 1969, 15

7. Paul A. Robinson, *The Freudian Left: Wilhelm Reich, Geza Roheim, Herbert Marcuse* (Harper and Row, 1969).

8. Houriet, "Life and Death of a Commune Called Oz."

9. Ralph Gleason, "Perspectives: Is There a Death Wish in the U.S.?" *Rolling Stone* (April 5, 1969), reprinted in *The Age of Paranoia*, Editors of Rolling Stone (Pocket Book, 1972): 417–20.

10. Michael Rossman, "American Revolution 1969," *Rolling Stone* (April 5, 1969), reprinted in *The Age of Paranoia*, 209–23.

11. Sale, *SDS*, 511–513, 533, 543.

12. Robert Scheer, *Playing President: My Close Encounters with Nixon, Carter, Bush I, Reagan, and Clinton and How They Did Not Prepare Me for George W. Bush* (Akashic Books, 2006), 163.

13. John Simon, "People's Park: Just the Beginning," *Liberation* (July 1969).

14. Langdon Winner, "The Battle of People's Park (Cont.)," *Rolling Stone* (June 14, 1969).

15. Thunderclap Newman, "Something in the Air" (1969).

16. McMillian, *Smoking Typewriters*, 123.

17. The Beatles, "The Ballad of John and Yoko" (1969).

18. Plastic Ono Band, "Give Peace a Chance" (1969).

19. Robert Christgau, "Rock 'n' Revolution," *The Village Voice*, July 1969.

20. Gitlin, *The Sixties*, 388; Sale, *SDS*, 569.

21. Bob Dylan, "Subterranean Homesick Blues" (1965).

22. Hearings, *Reports and Prints of the Senate Committee on Government Operations* (1969).

23. Lucian Truscott IV, "Gay Power Comes to Sheridan Square," *The Village Voice*, July 3, 1969.

24. David Carter, *Stonewall: The Riots That Sparked the Gay Revolution* (St. Martin's Griffin, 2010), 160.

25. James Lewes, *Protest and Survive: Underground GI Newspapers during the Vietnam War* (Praeger, 2003), 34.

26. Max Scherr, "Max the Pig," *Berkeley Barb*, July 11, 1969; Wallace Turner, Berkeley Paper Struck by Staff," *New York Times*, July 13, 1969.

27. *Easy Rider* (1969); *Easy Rider* (soundtrack) (1969).

28. Steven V. Roberts, "Some Enter Communal Seclusion to Escape Turmoil, Others to Find Religion," *New York Times*, August 2, 1969.

29. Roberts, "Some Enter Communal Seclusion to Escape Turmoil."

30. Steven V. Roberts, "Actress Is among 5 Slain at Home in Beverly Hills; Sharon Tate, 2d Woman and 3 Men Victims—Suspect Is Seized," *New York Times*, August 10, 1969.

31. Joel Rosenman, *Young Men with Unlimited Capital: The Story of Woodstock* (Scrivener Press, 1999); "Young Men with Unlimited Capital . . .," *New York Times*, March 22, 1968; Marley Brant, *Join Together: Forty Years of the Rock Music Festival* (Backbeat Books, 2008), 60.

32. Barnard L. Collier, "200,000 Thronging to Rock Festival Jam Roads Upstate," *New York Times*, August 16, 1969.

33. Jefferson Airplane, "Volunteers" (1969).

34. Abbie Hoffman, "The Hard Rain's Already Fallin'."

35. Peter Doggett, *There's a Riot Going On: Revolutionaries, Rock Stars, and the Rise and Fall of the '60s* (Canongate U.S., 2009), 272.

36. "Promoter Baffled That Festival Drew Such a Big Crowd," *New York Times*, August 17, 1969.

37. Barnard L. Collier, "300,000 at Folk-Rock Fair Camp Out in a Sea of Mud," *New York Times*, August 17, 1969.

38. Richard Reeves, "Fair's Financier Calls It 'Success'; But He Estimates Losses as High as $2-Million," *New York Times*, August 18, 1969.

39. Michael T. Kaufman, "Generation Gap Bridged as Monticello Residents Aid Courteous Festival Patrons: Clinic Is Set up in Town's School," *New York Times*, August 18, 1969.

40. "Farmer with Soul: Max Yasgur," *New York Times*, August 18, 1969.

41. "Nightmare in the Catskills," *New York Times*, August 18, 1969.

42. Patrick Lydon, "A Joyful Confirmation That Good Things *Can* Happen Here," *New York Times*, August 24, 1969.

43. "Woodstock—The Message of History's Biggest Happening," *Time* (August 29, 1969): 32–33.

44. "Woodstock," 32–33.

45. Andrew Kopkind, "Coming of Age," in *The Thirty Years' Wars: Dispatches and Diversions of a Radical Journalist: 1865–1994* (Verso, 1995), 171–74. "Coming of Age" initially appeared in *Hard Times* (August 25–September 1, 1969).

46. Kopkind, "Coming of Age," 175.

47. *Alice's Restaurant* (1969).

48. Vincent Canby, "Movie of Arlo Guthrie's 'Alice's Restaurant' Opens," *New York Times*, August 25, 1969; Vincent Canby, "Our Time: Arlo and Chicago," *New York Times*, August 31, 1969; *Medium Cool* (1969).

49. Jefferson Airplane, "We Can Be Together" (1969).

50. Joni Mitchell, "Woodstock," 1970.

51. Crosby, Stills, Nash and Young, *Déjà Vu* (1970); Crosby, Stills, Nash and Young, "Woodstock" (1970).

52. Crosby, Stills, Nash and Young, "Teach Your Children" (1970); Crosby, Stills, Nash and Young, "Our House"; Crosby, Stills, Nash and Young, "Almost Cut My Hair."

53. Theodore Roszak, *The Making of a Counter Culture: Reflections of the Technocratic Society and Its Youthful Opposition* (Anchor Books/Doubleday, 1969).

54. Robert Paul Wolff, "The Making of a Counter Culture," *New York Times*, September 7, 1969.

55. Paul Goodman, "The New Reformation," *New York Times*, September 14, 1969.

17. THE CONSPIRACY, STREET FIGHTING MAN, AND THE APOCALYPSE

1. Lytle, *America's Uncivil Wars*, 346.

2. Testimony of Abbie Hoffman, *Conspiracy in the Streets*, 157–65.

3. The Beatles, *Abbey Road* (1969).

4. The Beatles, "Come Together" (1969).

5. Plastic Ono Band, "Cold Turkey" (1969).

6. John Burks, "The Underground Press," *Rolling Stone* (October 4, 1969): 11–33.

7. Burks, "The Underground Press."

8. Burks, "The Underground Press."

9. Burks, "The Underground Press"; Dan Berger, *Outlaws of America: The Weather Underground and the Politics of Solidarity* (AK Press, 2006), 107–18; Jeremy Varon, *Bring the War Home: The Weather Underground, the Red Army Faction, and Revolutionary Violence in the Sixties and Seventies* (University of California Press, 2004), 74–112; Ron Jacobs, *The Way the Wind Blew: A History of the Weather Underground* (Verso, 1997), 38–65.

10. Sale, *SDS*, 600–614.

11. *New Left Notes* (October 21, 1969).

12. John Kifner, "300 in S.D.S. Clash with Chicago Police," *New York Times*, October 6, 1969; John Kifner, "Radicals Detect Gain in Chicago Strife," *New York Times*, October 14, 1969.

13. William F. Buckley interview of Jack Kerouac, *Firing Line* (taped September 3, 1968).

14. Joseph Lelyveld, "Jack Kerouac, Novelist, Dead; Father of the Beat Generation," *New York Times*, October 22, 1969.

15. Maher, *Kerouac*, 476.

16. Eric Ehrman, "Kerouac's Retrospective," in *The Rolling Stone Book of the Beats*, ed. Holly George-Warren (Hyperion, 1999), 139.

17. "End of the Road," *Time* (October 31, 1969): 10.

18. John Kifner, "Police in Chicago Slay 2 Panthers," *New York Times*, December 5, 1969.

19. The Rolling Stones, *Let It Bleed* (1969).

20. Ralph J. Gleason, "Aquarius Wept," *Esquire* (August 1970): 84–92, 48, 50.

21. Todd Gitlin, "The End of the Age of Aquarius," *Liberation* (December 1969). Reprinted in *Underground Press Anthology*, ed. Thomas King Forcade (Ace Books, 1972), 100–111.

22. "Let It Bleed," *Rolling Stone* (January 21, 1970): 1.

23. Michael Lydon, "The Rolling Stones—At Play in the Apocalypse," *Ramparts* (1970): 28–53; Michael Lydon, *RockFolk: Portraits from the Rock 'n" Roll Pantheon* (Dial Press, 1971), 191–200.

24. Gleason, "Aquarius Wept."

25. Robert Draper, *Rolling Stone Magazine: The Uncensored History* (Doubleday, 1990), 117.

26. Wiener, *Come Together*, 107–9.

27. Steven V. Roberts, "3 Suspects in Tate Case Tied to Guru and 'Family,'" *New York Times*, December 3, 1969.

28. Jeff Guinn, *Manson: The Life and Times of Charles Manson* (Simon and Schuster, 2013).

29. Guinn, *Manson*; Steven V. Roberts, "Head of 'Family' Is Held for Trial," *New York Times*, December 4, 1969.

30. Michael Walker, *Laurel Canyon: The Inside Story of Rock-and-Roll's Legendary Neighborhood* (Faber and Faber, 2007), xvii–xviii, 120–28.

31. "Many Religious Communes of Young People Are under the Sway of Compelling Leaders," *New York Times*, December 14, 1969.

32. "Many Religious Communes of Young People."

33. Steven V. Roberts, "The Hippie Mystique," *New York Times*, December 15, 1969.

34. Ed Sanders, *The Family: The Story of Charles Manson's Dune Buggy Attack Battalion* (Dutton, 1971).

35. Robert Christgau, "The Family," *New York Times*, October 31, 1971.

36. Jerry Rubin, *We Are Everywhere* (HarperCollins, 1971), 238, 240.

37. Sale, *SDS*, 623–29; Berger, *Outlaws of America*, 122–24; Varon, *Bring the War Home*, 151–71; Jacobs, *The Way the Wind Blew*, 66–89. Bill Ayers later insisted that Dohrn's statement regarding the Manson family was "agitated and inflamed and full of rhetorical overkill, and [delivered] partly as a joke, stupid perhaps, tasteless, but a joke nonetheless." Bill Ayers blog, March 3, 2008.

18. THE NOT SO SLOW FADE

1. Robin Morgan, "Goodbye to All That," *Rat* (January 1970).

2. *Sisterhood Is Powerful*, ed. Robin Morgan (Vintage, 1970).

3. Armstrong, *A Trumpet to Arms*, 225.

4. Tom Wolfe, *Radical Chic and Mau-Mauing the Flak Catchers* (Bantam Books, 1971).

5. Charlotte Curtis, "Black Panther Philosophy Is Debated at the Bernsteins," *New York Times*, January 15, 1970.

6. "False Note on Black Panthers," *New York Times*, January 16, 1970.

7. Felicia M. Bernstein, "Letters to the Editor of *The Times*: Panthers' Legal Aid," *New York Times*, January 21, 1970.

8. R. D. Laing, *The Politics of Experience* (Pantheon, 1967).

9. Marshall Berman, "The Divided Self" and "Self and Others," *New York Times*, February 22, 1970.

10. *Zabriskie Point* (1970).

11. Vincent Canby, "Screen: Antonioni's 'Zabriskie Point,'" *New York Times*, February 10, 1970; Richard Goldstein, "Did Antonioni Miss the Point?" *New York Times*, February 22, 1970.

12.   *Getting Straight* (1970); *The Strawberry Statement* (1970).

13.   Vincent Canby, "Ah, Youth! Ah, Sex! Ah, Revolution!" *New York Times*, June 14, 1970.

14.   Dotson Rader, "A Razzberry for 'Strawberry,'" *New York Times*, July 19, 1970.

15.   Sale, *SDS*, 633–34.

16.   Martin Waldron, "Militants Stockpile Illegal Guns Across the U.S.," *New York Times*, December 28, 1969.

17.   *Conspiracy in the Streets*; William R. Kunstler, *My Life as a Radical Lawyer* (Carol Publishing Group, 1996).

18.   Robert A. Wright, "Youths Battle Police on Coast," *New York Times*, February 27, 1970.

19.   Thomas R. Brooks, "U.S. 1970: The Radical Underground Surfaces with a Bang," *New York Times*, March 15, 1970.

20.   Rubin, *Do It!*.

21.   Christopher Lehmann-Haupt, "Isn't He the Person He's Been Warning Us Against?" *New York Times*, April 6, 1970.

22.   Bennett Kremen, "How to Do It," *New York Times*, July 12, 1970.

23.   Richard Todd, "'Walden Two': Three? Many More?" *New York Times*, March 15, 1970.

24.   Steven V. Roberts, "The Better Earth," *New York Times*, March 29, 1970.

25.   Roberts, "The Better Earth."

26.   Agis Salpukas, "Underground Papers Are Thriving on Campuses and in Cities across Nation," *New York Times*, April 5, 1970.

27.   Irving Howe, "Political Terrorism: Hysteria on the Left," *New York Times*, April 12, 1970.

28.   Richard Nixon, Informal Conversation during Visit to the Pentagon, May 1, 1970.

29.   Crosby, Stills, Nash and Young, "Ohio" (1970).

30.   The Beatles, *Let It Be* (1970).

31.   Paul McCartney, *McCartney* (1970).

32.   Thomas King Forcade, "Statement," May 13, 1970, to Commission on Obscenity and Pornography, Washington, D.C.

33.   Bernadine Dohrn, "First Communique," May 21, 1970, appeared in *The Berkeley Tribe* (July 31, 1970).

34.   "The Media Assassination of Charlie Manson: Last Interview from Jail," *New Times* (May 25, 1970).

35.   "A Special Report: Charles Manson: The Incredible Story of the Most Dangerous Man Alive," *Rolling Stone* (June 25, 1970): 1.

36.   "Manson Declares Nixon Guilty," *East Village Other*, August 11, 1970.

37. Frank Conroy, "Manson Wins! A Fantasy," *Harper's* (November 1970): 53–59.

38. Lee and Shlain, *Acid Dreams*, 257.

39. Jack Newfield, "Famous Long Ago," *New York Times*, June 28, 1970.

40. Sara Davidson, "Open Land: Getting Back to the Communal Garden," *Harper's* (June 1970): 91–102.

41. Davidson, "Open Land."

42. Steven V. Roberts, "Youth Communes Seek New Way of Life," *New York Times*, August 3, 1970.

43. William J. Craddock, *Be Not Content: A Subterranean Journal* (Doubleday, 1970), 11–145.

44. Craddock, *Be Not Content*, 225–40.

45. Craddock, *Be Not Content*, 274–75.

46. Craddock, *Be Not Content*, 327–28.

47. Tom Bates, *Rads: The 1970 Bombing of the Army Math Research Center at the University of Wisconsin and Its Aftermath* (HarperCollins, 1992).

48. Scott Bauer, "FBI Releases 1970 UW Bombing Documents," *Journal Sentinel*, April 6, 1970.

49. "Timothy Leary, Drug Advocate, Walks away from Coast Prison," *New York Times*, September 14, 1970.

50. Schou, *Orange Sunshine*, 233.

51. Timothy Leary, "Leary's Communique," *Harvard Crimson*, September 28, 1970.

52. Greenfield, *Timothy Leary*, 401; Timothy Leary to Allen Ginsberg, October 10, 1970.

53. Greenfield, *Timothy Leary*, 413–14; Lee and Shlain, *Acid Dreams*, 265–66.

54. Conners, *White Hand Society*, 232–33.

55. Conners, *White Hand Society*, 233–234.

56. Gilmore, *Stories Done*, 94.

57. Kenneth Keniston, "Three Books That Suggest a Radical Critique of Modern America," *New York Times*, September 6, 1970.

58. Keniston, "Three Books That Suggest a Radical Critique of Modern America."

59. Keniston, "Three Books That Suggest a Radical Critique of Modern America."

60. Charles A. Reich, "Reflections: The Greening of America," *The New Yorker* (September 26, 1970): 42–46, 48, 50, 53–54, 56, 59–64, 66, 69–70, 74–76, 79–80, 82–86, 89–92, 95–98, 100–102, 104–6, 108–11.

61. Peter Marin, "A Somber View of a Cheerful View of the Future; The Greening of America," *New York Times*, November 8, 1970.

62. George Kennan, "Con III Is Not the Answer," *New York Times*, October 28, 1970.

63. Herbert Marcuse, "Charles Reich—A Negative View," *New York Times*, November 6, 1970.

64. Tom Hayden, "At Issue: Peaceful Change or Civil War," *New York Times*, November 14, 1970.

65. George Harrison, *All Things Must Pass* (1970); George Harrison, "My Sweet Lord" (1970).

66. John Lennon, *John Lennon/Plastic Ono Band* (1970).

67. John Lennon, "God" (1970).

68. John Lennon, "Working Class Hero" (1970).

69. Weather Underground, "New Morning, Changing Weather," Weatherman Communique, December 6, 1970.

19. IT'S ALL OVER NOW

1. John Lennon, "Power to the People" (1971); John Lennon, "Imagine" (1971); John Lennon, "Woman Is the Nigger of the World" (1972); John Lennon, "John Sinclair" (1972); John Lennon, "Happy Xmas (War Is Over)" (1971); Jann S. Wenner Interview with John Lennon, *Rolling Stone* (January 21, 1971, February 4, 1971).

2. Bill Kovach, "Communes Spread as the Young Reject Old Values," *New York Times*, December 17, 1970.

3. Kovach, "Communes Spread as the Young Reject Old Values."

4. Steven V. Roberts, "Halfway between Dropping Out and Dropping In," *New York Times*, September 12, 1971.

5. Bennett M. Berger, "The Best Things in Life Are Free, or You Can Build Them Yourself," *New York Times*, November 14, 1971.

6. Berger, "The Best Things in Life Are Free."

7. Timothy Tyler, "The Cooling of America: Out of Tune and Lost in the Counterculture," *Time* (February 22, 1971): 15–16.

8. Peter Marin, "Tripping the Heavy Fantastic," *New York Times*, February 21, 1971.

9. Paul Starr, "Rebels after the Cause: Living with Contradictions," *New York Times*, October 13, 1974.

10. Thomas Frank, *The Conquest of Cool: Business Culture, Counterculture, and the Rise of Hip Consumption* (University of Chicago Press, 1997).

11. Stewart Brand, "We Owe It All to the Hippies," *Time* (March 1, 1995): 54–56.

12. John Markoff, *What the Dormouse Said: How the Sixties Counterculture Shaped the Personal Computer Industry* (Penguin, 2005); Fred Turner, *From Counterculture to Cyberculture: Stewart Brand, the Whole Earth Network, and the Rise of Digital Utopianism* (University of Chicago Press, 2006).

13. John Diggins, *The Rise and Fall of the American Left* (W.W. Norton, 1992), 275.

14. Allen J. Matusow, *The Unraveling of America: A History of Liberalism in the 1960s* (Harper & Row, 1984), 307.

15. Terry J. Anderson, *The Movement in the Sixties*, 422–23.

16. Irwin Unger and Debi Unger, *the times were a changing': The Sixties Reader* (Three Rivers Press, 1998), 160.

17. Christopher Gair, *The American Counterculture* (Edinburgh University Press, 2007), 9; Alice Echols, *Shaky Ground: The Sixties and Its Aftershocks* (Columbia University Press, 2002), 50.

18. Lee and Shlain, *Acid Dreams*, 294.

19. David Chalmers, *And the Crooked Places Made Straight: The Struggle for Social Change in the 1960s* (Johns Hopkins University Press, 1996), 100.

20. Farrell, *The Spirit of the Sixties*, 231.

21. Morris Dickstein, *Gates of Eden: American Culture in the 1960s* (Basic Books, 1977), 276–77.

22. Charles Dickens, *A Tale of Two Cities* (Penguin Classics, 2003), 5.

23. Timothy Leary, *Chaos and Cyber Culture* (Ronin Publishing, 1994).

24. Laura Mansnerus, "Timothy Leary, Pied Piper of Psychedelic 60's, Dies at 75," *New York Times*, June 1, 1996.

25. Rupert Cornwell Washington, "Timothy Leary, Sixties Messiah, Dies with the Words 'Why Not?'" *The Independent*, June 1, 1996.

26. The Friends of Timothy Leary, "An Open Letter."

27. Wilborn Hampton, "Allen Ginsberg, Master Poet of Beat Generation, Dies at 70," *New York Times*, April 6, 1997.

28. Ken Babbs, "Kesey's Belly," November 10, 2001.

29. "The Prankster's Death," *New York Times*, November 13, 2001.

BIBLIOGRAPHY

Aaron, Daniel. *Writers on the Left* (1992).

Allyn, David. *Make Love, Not War: The Sexual Revolution* (2001).

Altschuler, Glenn C. *All Shook Up: How Rock 'n' Roll Changed America* (2004).

Amburn, Ellis. *Subterranean Kerouac: The Hidden Life of Jack Kerouac* (1999).

Anderson, Terry H. *The Movement and the Sixties: Protest in America from Greensboro to Wounded Knee* (1996).

Anson, Robert Sam. *Gone Crazy and Back Again: The Rise and Fall of the Rolling Stone Generation* (1981).

Anthony, Gene. *Magic of the Sixties* (2004).

———. *Summer of Love: Haight-Ashbury at Its Highest* (1995).

Armstrong, David. *A Trumpet to Arms: Alternative Media in America* (1981).

Ashbolt, Anthony. *A Cultural History of the Radical Sixties in the San Francisco Bay Area* (2013).

Barber, David. *A Hard Rain Fell: SDS and Why It Failed* (2010).

Bates, Tom. *Rads: The 1970 Bombing of the Army Math Research Center at the University of Wisconsin and Its Aftermath* (1992).

Beatles, The. *The Beatles Anthology* (2000).

Bebergal, Peter. *Too Much to Dream: A Psychedelic American Boyhood* (2011).

Behnke, Alison. *Jack Kerouac* (2007).

Ben-Ami, Etan. Interview with Peter Coyote, January 12, 1989.

Berger, Dan. *Outlaws of America: The Weather Underground and the Politics of Solidarity* (2005).

Berniere, Vincent, and Mariel Primois. *Sex Press: The Sexual Revolution in the Underground Press, 1965–1975* (2012).

Bizot, Jean-Francois. *Free Press: Underground and Alternative Publications, 1965–1975* (2006).

Bloom, Alexander, and Wini Breines, eds. *"Takin' It to the Streets": A Sixties Reader* (2010).

Boal, Iain et al., eds. *West of Eden: Communes and Utopia in Northern California* (2012).

Brant, Marley. *Join Together: Forty Years of the Rock Music Festival* (2008).

Braunstein, Peter, and Michael William Doyle, eds. *Imagine Nation: The American Counter-culture in the 1960s and '70s* (2001).

Briggs, Robert. *Ruined Time: The 1950s and the Beats* (2006).

Brown, Norman O. *Life against Death: The Psychoanalytical Meaning of History* (1959).

———. *Love's Body* (1966).

Broyard, Anatole. *Kafka Was the Rage: A Greenwich Village Memoir* (1997).

Bugliosi, Vincent. *Helter Skelter: The True Story of the Manson Murders* (2001).

Burroughs, William S. *Junky: The Definitive Text of 'Junk'* (2012).
———. *The Letters of William Burroughs: Volume I: 1945–1959* (1993).
———. *Naked Lunch* (1959).
Campbell, James. *This Is the Beat Generation: New York-San Francisco-Paris* (2004).
Cannato, Vincent. *The Ungovernable City* (2002).
Cannon, Lou. *Governor Reagan: His Rise to Power* (2005).
Carroll, Lewis. *Alice's Adventures in Wonderland and Through the Looking-Glass* (1946).
Carroll, Paul. Interview with Allen Ginsberg, *Playboy* (April 1969).
Carter, David. *Stonewall: The Riots That Sparked the Gay Revolution* (2010).
Castaneda, Carlos. *A Separate Reality* (1972).
———. *The Teachings of Don Juan: A Yaqui Way of Knowledge* (1968).
Chalmers, David. *And the Crooked Places Made Straight: The Struggle for Social Change in the 1960s* (1996).
Charters, Ann. *Beat Down to Your Soul: What Was the Beat Generation* (2001)?
———. *The Portable Beat Reader* (2003).
Charters, Ann, and Samuel Charters. *Brother-Souls: John Clellon Holmes, Jack Kerouac, and the Beat Generation* (2010).
Christensen, Mark. *Acid Christ: Ken Kesey, LSD and the Politics of Ecstasy* (2010).
Clarke, Arthur C. *Childhood's End* (Books, 1953).
———. *2001: A Space Odyssey* (1968).
Clarke, Thurston. *The Last Campaign: Robert F. Kennedy and 82 Days That Inspired America* (2008).
Cohen, Allen. *The San Francisco Oracle: The Psychedelic Newspapers of the Haight Ashbury* (2005).
Conn, Scott, director. *Dirt Road to Psychedelia: Austin, TX during the 1960s* (2008).
Conners, Peter. *White Hand Society: The Psychedelic Partnership of Timothy Leary and Allen Ginsberg* (2010).
Cook, Bruce. *The Beat Generation: The Tumultuous '50s Movement and Its Impact on Today* (1971).
Cox, Craig. *Storefront Revolution: Food Co-ops and the Counterculture* (1994).
Coyote, Peter. *Sleeping Where I Fall: A Chronicle* (1999).
Craddock, William J. *Be Not Content: A Subterranean Journal* (1970).
Creighton, David. *Ecstasy of the Beats: On the Road to Understanding* (2007).
Cross, Charles R. *Room Full of Mirrors: A Biography of Jimi Hendrix* (2006).
Curl, John. *Memories of Drop City: The First Hippie Commune of the 1960s and the Summer of Love* (1971).
Dass, Ram, and Ralph Metzner. *Birth of a Psychedelic Culture: Conversations about Leary, the Harvard Experiments, Milbrook and the Sixties* (2010).
Davies, Hunter. *The Beatles* (1968).
DeBenedetti, Charles. *An American Ordeal: The Antiwar Movement of the Vietnam Era* (1990).
DeGroot, Gerard J. *The Sixties Unplugged: A Kaleidoscopic History of Disorderly Decade* (2009).
Dickstein, Morris. *Gates of Eden: American Culture in the 1960s* (1977).
Digger Archives, The (1995).
Diggins, John. *The Rise and Fall of the American Left* (1992).
Dobkin de Rios, Marlene, and Oscar Janiger. *LSD: Spirituality and the Creative Process* (2002).
Dodgson, Rick. *It's All a Kind of Magic: The Young Ken Kesey* (2013).
Doggett, Peter. *There's a Riot Going On: Revolutionaries, Rock Stars, and the Rise and Fall of the '60s* (2009).
Doglin, Gail, and Vicente Franco, directors. *Summer of Love* (2007).
Dormehl, Luke. *The Apple Revolution: Steve Jobs, the Counter Culture and How the Crazy Ones Took over the World* (2013).
Douglas, Susan J. *Listening In: Radio and the American Imagination* (2004).
Draper, Robert. *Rolling Stone Magazine: The Uncensored History* (1990).

Drummond, Paul, and Julian Cope. *Eye Mind: The Saga of Roky Erickson and the 13th Floor Elevators, the Pioneers of Psychedelic Sound* (2007).

Dunaway, David King. *Huxley in Hollywood* (1989).

Dunlap, Jane. *Exploring Inner Space: Personal Experiences under LSD-25* (1961).

Echols, Alice. *Shaky Ground: The Sixties and Its Aftershocks* (2002).

Edington, Stephen D. *The Beat Face of God: The Beat Generation as Spirit Guides* (2006).

Editors of *Rolling Stone, The Age of Paranoia* (1972).

Edmondson, Jacqueline. *John Lennon: A Biography* (2010).

Evans, Michael, and Paul Kingsbury, eds. *Woodstock: Three Days That Rocked the World* (2010).

Fadiman, James. *The Psychedelic Explorer's Guide: Safe, Therapeutic, and Sacred Journeys* (2011).

Fairfield, Richard. *Communes USA: A Personal Tour* (1972).

———. *The Modern Utopian: Alternative Communities of the '60s and '70s* (2010).

Farber, David. *The Age of Great Dreams: America in the 1960s* (1994).

———. *Chicago '68* (1994).

Farrell, James J. *The Spirit of the Sixties: The Making of Postwar Radicalism* (1997).

Feldman, Gene, and Max Gartenberg, eds. *The Beat Generation and the Angry Young Men* (1959).

Felton, David, Robin Green, and David Dalton, *Mindfuckers: A Source Book on the Rise of Acid Fascism in America* (1972).

Fogart, Robert S. *All Things New: American Communes and Utopian Movement, 1860–1914* (1990).

Forcade, Thomas King, ed. *Underground Press Anthology* (1972).

Fornatale, Peter. *Back to the Garden: The Story of Woodstock* (2009).

Fradkin, Philip L. *Wallace Stegner and the American West* (2008).

Frank, Thomas. *The Conquest of Cool: Business Culture, Counterculture, and the Rise of Hip Consumerism* (1997).

Freedman, Ralph. *Hermann Hesse: Pilgrim of Crisis* (1997).

Gair, Christopher. *The American Counterculture* (2007).

Gamson, Joshua. *The Fabulous Sylvester: The Legend, the Music, the Seventies in San Francisco* (2006).

George-Warren, Holly, ed. *The Rolling Stone Book of the Beats* (1999).

Gerzon, Mark. *The Whole World Is Watching: A Young Man Looks at Youth's Dissent* (1970).

Gibran, Kahlil. *The Prophet* (1923).

Gifford, Barry. *Jack's Book: An Oral Biography of Jack Kerouac* (2012).

Gilmore, Mikal. *Stories Done: Writings on the 1960s and Its Discontents* (2009).

Ginsberg, Allen. *The Book of Martyrdom and Artifice: First Journals and Poems 1937–1952* (2008).

———. *Collected Poems 1947–1997* (2007).

———. *Deliberate Prose: Selected Essays 1952–1995* (2000).

———. *Howl: Original Draft Facsimile, Transcript, and Variant Versions, Fully Annotated with Contemporaneous Correspondence* (2006).

———. *Howl and Other Poems* (2001, 2006).

———. *Indian Journals* (1996).

———. *Journals: Early Fifties, Early Sixties* (1994).

———. *Journals: Mid-Fifties: 1954–1958* (1995).

———. *Kaddish and Other Poems 1958–1960* (1961).

———. *The Letters of Allen Ginsberg* (2008).

———. *Spontaneous Mind: Selected Interviews 1958–1996* (2002).

———. *The Visions of the Great Rememberer* (1974)

Gitlin, Todd. *The Sixties: Years of Hope, Days of Rage* (1993).

Gleason, Ralph. *The Jefferson Airplane and the San Francisco Sound* (1969).

Glessing, Robert J. *The Underground Press in America* (1972).

Goffman, Ken, and Dan Joy. *Counterculture through the Ages: From Abraham to Acid House* (2005).

Goldman, Marion S. *The American Soul Rush: Esalen and the Rise of Spiritual Privilege* (2012).
Goldstein, Richard. *Reporting the Counterculture* (1989).
Goodman, Percival, and Paul Goodman, *Communitas: Means of Livelihood and Ways of Life* (1947).
Grace, Nancy M., and Jennie Skerl, eds. *The Transnational Beat Generation* (2012).
Graham, Bill. *Bill Graham Presents: My Life inside Rock and Out* (2004).
Gravzer, Bernard. Interview with Timothy Leary, *Playboy* (September 1966).
Greene, Joshua M. *Here Comes the Sun: The Spiritual and Musical Journey of George Harrison* (2006).
Greenfield, Robert. *Timothy Leary: A Biography* (2006).
Grov, Stanislav. *LSD: Doorway to the Numinous: The Groundbreaking Psychedelic Research into Realms of the Human Unconscious* (2009).
Gruen, John. *The New Bohemia* (1966).
Guinn, Jeff. *Manson: The Life and Times of Charles Manson* (2013).
Hayes, Kevin J. *Conversations with Jack Kerouac* (2005).
Heinlein, Robert A. *Stranger in a Strange Land* (1961).
Hentoff, Nat. Interview with Eldridge Cleaver, "Eldridge Cleaver: A Candid Conversation with the Black Panther Leader," *Playboy* (December 1968).
Hesse, Hermann. *Autobiographical Writings* (1972).
———. *Beneath the Wheel* (1968).
———. *Demian* (1965).
———. *Gertrude* (1969).
———. *The Glass Bead Game* (1970).
———. *Journey to the East* (1968).
———. *Klingsor's Last Summer* (1970).
———. *Knulp* (1971).
———. *Narcissus and Goldmund* (1968).
———. *Peter Camenzind* (1969).
———. *Rosshalde* (1970).
———. *Siddhartha* (1951).
———. *Soul of the Age: Selected Letters of Hermann Hesse, 1891–1962* (2013).
———. *Steppenwolf* (1962).
Hesse, Hermann, and Thomas Mann. *The Hesse/Mann Letters* (2005).
Higgs, John. *I Have America Surrounded: A Biography of Timothy Leary* (2006).
Hopkins, Jerry, ed. *The Hippie Papers: Notes from the Underground Press* (1968).
Hoffman, Abbie. *The Autobiography of Abbie Hoffman* (2000).
———. *Revolution for the Hell of It: The Book That Earned Abbie Hoffman a Five-Year Prison Term at the Chicago Conspiracy Trial* (2005).
———. *Soon to Be a Major Motion Picture* (1980).
Hoffmann, Albert. *LSD: My Problem Child* (2013).
Hollady, Hilary. *American Hipster: A Life of Herbert Huncke, the Times Square Hustler Who Inspired the Beat Movement* (2013).
Holmes, John Clellon. *Go: A Novel* (1952).
Horowitz, Michael, and Cynthia Palmer, eds. *Moksha: Aldous Huxley's Classic Writings on Psychedelics and the Visionary Experience* (1999).
Hoskyns, Barney. *Beneath the Diamond Sky: Haight-Ashbury 1965–1970* (1997).
Houriet, Robert. *Getting Back Together* (1971).
Howard, Mel, ed. *The Underground Reader* (1971).
Huxley, Aldous. *Brave New World* (1932).
———. *The Devils of Loudun* (2009).
———. *The Doors of Perception* (1954).
———. *Heaven and Hell* (1955).
———. *Island* (1962).
Hyde, Lewis, ed. *On the Poetry of Allen Ginsberg* (1985).
Isserman, Maurice, and Michael Kazin. *America Divided: The Civil War of the 1960s* (2008).

Jackson, Blair. *Garcia: An American Life* (2000).
Jacobs, Ron. *The Way the Wind Blew: A History of the Weather Underground* (1997).
Jacobs, Mark W. *San Fran '60s: San Francisco and the Birth of the Hippies* (2010).
Jamison, Andrew, and Roy Eyerman, *Seeds of the Sixties* (1995).
Jezer, Marty. *Abbie Hoffman: American Rebel* (1993).
Johnson, Joyce. *Minor Characters: A Beat Memoir* (1983).
Jonnes, Jill. *Hep-Cats, Narcs, and Pipe Dreams: A History of America's Romance with Illegal Drugs* (1996).
Kaiser, David. *How the Hippies Saved Physics: Science, Counterculture, and the Quantum Revival* (2012).
Kaplan, Geoff. *Power to the People: The Graphic Design of the Radical Press and the Rise of the Counter-Culture, 1964–1974* (2013).
Kaplan, Jeffrey, and Helene Loow, eds. *The Cultic Milieu: Oppositional Subcultures in an Age of Globalization* (2002).
Katz, Elia. *Armed Love: Communal Living—Good or Bad?* (1972).
Kerouac, Jack. *Big Sur* (1962).
———. *The Dharma Bums* (1958, 1991).
———. *On the Road* (1957, 1999).
———. *Selected Letters: Volume I: 1940–1956* (1995).
———. *Selected Letters: Volume II: 1957–1969* (2000).
———. *The Subterraneans* (1959).
———. *The Town and the City* (1950).
Kerouac, Jack, and Allen Ginsberg. *Jack Kerouac and Allen Ginsberg: The Letters* (2011).
Keyes, Gary, and Mike Lawler, *Wicked Crescenta Valley* (2014).
Kindman, Michael. *My Odyssey through the Underground Press* (2011).
Kinkade, Kathleen. *Walden Two Experiment* (1973).
Kopkind, Andrew. *The Thirty Years' Wars: Dispatches and Diversions of a Radical Journalist: 1865–1994* (1995).
Kornbluth, Jesse, ed. *Notes from the New Underground* (1968).
Krassner, Paul. *Confessions of a Raving, Unconfined Nut: Misadventures in Counter-Culture* (2012).
Krieger, Susan. *Hip Capitalism* (1979).
Kunstler, William R. *My Life as a Radical Lawyer* (1996).
Kurlansky, Mark. *1968: The Year That Rocked the World* (2005).
Kusch, Frank. *Battleground Chicago: The Police and the 1968 Democratic National Convention* (2008).
Laing, R. D. *The Politics of Experience* (1967).
Lang, Michael. *The Road to Woodstock: From the Man Behind the Legendary Festival* (2010).
Lardas, John. *The Bop Apocalypse: The Religious Visions of Kerouac, Ginsberg, and Burroughs* (2000).
Lasch, Christopher. *The Culture of Narcissism: American Life in an Age of Diminishing Expectations* (1978).
Lattin, Don. *The Harvard Psychedelic Club: How Timothy Leary, Ram Dass, Huston Smith, and Andrew Weil Killed the Fifties and Ushered in a New Age for America* (2010).
Leamer, Laurence. *The Paper Revolutionaries: The Rise of the Underground Press* (1972).
Leary, Timothy. *Chaos and Cyber Culture* (1994).
———. *Flashbacks: An Autobiography* (1989).
———. *The Politics of Ecstasy* (1998).
———. *Psychedelic Prayers and Other Meditations* (1997).
Leary, Timothy, Ralph Metzner, and Richard Alpert. *The Psychedelic Experience: A Manual Based on the Tibetan Book of the Dead* (1964).
Lee, Martin A., and Bruce Shlain. *Acid Dreams: The Complete Social History of LSD: The CIA, the Sixties, and Beyond* (1994).
Leland, John. *Why Kerouac Matters: The Lessons of On the Road (They're Not What You Think)* (2007).
Levin, Joanna. *Bohemia in America, 1858–1920* (2009).

Lewes, James. *Protest and Survive: Underground GI Newspapers during the Vietnam War* (2003).
Lewis, Roger. *Outlaws of America: The Underground Press and Its Context* (1973).
Lipton, Lawrence. *The Holy Barbarians* (1959).
Lucas, Philip Charles. *The Odyssey of a New Religion: The Holy Order of MANS from New Age to Orthodoxy* (1995).
Lydon, Michael. *Rock Folk: Portraits from the Rock 'n Roll Pantheon* (1971).
Lyman, Mel. *Mirror at the End of the Road* (1971).
Lytle, Mark Hamilton. *America's Uncivil Wars: The Sixties Era from Elvis to the Fall of Richard Nixon* (2006).
Maher, Paul. *Empty Phantoms: Interviews and Encounters with Jack Kerouac* (2005).
———. *Kerouac: The Definitive Biography* (2004).
Mann, Thomas. *Letters of Thomas Mann, 1889–1955* (1975).
Manso, Peter. *Mailer: His Life and Times* (2008).
Manzarek, Ray. *Light My Fire* (1999).
Marcuse, Herbert. *A Critique of Pure Tolerance* (1965).
———. *Eros and Civilization: A Philosophical Inquiry into Freud* (1955).
———. *The New Left and the 1960s: The Collected Papers of Herbert Marcuse*, Volume 3 (2004).
———. *One-Dimensional Man* (1964).
Mariani, Paul J. *William Carlos Williams: A New World Naked* (1990).
Markoff, John. *What the Dormouse Said: How the Sixties Counterculture Shaped the Personal Computer Industry* (2005).
Marler, Regina, ed. *Queer Beats: How the Beats Turned America on to Sex* (2004).
Masters, Robert, and Jean Houston. *The Varieties of Psychedelic Experience: The First Comprehensive Guide to the Effects of LSD on Human Personality* (1966).
Matthews, Mark. *Droppers: America's First Hippie Commune, Drop City* (2010).
Matusow, Allen J. *The Unraveling of America: A History of Liberalism in the 1960s* (1984).
Maynard, John Arthur. *Venice West: The Beat Generation in Southern California* (1991).
McClanahan, Ed. *I Just Hitched in from the Coast: The Ed McClanahan Reader* (2011).
McDarrah, Fred W. *Beat Generation: Glory Days in Greenwich Village* (1996).
McKeen, William. *Outlaw Journalist: The Life and Times of Hunter S. Thompson* (2008).
McMillan, John. *Smoking Typewriters: The Sixties Underground Press and the Rise of Alternative Media in America* (2011).
McNally, Dennis. *Desolate Angel: Jack Kerouac, the Beat Generation, and America.*
———. *A Long Strange Trip: The Inside History of the Grateful Dead* (1981).
Melville, Keith. *Communes in the Counter Culture: Origins, Theories, Styles of Life* (1972).
Merrill, Thomas F. *Allen Ginsberg* (1988).
Mileck, Joseph. *Hermann Hesse: Life and Art* (1978).
Miles, Barry. *The Beat Hotel: Ginsberg, Burroughs, and Corso in Paris, 1957–1963* (2001).
———. *Hippie* (2005).
———. *Paul McCartney: Many Years from Now* (1998).
Miller, Timothy. *The Hippies and American Values* (1991).
———. *The 60's Communes: Hippies and Beyond* (2000).
Montanareli, Lisa, and Ann Harrison, *Strange But True: San Francisco: Tales of the City by the Bay* (2005).
Moore, Heidi. *The Aesthetics of Place and the Comedy of Discomfort: Six Humorists* (2008).
Morgan, Bill. *The Beat Generation in San Francisco: A Literary Tour* (2003).
———, ed. *Howl on Trial: The Battle for Free Expression* (2006).
———. *I Celebrate Myself: The Somewhat Private Life of Allen Ginsberg* (2006).
———. *The Typewriter Is Holy: The Complete, Uncensored History of the Beat Generation* (2010).
Morgan, Robin, ed. *Sisterhood Is Powerful* (1970).
Morgan, Ted. *Literary Outlaw: The Life and Times of William S. Burroughs* (2012).
Mungo, Raymond. *Beyond the Revolution: My Life and Times since Famous Long Ago* (1990).
———. *Famous Long Ago: My Life and Hard Times with Liberation News Service* (1970).

Murray, Nicholas. *Aldous Huxley: A Biography* (2003).

Nachman, Gerald. *Seriously Funny: The Rebel Comedians of the 1950s and 1960s* (2009).

Nearing, Helen, and Scott Nearing. *Living the Good Life: Being a Plain Practical Account of a Twenty Year Project in a Self-Subsistent Homestead in Vermont, Together with Remarks on How to Live Sanely and Simply in a Troubled World* (1954).

Nearing, Scott. *The Making of a Radical: A Political Autobiography* (2000).

Norman, Philip. *John Lennon: The Life* (2009).

O'Neill, William. *The New Left: A History* (2001).

Peck, Abe. *Uncovering the Sixties: The Life and Times of the Underground Press* (1985).

Perry, Charles. *The Haight-Ashbury: A History* (1988).

Perry, Helen. *The Human Be-In* (1970).

Perry, Paul et al. *On the Bus: The Complete Guide to the Legendary Trip of Ken Kesey and the Merry Pranksters and the Birth of the Counterculture* (1990).

Pinchbeck, Daniel. *Breaking Open the Head: A Psychedelic Journey into the Heart of Contemporary Shamanism* (2003).

Placzek, Beverley R., ed. *Record of a Friendship: The Correspondence between William Reich and A. S. Neil* (1981).

Rabbit, Peter. *Drop City* (1971).

Raskin, Jonah. *American Scream: Allen Ginsberg's Howl and the Making of the Beat Generation* (2004).

Reed, T. V. *Fifteen Jugglers, Five Believers: Literary Politics and the Poetics of American Social Movements* (1992).

Reich, Charles A. *The Greening of America* (1970).

Reich, William. *The Function of the Orgasm: Sex-Economic Problems of Biology Energy: Volume 1 of The Discovery of the Orgone* (1973).

———. *The Mass Psychology of Fascism* (1933).

Rexroth, Kenneth. *Rexroth Reader* (1972).

———. *The Selected Poems of Kenneth Rexroth* (1984).

Richardson, Peter. *A Bomb in Every Issue: How the Short, Unruly Life of Ramparts Magazine Changed America* (2009).

Robinson, Paul A. *The Freudian Left: Wilhelm Reich, Geza Roheim, Herbert Marcuse* (1969).

Roby, Stephen, and Brad Schreiber. *Becoming Jimi Hendrix: From Southern Crossroads to Psychedelic London, the Untold Story of a Musical Genius* (2010).

Rorabaugh, W. J. *Kennedy and the Promise of the Sixties* (2004).

Rosen, Ruth. *The World Split Open: How the Modern Women's Movement Changed America* (2006).

Rosenman, Joel. *Young Men with Unlimited Capital: The Story of Woodstock* (1999).

Rossinow, Doug. *The Politics of Authenticity: Liberalism, Christianity, and the New Left in America* (1998).

Roszak, Theodore. *The Making of a Counter Culture: Reflections on the Technocratic Society and Its Youthful Opposition* (1969).

Rothchild, John. *The Children of the Counter-Culture* (1976).

Rubin, Jerry. *Do It!: Scenarios of the Revolution* (1970).

———. *We Are Everywhere* (1971).

Sale, Kirkpatrick. *SDS* (1974).

Sanders, Ed. *The Family: The Story of Charles Manson's Dune Buggy Attack Battalion* (1971).

———. *Fug You: An Informal History of the Peace Eye Bookstore, the Fuck You Press, the Fugs, and Counterculture in the Lower East Side* (2011).

San Francisco Tape Music Center. *1960s Counterculture and the Avant-Garde* (2008).

Scheer, Robert. *Playing President: My Close Encounters with Nixon, Carter, Bush I, Reagan, and Clinton and How They Did Not Prepare Me for George W. Bush* (2006).

Schou, Nicholas. *Orange Sunshine: The Brotherhood of Eternal Love and Its Quest to Spread Peace, Love, and Acid to the World* (2011).

Schumacher, Michael. *Dharma Lion: A Critical Biography of Allen Ginsberg* (1992).

Sculatti, Gene, and Davin Seay. *San Francisco Nights: The Psychedelic Music Trip, 1965–1968* (1985).

Scully, Rock. *Living with the Dead: Twenty Years on the Bus with Garcia and the Grateful Dead* (2001).

Selvin, Joel. *Monterey Pop* (1992).

―――. *Summer of Love: The Inside Story of LSD, Rock and Roll, Free Love and High Times in the Wild West* (1999).

Serrano, Miguel. *C. G. Jung and Hermann Hesse: A Record of Two Friendships* (1971).

Sharaf, Myron. *Fury on Earth: A Biography of William Reich* (1994).

Skinner, B. F. *Walden Two* (1948).

Shroder, Tom. *Acid Test: LSD, Ecstasy, and the Power to Heal* (2014).

Solomon, David, ed. *LSD: The Consciousness-Expanding Drug* (1964).

Stine, Peter, ed. *The Sixties* (1996).

Slick, Grace. *Somebody to Love?: A Rock-and-Roll Memoir* (1998).

Smith, Huston. *Cleansing the Doors of Perception: The Significance of Entheogenic Plants and Chemicals* (2000).

Snyder, Gary, and Allen Ginsberg. *The Selected Letters of Allen Ginsberg and Gary Snyder, 1956–1991* (2008).

Spitz, Bob. *The Beatles: The Biography* (2006).

Stanley, Rhoney Gissen. *Owsley and Me: My LSD Family* (2013).

Stark, Steven D. *Meet the Beatles: A Cultural History of the Band that Shook Youth, Gender, and the World* (2006).

Stein, Robert. *Media Power: Who Is Shaping Your Picture of the World?* (2005).

Stevens, Amy. *Daniel Shays' Legacy: Marshall Bloom, Radical Insurgency and the Pioneer Valley* (2005).

Stevens, Jay. *Storming Heaven: LSD and the American Dream* (1987).

Stickney, John. *Streets, Actions, Alternatives, Raps* (1971).

Stone, Robert. *Prime Green: Remembering the Sixties* (2007).

Strausbaugh, John. *The Village: 400 Years of Beats and Bohemians, Radicals and Rogues, a History of Greenwich Village* (2013).

Streitmatter, Rodger. *Voices of Revolution: The Dissident Press in America* (2001).

Summer of Love: Psychedelic Art, Social Crisis, and Counterculture in the 1960s (2006).

Sutton, Robert P., ed. *Modern American Communes: A Dictionary* (2005).

Suzuki, D. T. *An Introduction to Zen Buddhism* (1964).

Talbot, David. *Season of the Witch: Enchantment, Terror, and Deliverance in the City of Love* (2013).

Tamarkin, Jeff. *Got a Revolution! The Turbulent Flight of Jefferson Airplane* (2005).

Taylor, Derek. *It Was Twenty Years Ago Today* (1967).

Tendler, Stewart, and David May. *The Brotherhood of Eternal Love: From Flower Power to Hippie Mafia: The Story of the LSD Counterculture* (2007).

Theado, Matt, ed. *The Beats: A Literary Reference* (2002).

Thompson, Hunter S. *The Great Shark Hunt: Strange Tales from a Strange Time* (1979).

―――. *Hell's Angels: The Strange and Terrible Saga of the Outlaw Motorcycle Gangs* (1966).

―――. *The Proud Highway: Saga of a Desperate Southern Gentleman* (1998).

Torgoff, Martin. *Can't Find My Way Home: America in the Great Stoned Age, 1945–2000* (2004).

Troy, Sandy. *Captain Trips: A Biography of Jerry Garcia* (1995).

Tucci, Stanley. *Magic Trip* (2011).

Turner, Fred. *From Counterculture to Cyberculture: Stewart Brand, the Whole Earth Network, and the Rise of Digital Utopianism* (2006).

Tytell, John. *Naked Angels: The Lives and Literature of the Beat Generation* (2006).

Unger, Irwin, and Debi Unger. *America in the 1960s* (1988).

―――. *the times were a changing': The Sixties Reader* (1998).

Unterberger, Richie. *Eight Miles High: Folk-Rock's Flight from Haight-Ashbury to Woodstock* (2003).

―――. *Turn! Turn! Turn!: The '60s Folk-Rock Revolution* (2002).

Varon, Jeremy. *Bring the War Home: The Weather Underground, the Red Army Faction, and Revolutionary Violence in the Sixties and Seventies* (2004).
von Hoffman, Nicholas. *We Are the People Our Parents Warned Us Against* (1968).
Wachsberger, Ken. *Insider Histories of the Vietnam Era Underground Press, Part 1* (2011).
———. *Insider Histories of the Vietnam Era Underground Press, Part 2* (2012).
Waldman, Anne, ed. *The Beat Book: Writings from the Beat Generation* (2007).
Walker, Michael. *Laurel Canyon: The Inside Story of Rock-and-Roll's Legendary Neighborhood* (2007).
Watson, Steven. *The Birth of the Beat Generation: Visionaries, Rebels, and Hipsters, 1944–1960* (1995).
Wenner, Jann S. Interview with John Lennon, *Rolling Stone* (January 21, 1971).
Wetzsteon, Ross. *Republic of Dreams: Greenwich Village: The American Bohemia, 1910–1960* (2003).
Whitman, Howard. *The Sex Age* (1962).
Whitmer, Peter O. *Aquarius Revisited: Seven Who Created the Sixties Counterculture That Changed America* (2007).
Whole Earth Catalog: Access to Tools (1969).
Wiener, John, ed. *Conspiracy in the Streets: The Extraordinary Trial of the Chicago Eight* (2006).
Wiener, Jon. *Come Together: John Lennon in His Time* (1984).
———. *Gimme Some Truth: The John Lennon FBI Files* (2000).
Wilkerson, Cathy. *Flying Close to the Sun: My Life and Times as a Weatherman* (2011).
Wilson, Colin. *The Outsider: The Seminal Book on the Alienation of Modern Man* (1956).
Wolfe, Burton H. *Hippies* (1968).
Wolfe, Tom. *Radical Chic and Mau-Mauing the Flak Catchers* (1971).
Wolfe, Tom. *The Electric Kool-Aid Acid Test* (1968).
Yablonsky, Lewis. *The Hippie Trip* (1968).
Ziolkowski, Theodore. *The Novels of Hermann Hesse: A Study in Theme and Structure* (1967).

INDEX

ABOUT THE AUTHOR

Robert C. Cottrell has written over twenty books, including biographies of the radical journalist I. F. Stone, ACLU icon Roger Nash Baldwin, and Negro League founder Rube Foster. He is the author most recently of *Two Icons: How Hank Greenberg and Jackie Robinson Transformed Baseball and America*. Cottrell, professor of history and American studies at California State University, Chico, has also taught in London; Puebla, Mexico; and Moscow, Russia, in the latter instance as a Distinguished Fulbright Chair. He is currently working on a collective biography of four key members of the early twentieth-century American left: Crystal Eastman, John Reed, Inez Milholland, and Randolph Bourne.